ROBERT
THE BRUCE

ROBERT THE BRUCE

CHAMPION OF A NATION

STEPHEN SPINKS

AMBERLEY

First published 2019

Amberley Publishing
The Hill, Stroud
Gloucestershire, GL5 4EP

www.amberley-books.com

British Library Cataloguing in Publication Data.
A catalogue record for this book is available from the British Library.

ISBN 978 1 4456 8507 6 (hardback)
ISBN 978 1 4456 8508 3 (ebook)

Typesetting by Aura Technology and Software Services, India.
Printed in the UK.

For Alexander John Lee in respect of his many years of
friendship, peppered with the indomitable cries of...'*freedom*'!

Contents

Appendices

Acknowledgements

An author friend of mine once said that writing a second book is nothing like the first. The hiatus of the unknown, of when deadlines should or do roll in, the random requests that are made of you, become, by book two, something of a well-learned lesson. You definitely set out on this later journey more armoured and experienced. There are still pitfalls, of course, with the unknown trials and tribulations that come with bringing life to another book. It is, after all, part of what makes it all so exciting. So, armed with my research, my many tomes, notebooks, pens, pencils and of course a MacBook, I boldly stepped out on to that familiar path once more and began my new adventure. As I travelled along the dusty road, I also learned another truth. In exercising my craft, I soon rediscovered some familiar faces, like beacons of light guiding me along my way, whose help, support or simple encouragement kept me on my path. But along with the familiar, I also had the pleasure of meeting many new people. Together, each in their own unique way, these guiding lights have helped shape the writing of this book. For that I wish to thank every one of you. There are too many to name, but in the spirit of celebration and gratitude, I wanted to note at least a few here.

Firstly, I wish to thank my editor Shaun, who decided he was a glutton for punishment and offered me the opportunity to write a second book with Amberley. I had wanted to tell Robert's story for the last few years, and his support and encouragement has made that possible. I still smile every time I walk into a bookshop and see copies of *Edward II* on the bookshelves, and I can't wait to see *Robert the Bruce* there too. My thanks also extend to Alex, whose sharp eye for detail, boundless enthusiasm and flexibility

Acknowledgements

throughout the editorial and imaging process helped to bring polish to the final cut.

Secondly, I want to thank my close friends Ann Ryan, Simon Pickering, Hannah Mitchell and Catherine Taylor for their enduring friendship and commitment to marching up steep-sided Scottish lochs or battling across 'rather posh' golf courses all in search of a castle, a battle site or a location in King Robert's illustrious story; all this while enduring arctic December blasts of minus five! I also want to thank the wonderful Emma Dwan O'Reilly, who never fails to check in and proffer words of sound advice. Collectively, these amazing people have stood by me, fed me cake and wine, held out the hand of encouragement as well as celebrating the milestones over the last few years. Your friendship is a fellowship, and I for one feel very privileged to have you in my life.

I also want to thank Amy Schrepel from The Tudor Rose Shop on Etsy.com, whose handcrafted brass rubbings of historical figures, based on their tombs and effigies, are so beautiful I just had to have Robert's on the front cover of my book. Amy's speedy replies, kind permission and infinite support to make that happen, including sending a rubbing across the pond from sunny Florida, has produced something that I am sure we are both very proud of. Thank you from the bottom of my heart. Go check out her amazing shop if you can. You won't be disappointed.

Lastly, I want to thank my readers from around the world, and those of you who follow me on Twitter (@Spinksstephen) as well as my website (fourteenthcenturyfiend.com). I learn so much every day from you, and thoroughly enjoy talking about our shared passion for the past and our enthusiasm to hand on the history of our ancestors to anyone who will listen. Your advocacy and determination does much to keep history alive.

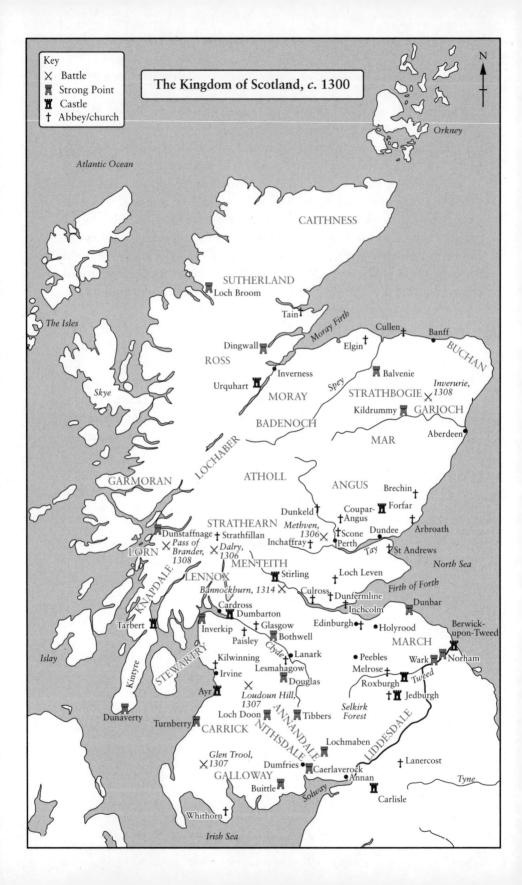

Key
✗ Battle
🏰 Strong Point
🏰 Castle
✝ Abbey/church

N

Atlantic Ocean

Orkney

CAITHNESS

SUTHERLAND
🏰 Loch Broom

Tain

Moray Firth

The Isles

Dingwall 🏰

Cullen ✝   • Banff

Elgin ✝   BUCHAN

ROSS

Urquhart 🏰   • Inverness

Spey

Balvenie 🏰

Skye

MORAY   STRATHBOGIE   *Inverurie, 1308* ✗

BADENOCH   Kildrummy 🏰   GARIOCH

LOCHABER   MAR   • Aberdeen

GARMORAN   ATHOLL

ANGUS   Brechin ✝

Dunkeld ✝   Coupar-   Forfar 🏰
Angus ✝

STRATHEARN   *Methven, 1306* ✗   Dundee •   Arbroath

Dunstaffnage 🏰 ✝ Strathfillan   Inchaffray ✝   Scone ✝

Pass of   *Dalry,*   Perth •
Brander, 1308 ✗   *1306* ✗   St Andrews ✝

LORN   KNAPDALE   MENTEITH   *North Sea*

LENNOX   Loch Leven ✝

Bannockburn, 1314 ✗   Stirling 🏰

Tarbert 🏰   Culross ✝   *Firth of Forth*

Cardross ✝   Dumbarton 🏰   Dunfermline ✝   Dunbar 🏰

Inverkip ✝   Glasgow ✝   Inchcolm ✝   Berwick-
upon-Tweed

Islay   Paisley ✝   Bothwell 🏰   Edinburgh ✝   • Holyrood

Kintyre   STEWARTRY   *Clyde*   Lanark •   • Peebles   MARCH

Kilwinning ✝   Lesmahagow 🏰   Melrose ✝   Wark 🏰   Norham 🏰

Irvine ✝   Douglas 🏰   Roxburgh 🏰   *Tweed*

Ayr ✗   *Loudoun Hill,*   *Selkirk*   Jedburgh 🏰
1307   *Forest*

Dunaverty   *Glen Trool,*   Loch Doon 🏰   Tibbers 🏰   LIDDESDALE

Turnberry 🏰   CARRICK   *1307* ✗   Lochmaben 🏰   Lanercost ✝

NITHSDALE   ANNANDALE

GALLOWAY   Dumfries •   Caerlaverock 🏰

Buittle 🏰   Annan 🏰   *Tyne*

Whithorn ✝   *Solway*   Carlisle 🏰

Irish Sea

The Scottish Succession and the Bruces

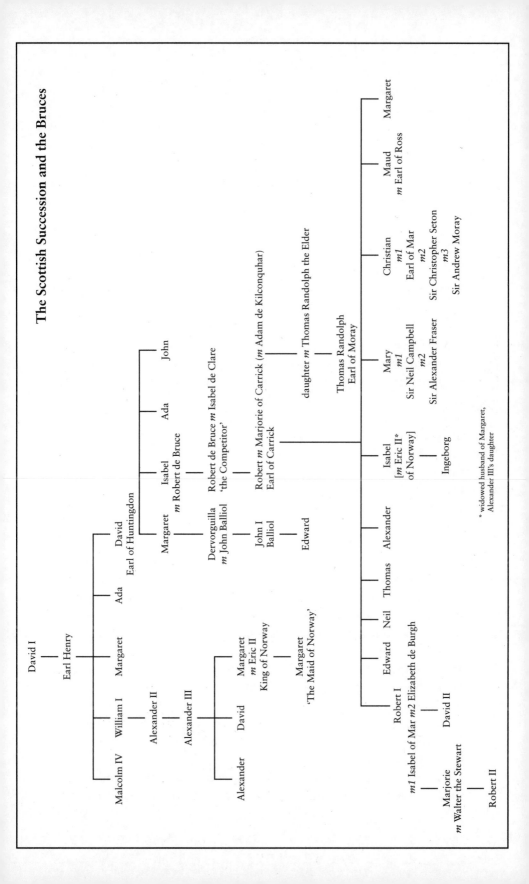

David I — Earl Henry

Malcolm IV, William I, Margaret, Ada, David Earl of Huntingdon

Alexander II

Alexander III

Alexander, David, Margaret *m* Eric II King of Norway

Margaret 'The Maid of Norway'

Margaret *m* Robert de Bruce, Isabel, Ada, John

Dervorguilla *m* John Balliol, Robert de Bruce 'the Competitor' *m* Isabel de Clare

John I Balliol, Edward

Robert *m* Marjorie of Carrick (*m* Adam de Kilconquhar) Earl of Carrick

daughter *m* Thomas Randolph the Elder

Thomas Randolph Earl of Moray

Robert I *m1* Isabel of Mar *m2* Elizabeth de Burgh

Edward, Neil, Thomas, Alexander, Isabel [*m* Eric II* of Norway], Mary *m1* Sir Neil Campbell *m2* Sir Alexander Fraser, Christian *m1* Earl of Mar *m2* Sir Christopher Seton *m3* Sir Andrew Moray, Maud *m* Earl of Ross, Margaret

Ingeborg

Marjorie *m* Walter the Stewart, David II

Robert II

* widowed husband of Margaret, Alexander III's daughter

Preface

Wherever I go, it seems there are few people who have not heard of 'Robert the Bruce'. It's hardly surprising. Synonymous with the underdog, King Robert's extraordinary career is ultimately characterised by gritty determination, clever and calculated ruthlessness, and a good dose of royal ambition. He's the outsider made great through his own ability and prowess, and his many victories and achievements, both for himself and his people, which were forged in the face of such overwhelming adversity, are all the more profound because of it. Born in 1274, and leader of the Scottish nation from 1306 to 1329, Robert I faced the very real threat of long-term English subjugation at the hands of successive Plantagenet kings of England. In desperation, he seized a vacant crown, outwitted his mighty English neighbour and resisted the stubborn and determined monarchs Edward I and II. In doing so, he secured both recognition of his status as king and the independence of the Scottish nation. Robert remains a national hero in Scotland to this day, even if his actual deeds are now shrouded in seven hundred years of almost impenetrable myth and legend. In England he is begrudgingly acknowledged as the hero of the Battle of Bannockburn, the monarch who dared defy the might of the English nation – and won. Around the world his name continues to resound, bold and triumphant. The many monuments erected in his honour stand testament not only to his valour and might but his continued appeal in our collective memory. In our world, increasingly marked out by division, intolerance and indifference, Robert's story is as profound and relevant as ever; his history is a lesson for us all.

I first discovered this enigmatic man as a teenager while glued to the silver screen watching Mel Gibson and Angus Macfadyen fight it out against the likes of the devilishly brilliant Patrick McGoohan, whose portrayal of Edward I was both salacious and tyrannical. Macfadyen's depiction of a carefully calculating Robert Bruce, torn in loyalty between what he knew to be right and what he needed to do in order to survive, reached into the heart of this near-mythical man, even if *Braveheart* is legendary for its many historical inaccuracies. Yet despite its many shortcomings, that film – and others since, such as the recent Netflix drama *Outlaw King* – inspired me to learn more about these characters from our past. As a writer who spent twenty years unearthing the life of Edward II, King of England, Robert's contemporary and something of a second nemesis, this man who later became King of Scots was never far from my mind. So closely entwined are the stories of these two men – King Robert and Edward II – that you cannot really tell one without exploring the other. Robert's unswerving determination to secure his crown and win the independence of his nation was as great and all-consuming as Edward II's desire to stop him. By the time that my biography of King Edward II was published in 2017, it was a simple fact that Robert's would soon follow.

In order to really grapple with the man, there must also be an exploration of his world and the politically charged environment in which he lived. The death of Alexander III, King of Scots in 1286, and that of his young granddaughter in 1290, was catastrophic for the Scottish nation. The subsequent outbreak of the First War of Scottish Independence saw noble houses divide as loyalties and betrayals became the bedrock of Scotland's rich history. At its darkest hour, the Scottish nation ceased to be a kingdom, instead becoming a simple appendage to the Kingdom of England. Amid the chaos, the House of Bruce, which had a claim to the Scottish crown, sat at the heart of this nightmare. Yet in murdering his rival, reaching out and seizing the throne in 1306, and then battling to hold onto it against all odds, Robert would become not only the champion of House Bruce but the champion of the Scottish nation.

Robert's twenty-three-year reign saw him beat the English, of course, but he also overcame many of his own Scottish enemies within his kingdom. He survived conspiracy and years of war, and went on to enjoy a famous victory at Bannockburn in 1314 and the near humiliating capture of Edward II in 1322. His invasion of Ireland alongside his brother Edward Bruce highlighted the breadth of his ambition, emphasising his desire to create a pan-Celtic alliance that would threaten the very core of English power. He was innovative, bold and demonstrated great strength of leadership. Yet even he failed to succeed at everything. His Irish campaign collapsed, his brothers and many supporters lost their lives defending his cause, and he himself spent twenty years dogged by illness that sometimes incapacitated him. The imprisonment of his wife and daughter at the hands of the English nearly cost him an heir, and his legacy was soon challenged and almost overcome in the immediate years following his death. Yet his life rightly remains the tale of a hero.

Throughout the telling of his story, I have been conscious to take you on a journey which not only allows you to peer through a window into his past but also to experience medieval Scotland, and the fortunes of the Bruce family from the early twelfth century through the intrigues, machinations and dramas of the Scottish and English courts. In telling this wider story, the rich tapestry of Robert's life suddenly makes all the more sense. In essence, you see what he saw. Despite what we think we know about Robert, some of his actual deeds and decisions are harder to unearth, complicated by the absence of certain medieval records. It is no surprise that where gaps exist, myth and legend are quick to emerge. While fourteenth-century record-keeping was relatively robust in England, Scottish royal records of the period are frustratingly limited, leaving much to be gleaned from charters and unreliable, often heavily biased chroniclers, out to either damage or embellish Robert's character and deeds. Yet these materials can also reveal a rich, bountiful catalogue of events and tell us much about how contemporaries saw and judged him.

The absence of key documents like Scottish exchequer rolls, which only survive from 1327 and would have given us intimate access into Robert's daily life, means we must seek far and wide to piece together his movements, spending habits and everyday decisions. In such details we unearth the true character of the man. Most frustrating of all, we do not know what Robert actually looked like, having no contemporary descriptions of his build, hair and eye colour, or court style. This must be left to our imagination. The recent facial reconstruction made from a plaster cast of his skull, and included in the plates of this book, can only allude to his features. Yet despite these limitations, with diligent research and a wider understanding of the world in which he lived, we can discover breath-taking glimpses into his past. Thankfully, enough survives to allow us to put this jigsaw together, faithfully recreating the often dramatic and colourful life Robert led.

In researching Robert's life, I quickly discovered there are a number of writers who have also made this journey and who have been a guiding light in helping me navigate and stay true to my course, even if they themselves do not always personally know it. The first is Michael Penman, Senior Lecturer at Stirling University, who has devoted a lifetime of work to King Robert I and his son King David II, and whose academic biography of Robert has been a sure-footed guide in helping to close some of those gaps in the historical record. His particular emphasis on Robert's patronage and his years of kingship after Bannockburn, especially between 1322 and 1328, were very helpful indeed. The second writer, biographer and historian is the late Caroline Bingham, whose last work, *Robert the Bruce*, was completed only months prior to her death in 1998. Her book, often calling upon John Barbour's colourful poem *The Bruce* from the 1370s, as well as her light-touch narrative, breathed life into Robert's story in ways that many others had failed to do. It was Caroline Bingham's book that inspired me to write my own. Lastly, no research into the life of King Robert would be complete without consultation of the lifetime works of the late Professor Geoffrey Barrow, as well as that of Colm McNamee. Both men have produced many academic works which have sought to emphasise Robert's kingship. I am also thankful to Professor Michael Prestwich, an authority on the life and reign of Edward I, and whose many works I have read. Beyond them, the boundless energy of many chronicles from the fourteenth and fifteenth centuries, including John Barbour's *The Bruce*, Walter Bower's *Scotichronicon*, John of Fordun's *Chronicle of the Scottish Nation*, the *Chronicle of Lanercost*, the *Vita Edwardi Secundi* and Thomas Gray's *Scalacronica*, to name but a few, add much colourful vibrancy and pleasure to the researching and writing of this work.

I hope that this book, a story of Robert's life and kingship as well as the First War of Scottish Independence, helps to cast a revealing light onto his life, giving the reader an opportunity to discover an enigmatic man who won the hearts of many while becoming anathema to his enemies. It has always been my ambition to keep history alive through the telling of stories, a medium in which we have been preserving our cultural heritage for thousands of years.

In this retelling, faithfully done, I hope with the academic integrity applied through rigorous historical interrogation and analysis as taught to me by my tutors at King's College London as a History undergraduate, I have tried to pass on Robert's story in a style that is accessible for everyone. In doing so, the actions, decisions and impacts of those who have lived before us can be preserved for posterity. In reading this book, you too have become the guardian of that heritage.

Stephen Spinks
Moseley
2019

PART ONE
Loyalty & Ambition

No man holds his own flesh and blood
in hatred, and I am no exception.
I must join my own people and the nation
in which I was born.

Walter of Guisborough

1

Scotland

In 1136, Geoffrey of Monmouth, that silver-tongued storyteller, finally set down his quill and parchment, completing the now world-famous *Historia Regum Britanniae*. In the following centuries, the *History of the Kings of Britain* became something of a medieval bestseller, and its legacy stretched out far and wide, influencing the likes of Shakespeare, Malory, Tennyson and Dryden. It isn't hard to see why. For Geoffrey painted, with great vivid imagination, the story of over two thousand years of British history, and it is in his work that we first discover King Arthur, King Lear and the founder of Britain himself, at least as Geoffrey believed it to be: the mighty Brutus.

Among the rich tapestry of tales, there is a telling story early within his work, which reflects the mood of his age. For in twelfth-century Britain, England especially, there was a growing sense among the populace of what we would now call national identity or nationhood. It was increasingly infectious, and the English became evermore preoccupied with their own position and status when compared to the remaining peoples of these islands. According to Monmouth, in ancient Britain, long before Julius Caesar set foot on the shores of the south coast, the brothers Belinus and Brennius, after years of warring against one another for the right to rule the whole of Britain, eventually made peace, and through the diplomacy of friends agreed to divide the kingdom in two. Belinus, the elder of the two, would inherit Loegria, Kambria and Cornwall, the lands south of the Humber – that is, England and Wales. Brennius, meanwhile, would possess the lands north of that great river as far as Caithness, essentially outlining Scotland. As the younger brother, in keeping with ancient Trojan custom, Brennius would remain subject to his elder sibling Belinus, who would, by virtue of his age, inherit the crown of Britain. Brennius would have to be satisfied with the lesser deal.[1]

This fable was just one of many known in medieval England. So why is it so important? This particular tale tells us something of Monmouth's inherent attitude, which was shared by his contemporaries. It is a tale of England's perceived right to dominate the Celtic countries, and Scotland in particular, borne out, as Geoffrey saw it, by ancient history and custom. In the view of the twelfth-century Englishman, England, and its kings, had the inalienable right to wear Belinus' crown, a right that they would jealousy guard for generations.

Monmouth's work was read widely among the literate class, being found in the growing libraries of noble families, but also spread through word of mouth among the wider populace, its stories entering the folklore of Britain. Avidly consumed by the English, its depictions saw Scotland and the other Celtic nations, Wales and Ireland, increasingly viewed as alien and undeveloped. The Celts, isolated by their stronger neighbour, were considered lesser, marked out against the more civilised, Eurocentric English kingdom. Yet, only a year after the *Historia Regum Britanniae* was completed, King Stephen I had seized the throne of England following the death of his uncle Henry I (r. 1100–35), dispossessing the Empress Matilda of her right as natural heir and successor to her father, the late king. As England descended into twenty years of brutal civil war, Scotland, under the enigmatic visionary King David I (r. 1124–53), had already begun an evolutionary journey towards something best described as an early medieval renaissance in politics as well as social and cultural diversification. David I was building on an already complex kingdom that in itself was far from the barbarous backwater the English thought it to be.

By the turn of the thirteenth century, the Kingdom of Scotland, with its population of 400,000 to England's 4 million, was a multicultural melting pot, a product of its rich and vibrant heritage.[2] Initially divided into a multitude of smaller kingdoms, in the fourth century AD, Gaelic-speaking tribesmen from the Kingdom of Dalriada, now County Antrim in Northern Ireland, set sail across the Irish Sea, raiding the lands along the modern Scottish west coast. Within a century they had settled, establishing a kingdom, also called Dalriada, along the Western Isles and the coast of Argyll. With their settlements growing under the leadership of their king, Fergus Mór MacEirc, their kingdom was both confident and their successors assured; indeed, from King Fergus himself would spring the long line of later Scots kings.[3] As generations came and went, Dalriada became known as Alba, and the Gaelic people of that western kingdom were referred to as the Albanach. To the Latin-speaking world, Alba was simply known as Scotia, and its people the Scoti.[4]

To the north in Shetland and to the east on the mainland, north of the Forth, lived the Gaelic-speaking Picts, neighbours of the Scoti. The Celtic world, known as the Gaeltacht, was a well-connected one, rich in culture, technology and social ties, stretching from the Northern and Western Isles and west through Ireland, and in centuries past had included England, Wales and northern France before the arrival of the Romans.[5] Yet the Picts and the Scoti, despite their cultural similarities, were often in conflict, both burdened with unstable lordships and competing self-interests. In AD 850, the two warring kingdoms came together under a single king, Kenneth MacAlpin, and as a single kingdom, Scotland. These foundations were substantially developed by Kenneth's successors including Constantine I and Donald II. There was strength in numbers after all. This important moment was the beginning of a seismic power shift in the Kingdom of Scotia. Its political heart moved from Dunadd in Argyll to Dunkeld in Perthshire, and the Christian religious nerve centre relocated from the Isle of Iona, whose famous saint was Columba, to Scone, which became the inauguration site for the King of Scots.[6] Scotia then extended its borders further still, absorbing the old Celtic Kingdom of Strathclyde in the south-west and the Anglian area of Lothian, which was once under the control of the Saxon Kingdom of Northumbria.[7] Here in Lothian, the majority of the population, be they lord, cleric or commoner, spoke not Gaelic but northern English or French, while those in the old Celtic heartlands in the Western Isles, north of the Forth and in the south-west in Galloway continued to speak Gaelic.[8] Walking through eleventh-century Scotland, a traveller or pilgrim would have heard a multitude of languages.

With such a mix of cultures, it was only a matter of time before people began to intermarry and customs began to merge. Names in Scotland became increasingly anglicised, with new arrivals like William, Henry, Alexander and David taking precedence over Celtic names such as Duncan, Malcolm and Kenneth, especially in the south.[9] Over the coming centuries, and under the rule of David I in particular, people from England, the Low Countries and northern Europe were encouraged to settle in Scotland, especially in the rich fertile lands south of the Forth, bringing with them their own cultures, adding to the already rich tapestry of daily Scottish life. The names of even the most ordinary folk began to change, with official records turning up surnames like Whitefield and Stinchende, or Stinking Howen, over their Gaelic counterparts.[10] The kingdom of Scotia was therefore becoming culturally diverse as it amalgamated lands and peoples into a complex, homogeneous kingdom. By the twelfth and thirteenth centuries, the English earls of Norfolk, Kent and Pembroke had all married Scottish royal women. John Balliol's father, also called John, married Dervorguilla of Galloway, and Robert Bruce the Competitor married Isabel de Clare, daughter of the Earl of Gloucester.[11] Ties north and south of the border could only strengthen relationships, and cross-border interests flourished as a consequence.

As the twelfth century dawned, political and economic prosperity was principally, but not exclusively, focused in the lowlands to the south and east of the kingdom. Under David I, Edinburgh effectively became the capital, and castles such as Roxburgh and Stirling were beginning to appear on the landscape.[12] Many of the Anglo-Norman settlers in the region, whether large landowners or small, began to encastellate much of the area, and as many as 318 possible motte-and-bailey sites have since been identified, the majority between the Clyde and the Solway and the Firths of Forth and Moray.[13] Although the Norman Conquest fell short of Scotland, the Scottish south underwent a gradual process of anglicisation, created and encouraged by successive Scots kings who appreciated and benefitted from the rewards that came with such a visionary policy.

In tandem, there were also developments to religious houses and institutions. God, after all, remained central to the daily lives of all those living in Scotland. The founding of places such as Holyrood, Melrose and Kelso were quick in the coming.[14] Veneration of the saints was an important daily ritual for all in the medieval world, and Scotland was no exception. The patron saint of Scotia had been St Columba. Yet when Norse raiders from Scandinavia invaded and took possession of the Western Isles, Columba fell into obscurity, eclipsed by the growing cult of the apostle St Andrew, which was favoured originally by the eighth-century

Pictish kings. The town which housed his relics, Kinrymont, was renamed St Andrews. Despite St Andrew's elevation as patron saint of the Scots, Columba remained an important part of Scottish ecclesiastical heritage; his reliquary, known as the Brecbennach, was still taken by the Scots into battle as late as the thirteenth century, their hopes for victory pinned on his saintly intercession. The kingdom boasted other saints, too, including St Ninian and St Nicholas, and closer to home was St Margaret, the wife of King Malcolm Canmore and ancestress of medieval Scottish kings, who was canonised in 1250.[15]

Trade with other kingdoms was a backbone to economic success. A rich supply of timber, hides, wool from the fertile southern uplands and copious catches of fresh and seawater fish, coupled with unlimited access to the North Sea, ensured a thriving and sustainable trade network. Trade meant wealth and prosperity. Ports in the west, such as Glasgow, Irvine, Dumfries and Renfrew, were ideally located to reach out to Ireland and western England. As these towns or burghs developed, so too did those on the east coast, including the ever-important St Andrews and Dundee, plus Montrose, Roxburgh and Berwick. In Edinburgh, now the capital, the twin ports of Leith and Musselburgh brought wealth directly into the growing town. The Scots were also building boats to order for wealthy patrons from the Low Countries, highlighting very clearly that the kingdom was far from isolated and remote, in fact intricately connected to Ireland, Scandinavia, northern Europe and, of course, England through its extensive trading network. As a result of this interconnectivity, traders from Flanders, Cologne and elsewhere were encouraged to settle in Scotland, taking up residence in areas particularly focussed on the east coast, such as Berwick, allowing them easy access to Continental trading routes. The Flemish migrants had their headquarters at the town there, building themselves the Red Hall, while their rivals from Cologne set themselves up in the White Hall. They quickly assimilated into daily Scottish life, so much so that when Berwick lay under siege by Edward I and his English army in 1296, it was the Flemish who were noted for their fierce resistance, defending themselves and their neighbours to the death.[16]

As Scotland grew in prosperity, so too did its need for greater governance to best meet the complex demands placed upon it, and the systems of government that subsequently arose would greatly aid Robert Bruce in his kingship after 1306. Unlike England,

Scotland had thirteen earls, and these great men held offices that found their roots in the kingdom's Celtic ancestry. These leading men were the successors to the *mormaers*, also known as great officers or sea-stewards, whose key responsibilities had been to act as local lords, providing local justice as well as military leadership within the regions that they governed. First among them was the Earl of Fife, who retained the hereditary right to place any new king on the Stone of Destiny during their inauguration at Scone. All thirteen earls held the right to elect the next king, although by the twelfth century kingship mostly passed from father to son through the legal right of primogeniture.[17] Adopting such a solid system of succession, which mirrored that in England and France, spared the Scots the internecine strife prevalent among the Celts.

The Scots kings themselves were not enthroned by rite of coronation like their English counterparts. Instead they went through the inauguration known as enkinging, derived from ancient Celtic custom, where the king was placed above the Stone of Destiny, a symbolic object brought to Scotland from the ancient kingdom of Dalriada; according to legend, it had been brought there from Egypt by Scota, daughter of one of the Pharaohs.[18] As part of the ceremony, the king and congregation listened to the recital of a long list of names which marked out his royal predecessors as far back as the earliest of kings. If anything, this nostalgic sojourn through the annals reinforced that the current occupant descended from an impressive pedigree, his credentials rooted deep in history. At no point during the ceremony was the king anointed with holy oil, despite more recent attempts to gain papal approval to do so; the English kings, themselves anointed in this way, felt that it would be prejudicial to their own status, and vehemently lobbied the Curia to prevent it.[19] There was, after all, only one crown which had been worn by Belinus.

Scotland's earls, including Moray, Atholl and Mar, were powerful, but only in their immediate lordships and retinues, or *meinye*, with whom they travelled around the country. Unlike their English counterparts, such as the earls of Gloucester, Cornwall and Lancaster, the Scottish earls held lands associated with their title only. For instance, the Earl of Atholl had his chief seat at Moulin and the majority of his lands were close by.[20] Meanwhile, an earl in England could own lands all across the kingdom, so someone like the Earl of Surrey held lands in Sussex, Norfolk and Yorkshire, giving him power and lordship across a much wider area, and with it greater influence.[21] To broaden their influence north of the border, Scottish earls could find themselves seeking royal patronage through offices within the royal household, but this was not an automatic right. Robert Bruce would later capitalise on this need.

Under David I and his successors, Scotland saw the ascendancy of the three justiciars, the chief judicial and administrative officers of the Crown, a system developed in England. The Justiciar of Scotia took on the key role for Scotland north of the Forth and the Clyde, while the remaining two were appointed to Lothian and Galloway respectively.[22] Reporting to the justiciars were the twenty-six sheriffs, again based on the English model, who were appointed to represent the king in the localities, collecting revenues as a result of imposed taxation, presiding over courts and hearing complaints, and increasingly given roles such as constabling castles within their sheriffdoms when necessary.[23]

Along with these came other major titles of the realm. The steward, for instance, held responsibility for managing the ever-growing royal household. So important was this office that before the fourteenth century was out, a steward, or stewart, would become King of Scots in their own right. The chamberlain, meanwhile, acted as a treasurer, maintaining a careful watch over the royal revenues, while the constable and the marischal were appointed to organise the royal military resources, the marischal having the specific role of overseeing the royal cavalry in times of war. The role of chancellor developed at this time as well, but unlike the others it was not hereditary; those who undertook it were often drawn from the clergy. The holder was responsible for the king's spiritual welfare, presiding over his chapel, but also acted as his chancery. Through them, royal writs or *brieves*, essentially the written word of the king, were prepared and issued, and his seals, the authentication of his royal will, were kept safe and strictly regulated. As the reliance on written records grew, so did the number of clerks and chaplains who were drafted in to support the chancellor in his work.[24]

As the royal administration evolved and professionalised, it would have felt indistinguishable from the royal households of the kings of England and France.[25] In all, the growth of a sophisticated royal household ensured that the Scottish system of government was both efficient and stable, creating a powerful monarchy that was able to exercise its will over the majority of its subjects.

Knights were also an important part of medieval Scottish society; indeed, they proved crucial to Robert I's accession and subsequent rule. Providers of military might, the knights were often given fertile lands, which were organised into baronies and knights' fees, giving them both local power and an income. Some held their lands directly from the Crown, while others were retained as sub-tenants by virtue of service to local lords, earls or the Church. Another product of King David I's vision, Scotland's knightly class became the core military strength of the Crown. Tournaments, those chivalric events which provided opportunities for knights to come together, hone their martial skills and display their prowess in order to gain worldly reputation but also employment, were a feature of Scottish life, and by competing in tournaments all across Europe they fostered a broader cultural connection.[26] These colourful events would have been rich with heraldry, some of which survives in the Bannatyne mazer, which preserves their knightly armorial bearings.[27]

Scottish lords, whether the king, the earls, the churchmen or the knights, would farm out their lands to tenants. Payment was either in coin or in kind, and occurred at set times during the year. In times of war, tenants could be called upon to fight if they had the necessary skill. In the Western Isles, the lordships often provided galleys in lieu of men at such times, which was known as ship service.[28] As the Scottish Wars of Independence got underway, a regular provision of local inhabitants was critical in raising arms to fend off repeated attacks from the English.

England, of course, was the dominant player in the British Isles. After the Normans conquered the kingdom, they continued to polish the complex system of governance left by the Saxons, which helped to centralise and bind the kingdom as a single political unit. Capitalising on its size, wealth and powerful lordships, the English Crown could command significant armies in times of war and have the money and might to dominate its neighbours when it was focussed and determined behind a single cause. It often, but not exclusively, had the ear of the Curia in Rome, and could call upon long-established diplomatic relationships across the European kingdoms and beyond, which could be employed to Scotland's detriment. The ten English earls wielded far more power and influence than their Scots counterparts, and the English king could call upon his extensive royal household, in which knights, the core nucleus of any royal army, held great status. Scotland, however, was more decentralised and culturally diverse. Throughout the thirteenth century, the western lordships, while technically subjects of the King of Scots, continued to exercise independence from the monarchy in daily life. They had their own laws, still levied the wergild or 'blood price' for murder, and could, if challenged, pose a significant threat to the king.[29] But in many aspects, as a result of centuries of political and social development, the Scottish kingdom was not altogether dissimilar to its much larger neighbour.

The greatest bone of contention between the two neighbours, and one which was to be repeatedly revisited during the Middle Ages, was the exact location of the border between the two kingdoms. King David I, when heir to the throne, spent much of his youth at the court of King Henry I of England. Henry had married David's sister, Edith Matilda, and the brothers-in-law seemed to form a genuine affection. It was during this prolonged stay that David saw English government and custom at first hand, and he very much liked what he saw. As a genuine friendship grew, Henry rewarded David with the earldom of Huntingdon in 1114, as well as granting him by royal licence the right to marry Matilda, the widowed daughter of the Saxon rebel Earl Waltheof, who had challenged the rule of William the Conqueror in 1075 only to find his head in a basket for his ill-ventured effort. David acquired wealth from this marriage and extensive estates in the Midlands, and this show of royal favour created a long-term bond between the Scottish and English rulers.[30]

When David I succeeded his elder brother Alexander I (r. 1107–24), he returned north with many boon companions who owed him service, including Robert de Brus, who had originally hailed from Brix in Normandy where Henry I had spent much time before his rule commenced. Brus was given lands in Scotland and encouraged to settle.[31] Many more followed him.

Eleven years into David's eventful reign, King Henry I died and England was plunged into civil war between the cousins Stephen and Matilda. The King of Scots saw his opportunity. Capitalising on this strife, he marched his army, along with own son Henry, into the Scottish Marches, capturing lands there. King Stephen, forced to fight wars on multiple fronts, had no real choice but to acknowledge David's possession of Carlisle, Cumbria south of the Solway and the earldom of Huntingdon, the latter, of course, having been bequeathed to him by Henry I. Stephen also granted David's son Henry the lands in Northumbria between the rivers Tweed and Tyne, except for the castles of Bamburgh and Newcastle. In return, father and son gave their fealty to Stephen, who likely felt confident that he had closed down one front in his seemingly never-ending family war.[32] If so, he was mistaken; before long, David had possession of both Bamburgh and Newcastle.

But such gains, achieved in times of war, could only really be maintained by the key personalities involved. Once they were removed from the field, everything was to play for once again. David died in 1153 and was followed shortly after by King Stephen. Henry of Huntingdon, David's son, also lay dead, so the Scots crown passed to David's grandson Malcolm IV (r. 1153–65), who inherited the unenviable task of facing the energetic and determined Henry of Anjou, the founder of the Plantagenet dynasty in England and ruler of the vast Angevin Empire. As King Henry II, he brought a vigorous determination to restore order to England after twenty years of war and reclaim the historic lands and privileges enjoyed by the English Crown under his grandfather Henry I. By 1157, the English king had wrested back Newcastle, Bamburgh and Carlisle, as well as the lands in Northumbria. At a stroke, the clock had been turned back to 1135.

Malcolm's defeat rankled, and he seethed resentfully for the rest of his life. Following his death in 1165 without direct male issue, the crown passed to his brother William I the Lion (r. 1165–1214). William also inherited his brother's burning desire to reclaim the lands taken back by Henry II, and when the English king faced an internal rebellion across his extensive lands in England, Ireland and France, the King of Scots joined the English rebels and invaded northern England in 1173. Unlike David I's campaign years earlier, however, William's was far from successful. In 1174, he was captured at the Battle of Alnwick and taken south to meet Henry at Northampton. Over the following months, an indignant King of England extracted the ultimate penalty from his rebellious neighbour. The Lion was forced to render homage for his kingdom, Henry claiming overlordship in a way captured vividly by Geoffrey of Monmouth in *Historia Regum Britanniae*.[33] This was a significant blow to the Scottish Crown, for in bending the knee and acknowledging Henry II as his liege lord William I had subjected himself and his kingdom to external interference. England would, and could, dominate to Scotland's detriment, if it so chose.

Yet Henry felt magnanimous in victory, and by 1185 he had granted the confiscated earldom of Huntingdon to William's brother David, who paid homage to the English king for its possession. William continued to protest the terms under which he had been released, claiming that an oath extracted under duress was no oath at all, and generally this was the view of the medieval political world. Nonetheless, it stood. By 1189, the King of Scots was able to find some relief at the court of Richard I, son and successor to Henry II; in return for a cash settlement to help fund the Crusades, Richard was prepared to forgo English claims to Scottish overlordship. It was a get-out-of-jail-free card. However, although this was to Scotland's advantage in the short term, it was a somewhat ambiguous arrangement and left an uneasy political minefield for all future royal successors to both kingdoms. They would navigate it, or manipulate it, as each saw fit.

In the thirteenth century, the question of the border and the growing issue of homage continued to vex minds north and south. Effort was put into forging closer links between both royal houses, and to this effect, William I's successor, Alexander II (r. 1214–49), married Joan, daughter of King John of England (r. 1189–1216). While they had no children, the marriage helped to bring peace between the two countries, especially after King John was succeeded by his nine-year-old son Henry III in 1216. Henry and Alexander were brothers-in-law, and in 1237 the border between the two countries was finally fixed in the very place it remains today. The King of Scots renounced his claim to Cumbria, Westmoreland and Northumberland in return for English lands in Tynedale (an earlier gift made by Henry II) and Penrith, which were valued jointly at £200.[34] Alexander II successfully avoided the thorny issue of homage.

Despite his losses in England, the King of Scots set his sights on a different prize altogether. Centuries before, the Western Isles of Scotland had been wrenched from Scots control by invading Norsemen. By 1249 they remained in Norwegian hands, under the remote rule of King Haakon IV. Alexander turned aggressor, raising a fleet and sailing around the Mull of Kintyre and into the Firth of Lorn. But when he landed on the Isle of Kerrera, opposite Oban, he was taken ill and died suddenly on 8 July, hopes of reconquering the Western Isles fading with him.[35]

This remained the case until 1261, when Alexander II's successor and namesake, Alexander III (r. 1249–86), decided to take up his father's cause. Initially he hoped to find a peaceful way to expand his authority into the traditional heartlands of Scotia. Yet when Haakon IV, now very old but still in power, imprisoned the Scottish diplomatic embassy sent to pursue Alexander's offer, the signal was clear. If the King of Scots wanted them back, he would have to fight for them like his father before him. In 1262, he responded, sending a force commanded by William, Earl of Mar to the Isle of Skye, where he devastated the island. The gambit worked, for Haakon, despite his age, was determined to meet his enemy in the field. Crowning his son Magnus Lagaboater ('the law mender') in his stead, Haakon set sail late in the summer of 1263 and headed to his far-flung territories.[36]

Haakon's campaign did not get off to a good start, and even though he was joined by Magnus and Daguld of Guimorra, many of the Chieftains in the Western Isles decided to support the King of Scots. It was all over by 2 October 1263, when Haakon's fleet was forced to land after being battered by storms and subsequently defeated in a minor skirmish known as the Battle of Largs. With no choice but to retreat, on 29 October the Norwegian king fell ill and died in the Bishop's Palace at Kirkwall on 16 December.[37]

Despite the military victories, Scotland did not secure the return of the Western Isles until 1266, when Alexander III and Magnus Lagaboater agreed the Treaty of Perth. This agreement did not include Shetland, which remained outside the Scottish kingdom until 1466. In return for his gains, Alexander agreed to pay 4,000 marks and an additional 100 marks every year in perpetuity.[38] Despite the levy, which lapsed within a century, Alexander had achieved something that his father had not, and – with the exception of Shetland – had asserted his influence across the western part of his kingdom. The central governance and military arrangements that had been developing in Scotland since the twelfth century were now paying dividends.

At the same time that he was flexing his muscles in the west, Alexander also brought his military reputation to bear on the Isle of Man. In 1264, the year after King Haakon's death at Kirkwall, King Magnus of Man offered to bend the knee and give homage to the King of Scots in return for recognition as king of the island. Alexander agreed, and without any military intervention had secured a strategic asset of immeasurable value. The Isle of Man lies only 30 miles off the coast of England, 50 miles from Wales and a stone's throw from Ireland. The King of Scots possessing such a strategic piece of land did not go unnoticed in England, where Henry III ruled.[39] When King Magnus died within a year without legitimate issue, the benefit was all the greater, the island defaulting to Alexander. When the local populace rebelled in 1275 under an illegitimate son of King Magnus, Alexander III had no problem in quashing the rebellion.

The relationship between Scotland and England continued on good terms. Like his father before him, Alexander III had married into the English Plantagenet royal line; his wife was Margaret, daughter of Henry III. Alexander was, after all, the possessor of a good bloodline; his mother was Marie de Coucy, daughter of Inguerrand III, Lord of Coucy in Picardy, France. Alexander and Margaret had married at York during Christmas 1251, when he was but ten and his bride eleven. On Christmas Day, the infant king had been ceremonially knighted, along with twenty others, and his father-in-law had been careful to present to him 'a beautiful sword with a silk covered scabbard with decorated silver pommel and accompanying belt'.[40]

Unlike his father, and perhaps due to his vulnerable age, Alexander was urged by Henry III and his ministers to pay homage for the kingdom of Scotland. Alexander had been well advised, however, and the young boy replied with some courtesy that he had come to York 'to be married and not to answer so difficult a matter'.[41] This evasion worked, for Henry did not pursue the issue, but did, through affection for his daughter, maintain an interest in affairs north of the border – especially when Margaret took time to settle, writing to her father, according to chronicler Matthew Paris, that she felt imprisoned in Edinburgh Castle, that 'dreary and solitary place'.[42]

Despite these early reservations, the marriage bloomed into an intimate and supportive relationship. Alexander visited England with Margaret in 1260, and there she gave birth to her only daughter and namesake, returning to Scotland the following year. The King of Scots was criticised at home for allowing his queen to give birth in England, for had the child been a boy the heir's status would have been complicated, keeping in mind the tricky political machinations surrounding the thorny issue of homage. Two other children followed: Alexander, born on 21 January 1264, and David, born on 30 March 1273. The queen died just two years after David's birth, on 26 February 1275, at Cupar in Fife, at the young age of thirty-five. Alexander was bereft. So much so that he did not remarry for ten years, labouring under the pretence that the Scottish succession was secure, with an heir and a spare. Even the chronicler of Lanercost was forced to admit that Margaret 'was a woman of great beauty, chastity and humility, three qualities seldom united in one individual'.[43]

In England, Henry III died on 16 November 1272, after a long and often challenging reign that had lasted fifty-six years. His son, the lord Edward, inherited the throne while in Sicily on Crusade, and when he returned in 1274, Alexander III was invited to attend his brother-in-law's coronation at Westminster on 19 August. It may have been that the King of Scots was asked to carry one the swords of state into the abbey as part of the ancient coronation ritual, but Alexander wanted written assurances that this would not prejudice his status as the King of Scots. In the end, he did not perform the role, nor was he asked to perform homage either for Scotland or more rightly for the lands he held from the king in England at Tynedale and Penrith.[44]

However, Alexander would not be able to avoid his homage forever, and four years after the coronation he was back in England. Meeting Edward I at Tewkesbury on 16 October, he offered to perform his homage for Tynedale and Penrith. Edward deferred, wanting him to perform it in front of his council at Westminster twelve days later, which Alexander agreed to do. The King of Scots must have sensed a ruse, however, for such a public appearance had to be to Edward's benefit, so when he entered the chamber at Westminster on 29 October, he was prepared. Bending the knee to another king offered a difficult political and social predicament. Edward I, like English kings before and after him, was required to do the same for the lands held in Aquitaine, Ponthieu and Montreuil in France; he had done so before Philip III in 1274 when returning through that kingdom. On this occasion, Alexander III, to help protect his dignity, and no doubt suspicious that there was a bigger game afoot, asked for Robert Bruce VI, Earl of Carrick, to represent him in the room and act as his proxy. This way, Alexander did not need to physically bend the knee, although he was nevertheless bound by the homage performed. Edward agreed. Records of the event are conflicting. According to the English account, Robert said,

I Robert, Earl of Carrick by virtue of the power given me by the lord the King of Scotland in the presence of the King of Scotland and by his command, do thus swear fealty to Edward, King of England. I, Alexander, King of Scotland, will keep true faith with

Edward, King of England in matters of life, limb and earthly honour and will faithfully perform the services due for the lands and tenements that I hold of the King of England.[45]

In another version, this time captured in the 1320s in the Cartulary of Dunfermline, Robert's words on behalf of his master were much simpler: 'I become your man for the lands which I hold of you in the realm of England, for which I owe you homage, reserving my kingdom.'[46] The latter was a much clearer and more direct assertion, but was possibly written with the considerable benefit of hindsight for much had happened between Scotland and England by the time it was committed to the page.

What happened after the act of homage is a matter of accepted record. Alexander had been right to suspect trickery, for at that moment the Bishop of Norwich, William de Middleton, interrupted and added, 'And let it be reserved to the King of England, if he should have right to your homage for the kingdom.' Alexander, half-expecting this, was able to confidently rebuff the ambitious bishop, who had no doubt been put up to the task by his king, replying, 'Nobody but God himself has the right of the homage for my realm of Scotland, and I hold it of nobody but God himself.'[47] It was a decisive and unambiguous response that closed down the debate. Edward, probably as he expected, had been unable to advance his claim of overlordship, but had kept the issue live in the records for his successors. The Earl of Carrick completed the homage while still holding the Gospels, with Alexander interjecting at the end again to reiterate that his homage was 'for the lands that I hold of you in the kingdom'.

The events at the English council in Westminster in 1278 did not sour the brotherly relationship between the two kings. There is much correspondence between the two men that goes beyond the usual formal written custom of royal affection. In 1284, while Edward was finishing his conquest of Wales, Alexander had written to him enquiring after his health and sending him four fine gyrfalcons.[48] When Alexander's eldest son died at Ladoies Abbey, Fife, on 28 January 1284, at the tender age of twenty, the King of England sent his condolences to his grieving brother-in-law. The King of Scots replied on 20 April writing that 'faithful friends know not fickleness in their affection, and after our long experience we ought with good reason to praise the faithfulness of your excellency for the many kindnesses we have received'.[49]

The death of Alexander's son was all the more significant because just three years earlier, in 1281, his youngest son, David, had also perished. Later that year, Alexander's only daughter, Margaret, was sent to Norway to marry its new king, Eric II Magnusson. The marriage was successful albeit short lived, Margaret herself dying in childbirth giving life to her only daughter and namesake. In January 1284, this young child, the so called 'Maid of Norway', had unexpectedly become the heir to the throne of Scotland as a result of the death of her mother and two uncles. Suddenly, Alexander III found himself with a succession crisis, for no female heir had ever inherited the throne of Scotland, and he had not remarried following the death of his own wife in 1275, believing his royal line secure. In a desperate attempt to avert catastrophe, Alexander struck up a match with Yolande de Dreux, the daughter of Robert II, Count of Dreux in France. They married at Jedburgh Abbey on 14 October 1285. The count boasted a good pedigree, having descended from King Louis VI of France, and so Yolande was a suitable wife for the king.[50]

What happened next was catastrophic for Scotland. On 18 March 1286, Alexander III attended his council in Edinburgh Castle. Following the day's work, he spent the evening feasting in the hall. Afterwards, despite the late hour and the onset of terrible weather, he was determined to head out with his squires and make the short but treacherous journey to Kinghorn, where Queen Yolande was in residence. According to the chronicler of Lanercost, the journey was fraught with peril:

> When he arrived at the village near the crossing, the ferry master warned him of the danger, and advised him to go back; but when [the king] asked him in return whether he was afraid to die with him; 'By no means,' quoth he, 'it would be a great honour to share the fate of your father's son.' Thus he arrived at the burgh of Inverkeithing, in profound darkness accompanied by only three squires. The manager of his saltpans, a married man of that town, recognising him by his voice, called out; 'My Lord, what are you doing here in such a storm and such darkness? Often I have tried to persuade you that your nocturnal rambles will bring you no good. Stay with us, and we will provide you with decent fare and all that you want till morning light.' 'No need for that,' said the other with a laugh, 'but provide me with a couple of bondmen, to go afoot as guide to the way.' And it came to pass that when

they proceeded two miles, one and all lost all knowledge of the way, owing to the darkness; only the horses, by natural instinct, picked out the road. While they were thus separated from each other, the squires took the right road.[51]

Alexander became separated from his escort, and in the darkness of the night, made inhospitable by dense fog, his horse stumbled as it travelled along the cliff edge, throwing the king off his mount. His body was discovered the next morning on the foreshore, his neck broken. As his remains were recovered and transferred to Dunfermline Abbey, where he was entombed in the south aisle, the Kingdom of Scotland was suddenly confronted with a crisis. The heir to the throne was the Maid of Norway, who was not yet three years old. Queen Yolande insisted that she was pregnant, but after three months, whether the baby was miscarried or was never there at all, it was clear that there would be no new heir.[52] On 28 April 1286, at Scone, the lords of the land swore fealty to the Maid of Norway as Queen of Scotland, promising to preserve and protect her kingdom and maintain peace.[53] The Scottish nobility were about to tread a treacherous path fraught with danger and uncertainty. Many would succumb to the peril.

2

The Bruces of Annandale

Robert Bruce was descended from a distinguished family line. His pedigree, by the time of his birth on 11 July 1274, was long established in Scotland, the family first settling under the patronage of David I shortly after the king's accession in 1124. Their ascent – from lords of Annandale to earls of Carrick and later kings of Scotland – is a tale of ambition, loyalty and gritty determination.

Robert de Brus I, the founder of the dynasty, began his life in the duchy of Normandy, which belonged to Henry I of England. The holder of strategically important lands in Brus or Bruis, now Brix, just south of Cherbourg, Robert was a powerful player and boon companion at the court of his patron. Much like Henry, Robert may have descended from the Vikings, whose raiding parties and later settlements in Normandy – the home of 'the North Men' – occurred two centuries before. Given the size and importance of his landholdings, it may well be that de Brus was related to Henry himself in some degree or other, enjoying a close bond of loyalty.[1]

When Henry I sought to bring his followers over to England and build up a loyal base of supporters there, he rewarded his long-time friend with the lordship of Cleveland, a gift of significant value, which meant that Robert soon headed across the Channel to enter into his lands and enjoy his new-found position in medieval English society. As his wealth grew, de Brus established an Augustinian priory at Guisborough in Yorkshire, which the family continued to patronise right up until the early fourteenth century. Indeed, so important was this abbey to them that, despite their conventional piety, they never established another ecclesiastical foundation,

35

even in Scotland after they settled across the border.[2] Guisborough Priory, it would seem, stole their hearts.

As well as men like Robert de Brus, Henry I attracted others to his banner. The son of the King of Scots, later King David I, was another to whom Henry granted gifts of royal patronage. These good friends, tied by a knightly code, were well acquainted, having fought side by side in previous campaigns. When David ascended the throne of Scotland in 1124, he was quick to grant to their mutual friend de Brus the lordship of Annandale in south-west Scotland, a lucrative and strategically important demesne on the border between the two countries. For David, the appointment of de Brus was part of a much larger and ambitious plan to anglicise the south, and Annandale gave Robert the task of protecting the west, where Galloway remained distinctly Gaelic-speaking, with its own laws and entrenched customs.

The trustworthy de Brus quickly secured his position and status in the Scottish kingdom, becoming something of an unofficial warden of the west, long before that title was formally recognised. He would not be alone, for David and his successors drew other Norman lords into Scotland and into the Dumfries and Galloway region, including the Stewarts, who had originated from Dol in Brittany and now held lands at Renfrew and North Kyle, while Cunningham was granted to Hugh de Morville, the constable, the Crown retaining South Kyle. In the following century, the Balliol family, originally from Bailleul-en-Vimeu in Picardy, would marry into the lordship of Galloway.[3] This conglomeration of Norman and Breton lords did much to secure the Scottish Crown's hold in the south-west, as well as other areas in the kingdom, creating an Anglo-Norman lordship with roots deep in the Scottish kingdom by the dawn of the fourteenth century.

The lordship of Annandale was strategically sited. In the twelfth and thirteenth centuries, the main route across the western border between Scotland and England was not past Gretna like today. Instead, travellers crossed the upper Solway to the west of Gretna at low tide, reaching Scotland nearer to Annan, as here the grounds were safer and less marshy. The regular flood of people making the crossing travelled through or near Annan and Lochmaben castles, both under the command of House Bruce, making both fortifications a gateway into the Scottish kingdom.[4] Annan initially became the heart of the lordship, with its castle used as the *caput* or seat of the administration, but following a significant flood in the twelfth century, which saw a substantial part of the motte and lower bailey swept away in the raging torrents, Lochmaben became the centre of the lordship instead, the officials relocating there with the administrative records.[5] Lochmaben was well situated, too. The castle sat on a promontory that extended out into the loch, with a moat cut on the landward side, effectively creating an impressive defensive island.[6] Those defences would be much tested in the coming years.

With landholdings in both England and Scotland, the Bruces would soon discover that loyalty to two masters placed them in a compromised and unenviable position. Within three years of Henry I's death, England was torn apart by the civil war between King Stephen and Matilda. When King David ventured south with war banners unfurled, Robert de Brus weighed his conscience and threw his lot in with the English king. Out of respect for the King of Scots, who had given him everything in Scotland, de Brus forfeited his lordship of Annandale before engaging the Scots at the Battle of the Standard, fought at Cowton Moor near Northallerton in Yorkshire in 1138. Whether a cleverly devised strategy of hedged loyalties or a simple act of conscience, Bruce's younger son, also called Robert, and known as le Meshin (meaning the younger or the cadet), joined the forces of King David, placing father and son on opposite sides of the battlefield. On the eve of the coming clash, according to the chronicler Aelred of Rievaulx, both father and son met in an attempt to dissuade the other from fighting the following day; neither achieved his goal. In any event, it mattered not. Both men survived the battle, in which the English prevailed, and de Brus resumed his lordship in Scotland once more.[7]

Following his death in 1141, Robert de Brus was laid to rest in the very foundation he had created at Guisborough Priory. He was succeeded by his eldest son, Adam, but by 1171 that line came to an end, leaving the estates to be divided among four co-heiresses. Annandale passed to Robert le Meshin, who spent considerably more time north of the border than his father had. He attracted a band of knights including the Herrieses, Kirkpatricks, Crosbies and Johnstones to him, gifting lands within his lordship for them to settle, reinforcing a burgeoning feudal life in the southern part of Scotland.[8] In return for land, Robert Bruce II and his son Robert Bruce III cultivated tight bonds of loyalty within the confines of their lordship, which further improved their status, position and power in the region.

Like his namesakes before him, Robert Bruce III continued to cultivate a close relationship with Scotland's successive kings. He went on to marry an illegitimate daughter of William the Lion, but despite such favour, the marriage was childless. Upon Robert's premature death, his titles passed to his nephew, also called Robert, son of his brother William. Robert IV, Lord of Annandale, was unwittingly to have the most profound impact on his dynasty's future fortunes, for in 1219 he married Isabel, second daughter of David, Earl of Huntingdon, who was brother to the King of Scots.[9] Isabel of Huntingdon's pedigree far outweighed any illegitimate daughter of a king, and this marriage proved a fruitful one, with Robert IV and Isabel producing offspring, in particular the heir, Robert V.

Robert V, Lord of Annandale, was born a year after his parents' marriage and was to become a man of renowned energy and vigour, being granted the title of 'the Noble' by his contemporaries. To history he is remembered as 'the Competitor'. He would live a long life, reaching the respectable age of seventy-five – a significant milestone in the medieval world, when many baronial males died in their fifties and the common folk were lucky to reach forty. It would almost grant him mythical status, with the chronicler of Lanercost making special reference to his piety as the reason for his survival into his dotage.[10] God seemed to favour him, or at least that's what contemporaries thought. His qualities were celebrated, and the aforementioned chronicler, who appeared to take a particular liking to him, wrote,

> He was of handsome appearance, a gifted speaker, remarkable for his influence, and, what is more important, most devoted to God and the clergy … It was his custom to entertain and feast more liberally than all the other courtiers, and was most hospitable to all his guests, nor used the pilgrims to remain outside his gates, for his door was open to the wayfarer.[11]

Already respected by many, Bruce's status was about to soar. On 4 March 1238, Queen Joan, daughter of King John of England and wife to Alexander II of Scotland, died without issue. The king was left without a direct heir. Before he could remarry – he later chose Marie de Coucy and begat a son – Alexander II named Robert Bruce V as his immediate heir following the death of Robert's elder cousin John of Scotland, who had perished in 1237.[12] As a grandson of

David, Earl of Huntingdon through his mother Isabel, Robert had a direct claim to the Scottish throne, and Alexander's public recognition of that at a gathering of the magnates in 1238 ensured the nobles knew where to place their loyalty should the king die without direct issue.[13] This recognition fell redundant in late 1241 when the king's son was born, but in the three years that he had been marked out as heir apparent, Robert must have felt an elevated sense of his own position among his peers, and it was something that he would fail to shake off for the rest of his life.

In May 1240, he secured a valuable, if not richly endowed marriage contract. Riding high, his wife was Isabel de Clare, daughter of the English Earl of Gloucester. Despite her meagre dowry of a single manor in Sussex, Isabel brought something much more appealing to her husband: prestige. The de Clare family were preeminent earls in England, and this marital tie bound the Bruce family much closer to a well-respected noble house. This only helped to increase Robert's sense of his exalted position further.[14] England's Henry III also gave Bruce, who still held estates in England, custody of Carlisle Castle, well sited immediately south of his Annandale lordship yet just across the border in England.[15] In 1237, following the death of his uncle John of Scotland, who had died without male issue, John's lands as Earl of Chester and Huntingdon were divided between his sisters, which included Robert's mother, who inherited a one-third share of the honour of Huntingdon and 'a third of the lordship held by Earl David north of the border, a lordship which included Garioch in Aberdeenshire and the growing Burgh of Dundee'.[16] These lucrative endowments came to Robert upon his mother's death in 1252, adding as much as £170 annually – a considerable sum in the mid-thirteenth century – to his overall wealth.[17]

These additional landholdings raised Bruce's importance in England, and his close connection with the English royal family continued. In 1264, during the bitter baronial conflict between Henry III and his overmighty vassal Simon de Montfort, Robert Bruce V was called upon to fight, which he duly did for the English king. In April he took a large force to Nottingham.[18] At the Battle of Lewes, fought that year in Sussex, Henry III, his son and heir the future Edward I, and Robert Bruce were all captured. Bruce was immediately ransomed, and his son and namesake, Robert, later sixth lord of Annandale, made haste from Scotland to settle the debt.[19] In the end, Henry III, his eldest son and their royalist supporters overcame Simon de Montfort at the Battle of Evesham in 1265, while the wider rebellion was crushed as a whole the following year after a protracted siege at Kenilworth Castle, the longest in English history.

As England settled back into a period of relative peace, Robert Bruce and his son followed the fervour of the day and joined the retinue of Henry's sons Edward and Edmund of Lancaster on Crusade to the Holy Land in 1270, where they stayed for two years with the Plantagenet brothers.[20] This was an impressive feat given that Robert V was fifty when he departed on what he thought was God's Holy mission to recover the Kingdom of Jerusalem, which had fallen in 1187 to the armies of Saladin, Sultan of Egypt and Syria and founder of the Ayyubid dynasty.[21]

It was on his return in 1272 that Robert took the opportunity to visit the Abbey of Clairvaux in penitence, hoping to settle a long overdue curse which had been placed on his family since the time of Robert de Brus in the 1140s. The curse, as it was later remembered, had been pronounced by an indignant Maelmaedhoig Ua Morgair, otherwise known as St Malachy O' Moore, who had been Archbishop of Armagh. He was a renowned Irish Church reformer whose later life had been spent on various pilgrimages to and from Rome. Whenever he travelled, he would ensure a sojourn in south-western Scotland, having sailed from Antrim. According to the Lanercost chronicle, on such a journey in 1140, St Malachy arrived at Annan:

> [He] enquired of the inhabitants who would deign to receive him to hospitality. When they declared that an illustrious man, lord of that district, who was there at the time, would willingly undertake that kindness [Robert de Brus], he humbly besought some dinner, which was liberally provided for him. And when the servants enquired of him, seeing that he had been travelling, whether they should anticipate the dinner hour or await the master's table, he begged that he might have dinner at once. Accordingly, a table having been dressed for him on the north side of the hall, he sat down with his two companions to refresh himself; and, as the servants were discussing the death of a certain robber that had been taken, who was then awaiting the sentence of justice, the baron entered the hall, and bade his feasting guests welcome. Then the gentle bishop relying entirely upon the courteousness of the noble said 'As a pilgrim, I crave a boon from your excellency,

that, as sentence of death has hitherto polluted any place where I was present, let the life of the culprit, if he has committed an offence, be given to me'. The noble host agreed, not amiably, but deceitfully and according to the wisdom of his age, which is folly before God, privily ordered that the malefactor should suffer death. When he had been hanged, and the bishop had finished his meal, the baron came in to his dinner; and when the bishop returned thanks to God and to his host, he said 'I pronounce the blessing of God upon this hall, and upon this table, and upon all who shall eat thereat hereafter'. But, as he was passing through the town, he beheld by the wayside the thief hanging on the gallows. Then, sorrowing in spirit, he pronounced a heavy sentence, first on the lord of the place and his offspring, and next upon the town [Annan]; which the course of events confirmed; for soon afterward the rich man [Robert de Brus] died in torment, three of his heirs in succession perished in the flower of their age, some before they had been five years in possession, others before they had been three.[22]

Robert de Brus' unforgiving treatment of the local thief had apparently cast a shadow on the Bruce lordship for more than a century. Anything that went wrong, including the major flood at Annan or the premature death of an heir or family member, was quickly attributed to the curse of St Malachy. Robert V, over 130 years later, certainly believed in it enough to regularly visit the tomb of the dead saint at the Abbey of Clairvaux to render penance for his family's previous misdemeanours. In 1272, he donated 'three silver lamps with their lights', no doubt to burn in perpetuity; these were pointed gifts, possibly in reference to the saint's reputation that through his reforms he had cast light on the Irish Church.[23] Either way, such acts of spiritual devotion were typical of the medieval age, and show that Robert Bruce took his declarations of piety seriously.

A year after his offering, Bruce, now fifty-three, married a second time following the death of Isabel de Clare, choosing the twice-widowed Christine de Ireby, daughter of William Ireby, a knight of Cumberland.[24] By the time of the marriage, Robert V already had at least three children, including his son and heir Robert, a second son named Richard who died in 1287, and a daughter, Isabel, who married Sir John Marmaduke. The prospect of another maternal figure in the family was not well received by all, and tensions grew between Robert V and his heir.

The younger Robert was soon preoccupied with a marriage of his own, although the events leading up to it would draw far more commentary than any disgruntled family member's views on the suitability of the union. While crusading in the Holy Land, Robert had served alongside Adam of Kilconquhar, from the cadet branch of the earls of Fife, who, through right of his wife Marjorie, was Earl of Carrick. At the Siege of Acre, Kilconquhar was mortally injured, and Robert was charged with taking news of his death and possibly any last words to his widow. On his return, he dutifully set out into Galloway to visit the Countess of Carrick, a neighbour of the Annandale lordship. He found her out hunting:

> ... she met a distinguished and very handsome young knight by the name of Robert de Bruce ... When greetings and kisses had been given on each side, as is the custom of courtiers, she begged him to stay for hunting and walking about; when he resisted, she by force, so to speak, with her own hand pulled back his reins and brought the knight to her, unwilling though he was, to her castle of Turnberry. And while staying there, along with his followers for the space of fifteen days or more, he secretly married the Countess, the friends and well-wishers of both knowing nothing about it. They had in no way obtained the royal consent for the marriage, and because of this it was the common talk of the realm that she had all but carried off this young man into marriage by force.[25]

It would seem highly unlikely that Marjorie, Countess of Carrick, kept her young, handsome knight hostage until he chivalrously agreed to marry her. It is more likely that this was a love match or one of political expediency, and Bruce and Marjorie wasted no time in binding themselves in union before she could be married off to another.[26] Widowed or unmarried women of her status were often vulnerable to the aggressive advances of unscrupulous lords, so marriage to Robert, a man of her own choosing, would prevent a more troubling outcome. The failure to seek King Alexander III's consent posed a significant dilemma, for he controlled the rights to all noble marriages within his kingdom. Yet a marriage vow made between two consenting parties was beyond his or the Church's gift to put aside. He could, if he chose, imprison them both – or, worse, strip their lands from them – but the years of loyal service to the Crown paid dividends, and the king, after exacting a fine on the presumptuous couple, allowed Robert to assume the title Earl of Carrick in *jure uxoris*, meaning in right of his wife. Things were looking good for the Bruces. Overnight, Robert had become a significant player, one of Scotland's thirteen earls. In social terms, he now held precedence over his father, who was only a lord, yet the elder Robert still dominated as head of the family. As well as the Carrick earldom, which in 1260 was valued at £168, the younger Robert's wife also held lands in the north of Ireland in Larne, focussed around Olderfleet and Glenarm, which had been granted to her grandfather Duncan, Earl of Carrick, over seventy years before by England's King John, who claimed overlordship.[27]

By the time Robert became the sixth lord of Annandale in 1295, he also inherited estates beyond Annandale in Tottenham near London, manors at Hartness and Writtle in Essex, as well as estates in Yorkshire, Northumberland and Cumberland.[28] Back in May 1283 he had also became constable of Carlisle Castle and Sheriff of Cumberland.[29] In just over 160 years, the Bruce family had become significant landholders, with their chief residences at Lochmaben, Turnberry and Loch Doon.[30] The close relationship with the King of Scots continued, a consistent theme through their years in Scotland since 1124, and it is no surprise that it was Robert VI, Earl of Carrick, whom Alexander III chose as his proxy to perform his homage for his lands in England at the court of Edward I in 1277. Such public acts of loyalty and reward represented a high point in the relationship between the two men, emphasising their trust in one another as king and subject.

As well as lands, the Earl of Carrick had also inherited a longstanding rivalry which had persisted in the old principality of Galloway since the days of Fergus, its former ruler. His two sons, Gilbert and Uchtred, had fought bitterly until Gilbert murdered Uchtred in revenge for damage done to his lands. Such crimes within a family were not quickly forgiven or forgotten, and the longstanding enmity was passed on to their successive descendants in the Gaelic tradition as the lands of Fergus remained partitioned. By 1270, the heirs were his two great-granddaughters Marjorie, Countess of Carrick and Dervorguilla, Lady of Galloway. Dervorguilla, whose lands centred on Wigtownshire and Kirkcudbright, married John Balliol the Elder, whose son was to play a major role in events following the death of King Alexander III in 1286. When her husband died, Dervorguilla founded Sweetheart Abbey in her husband's memory and had his embalmed heart placed in an ebony-and-silver casket which she is said to have kept beside her at all times. The heart would be buried with her following her own death in 1290 on the festival of St Agnes. The Lanercost chronicler, who knew of Dervorguilla's reputation, recorded for posterity the inscription which was found upon her tomb:

> Thy peace, of King of Kings! may we implore
> For noble Dervorguilla, now no more?
> Given her among the sacred seers a place
> Uniting Martha's faith with Mary's grace.
> This stone protects her and her husband's heart
> So closely knit not even in death could part.[31]

Robert's marriage to Marjorie and John's to Dervorguilla placed both Bruce and Balliol at odds in an already historic feud.[32] It was set to deteriorate further in the coming decades.

Robert and Marjorie's marriage resulted in eleven children: five sons and six daughters. Their eldest son and heir, named Robert in keeping with family tradition, was born on 11 July 1274. This is our Robert Bruce, whose extraordinary future would see him inherit not just the lordship of Annandale and the earldom of Carrick but, from 1306, the throne of Scotland itself. Yet despite his staggering career, little is known of his childhood. Until the age of twelve, nothing is recorded about him.

Even Robert's place of birth has been held in contention over the centuries. The most likely location is Turnberry Castle, sat precariously on the Ayrshire coast, the seat of his parents in the earldom of Carrick, and not Lochmaben, which was the principal seat of his grandfather Robert V, Lord of Annandale. In the seventeenth century the people of Lochmaben claimed him as their own, proudly adding to the arms of the Burgh, '*E Nobis Liberator Rex*', 'From Us came the Liberator King'. However, evidence for this remains absent.[33] The mystery does not stop there, either. Further speculation has long abounded since the medieval chronicler Geoffrey le Baker of Swinbrooke wrote that Bruce, 'who later became King of Scotland', was born at the Bruce manor of Writtle in Essex.[34] While this is possible, le Baker is the only one who makes this assertion, and he was writing long after his subject's death, later in the fourteenth century. He may have been labouring under a false impression, knowing that Robert's father favoured his manors at Writtle and neighbouring Hatfield Regis, but this was only during his final years, between 1295 to 1304. Le Baker's work is also notoriously littered with factual errors. When compared to more reliable works like Walter of Guisborough, who refers to Bruce as a 'native' of Scotland in his medieval chronicle, it becomes increasingly likely that Robert Bruce was born in Scotland within the earldom of Carrick, most likely at Turnberry Castle.[35]

Just as Robert's place of birth is unclear, so too is his childhood. Nothing survives to offer an intimate glimpse of his young life, and there are no contemporary accounts of his appearance. What is certain, however, is that Robert would have grown up speaking French as his first language, the tongue of his father and grandfather before him. Yet he would also have been able to speak Gaelic, the common tongue of his mother's lands. He most likely had a working knowledge of northern English, too, which had evolved into Lowland Scots vernacular, and quite possibly even Latin, although is by no means certain. In short, he was certainly trilingual in varying forms and this was a product of the rich, diverse world in which he lived in late thirteenth-century Scotland. It would have stood him in good stead, for a working knowledge as broad as his allowed him to communicate with people from all over the country. John Barbour records scenes from 1306 in which Robert, then a fugitive king fleeing the might of Edward I and the English army, was able to command and speak to his men drawn from the south-west, as well as reciting in Gaelic some stories he had heard growing up, including the Charlemagne romance known as *Fierabras*, as well as conjuring up tales of other great underdogs like Hannibal, who took on the might of Rome.[36] He was clearly well read, or at least had been read to, and had demonstrated both a curious nature and a good memory – two skills critical for successful leadership.

As a young boy and heir to his father's estates, Robert would have been educated in the arts of war along with his other brothers. At a very tender age he would have picked up his first wooden sword to be taught the basics of swordsmanship, a skill which would prove essential in his later life. His training did not stop there. He would have learnt how to wield a variety of weapons, from the axe to the lance and the mace. He would have spent hours learning to ride, to hunt and to tourney. His earliest teachers may well have been chosen from among the ranks of his grandfather's retinue, those expert knights who had returned from Crusade only a few years earlier.[37] He would also have been taught the social etiquette demanded of him at court, being expected to dance to the latest songs and understand music and courtly love. He would have been taught the role of the chivalric knight, whose knightly conduct was a code that bound this class of men together across Europe, setting out the rules of the chessboard, never more so than in times of war. If he was to gain a noble reputation, then his manners were as important as his swordplay. All of this he would have grasped before the delicate age of ten.

At this time it was customary in Gaelic culture for elder sons to be sent in fosterage to other suitable noble families for a number of years to hone their skills and toughen their characters.[38] For those families involved, it not only gave them a mark of high honour but bound them to other houses in ties of loyalty and obligations of kinship that could last a lifetime. Trust was at the heart of it. Robert Bruce, advancing in age, confidence and skills, was no exception to this practice. We do not know where he was sent, but there is tantalising evidence that his eldest younger brother, Edward Bruce, was sent to a great family in Ireland, possibly the O'Néills, on account of a contemporary chronicle fragment that records Edward Bruce being invited to become High King of Ireland in 1315 at the invitation of those 'who had educated him in his youth'.[39] But an Irish placement is not certain for Robert, and there were great families much closer to home who could easily have obliged such as the Torthorwalds, Boyds, De Boscos, Carruthers and others. Further north-west there were the MacDonalds and the Campbells of Lochawe.[40] As they completed their fosterage, the brothers may also have proffered their services to more politically significant lords, for in 1304 Edward Bruce was in the retinue of Edward of Caernarvon, the eldest son of Edward I and the future King of England.[41]

The Bruce siblings would have grown up with a religious education that led to a conventional piety. The presence of St Malachy must not have gone unnoticed given Robert's grandfather's regular pilgrimages to the dead saint's tomb. But there were also other saints to whom the family made devotions and votives, including St Cuthbert and St Ninian, the latter's cave being in striking distance, near Whithorn in Galloway, and whose cult may well have been favoured by Bruce's mother, Marjorie. The family still retained their patronage on Guisborough Priory in Yorkshire, founded by their ancestor. Like many of their contemporaries, the Bruce family also favoured St Thomas Becket, whose murder in

Canterbury Cathedral in 1170 and subsequent reported miracles resulted in his canonisation. The Bruces, particularly Robert Bruce VI, Earl of Carrick, visited the shrine often from their family manors in the south-east of England.[42]

So Robert Bruce VII, later King of Scots, grew up with a conventional piety expected of his noble class and exercised his devotions frequently throughout his lifetime. His childhood would have been busy as he grew up alongside his four brothers and six sisters, as well as forging new ties of kinship through fosterage. The first time we see Robert stepping out from the shadows is in 1286, at the age of twelve, when he witnessed a charter, a deed of Alexander MacDonald of Islay to the Cistercian abbey of Paisley.[43] Perhaps MacDonald was the man who fostered Robert. Along with young Robert and his father, the Bishop of Argyll, the vicar of Carrick and others also acted as witnesses. This would be a tumultuous year for Robert's family, for this was when Alexander III of Scotland died, and the Scottish succession hung on the survival of one little girl living in an overseas kingdom. What happened next would set the young man on a path that no one would have seen coming.

3

The Great Cause

Alexander III was laid to rest at Dunfermline Abbey on 29 March 1286. The magnates then swiftly gathered at Scone on 2 April to determine who should succeed the late king and how, in the interim, the government of the kingdom should continue to run. There were two possible successors: the Maid of Norway and the unborn child of Queen Yolande. In such uncertain times, Robert Bruce, Lord of Annandale, sensed that this was the best opportunity he would have to reach out and claim the throne for himself and his dynasty. He had, after all, been briefly made heir apparent in 1238 by Alexander II. Striding into the parliament at Scone, the Lord of Annandale gave an impassioned speech protesting against the rights of any female to inherit the ancient Scottish crown. There was no precedent for it, and Bruce argued that the succession choices in front of them should therefore be rejected. Conveniently, he felt that only a male of close degree should assume the role, and as a direct descendant of David I through David, Earl of Huntingdon, he was the man best placed to undertake the job.[1]

Robert's peers were not so convinced. Sensing trouble, they decided to adjourn until another claimant could state his case with equal passion. John Balliol did not need much encouragement and soon arrived at Scone, where, after much 'bitter pleading' between the two men, those assembled decided it was in everybody's interest to side-step the now somewhat heated debate. All took an oath to maintain the peace of the kingdom and offered fealty to 'the nearest by blood who by right must inherit'.[2] This clever construction effectively meant the issue had been left unanswered, for this could mean the Maid of Norway, any posthumous child of Alexander III, or, failing that, Bruce or Balliol. Ambiguity was in Scotland's best interest.

To guarantee continued peace, it was agreed that government would be undertaken not in the name of any single individual but by six appointed Guardians who would act on behalf of the Crown during such a precarious time. This body of men, made up of two bishops, two earls and two barons, would act in the name of the Community of the Realm. As ever in the medieval age, the community essentially meant the higher levels of society: the bishops, abbots, priors, earls and barons, and, through them, the free tenants of Scotland.[3] The appointment of six instead of one was a shrewd move that helped to create a sense of calm when political stability was most needed.

The appointed panel offered a healthy cross section, representing territorial influences from across Scotland, which theoretically meant no single Guardian would or should dominate the rest. Yet it is not surprising that three of the Guardians – Duncan, Earl of Fife, the premier earl in Scotland, James Stewart, hereditary High Steward of Scotland, and Robert Wishart, Bishop of Glasgow – had sympathies for Robert Bruce of Annandale. Alexander Comyn, Earl of Buchan, and John Comyn, Lord of Badenoch, were both supporters of John Balliol, themselves connected to him through marriage. The sixth Guardian, William Fraser, Bishop of St Andrews, who was the leading bishop in Scotland despite the kingdom having no primatial see like Canterbury in England, was also highly in favour of Balliol.[4] It was envisaged that all six would act in unity to defend and govern the kingdom, and as such, to authenticate their decisions and judgements, a Great Seal was made bearing the motto *ANDREA SCOTIS DUX ESTO COMPATRIOTIS*, 'St Andrew be the leader of the compatriot Scots'.[5] In the absence of a king, St Andrew, the nation's patron saint, was to be their ultimate protector and guiding light.

The Lord of Annandale was far from impressed with this outcome. Leaving Scone, the frustrated patrician raised a force with his son the Earl of Carrick and marched on Galloway, attacking the castles of Dumfries and Wigtown, as well as that of Buittle. It was a strategic move designed to better connect Annandale with Carrick, for these three castles sat between them, but it was also a pointed attack against John Balliol and

Dervorguilla of Galloway. The Guardians were quick to respond to such heavy-handedness, and under the leadership of four of them, including the two Comyns, James Stewart and Bishop Wishart of Glasgow, entered the south-west and laid waste to the region. Their campaign, designed to weaken the economic power base of the Bruces, was clearly successful; two years later, both Dumfries and Wigtown were still unable to contribute tax returns via the sheriffs of that region because of the violence that had taken place.[5] The Guardians had made their point. The Bruces' aggression had stirred a hornet's nest and gained them nothing but a reputation as troublemakers, all too willing to resort to force to drive their point home.

Sensing their vulnerability, the House of Bruce quickly built up a confederacy of like-minded men, in part as a show of strength designed to protect their individual and collective interests. Their call to action rested on an age-old presumption of safety in numbers levied against any unwelcome opposition from Balliol and the Comyns. On 20 September 1286, at Turnberry Castle, Annandale and his son gathered supporters and sealed the Turnberry Bond. The bond itself offered support to Richard de Burgh, Earl of Ulster, and Thomas de Clare of Thomond in their activities to curb the power of local enemies in Ireland, where the Bruces had interests. Those Scots sealing the document also offered their fealty to whoever would inherit the throne of Scotland 'by reason of the blood of the Lord Alexander'.[6] Although focussed essentially on Irish affairs, this display of unity among noble families in the south-west and western part of Scotland, orchestrated by Bruce of Annandale, was a strategic show of strength. After all, such a gesture would have been equally applicable to mutual aid in Scotland, and the Bruces' rivals would have understood this. They were trying to make themselves untouchable.

The names of those who sealed the indenture are telling, counting among them Patrick, Earl of Dunbar and Walter, Earl of Menteith along with Walter's two sons Alexander and John. It also included the Guardian James Stewart and his brother John of Jedburgh Forest, as well as Angus Mór MacDonald of Islay and one of his sons, Alexander.[7] To reinforce the closeness of their relationships, discussions of marriage between the sons and daughters of these great men may well have taken place, although no records survive. In the following three years Annandale would go on to reach understandings with others including John, Earl of Atholl and

Donald, Earl of Mar, whose lands were in the north and north-east of the kingdom. Donald's son Gartnait was soon married to one of the Earl of Carrick's daughters.[8]

Annandale was playing the game well by capitalising on the fear of a common enemy. The Earl of Menteith was convinced that the Comyns would make for his title and the lands that Alexander III had settled on him in 1260 to the detriment of his Comyn rivals. The MacDonalds worried that the Comyn Guardians would continue the policy of extending royal influence through the sheriffdoms into Kintyre, Lorn and Skye, which would inevitably encroach upon the autonomy of the MacDonalds within their own lordship.[9] Fear, and the exploitation of that fear by the Bruces, allowed them to call to their side a sufficient number of noble families under a single banner, all the while bolstering the family's position. It was a clever strategy, and well executed.

Given the closeness of England and Scotland during the majority of the thirteenth century, and the family ties between its monarchs, news of Alexander III's death had been quickly dispatched south with two Dominicans. In September, Bishop Fraser of St Andrews caught up with Edward I at Saintes in France, where the English king was preoccupied with affairs which would keep him busy until 1289. Fraser, later joined by William Comyn, Bishop of Brechin, and Geoffrey Mowbray, informed their royal neighbour of the Guardians' election, and by all accounts the King of England viewed the decision favourably and wished them well.[10] However, his apparent neighbourly disinterest was not set to last long.

By 1289, Edward had returned to England. That May, the six Guardians became five as the elderly Earl of Buchan passed away. Rather more dramatically, four months later, on 10 September, Duncan, Earl of Fife was ambushed while out riding and murdered by Sir Hugh Abernethy and his followers. With a third of their number now gone, the Guardians chose to carry on without replacing their dead. More importantly, it had become clear shortly after Alexander's death that Queen Yolande was either not pregnant at all or had miscarried. Margaret, the Maid of Norway, was now Scotland's hope, but the prospect of a young girl inheriting the throne as the heir to the House of Dunkeld elicited very little enthusiasm. Margaret's concerned father, Eric II, King of Norway, was growing impatient. To help refocus attention and ensure that his daughter would be formally recognised as Scotland's queen, he sent envoys to Edward I to help discuss her status. As a powerful neighbour with international prestige, the King of England would be well placed to offer friendly support.

Following his return from Gascony, Edward I now turned his attention to the Scottish succession. Sensing an opportunity, he was quick to respond to Eric's invitation, writing to the remaining Guardians asking them to attend him on 3 October 1289 at Salisbury. Edward also chose to invite Robert Bruce, Lord of Annandale.[11] The king, it seemed, felt Bruce could not be ignored – possibly because he had been corresponding in private with him for some time. If the Maid was to be recognised as queen, Edward needed to make sure Bruce would stomach it.

The delegation that arrived at Salisbury brought the Scots and the Norwegians together under the arbitration of the king. After debate in this already ancient English town, the Scots agreed to accept Margaret as their undisputed 'Lady, Queen and heiress', and under the terms of the Treaty of Salisbury, agreed on 6 November 1289, she was to set sail and arrive in Scotland by 1 November 1290. Outmanoeuvred, Bruce was determined not to be thwarted. Never a man to miss an opportunity, it may well have been at these negotiations that he first proffered the helpful suggestion that the Maid marry his grandson, the young Robert VII, then only fifteen;[12] through such a marriage Robert would have inherited the throne of Scotland *jure uxoris*. The proposal came to nothing.

Three years later, one of Annandale's granddaughters, Isabel, sister to Robert VII, married Eric II in Norway; perhaps this was something of a consolation prize. The kings of England and Norway were clearly aware that Bruce was not the only one harbouring dynastic ambitions, and to prevent any misguided marital matches now or in the future, the Treaty of Salisbury ruled that the Maid was to arrive 'free and quit of all contract of marriage or betrothal'.[13] Once again, the Lord of Annandale had been beaten back in his quest for Scotland's crown.

The Scots came together at Birgham in March 1290 to ratify the Treaty of Salisbury, and it was there that rumours arrived in the corridors of power that Edward I had sent an English delegation to Pope Nicholas IV at Avignon seeking dispensation for his only surviving son and heir, Edward of Caernarvon, to marry Scotland's new queen – the two were related within the forbidden degrees of affinity. The Lord of Annandale would no doubt have felt exasperated, but the Guardians and nobles of Scotland held a different view. After all, such a marriage was in keeping with the last one hundred years of forged relationships between the two crowns, albeit this time it would be a boy marrying a queen, not a girl marrying a king. A marriage such as this would only strengthen the Scottish kingdom at a time when it was most vulnerable, and given that Edward had not reasserted his ancient claim of overlordship at their last meeting, such a prospect looked like a satisfactory outcome. Therefore, the Guardians sent a letter to the King of England on 17 March, consenting to the marriage so long as certain terms defining the position and status of Scotland were guaranteed and enshrined by treaty.[14] Edward, of course, was quick to agree.

In July, the Scottish nobles again assembled at Birgham to meet their English counterparts and negotiate the terms of a marriage contract, taking pains at the same time to safeguard the rights and liberties of the kingdom. It was quickly established that the two countries would retain their separate identities, Scotland's terms noting that the kingdom 'shall be free in itself and without subjection'. Homage and fealty to England was not demanded, and never again would a tenant-in-chief of Scotland have to leave the kingdom to perform homage and fealty for their Scottish lands. Scottish parliaments were to be held in Scotland, meaning Scottish affairs remained and were dealt with in the kingdom. The institutions of government would be left intact, and records and ancient relics would remain where they were.[15] It was, *prima facie*, a good deal, with the cautious Scots safe in the knowledge that they had done everything possible to safeguard their rights and that of their queen regnant, upholding the oaths they took at Scone in 1286.[16] Edward I did not protest either, promptly ratifying what became known as the Treaty of Northampton on 28 August 1290.

Yet what quickly followed was a change in attitude by that steely leopard, Edward I. In June, the king had already sent a so-called peacekeeping force to the Isle of Man under the leadership of Sir Walter de Huntercombe and occupied the island, effectively annexing the territory.[17] Further still, at Northampton, following the ratification of the treaty, the king appointed the Bishop of Durham, Anthony Bek, as Lieutenant of Scotland, whose role was 'to administer justice and set the realm in order' on behalf of Queen Margaret and Edward of Caernarvon.[18] This appointment was most certainly presumptuous given that the marriage between the two children had not yet taken place and neither was resident in Scotland. The King of England had no authority to make the appointment, and to ease Bek's transition into his role Edward asked the Guardians and nobles of Scotland to receive him 'kindly and courteously ... putting yourselves at his bidding in all matters needful for the foremost and peaceful state of the kingdom'.[19] It was the first time that Edward's underlying intentions got the better of him and began to show through the veneer of neighbourly support and mutual best interest. To contemporaries like the chronicler of Waverley Abbey, it seemed that the King of England would soon gather his men and magnates about him and announce that he intended to bring Scotland to heel, just as he had done to Wales.[20] The friendly neighbour was quickly becoming a wolf descending on the fold.

By the summer of 1290, preparations were underway both in England and in Norway for Margaret's arrival. Edward sent a ship from Great Yarmouth, provisioned with luxurious fabrics, sweetmeats, gingerbread, dried fruits and even an organ, to Norway on 20 May. However, either Margaret and her retinue were not ready to sail, or King Eric refused to send her on an English ship, bristling against the over-mighty gesture from the King of England, who was already acting like a master puppeteer. The ship was sent packing, and it returned to England the following month with a crew greatly weakened by sickness and with many of their number deceased. For Margaret it had been a lucky escape.

By September, preparations were complete and the seven-year-old Maid of Norway waved her father goodbye, setting sail to her new kingdom in the company of Narne, Bishop of Bergen, and others including Ban Thorir Haaknson and Fan Ingebirorg Erlingsdottir.[21] Whether because of storms or sickness on board, the ships detoured and put in at the Norwegian island of Orkney. There, having taken ill, young Margaret died unexpectedly in the arms of the Bishop of Narne.[22] Her little body was promptly taken back to her grieving father in Norway rather than completing the journey on to Scotland, and was later buried in the north aisle of Bergen Cathedral. With her premature death came the abrupt end of the ancient Celtic House of Dunkeld and the opening of a difficult chapter in Scotland's history.

The death of Margaret had profound implications for the Scottish succession. The nobles had foregathered in September at Perth, anticipating the arrival of their new queen, and once news began drifting in of the tragedy that had unfolded in Orkney, civil war looked imminent. Annandale wasted no time in reasserting his claim, raising a large armed force and marching to Perth to back up his words. John Balliol, whose mother Dervorguilla of Galloway had died on 28 January that year, was now head of his branch of the family and he too wasted no time in proclaiming himself heir to Scotland. With two well-supported powerhouses claiming the throne, political tension in Scotland quickly approached breaking point. Suddenly, everything was to play for. Neither Bruce nor Balliol would back down. In a frantic bid to maintain the peace, and in support of the latter, William Fraser, Bishop of St Andrews, took it upon himself – without the consent of the remaining Guardians or the nobles lay and ecclesiastical – to write to Edward I:

> There is a fear of a general war and a great slaughter of men, unless the Highest [God], by means of your industry and good service apply a speedy remedy ... We have agreed among ourselves to remain about Perth, until we have certain news, by the knights who are sent to Orkney, what is the condition of our Lady - would that it be prosperous and happy ... If Sir John de Balliol comes to your presence we advise you to take care so to treat with him that in any event your honour and advantage may be preserved. If it turns out that the aforesaid Lady has departed this life ... let your excellency deign if you please to approach toward the March [Scottish/English border] for the consolation of the Scottish people, and for saving the shedding of blood ... and set over them for King him who of right ought to have succession, if so he that be will follow your counsel.[23]

His invitation to the English king to intervene directly was personally motivated, advocating the position of John Balliol as likely successor. What Fraser did not realise was that his actions invited catastrophe to befall Scotland.

The Lord of Annandale was also quick to appeal to Edward, who by this point was seen as the natural arbiter, holding sufficient power to bring about a much-needed resolution. Bruce rallied support, and an appeal from seven earls was sent to the king, which proclaimed that these seven alone had the authority to choose the next King of Scots and that their preferred candidate was Robert Bruce, Lord of Annandale. They also claimed that John Comyn, Lord of Badenoch, and Bishop Fraser of St Andrews, both Balliol supporters, were abusing their positions as Guardians, inflicting 'injustices, losses and arsons' in Moray and elsewhere.[24] The identity of these seven earls remains unknown, given that the seals attached to this document have long been lost to history. Yet all was not as it seemed even before these seals were lost. Given that there were thirteen earls in Scotland, and all, by virtue of their position, had the right to choose the next king, the implication provided in this 'appeal of the seven' was that they as a collective of thirteen were united in their wish to see Bruce as king; this clearly wasn't reflective of the true political landscape, given the earls were divided between Bruce and Balliol. Edward I, both letters in hand, would have known this. Bruce's appeal was therefore a desperate attempt at deception.

Irrespective of which letter motivated him, Edward I needed little encouragement to intervene directly in Scottish affairs now that his plans to marry his son and heir to the Queen of Scotland had been cut short. He headed north at the start of November, but stopped abruptly when news arrived that his wife, Queen Eleanor of Castile, who had been ailing all year, had died at Harby on 28 November, most likely from some form of long-term coronary disease.[25] Edward, who had been married to his wife for thirty-six years, was uncharacteristically distraught and withdrew temporarily from public life. Re-emerging two months later, in January 1291, he poured his grief into resolving the Great Cause of Scotland, requesting that those claiming the crown go to the Bishop of Durham's castle at Norham in England on the border between the two countries to present their cases to him in May. He also gave a guarantee that meeting the claimants on English rather than Scottish soil would not set a precedent which would infringe upon their status or that of the Scottish kingdom. It would be the start of many duplicitous assertions.[26]

The King of England was a man of great complexity and cunning. A contemporary who wrote the Song of Lewes captured his character beautifully:

He is valiant as a lion, quick to attack the strongest and fearing the onslaught of none. But if a lion in pride and fierceness, he is a panther in fickleness and inconstancy, changing his word and promise, cloaking him by pleasant speech ... the treachery and falsehood by which he advanced he called prudence ... and whatever he likes he says is lawful.[27]

The Scots were about to feel the full force of his panther-like character.

The key lay and ecclesiastical nobility of Scotland assembled as instructed at Norham, hopeful that their friendly neighbour would help guide them and resolve the Scottish succession crisis.[28] However, they were to be disappointed when, as a preliminary shot across the bows, Edward demanded that the Scots recognise him first as overlord and suzerain of Scotland. They were both shocked and dumbfounded. Those royal velvet gloves had suddenly slipped off. Edward claimed that he could not determine the succession if his rights and therefore authority were not recognised. In the late thirteenth century, simply holding a right was one thing; being seen to assert and then exercise it was altogether different and, to Edward, all the more important. He knew that this was the moment he had been waiting for, and he wasn't going to give it up.

The Scots, stricken with panic, were at a loss; more so given Scottish sovereignty had only recently been secured in the Treaty of Northampton, which made no mention of the restoration of the English king's claims to overlordship, let alone suzerainty or absolute sovereign lordship. They had been lured to Norham under a false sense of security. Edward went further, claiming that the onus was on the Scots to prove that he was not suzerain. It was a pointed and unfair attack, and one designed to hamstring the Scottish delegates. To add insult to injury, they were given twenty-four hours to respond, and only when they fought back was this extended to three weeks.[29] In despondency, the Scots withdrew and began the agonising debates about how to protect Scottish sovereignty while resolving the succession crisis at the same time.

While they were absent, Edward I, sensing that his power grab may be more difficult than he had planned, made preparations to apply further pressure. He had already invited sixty-seven northern magnates to Norham, giving a touch of menace to proceedings, but he went on to order a large armed English force made up of crossbowmen and archers to assemble in the area for 2 June, just at the point when the Scots were in private deliberation.[30] It was a calculated and unjust use of force with a clear motive. The Scots had been decisively outmanoeuvred.

In the end it was Bishop Wishart of Glasgow, that indomitable defender of Scottish independence, who composed himself and the Scottish delegation sufficiently to fire off their considered and somewhat courteous response:

> Sir. To this statement [of overlordship] the good people who have sent us here make answer that they do not in the least believe that you would ask so great a thing if you were not convinced of your sound right to it. But they have no knowledge of your right, nor did they ever see it claimed or used by you or your ancestors; therefore they answer ... that they have no power to reply to your statement in default of a lord [Scots King] whom the demand ought to be addresses and who will have power to make answer about it ... But the good people of the realm earnestly demand that he who shall be king in the aforesaid kingdom shall do to you whatsoever reason and justice may demand, for he, and no other, will have power to reply and to act in the manner.[31]

Their vulnerability became their justification to defer the issue, the only response that the Scots could muster from their ammunition. If Edward wanted recognition of his overlordship, then he ought to seek it from the next king once he had been chosen.

Furious, Edward I dismissed the response as 'nothing to the purpose'.[32] Now he changed tack. If the Guardians of Scotland were unmovable, then he would dangle the prize of a crown in front of the claimants, demanding recognition of his overlordship as a precondition for starting the race. It worked. Bruce and Balliol, and many of the others who had come forward presenting claims, had no choice but to recognise the King of England's suzerainty of Scotland as a prerequisite to being its next king. On 5 June 1291, they submitted and set their seals to a document that captured that recognition. With the claimants having capitulated, the Guardians and the rest of the Scottish nobility had little choice but to follow suit, although not until they extracted three concessions from their overmighty neighbour.

First, until a successor was proclaimed Edward would 'maintain the customary laws, liberties and usages of Scotland, saving only the homage of whosoever should become king'. Edward agreed to this on 6 June; it wasn't a big ask, after all. The remaining two concessions were left unanswered for the next five days. One stipulated that the decision on the next Scottish ruler would be taken in Scotland, and not England, thereby protecting the kingdom's status; the other sought the king's confirmation that if he took possession of the royal castles in Scotland as well as the kingdom itself, he would return them to the new king within two months of the award, on condition that Edward himself received the homage of the new King of Scots.[33]

Eventually, a satisfied Edward gave the royal nod. On 11 June, the four Guardians submitted and resigned their commission, immediately being reappointed by the king with a fifth, the English baron Brian Fitzalan of Bedale. They were now legally Edward's men. Two days later, at Upsettlington on the Scottish bank of the River Tweed, in the shadow of Norham Castle, the king received the homages and oaths of fealty of some of Scotland's principal magnates, lay and ecclesiastical. According to the chronicler of Lanercost, 'by the feast of the Holy Trinity the king was acknowledged and installed as Lord Paramount of Scotland'.[34] It had taken him a month to achieve his ultimate goal of overlordship, and to emphasise the point he quickly went on a six-week progress to receive further nobles on bended knee, stopping at Linlithgow, Edinburgh, Haddington, Stirling, Dunfermline, St Andrews and Perth.[35] On his return, he promised to hear the claimants' pleas through a novel Court of Claims that he had devised, which was to sit at the castle of Berwick starting on 3 August 1291.[36]

In all, thirteen claimants came forward. Initially, as noted at Norham, Robert Bruce, Lord of Annandale, and John Balliol, Lord of Galloway, were the clear front runners. In close proximity were the claims of John de Hastings, Lord of Abergavenny, and Florent, Count of Holland. The others included John Comyn, Lord of Badenoch, a Guardian of Scotland; Patrick, Earl of Dunbar; William de Vesci; Nicholas de Soules; and William de Ross. As the court got underway, a further three claims were registered from Patrick of Galithley, Roger de Mandeville and Robert de Pinkey. These last three were outsiders with little hope of being seriously considered, but registering their claims was a way to safeguard their interests should the royal line ever end without an undisputed heir again; it was, in essence, an insurance policy indemnifying successors as yet unknown. Later in proceedings, King Eric II of Norway also rather remarkably staked his claim, this by 'ascent' rather than 'descent' as the justification for it. As father to the late queen, he felt obliged to plea, even though his argument was fundamentally a weak one.[37] The court itself was a highly charged place, where debates were held behind closed doors and evidence was demanded to support every assertion. This evidence, once presented, would then be sewn into a leather sock and retained at Berwick for reference.[38]

The claims of the Lord of Annandale, the Lord of Galloway and the Lord of Abergavenny rested on the key argument that they were all descended from David, Earl of Huntingdon, who had been the grandson of King David I of Scotland and brother to Malcolm IV and William the Lion. Balliol was the grandson of the Earl of Huntingdon's eldest daughter, Margaret. Hastings was the grandson of the third daughter, Ada. Robert Bruce was the son of the second daughter, Isabel, and he claimed in particular that as a son, rather than a grandson, he was closer to the royal line and therefore took precedence over the other two even though he descended from the second and not the first daughter. Given he was now seventy-one, settlement of his claim needed an urgent judgement; if he died beforehand, his son would not benefit from this precedence. As insurance, Bruce also asserted that he had been designated as heir apparent by Alexander II, son of William the Lion, as well as having support of the 'seven earls', as shown by their recent appeal. All had compelling arguments, although Hastings, who was the least likely of the three to inherit, suggested to the court that the kingdom should be divided into three, as any earldom would be when co-heiresses were left to inherit.

Florent, Count of Holland rested his argument on the claim that his descent from Ada, a sister of David, Earl of Huntingdon, gave him precedence over David's daughters and their subsequent descendants. According to Florent, David had given up his rights to inherit the crown in return for lands in Garioch in the north-east of Scotland, and William the Lion, then king, had secured the succession on his sister Ada, Florent's ancestor, in the event his royal line failed. It seemed a tenuous argument, but Florent insisted that firm evidence existed and he pleaded with the court for time to seek out the necessary documents.[39] With time on his side, Edward I was inclined to agree. The Court of Claims was adjourned for a long recess until 2 June 1292, and then shortly after that was adjourned again until 14 October. If the claimants had thought a quick resolution was in the coming when they had first assembled at Berwick in August 1291, they were to be sorely disappointed.

As the King of England left Berwick at the end of 1291 and headed south, he may well have taken with him in his retinue the young Robert Bruce VII since it is likely that Robert was sent to join Edward I's household around 1290 after his fosterage in the Western Isles, south-west Scotland or Ireland. If this were indeed the case, like his brother Edward Bruce, who later joined the retinue of Edward of Caernarvon, Robert would have been in the company of the king during this difficult and tense period for the Bruce family. He would have seen at first hand the events as they unfolded, not from his grandfather's vantage point but from the English side. As a squire, Robert would have been housed and fed by the king, given robes to wear and expected to travel with the itinerant court as it moved from castle to castle, manor to manor across England. Any loss of horses during his service would have been compensated for.[40] During his time there he would also have polished his manners and seen the might of the English political and administrative machine, not to mention a king who was most certainly at the height of his power. It would have made a deep impression. It is also quite possible that the young Robert was an insider for the Bruce family and well placed to keep his father, the Earl of Carrick, and his paternal grandfather, the Lord of Annandale, abreast of events as he inevitably heard rumour and gossip at close quarters.

In October 1292 the Court of Claims finally reconvened, its 104 auditors settling down again to hear the more convincing of the claimants' arguments. Of their body, forty had been appointed by Robert Bruce, Lord of Annandale, another forty by John Balliol and the remaining twenty-four by Edward I himself. Bruce had fewer ecclesiastical men supporting him than Balliol, but boasted among others the ever-faithful Robert Wishart, Bishop of Glasgow; Matthew de Crambeth, Bishop of Dunkeld; the abbots of Melrose and Jedburgh; and the archdeacon of Lothian. He also drew in the support of Donald, Earl of Mar; Walter, Earl of Menteith; John, Earl of Atholl; the Earl of Lennox; and Guardian James Stewart.[41] It was an impressive gathering, but so was Balliol's cohort.

John Balliol commanded greater support among the more important ecclesiastics, including William Fraser, Bishop of St Andrews, Guardian of Scotland; Henry, Bishop of Aberdeen; William Comyn, Bishop of Brechin; the bishops of the Isles, Galloway and Ross; and abbots of many seats including Dunfermline, Holyrood, Scone and Coupar-Angus.[42] The list went on. This show of spiritual support for Balliol evidently dwarfed that shown for Bruce. Balliol could also count on his natural allies the Comyns, best represented by the presence of John, Earl of Buchan. He also had Gilbert, Earl of Angus and his brother Ingram de Umfraville, as well as the earls of Strathearn and Ross and other significant members of the baronage.[43] In short, John Balliol was perhaps in the strongest position to advance his claim.

However, the remaining twenty-four auditors were appointed by Edward I and nearly all of them were lawyers, drawn from Oxford, Cambridge and Paris, including the French jurist Bonet de St Quentin and the Master General of the Minorities. Between them, the Scottish auditors had to agree upon which rule of law to apply in order to settle the case. Debate inevitably raged. If primogeniture was applied then Balliol, who was descended from the eldest daughter of the Earl of Huntingdon, would succeed. However, while primogeniture was increasingly accepted as the route by which to transmute titles and lands, it was not universally applied in the late thirteenth century. Equally, the French jurist Bonet de St Quentin and the Master General of the Minorities both agreed that primogeniture in this instance did not apply, and that the succession should by virtue pass to the one who was born first; that meant Robert Bruce, Lord of Annandale.[44]

The debates went on. If we are to believe the chronicler Walter Bower, who wrote the Scotichronicon, it looked increasingly likely that the court was going to favour the law that supported Annandale's claim before Anthony Bek, Bishop of Durham, warned the king against it, eliciting Edward's thanks for 'singing so well'.[45] This seems unlikely, however, and the argument put forward by Bower that the King of England did not favour Bruce because he was already powerful in Scotland, unlike Balliol, is clearly not true given that notable men sat on Balliol's bench at court. Bower, writing as a pro-Bruce source, was clearly recounting his story with the benefit of hindsight and a good application of whitewash.

In the end, the eighty Scottish auditors could not agree which law should be applied to Scotland. The English then put forward the suggestion that English law and custom could be adopted, and the protracted stalemate was broken. Edward I, with one surviving son and five daughters from a line of sixteen children, knew all too well that his own crown lay vulnerable to a similar succession crisis. To avoid any confusion, he had it confirmed in law that should his male line ultimately fail, then his daughters and their heirs would inherit on the basis of seniority. Only when the eldest daughter's line had perished would the crown then pass down to the heirs of the next daughter's line and so forth. Once due process was agreed, the decision of the auditors was ultimately much more straightforward.

On 6 November 1292, the Lord of Annandale was summoned before the court. He must have entered the chamber with great anticipation and expectation, being the first to be called in. Once inside, he was promptly informed that his claim had failed. It must have been a devastating blow. He left the court furious yet stubbornly determined to continue, the next day making a quitclaim witnessed by the Earl of Gloucester, his first wife's nephew, passing his right to the throne onto his eldest son, Robert Bruce, Earl of Carrick. It made sense, given that he was seventy-one years of age, and he needed to guarantee his claim would be inherited by his heir, which at this point was not a given. Two days after that, on 9 November, Robert Bruce VI resigned his earldom of Carrick, which he held by right of his late wife Marjorie, and granted it to his eldest son, the young Robert Bruce VII. For the first time in the eighteen-year-old Bruce's life, he came into a substantial part of his inheritance.[46]

The Lord of Annandale may have failed to have his own claim upheld, but he doggedly held on to the vain hope that he and his heirs could still pursue the matter. Five months before the court's judgement, Annandale had agreed and sealed an indenture with Count Florent stipulating that if either of them had become king he would grant the other one-third of Scotland as a fief. Robert was all too aware that the potential value of one-third of Scotland equated to all his lands in England, and so by virtue of this deal, had he won, he would have given up these English lands in favour of Florent and been able to secure the whole of the Scottish kingdom for himself and his heirs. Had he not secured the crown, and Florent had instead, then at least he held one-third of Scotland, giving his heirs the chance not only to rule that fief but to eventually try and reclaim the remaining two-thirds at some future date. However, this clever long-term strategy came to nothing as Florent failed to produce the documents supporting his rights. He complained to the court that his evidence was being unfairly withheld by the Prior of Pluscarden. Documents that survive today which corroborate Florent's claim are most certainly forgeries, perhaps drawn up at the time, so either way something was much amiss here.[47]

Annandale's desperate final attempt to gain recognition of his rights on 7 November was almost pitiful, but shows the sheer unrelenting determination of his character. Having no other avenue open to him, he threw in his lot with John de Hastings, Lord of Abergavenny, supporting the idea that Scotland should be divided into three equal parts between the co-heiresses of David, Earl of Huntingdon. Much in the same vein as before, Bruce would have given his English lands to Hastings in return for Hastings' claim in Scotland, meaning Bruce would command two-thirds of the former kingdom to Balliol's one-third. Naturally, Edward I and the auditors did not favour the idea, the king perhaps all too aware of the precedent it may set in his own realm and the likelihood of subsequent civil war. The court declared that the Kingdom of Scotland was not like any earldom and was by its nature indivisible. With that final decision announced, the Lord of Annandale had run out of options. His claim had failed. He retired in disgust to his castle at Lochmaben while his son, the former Earl of Carrick, headed to Norway, thereby avoiding any obligation to bend the knee and give homage to a Balliol king.[48]

There was now only one thing left to do. On 17 November 1292, Edward I's judgement was given by the Chief Justice, Roger Brabazon, proclaiming that John Balliol, Lord of Galloway, was now King John I of Scotland. Formal legal recognition followed two days later on the 19th.[49] On 30 November, St Andrew's Day, John was escorted by the earls to Scone for his inauguration as king. There he was placed over the Stone of Destiny and wrapped in the royal mantle and handed the traditional regalia of the ceremony. As the Earl of Fife was but a child, this ancient Scottish crowning was instead conducted by an English proxy, Sir John de St John. The meaning of this symbolic appointment must have been clear to everyone in attendance. Unlike Alexander III, this king owed his crown, and now homage and fealty, to an English master.[50] Everything now depended on how John would establish his rule. The eighteen-year-old Robert needed to figure out how he could serve his new king while retaining and protecting his earldom and his family's claim to the Scottish crown, at this moment seemingly beyond his grasp.

4

A Nation in Peril

King John I of Scotland did not cut the greatest of royal figures. Contemporaries, particularly English ones, would in the following years pour scorn on his character, marking him out as a weak and highly indecisive man. The chronicler of Lanercost went so far as to call him 'brainless', while Rishanger described him as 'stupid' and 'simple' and a 'lamb among wolves'.[1] If the people of Scotland wanted a king to follow in the footsteps of the illustrious Alexander III, they were to be bitterly disappointed.

Shortly after his inauguration at Scone, the king and his court travelled across the border to Newcastle, where John formally bent the knee on 26 December 1292, paying homage for his kingdom of Scotland, thereby recognising Edward I as suzerain once more. By February, the king had assembled his first parliament at Scone, summoning the nobles to attend him. All three Bruces pointedly refused, continuing to avoid the delicate issue of homage, preserving their royal claim. Balliol was quick to use the occasion to reward his followers, and it is no surprise that he gifted lands and offices to his Comyn relatives, his sister having married the Earl of Buchan, the former Guardian. Outstanding legal cases brought against the Bishop of St Andrews were settled in his favour, and the Earl of Ross received the sheriffdom of Skye while MacDougall became the sheriff of Lorn. James Stewart, albeit it a Bruce supporter, was too important to be ignored, and was granted the third new sheriffdom of Kintyre.[2]

The king, attempting to mirror his predecessor, was set on extending Alexander III's policy of royal expansion into the west. Despite John's character, he had no appetite to let his enemies overcome him. As he handed out gifts to secure alliances and reinforce existing bonds of loyalty, John was also quick to cite Robert Bruce VI for default – failing to appear before him in parliament – along with others including Bruce's ally Agnus MacDonald of Islay. Sheriffs were sent out with orders demanding those protagonists conspicuous by their absence to attend another parliament later that year. Young Robert Bruce VII, now Earl of Carrick, had little real choice; his earldom could only be bequeathed to him with the blessing of the Crown, and navigating this thorny issue presented him with an immediate predicament.

Entering the parliamentary chamber at Stirling on 2 August 1293, Robert was obliged to present Donald, Earl of Mar, and James Stewart, High Steward of Scotland, as his men, who underwrote the relief or fee owed to the King of Scots for the inheritance. Malcolm, Earl of Lennox, Sir John Soules and Gilbert of Carrick confirmed that Robert Bruce VI had in fact resigned the earldom in favour of his son on 9 November 1292, which Parliament duly accepted. In his capacity as sheriff, James Stewart, as was custom, was charged to value the earldom before the king was obliged to grant it to its successor, thereby officially recognising Robert as earl. John obliged.[3] If there was any hostility between the king and young Robert, it did not show during these events. John was holding out an olive branch.

However, the king was not so fortunate in his relationship with his master Edward I. The King of England was growing increasingly restless on the back of such power brokering following the events of the Scottish succession, and with the benefit of hindsight it would appear that he was more determined than ever to rule in Scotland. Almost immediately after John's inauguration, Edward began to hear appeals from disgruntled Scots who were seeking justice in the Scottish kingdom and had not found it through John's courts. As king, John's status was immediately undermined, for one of the cornerstones of his kingship was to dispense secular justice. If his final judgements were to be challenged by a higher authority, then his position and status as king was fundamentally weak, and he himself nothing more than a regional governor. Edward I, with steely cunning and razor-sharp political astuteness, knew this all too well, and by accepting regular appeals from Scotland was sending a clear and barbed message north of the border.

It began with John de Mazun, a wine merchant from Bordeaux who had spent more than a decade claiming settlement of a large outstanding debt owed to him by the Scottish Crown. Despite offers of settlement from Alexander III, later the Guardians of Scotland and then John Balliol himself, the disgruntled and litigious de Mazun headed to London and to the Court of the King's Bench for final recompense. Edward ordered the court to summon the King of Scots to the Bench in May 1293 for failure to provide justice, but John, sensing the trap, refused to attend.

Not to be outmanoeuvred, Edward's justices then drew up rules to govern appeals from Scotland. As part of this dictate, John himself would be required to personally attend in all cases brought before the English court and account for his apparent poor decisions. It was an extraordinary affront to his royal dignity. To drive the point home, if the King of Scots refused to attend as he had in the de Mazun case, John would be held in contempt and might forfeit his lordship over the lands or fief of the appellant if judgement was not found in his favour.[4] It was an outrageous document, heavily weighted to disadvantage an indecisive monarch, but King John had to accept it.

Shortly after, a further appeal was received from MacDuff of Fife, brother of the murdered premier earl, who claimed he was unable to take possession of lands willed to him by his father and that he had temporarily been wrongfully imprisoned by his new king. It was exactly the kind of case Edward I needed, and he promptly reacted by demanding that John attend an English parliament in November to account for his alleged heavy-handed actions. Balliol, unable to resist and in fear of losing lordship over MacDuff's estates, had no choice but to gather a small group of councillors and court clerics and travel south and present himself like a chastised child before Parliament, forced to stand at the bar to hear the appeal against him.

By this point, the crushing humiliation was all too much. John fought back, claiming he ought not to answer the court's questions without first consulting with the great men of his kingdom and thereby immediately sought an adjournment. The tactic backfired. In doing so, he was effectively refusing to recognise the authority of Edward's court, and in consequence he was held to be in extreme contempt and was promptly sentenced to the loss of the castles and towns of Edinburgh, Roxburgh and Berwick. Bewildered and embattled by the exercise of such heavy justice, John made a humble petition requesting an adjournment to 14 June 1294, promising to return at the next parliament, which was duly granted.[5] Returning home to Scotland, it must have been clear to his people that John Balliol was far from an Alexander III, and that the King of England would stop at nothing in humiliating both the king and the kingdom of Scotland. It was apparent to all that Edward was goading the King of Scots into open and possibly violent confrontation.

Even the weather appeared to conspire against him. The winter of 1292/3 was a particularly hard one, with heavy snow and high gales sweeping the country, uprooting trees, unroofing houses and dealing considerable damage to property.[6] The poor weather continued into the spring and crops began to fail, leaving a great 'scarcity of victuals', which resulted in a threefold increase in the price of wheat.[7] Widespread famine was to follow, and in such a superstitious age, King John's failure to provide a resolution was seen as a bad omen. But the weather took its toll on England, too. On 20 April 1294, Edward I granted the new Earl of Carrick permission to travel to his estates in Ireland to requisition victuals for consumption back on his English and Scottish estates. That year the English king also remitted Robert's debts to the Exchequer, perhaps highlighting a policy in which Edward I sought to keep the Bruces relatively close and at odds with their Balliol and Comyn rivals in Scotland.[8] It was a well-executed strategy that did not need much encouragement.

If relations between the two kings were already fraught, what happened next could only break the bond altogether. Edward's ancient possessions included the Duchy of Aquitaine, located in the south-west of France. Inherited by successive English kings from Edward's great-grandparents Henry II of England and Eleanor of Aquitaine, the duchy centred on Gascony and had for generations remained in the hands of the English, albeit it at a somewhat reduced scale. Edward I, as ducal vassal of his French overlord, was caught in a complex relationship in which he was both an independent monarch of an English kingdom but required to bend the knee to Philip IV of France for his French dukedom. The relationship between the two kings was increasingly strained, in part due to frequent and growing acts of English and French piracy committed in the Channel. Philip IV was also a match for the English leopard, equally cunning and just as politically dangerous.

When Edward I ignored a summons to attend the King of France at a *parlement* in Paris, an incensed Philip IV confiscated the duchy on 19 May 1294. It was an all too similar situation to the one unfolding in Scotland, albeit it on this occasion Edward was merely the Duke of Aquitaine and his independent status as King of England was in no way threatened or undermined. Unlike the wavering, lamb-like Balliol, Edward was not about to accept defeat. Instead, he issued a *défi*, an act of formal withdrawal of homage to the King of France, freeing him to retaliate in arms without fear of incurring a charge of disloyalty as an oathbreaker.[9]

War between England and France was now inevitable, and in order to recover his lost possessions the King of England sent out summons to muster his Welsh, Irish and Scottish subjects, providing additional men for military service to fight in his overseas campaign, even though these men held no lands in Aquitaine. It was a highly unusual and somewhat autocratic request. Named in the writs on 29 June were King John, Robert Bruce V and sixteen other Scottish magnates.[10] For many this was a step too far, and the Welsh, under the leadership of Madog ap Llewelyn, rose up in arms, chafing under the ten-year rule of their English conqueror.[11] Facing a war on two fronts, the King of England had no choice but to tear up his plans and instead march into Wales to settle the revolt, which he overcame with his usual military efficiency.[12]

War in Wales had an unintended impact in Scotland. Seeing that the Welsh were restless and that opposition to Edward I had placed pressure on his foreign policy, the seemingly bewildered and humiliated members of the court of King John began to finally find their own fierce sense of resistance. Angered by the contempt shown to both their king and their kingdom, they were all too aware that John Balliol did not possess the strength of character to oppose Edward's ongoing bullying tactics alone. In consequence, there was but one viable option to help shore up the king's embattled leadership. In July 1295, only two months after the Welsh were defeated, the Scots formed a governing body. Its composition was similar to that of the six Guardians, only this time it was twice as large – being made up of four earls, fours bishops and four barons – and, more importantly, had the authority to make policy.[13] While in any normal year the presence of a governing body itself may have been prejudicial to the ancient rights of the Scottish Crown, at this delicate juncture its formation and its status were used to uphold rather than infringe upon the royal sovereignty. Together, John and his councillors were united and bound as one with a clear central purpose: legitimate opposition.

The mood of defiance deepened. Sometime in late 1294 or early 1295, the Scots sent delegates to Avignon to the newly elected pope, Boniface VIII, in an attempt to secure papal absolution from their oaths of fealty to the King of England.[14] The plan was gaining pace. At the same time, they opened talks with Edward's rival Philip IV of France; by October 1295 they had negotiated the Treaty of Paris, thus beginning the Auld Alliance. Its ratification at Dunfermline on 23 February 1296 was the Scots calling card to open war against their hostile, over-mighty English neighbour. The terms were simple enough. The French and the Scots would go to war against Edward I on two fronts. To guarantee a commitment, King John's only son, Edward Balliol, would marry Philip's niece Jeanne de Valois. Philip, possibly all too aware of John's indecisive nature, demanded that the Scottish Community of the Realm also seal the treaty, which they duly did. However, the Balliol–Valois marriage contract would never be solemnized.

By the end of February, the deal was done. To bolster the agreement, the King of France also made an alliance with King Eric II of Norway, to provide ships for the French and also to secure a guarantee that they would not go to war against the Scots, given that the relationship between Eric II and King John had deteriorated rapidly since the latter's inauguration.[15] The King of Norway had been attempting to enforce the terms of the Treaty of Perth, which had been agreed by Alexander III, when the Norwegians had ceded to Scotland the Western Isles as a result of war in return for an annual fee of 100 marks in perpetuity, which had already long fallen into arrears.

With such a committed force against him, Edward I was caught temporarily on the back foot. Yet the Scots had nonetheless played directly into his slippery hands. By attaching his seal to the Franco-Scottish Treaty, John Balliol had acted as a contumacious vassal, and Edward I, as suzerain of Scotland, had the legal right to act. Without hesitation, the King of England sent out writs summoning men to take up arms and muster at Newcastle for 1 March 1296. He also ordered a fleet, provisioned and ready for war, to sail up the North Sea to rendezvous with the army. The gloves were well and truly off.

Against this backdrop of growing tension, treaties and war preparations, Robert Bruce V, Lord of Annandale and claimant to the Scottish throne, finally succumbed to his old age on Maundy Thursday, 31 March 1295. At seventy-five he had already far outlived his contemporaries, and in the quiet of his castle of Lochmaben he finally breathed his last. It is likely that Robert Bruce VI, now Lord of Annandale, and his son, the Earl of Carrick, along with his siblings and the wider Bruce family, headed to Guisborough Priory in Yorkshire to see the veteran interred there on 17 April.[16] Yet even before his death, Annandale had continued to be a thorn in the side of the much-troubled Scottish king. Following the death of the Bishop of Galloway, Robert had secured the vacant see, either by good fortune or abject bribery, for his candidate, Master Thomas Dalston of Kirkcudbright. John Balliol was positively furious, and protested the result, but in the end was powerless to prevent the appointment of a Bruce nominee into a see that sat within the Balliol ancestral lands of Galloway.[17] As Bruce lay dying in 1295, he can only have met his maker with the brief satisfaction that even at this eleventh hour he could, at least on some things, outmanoeuvre his long-standing opponent.

To add insult to injury, the Bruce family remained in favour with the English king. Only two years earlier, the Earl of Carrick had been granted permission to draw a loan from the Royal Exchequer, which he used to purchase and send rich gifts – blue, scarlet and fur-trimmed gowns, table silver including twenty-four plates, twelve cups, four pitchers and four basins, among many other things – overseas as wedding gifts for his sister, the newly married Queen of Norway.[18] On 19 September 1295, Robert's father gained Edward I's permission to remarry, and on 6 October was granted custody of the strategically important castle of Carlisle, an office he had held briefly some twelve years earlier following in the golden footsteps of the old Lord of Annandale before him.[19] Even without Edward I stoking the flames of resentment, the Bruce and Balliol enmity was still very much alive, even if the ancient Annandale himself was now dead.

The year 1295 was therefore one of great change in the Bruce family, particularly for the Earl of Carrick. Not only did he lose his grandfather, who had perhaps been something of an inspiration to him since his own childhood, but more importantly Robert gained a wife. For in that year, at the age of twenty-one, he married Isabella, the daughter of Donald, Earl of Mar, and wasted no time in consummating the marriage. Within a few months, Isabella conceived. In 1296, she gave birth to their daughter Marjorie, named in honour of Robert's mother, the late Countess of Carrick. But the birth was to be bittersweet, for Isabella soon sickened following the labour, and despite the efforts of her attendants was unable to recover, dying shortly thereafter.

In just under a year, Bruce had gained a daughter but lost a wife and grandfather; the effect this had on him is unrecorded but can only be guessed at. Mortality as a result of labour was perilously high in medieval Britain, irrespective of social status. All the prayers said to St Margaret for her saintly intercession could not guarantee life after all. Isabella was just one more unfortunate victim of the birthing chamber.

Edward I's summons to war was met in Scotland with calculated coolness. King John and his governing body sent out an ultimatum to English nobles who held lands in Scotland: join us in the forthcoming war against the English king or forfeit your lands to the Scottish Crown. It had mixed results. As men were forced to take sides, often heading to England as their landholdings were more substantial there, King John went one step further, expelling English members of Scottish monastic houses. It was a futile gesture that did little to advance any strategic gains. Edward responded in kind, forfeiting Scottish-held lands in England including Balliol's manor at Kempstone, citing the Scots king's 'fraudulent alienations' as the reason.[20] As both Bruces gave their services to the King of England and refused to attend the Scottish parliament, John immediately confiscated *in absentia* the lordship of Annandale and the earldom of Carrick, granting the former to John Comyn, Earl of Buchan.[21] It was deliberately provocative.

A Scottish summons went out for all able-bodied men between the ages of sixteen and sixty to perform the *Servitum Scoticanum*, Scottish military service, and to muster at Caldenley on 18 March 1296, in Holy Passion week.[22] Unlike their English counterparts, the Scots were not paid wages after their feudal obligations of forty days at war were expended, and so Scottish military numbers and abilities lagged behind the English. Their use of weaponry was relatively inferior, too, for the English relied on heavy cavalry, which King John lacked in sufficient numbers.[23] Edward I had ordered the Exchequer to fund a staggering and slightly megalomaniac 60,000 infantry and 1,000 men-at-arms; while he eventually raised the much more reasonable 20,000 men, Balliol nonetheless had fewer than half that.[24]

The military campaign began in earnest in March, and it was set to be both targeted and bloody. First, the Lord of Wark in Northumberland, Robert de Ros, unexpectedly changed allegiance, forsaking Edward I and declaring for King John. The English Ros – who was about to marry a Scot, which only emphasises how the two countries were heavily interwoven culturally – had in a stroke handed Wark Castle to the Scots. However, Ros's brother, who remained loyal to the English, appealed to Edward to besiege the castle and recover his family's reputation. The King of England in turn sent a relief force to recover it, but Robert de Ros, who was garrisoned with men nearby at Roxburgh Castle, rode out and defeated the English relief force, leaving the king himself to march on Wark. In the ensuing siege, the castle quickly fell to the king and Edward, satisfied with this initial victory, set up his Easter Court there, celebrating Easter Sunday on 25 March. On the same date, Robert Bruce junior and senior, with the Earl of Dunbar and the Earl of Angus, issued letters patent which contained their promises of homage and fealty to the English king.[25] The Bruces at this juncture were sure to back the stronger of the two men and were willing to do almost anything to curry favour, and possibly win a crown.

The Scots were quick to enter into the fray as well. King John appointed John Comyn, Earl of Buchan, with the task of invading England from the south-west of Scotland, first attacking Carlisle Castle, held by the Bruces. For the younger Robert, this campaign was the first large-scale military action that he would have experienced in his career. What he felt and thought can only be guessed at. For the former Lord of Annandale, watching from the parapet as Comyn revelled in his new-found status at his expense must have been a bitterly galling experience. Yet in such deep-rooted hatred, the Bruces were able to galvanise their efforts and repel the Comyn attack, saving the castle from loss and destruction. In defeat, the Earl of Buchan had no alternative but to sweep south-east across the northern march, inflicting devastation through Northumberland.[26] At either Corbridge or Hexham, he supposedly ordered the massacre of two hundred schoolboys, locking them into a school and setting it ablaze. The numbers involved appear unlikely given the size of these villages, but whether true or not, this incident was just a taste of the bitter bloodshed that was to unfold on both sides of the conflict.

Edward set his focus on the Scots town, castle and port of Berwick, which Balliol had forfeited the previous year at the English parliament but failed to hand over to the king. A consistently profitable trading post linking Scotland to Norway and northern Europe, Berwick lay vulnerable to attack, its defences made up of earthworks and timber palisades. A century of peace between the two countries meant Berwick's inhabitants had neglected to strengthen its defences in stone, and as the English marched towards its ill-prepared walls, the townsfolk were effectively defenceless. Edward unleashed his fleet to attack from the sea, but one of his ships quickly ran aground, allowing the Scots inhabitants to set it alight, while a further two vessels got caught up in the blaze. Seeing his ships burning, the king ordered the advance of his army. The garrison sang ribald songs from the timber walls, taunting the English and accusing them of being tailed dogs, a long-established medieval slur that won them no favour.[27] On 30 March, the town fell. The English army poured into the streets, their bloodlust up, and indulged in an orgy of violence that lasted for two days. A contemporary noted that bodies 'fell like autumn leaves'. The chroniclers estimated anywhere between 7,500 to 15,000 inhabitants; men, women and children, were slaughtered.[28] Edward allegedly only called a halt when he witnessed the murder of a pregnant woman in which her unborn child spilled from her body onto the street.

Sir William Douglas, seeing the futility of defending the castle, surrendered shortly afterwards, offering himself up as a hostage on condition that his defending garrison could depart unmolested, which Edward confirmed according to the chivalric custom of the day.[29] The townspeople were not spared, however, due to the simple fact that they were common folk who, despite offers to surrender peaceably, had failed to grasp the olive branch early enough. Nevertheless, the atrocity at Berwick remains the most savage act committed on home territory during a time of war in Britain's long and blood-stained history. Even contemporaries poured scorn on both sides for the bloodshed and its timing, falling so close to Holy Week.[30] Edward set up his quarters at Berwick Castle for the next four weeks, and on 5 April two Franciscan friars dutifully arrived to deliver John Balliol's renunciation of homage. Edward, in typical form, simply replied, 'Be it unto the fool according to his folly.'[31]

For the King of Scots, the fall of Berwick presented something of a poor omen, and rumours of the massacre must surely have quickly found their way to his camp. If he was in any doubt about the strategy of his enemy, it was now all too clear that this was to be a bitter struggle in which the loser could expect little clemency. Dunbar Castle, held for the English by the Earl of Dunbar, who was fighting in Edward's ranks, had been surrendered to the earls of Ross, Mar and Menteith by Dunbar's wife in his absence. Sensing an opportunity, the English king sent Earl Warenne to relieve it. It was a pointed choice, for Warenne was the father-in-law of King John. As the English began to lay siege to the castle, news arrived on St George's Day that the Kings of Scots was gathering nearby with a large army to relieve it, and as such, Warenne divided his army, taking the most experienced of his men with him and leaving a much smaller force to continue the siege at Dunbar.

Before long, the two armies got sight of each other at Spottsmuir. The Scots had taken up the prime position on the upper side of the valley, and as the English advanced they temporarily disappeared into the valley basin carved out by the Spotts Burn. The Scots, thinking the English had fled, broke their defensive ranks and charged headlong down the valley, forgoing their strategic advantage, expecting to pick off soft targets. Much to their surprise, they found Warenne and his army advancing in solid formation, and with the Scots suddenly in disarray, the English army was able to break through the Scottish advance and quickly overcome the army, massacring the infantry.[32] It was a devastating defeat for King John. Without any hope of overcoming his English adversary, the King of Scots and his councillors must have known that utter ruin now awaited them.

On 16 May, growing numbers of Scottish prisoners were transferred south to England to be locked up in twenty-four castles around the country. The earls of Ross, Atholl and Menteith, who were captured at the fall of Dunbar Castle, plus Andrew Murray and the son of John Comyn of Badenoch were all were all sent to the Tower of London. Others were incarcerated at Windsor, Wallingford, Conway, Kenilworth, Winchester and elsewhere.[33] Their lands and estates in Scotland were temporarily forfeit.[34] In the face of such overwhelming defeat, on 2 July 1296 at Kincardine, John Balliol issued his surrender:

Seeing that we have by evil and false council, and of our own folly, grievously offended and angered our lord Edward, by the

Grace of God, King of England ... Therefore we, acting under no
constraint and of our own free will, have surrendered to him the
land of Scotland and all its people.[35]

Five days later, the beleaguered king renounced the Treaty of
Paris. The following day, at Montrose, he formally resigned the
Kingdom of Scotland to Edward I.[36] In a ceremony carefully
designed to humiliate, John Balliol was physically stripped of his
tabard on his surcoat bearing the Lion Rampant, the heraldic
insignia of the King of Scots, and was thereby stripped of his
symbolic power. It is from this act alone that he is remembered
by history as '*Twme Tabart*' or '*Toom Tabard*'. His regalia was
also removed. Edward was certainly pleased and declared, 'He
does good business, who rids himself of shit.'[37] The Scottish
royal castles were also quickly overcome, including Roxburgh,
Jedburgh, Dumbarton and, shortly after that, Edinburgh. So
utterly complete was the Scottish defeat that the garrison at
Stirling Castle simply abandoned their post before the English
arrived to take possession.[38] John Balliol and his son and heir,
Edward, were escorted to the Tower of London where they were
to remain in close confinement. Edward Balliol, along with sons
of other Scottish noble prisoners, later entered for a time into
the household of the young Edward of Caernarvon, the future
Edward II of England.

The King of England, drunk on victory and determined to
assert his unequivocal authority over the Kingdom of Scotland,
had not yet finished with his symbolic gestures. During his
progress through Scotland as far north as Elgin and Banff
following Balliol's abdication, Edward began to confiscate both
the regalia as well as the symbols of Scottish power, including
relics and records.[39] When he reached Perth, he had the ancient
Stone of Destiny, that relic central to the inauguration of Scots
kings, removed and transferred to Westminster Abbey. The
chair that was made to house it there was later used in the
coronation service for the monarchs of England.[40] Other relics
were transferred to the royal wardrobe, while some were sent to
the Shrine of St Thomas Becket at Canterbury.[41] More, including
fragments of the True Cross once belonging to Scotland's queen,
St Margaret, were parcelled out to the Shrine of St Cuthbert at
Durham.[42] As if this degradation was not yet sufficient, Scotland
was temporarily reduced to the legal status of a land, no longer

a kingdom, and from the ashes Berwick was to rise as the new centre of an administration set up to govern the kingdom.[43]

Before he left for England, Edward appointed Earl Warenne as Lieutenant of Scotland, most likely in reward for his success at the Battle of Dunbar earlier that year. Warenne, however, was far from overjoyed with the commission, preferring to stay in the south and leave the government to three other principal royal appointments: Hugh de Cressingham, Treasurer; Walter of Amersham, Chancellor; and William Ormesby, Chief Justice. Custodians of Scottish castles were promptly replaced with men loyal to the English Crown, as were the sheriffs.[44] In August 1296, a parliament was held at Berwick in which the King of England sought to finalise his victory by demanding that all significant freeholders appear in person or by proxy with sealed evidence that proved their fealty to the English king.[45] So enormous and successful was this task that the roll in which these oaths were registered became known as the Ragman Roll, on account of the number of seals that protrude from the record.[46] For the Scottish Community of the Realm, the Ragman Roll would represent nothing short of abject humiliation and subjugation, in stark contrast to the position they had found themselves in ten years earlier, immediately before the premature death of Alexander III.

Robert Bruce VI, however, saw this moment as an opportunity, and pressed his right to the Scottish crown. Edward I, in a position of absolute power, had no time, inclination or desire to appoint another king to rule in Scotland, least of all in the foreseeable future. His curt and somewhat waspish response – 'have we nothing else to do than win kingdoms for you?' – left Bruce in no doubt that, once more, his family claim would be left in abeyance, the crown beyond their immediate grasp.[47] In disgust, he retired to his English estates, never to set foot in Scotland again. This failure to passionately pursue his claim left his son in a compromised position. Young Robert knew all too well that he would one day inherit the claim, and he needed to play a careful game in order to protect his rights and also defend himself and his family's landed interests in the interim, even if his father appeared reluctant to do the same. In short, while his father lived, Robert could not advance his ambition, which can only have frustrated him.

To make matters worse, the Bruce family had won no material advantage from the fall of John Balliol or the Comyns. They received neither additional land nor title as reward for their service to Edward I, and had to watch as Sir Henry Percy was granted the Justiciarship of Galloway in September and Sir Reginald received that of Ayr four months prior.[48] A temporary relief for the repayment of a debt Robert owed to the English Exchequer on 15 October 1296 was a poor attempt at reward by Edward.[49] Worse still, while the English king had imprisoned many of Balliol's supporters, including the Comyns and other Scottish nobles, he had failed to confiscate their estates in the long term, sending out a clear signal that in time they could regain favour so long as they supported their English master. The young Earl of Carrick knew that if this proved to be the case, he and his family had gained enemies to no benefit. Resentment and conflicted loyalties were almost inevitable companions for Robert Bruce as he strove to walk the tightrope of Anglo-Scottish politics in the late thirteenth century.

5

Precarious Ambition

If Edward I thought peace was now assured in Scotland, he was in for a rude awakening. The Scots would not be so easily conquered. Robert Wishart, Bishop of Glasgow, and James Stewart were more determined than ever to resist the king's vaulting ambition. Wishart, born in 1240 to a family in the Mearns, and bishop since 1273, was a dedicated champion of the Church. When the King of England sought to undermine the Scottish Kirk, starting on 1 October 1296, Wishart was quick to act. Scotland's ecclesiastical body had been placed under the special protection of the Holy Roman See, and as a 'special daughter' was afforded the privilege of guaranteeing Scots to vacant Scottish benefices. To consolidate his ill-gotten gains, Edward simply ignored the papal ruling and began to appoint English candidates to ecclesiastical offices in Galloway. Within a year, this pro-English discrimination became more or less the norm. Facing foreign interference in the governance of the Church of Scotland, Wishart made his first move. Having sworn fealty to England by attaching his seal to the Ragman Roll the year before, his resistance was at first discreet. Along with James Stewart, he sought out a man whose circumspection was not necessary and whose determination to hold out against the English has passed down the ages as legend.[1]

William Wallace, second son of Malcom Wallace of Elderslie, was a vassal of James Stewart, High Steward of Scotland. The names of the Wallace brothers do not appear on the Ragman Roll, and it is clear that neither man was willing to bend the knee to their new English overlord. Facing outlawry, they fled into the vast Selkirk Forest, meeting up with many others who would not kneel to Edward I. According to the Scotichronicon, written in the fifteenth century, Wallace in 1297 'raised his head'.[2] Little is known of William's early life, but he married Marion Braidfoot, who lived in Lanark, and despite his dubious status as an outlaw he visited her home often. The English authorities soon got wind of this, and Wallace was forced to flee Lanark for the Cartland Crags. Marion and her household were rounded up and slaughtered, while her house was put to the torch.

On hearing the devastating news, Wallace, distraught with grief and seeking revenge, raised a band of men and on 3 May 1297 killed Sir William Hazelrigg, the English sheriff of Lanark, hacking the man's body to pieces.[3] With bloodlust coursing through their veins, further attacks would not be long in coming. Encouraged by Wishart and the High Steward, the flames of rebellion were soon spreading like wildfire.

Wallace joined his forces with Sir William Douglas, known as 'Le Hardi', the former governor of Berwick, who had secured a safe conduct for himself and his men when he had surrendered the castle to Edward I after the massacre there only the year before. Douglas, whose first wife was the High Steward's sister, had taken for his second an Englishwoman, Eleanor Ferrers, whom he had abducted and forced into marriage, presumably for her wealth and position.[4] However unsavoury Douglas might have been, he was just the kind of man required to help Wallace raise a rebellion. Joining forces, they marched on Scone, hoping to slay the English Chief Justice in Scotland, William Ormesby, who was holding court there. Ormesby narrowly escaped with his life, but the English now looked increasingly vulnerable. The Bishop of Durham, Anthony Bek, wrote to Edward I, warning the king that rebellion was spreading quickly through parts of Scotland and threatening their position. He requested urgent aid.[5]

As the hearts of rebellion were beginning to beat stronger, Robert Bruce was ensconced at Carlisle Castle. Having made his homage and fealty to Edward, as evidenced on the Ragman Roll, Bruce must have watched with some degree of anxiety. Although he was no supporter of John Balliol, or the Balliol–Comyn hegemony, he was clearly devoted to his country, which he did not wish to see torn apart again under the yoke of English power. His loyalty was ultimately to Scotland, but without the political might to overcome his rivals, and with his father very much alive, Bruce was caught between a rock and a hard place. He must have felt great confusion.

The King of England was quick to send orders to Bruce to amass a force and march on Douglasdale to seize the castle of Sir William Douglas, which was being held by the latter's English wife. Perhaps sensing an outward tension or conflict of conscience, Robert was required to swear an additional oath of fealty to the king, those around him seemingly uncertain of his immediate intentions.[6] They were right to be wary, for no sooner had he marched through Annandale, collecting his father's fighting men, than the Earl of Carrick reconciled his conscience. Turning to his men, he declared,

> No man holds his own flesh and blood in hatred, and I am no exception. I must join my own people and the nation in which I was born ... choose then whether you go with me or return to your homes.[7]

For Robert this was something of a watershed moment. For his men it was not. Having been summoned to fight for the earl, whose father was still in England and a supporter of the English Crown, many of Annandale's vassals would not risk supporting his son's new-found loyalty. Without much to gain, many decided to return to their homes rather than fight the might of the English.

With much-depleted forces, an undeterred Robert rode on to Douglasdale. When he arrived outside the walls of the castle, he was able to convince Eleanor Douglas, née Ferrers, of his change of allegiance. Throwing in her lot with Bruce, and knowing that a second, more loyal English contingent would be sent to capture the castle, Bruce and Eleanor rode out together for Irvine to join the Scots who were now encamped there. As Bruce rode across the war-torn countryside that was his homeland, he must have been excited with his choice, full of hope and determination. En route, he was able to strengthen his forces with men from his own lands of Carrick, who, unlike those in his father's patrimony of Annandale, responded to their master's jubilant call.

Seething at Bruce's betrayal, Edward sent Henry de Percy and Robert de Clifford across the northern march to answer Anthony Bek's pleas for aid. Taking a band of knights and the shire levies of Cumberland, Westmoreland and Lancashire, they soon arrived a few miles south of the Scots encampment at Irvine. Caught off guard and facing a serious and focussed English response, the Scottish leaders, including Wishart, James Stewart, Robert Bruce, Sir Alexander Lindsay and William Douglas, had no choice but to parley. Denying the truth, they claimed their opposition, which mirrored the contemporary arguments of their English counterparts against Edward I, rested on the extent of the king's exorbitant taxation and the request for military aid in the king's ongoing overseas wars. Nevertheless, backed into a corner, they surrendered on 7 July 1297. If there was hope of a glorious rebellion, it had abruptly hit a major setback.

Clifford and Percy demanded Scottish hostages as tokens of goodwill, but Bruce, whose only daughter, Marjorie, had been singled out in the demand for the earl, refused to offer her up, and instead proffered three sureties in the guise of Wishart, James Stewart and Alexander Lindsay.[8] Robert had no intention of giving up his only child, and if his conscience was now clearly set, he equally had no intention of remaining loyal to the English king hereafter. He would therefore not risk his only daughter to an increasingly irascible and arbitrary English monarch who was becoming more violent and unpredictable as he grew older. Wishart fared less favourably, and was promptly imprisoned, as was Douglas. The king, as an extra precaution, stripped Bruce's father, the Lord of Annandale, of the governorship of Carlisle Castle, replacing him with Bishop Halton.[9] Edward clearly felt that loyalty and honour among family members could not be assured, especially where strategic castles were involved.

Despite the setback, there was still hope. William Wallace had been absent from the debacle, and in August, commanding the common army of Scotland, made up of men between the ages of sixteen and sixty, he marched east to Dundee and laid siege to the castle there. His plan was simple. If the rebellion was to grow, he needed to unite his forces with another rebellion that had begun in the north under Sir Andrew de Murray, son of Andrew Murray of Petty, Justiciar of Scotia. Heir to his father's lands of Murray and Cromarty, Murray had been captured with his relatives at the Battle of Dunbar, but had subsequently escaped his English captivity at Chester Castle. In May 1297, Murray raised his vassals at Aroch Castle in the Black Isle. Having captured Urquhart Castle on the shore of Loch Ness, the band went on to take Inverness, Elgin and Banff. Aberdeen fell to them when the English sheriff, isolated in the north, decided his fate lay in the hands of the Scots, and so promptly switched sides rather than await English relief.[10] The northern rebellion quickly gained momentum, and Macduff of Fife, the noble who first took his litigious action to Edward I in opposition to King John Balliol, joined Wallace and his men, taking his sons with him. On 24 July, Wallace and Murray finally combined their forces. The rebellion was once more in full flame.

The English were quickly losing control. Sir Hugh de Cressingham, Edward I's unpopular Treasurer, dispatched anguished news south to the king's thirteen-year-old son, who was acting as regent while his father was in France. The reports were predictably gloomy. English officials across the Scottish kingdom were either murdered, imprisoned or besieged, Cressingham wrote. Many had been thrown out of their offices, and the emboldened Scots had appointed their own men to administer instead. Command of the kingdom was now only effective in Berwickshire and Roxburghshire, turning back the tide of English gains made only one year prior.[11] The King's Council ordered Earl Warenne back across the border to restore some semblance of law, and Warenne, as lacklustre as ever in his appoach to Scottish affairs, slowly gathered his men and begrudgingly headed north. In the earl's mind any conflict with Wallace and Murray would surely be nothing more than a simple, light campaign, given the Scots commanded the common army and not swathes of heavy cavalry. Furthermore, many of the Scots earls were still in the south, either in English custody or fighting for Edward on the continent as a means to buying their freedom. The recent defeat of the noble rebels at Irvine also made the job of subjugating Wallace and Murray all the easier, as any hope of aid was unlikely to be forthcoming. Warenne was overconfident.

The two armies met at Stirling Bridge on 9 September 1297. The Scots had chosen their position carefully, defending the crossing of the Firth of Forth from the high ground at the Abbey of Craig overlooking the bridge. In order to reach Stirling, Warenne and his men would be forced to make the crossing, the bridge only two horses wide, and then navigate a narrow causeway through boggy terrain. On the 9th and 10th the battle began, initially with two parleys. In the first, James Stewart and the Earl of Lennox arrived with large contingents but did not commit to either side. Instead, they offered to act as negotiators between Warenne, Wallace and Murray, but the latter two refused to enter talks, Stewart's intervention perhaps giving the Scots further time to prepare.[12] This was most likely a calculated, pre-planned smokescreen. Later, two Dominicans, seeking the avoidance of bloodshed, were sent by the English to encourage the Scots to surrender. Wallace replied, 'Tell your commander that we are not here to make peace but to do battle to defend ourselves and liberate our kingdom. Let them come and we shall prove this in their very beards.'[13] With such open defiance, only one course of action was now possible.

Battle was joined on 11 September amid some confusion. Warenne overslept, and his infantry, which had been ordered to cross the bridge without his authority, had to be called back. Eventually, the earl was up and readied for war, giving his first order to Hugh de Cressingham to lead the cavalry across the bridge to crush the Scottish resistance. Heading out two abreast, the long column of mounted men quickly became overstretched, and eventually Wallace and Murray saw their opportunity. They launched their attack, the Scots infantry slamming into the exposed English flank, forcing the cavalry off the causeway and into the waterlogged fields. As the horses became stuck in fetlock-deep water, the knights were massacred. At the same time, a second contingent of Scots were dispatched to the bridge. Deploying their Lochaber axes, they were able to bring it crashing down, preventing the English infantry or Earl Warenne from crossing. All that was left was to finish off the English cavalry, man by man, which James Stewart and the Earl of Lennox now obliged, joining their forces with their fellow countrymen. With calculated precision, the Scots took the field and secured a significant victory. The defeat at Dunbar had been avenged.

A dumbfounded Warenne, seeing that all was lost, took flight. In his desperation to escape, he rode his horse to Berwick without stopping, and the exhausted destrier collapsed and died upon arrival.[14] Cressingham's fate was worse; having been cut down and killed in the rout, his body was flayed and small pieces of skin were gifted throughout the country as macabre mementos of victory. Wallace himself allegedly made a skin belt to wear as a reminder of his greatest achievement.[15]

The victory at Stirling Bridge was a pivotal moment for the rebellion. It broke the perceived invincibility of the English war machine and emboldened those who were wavering. On 11 October, one month after the battle, Murray and Wallace sent a joint letter to the mayor and communes of Lubeck and Hamburg, informing them that Scottish ports were once again open to German merchants.[16] Rebel control of the Scottish machine of government may not have been so certain, but it was a message that the Scottish patriots sought to promote and cultivate. The kingdom needed to continue if Scotland was to survive. But for Andrew de

Murray, luck was running out. Wounded at Stirling Bridge, he failed to recover and was dead by the end of the month. Robbed of a capable commander, Wallace took up the mantle of sole leadership and marched the common army into northern England, turning the aggrieved into the aggressors, and through the autumn months harried the northern march, driving the English population south as their homes were put to the torch.[17] In return, a somewhat chastened Warenne, along with Robert de Clifford, retaliated in kind, burning the villages and tenements of Annandale, which only yet further weakened the financial resources of the Bruce family.

Following his return to Scotland, Wallace met with other patriots in March 1298 at the so-called Forest Parliament, held in the great wooded expanse that was Selkirk Forest. There, attended by the earls of Buchan, Lennox, Carrick and Strathearn, along with many nobles and clergy, Wallace was appointed as the sole Guardian of Scotland in recognition of his extraordinary achievements and the confidence he evoked in others. At the same time, to impove his status, he was knighted by one of the earls; it is not clear which earl it was, although legend suggests it was Robert Bruce.[18] With clear patriotic leadership, the rebellion had a strong focus, proven God-given success and political momentum. Faced with such united opposition, the King of England, returning from France on 14 March, had no choice but to muster an army and head in person to curb the insurrection.

Freed from his conflict with King Philip IV of France following a truce that was to last until 6 January 1299, the king hastened north, having amassed a considerable force of up to 3,000 cavalry, Welsh longbowmen, Gascon crossbowmen, and 10,900 infantry from Wales and a further 14,800 English foot.[19] As in previous campaigns, a fleet of ships was sailed up the coast to meet the army at Leith in order to provide a lifeline in the form of provisions.[20] Entering Scotland on 1 July, Edward headed east, despoiling the lands of the new Bishop of St Andrews, William Lamberton, who had recently replaced Bishop Fraser following the latter's death. Elected by the Scots cathedral chapter at Wallace's instigation and not Edward I's, Lamberton had been consecrated bishop by Pope Boniface VIII in June 1298, much to Edward's chagrin. Attacking his lands now was tit-for-tat.

Despite delays in provisions caused by storms in the North Sea, Edward moved his army north in response to news that the Scots army was encamped near Falkirk. On the evening of 21 July his forces bivouacked, the army bedding down under the stars besides their horses. In the night, two of the king's ribs were broken when his mount trod on him, but undeterred by the excruciating pain Edward refused to halt and rode at the head of his troops.[21] The old leopard was still very much a Caesar.

Battle was joined on 22 July. As before, Wallace had been careful to choose strategically advantageous ground, positioning his men on a hillside with a loch and marsh at the foot of it, restricting access. Around them a palisade of stakes stretched across the slope to slow down any English cavalry charge. The Scots then divided into four contingents, each forming up in a schiltron, a highly flexible circular or square formation of spearmen whose closed position gave their contingent the appearance of a hedgehog or porcupine. It was a shrewd move designed to ward off the dangers of heavy cavalry but was vulnerable to archers. Between the individual schiltrons, Wallace placed the archers of Selkirk Forest for added protection. In all, the Scots numbered approximately 15,000 men, but they faced a superior English force of between 24,000 and 27,000.[22] Wallace, who most certainly sensed the enormity of the task, addressed his men, saying, 'I have brought you to the ring, now dance the best you can.'[23]

Dancing was not enough on this occasion. Edward gave the command to advance, and the cavalry, led by Anthony Bek and the earls of Norfolk, Hereford, and Lincoln, swept forward, dividing in two, swinging around the loch and into the Scottish flanks simultaneously. The Scottish cavalry fled as their light archers were taken out, and their commander, John Stewart, brother of the High Steward, was killed. The King of England then brought his Welsh longbows and Gascon crossbows into play, decimating the schiltrons. With a final cavalry charge, the schiltrons collapsed as the Scots broke rank and were slaughtered in the ensuing retreat, including Macduff of Fife and his two sons. Wallace and his immediate men, who had fought hard throughout the battle, seeing all was lost, fled the field for Torwood and eventually the security of Selkirk Forest.[24] It was over. In the face of such bloody defeat, the illusion of Wallace's invincibility, which had for the last eighteen months propelled the patriot cause forward, now lay exposed. In defeat, Wallace resigned the Guardianship.

Robert Bruce did not witness the horrors of the Scottish defeat at Falkirk. However, he did benefit from it inasmuch as Wallace's resignation thrust Bruce into the centre of the patriot cause. As

Wallace gave up his mantle, Robert Bruce, along with John 'The Red Comyn', Lord of Badenoch, became joint Guardians of Scotland.[25] It may well have been the design of Wishart, Buchan and others to achieve some balance in the patriotic cause by appointing two men who represented the two very different political positions of Balliol and Bruce. Together they were united by one greater common thread: the survival of Scottish independence. Despite Badenoch's hot-headed temper and fierce support for Balliol, Robert knew that his best chance of securing his family's claim in the future was to work here and now for the common cause, winning respect along the way. In his mind, it was the shrewd choice at this juncture.

However, by June 1299 tensions had begun to mount. William Lamberton, the newly consecrated Bishop of St Andrews, returned from Avignon with David de Moravia of Moray, newly crowned Bishop of Moray. With them they brought news that Lamberton's intercession with Pope Boniface VIII had helped to secure John Balliol's release from Edward I's captivity into papal custody on 18 July.[26] While Balliol was not yet free, his transfer to papal authority was a positive step forward and one that was quickly welcomed by his compatriots back in Scotland, who still fiercely upheld his rightful claim. For Bruce, the news was a bitter blow. It threatened to undermine his position as Guardian and had ramifications for his wider ambition.

Events worsened over the coming months. When the patriots met again in Selkirk Forest in August following their failure to capture the English-held castle of Roxburgh, tempers ignited and violence quickly ensued. According to an English spy who reported back to Edward and whose account is preserved in the English archives, John Comyn leapt at Robert Bruce and seized him by the throat, while the Earl of Buchan turned on the Bishop of St Andrews, shouting accusations of treason.[27] It seems that Bruce was suspected of working against the interests of the captive King John, perhaps having laid out his ambitions too clearly. It was only with the direct intervention of James Stewart and others that bloodshed was avoided.[28]

Either way, Bruce was failing to win greater support for his father's claim; if anything, he was becoming increasingly isolated. In the interests of keeping the peace, it was agreed that Bishop Lamberton would assume the role of Senior Guardian and with that position would exercise control of all Scottish-held castles in the kingdom. It was a move designed to appease, and had the desired effect in the first instance, allowing the patriots the opportunity to gather together in November and lay siege to the strategically important Stirling Castle, which promptly fell to them.[29]

Despite the fractious patriotic leadership, the King of England, sensing an opportunity and unable to ignore the fall of Stirling, on 30 December ordered a muster at Carlisle for 24 June 1300. Against the threat of further invasion, the Scots gathered on 10 May at Rutherglen in Lanarkshire to hold another parliament. Here, amid growing political distrust among the gathering, Robert Bruce was either engineered out of the Guardianship or resigned his commission, being replaced by the pro-Balliol Ingram de Umfraville. Now without official office and facing a political future in which the Balliols would continue to hold sway, Bruce was yet more isolated. With the threat of invasion imminent, and his family's estate just north of the border, he knew he needed to turn his attention to Annandale and Carrick to mitigate any potential damage. The loss of these lands would be catastrophic to him.

On 4 July, Edward I crossed once again into Scotland by way of the north-west, his aim being the invasion of Galloway. Bringing with him 850 cavalry and 9,000 infantry, he headed first to Caerlaverock Castle, near Dumfries on the shores of the Solway Firth, besieging the garrison there.[30] With him was his new second wife, Marguerite of France, sister of Philip IV, and the king's son and heir, Edward of Caernarvon, who was experiencing his first taste of war. The event is captured in detail by the herald who composed the poem the Caerlaverock Roll, which lists the arms, including the much smaller Scottish garrison, which only surrendered when the English siege engines significantly damaged the castle.[31] Buoyed by his success, the king advanced west into Balliol-held Galloway, reaching as far as Wigtown without meeting any significant resistance. At Kirkcudbright, the Earl of Buchan and the Lord of Badenoch reached the king and offered terms. They claimed their peace was to be secured only with the return of John Balliol as King of Scots, and the release of those magnates taken at Dunbar, who should also be able to re-purchase their confiscated estates from the king. Edward had no need to back down and simply refused, allowing the Comyns the opportunity to return to their forces under safe conduct. In retaliation, the dismayed Scots appeared to challenge Edward's return march east at the crossing of the River Cree, but the king was able to deploy his cavalry, who routed the Scots before any significant injury could be inflicted on either side. It is highly unlikely that Robert Bruce was part of this action; he was probably focussing his energies in preparing the defence of his lands in Carrick.[32]

If the Comyns were unable to bring the King of England to heel, the next hope came in the unlikely form of Robert Winchelsey, the bombastic Archbishop of Canterbury, who was increasingly a thorn in Edward's side. While the king was encamped at the Cistercian abbey of Smeetham, founded by John Balliol's mother, Lady Dervorguilla, Winchelsey promptly unfurled the latest papal decree, *Scimus Fili*, which demanded that Edward I cease his campaigning in Scotland on the basis that the Scottish kingdom was a fiefdom of the Holy Roman See.[33] Winchelsey lectured the king, declaring his actions harmful to the Crusades of this time, which required Christian knights to support one another against the perceived infidel. The king snorted back, 'By God's blood I will not keep my peace ... but while there is breath to my nostrils I will defend my right, which all the world knows, with all my power.'[34]

With yet another opportunity lost, Scotland was still at the mercy of a king bent on its subjugation. In the end, though, Edward's campaign petered out for a much more prosaic reason: desertion. Lacking the financial reserves to pay for many salaried troops, and with his army thus largely comprised of the feudal levy, which had now performed its appointed term in the field, many simply left the campaign. With limited ability to take his dwindling forces north of Galloway into Carrick and beyond, Edward fell back on the diplomacy of the French king, who had offered to act as negotiator between the Scots and the English. Bruce had been given a temporary and somewhat lucky respite.

In the end, a truce was agreed between the two countries which was to extend until 21 May 1301, giving both parties the opportunity to regroup through the winter.[35] During the interlude, a war of words broke out between the parties in a legal bid to convince the pope of their just cause. Edward's camp argued that England had held superiority over the Scots and the Welsh since the time of the Trojans, resting their claim on the fable of the three sons of Brutus, by which Locrinus ruled England, Albanactus Scotland and Camber Wales. As Locrinus was the eldest brother, he held precedence therefore over Albion, setting a precedent that was presented as justification for Edward's position.[36] Not to be outdone, the Scots' argument, led by Master Baldred of Bisset, claimed that Scotland was named after the Egyptian pharaoh's daughter Scota, and as a consequence was no concern of the English king. Edward, they declared, had no more claim over Scotland than did the Egyptians.[37] The war of words, much like the war of arms, was set to continue for many years.

In early 1301, the Guardianship was once again changed. This time, Comyn of Badenoch, Lamberton of St Andrews and Ingram de Umfraville were replaced by the lone figure of Sir John de Soules, who was nominated by King John Balliol while still in exile. The patriotic government was once more conducted in the name of the absentee king. As May arrived and the truce between the two countries expired, King Edward immediately took up the campaigning season. This time the Scots had to prepare to ward off a two-pronged attack. The King of England would march into Scotland from Berwick, through Tweeddale and down to Clydesdale, while his son and heir, now recently created Prince of Wales, would take the western approach via Carlisle into Galloway and march north to Ayr, under the guidance of the stalwart Earl of Lincoln.[38] Together, they would act as a pincer and join up in the middle.

Edward I captured Bothwell Castle while Edward of Caernarvon, bolstered by conscripts from Ireland including 1,617 foot, 391 hobelars, 14 knights, 242 squires and 8 bannerets, made for and subsequently captured Robert Bruce's castle of Turnberry.[39] Bruce, isolated and without political power in the patriotic government, was forced to defend his lands as best he could. Despite losing Turnberry, a symbolic blow to his prestige, Robert carried out lightning attacks on the Prince of Wales' army, inflicting injury and causing Edward of Caernarvon and the Earl of Lincoln to return to Carlisle. Unable to close the trap, Bruce had been effective in thwarting English plans. Both Edward and his son, the latter only temporarily, hunkered down for the winter at Linlithgow.

With the loss of Turnberry, Robert's position was growing weaker. To compound matters, in the autumn of 1301, while he was defending his lands in Carrick, news reached him that John Balliol had been released from papal custody and handed over to the King of France, who had given him his freedom. Balliol returned to his ancestral castle of Bailleul-en-Vimeu in Picardy. Rumour began to sweep through Scotland that Balliol would return, bringing with him a French army to regain his crown and overthrow the English. Robert perceived this as a real threat, and it was one he could not countenance.[40] If Balliol returned to Scotland, his chance of ever pursuing his ancestral claim to the throne of Scotland would be lost, especially as his father was still living in England and had no appetite to press it.

To make matters worse, during the winter the English and French forged a new truce which received formal recognition on 26 January 1302, guaranteeing respite in Scotland. During the peace, until formal peace could be assured, Edward was to hand over to French custody the castles he had captured during his campaign, which included Bothwell as well as Robert's castle at Turnberry. This exposed the Earl of Carrick to yet more danger, for under such circumstances there was no guarantee that Turnberry would be granted back to him while he remained in opposition. Edward could choose to retain it, or, worse still, John Balliol could grant it to one of his relatives or supporters.[41] When Balliol was last in Scotland, he had also confiscated the lordship of Annandale and granted it to the Earl of Buchan. There was nothing to say he would not do the same again. If John did return, Bruce could not offer his homage either, without damaging his own claim to the throne. In a Balliol-run kingdom, Robert and his family had no future. Drifting between Scylla and Charybdis, he looked set to be outmanoeuvred. With no real voice in the patriotic government, with his lands significantly damaged from years of war, and estranged from his father, Robert had few options left open to him. If he was to survive, he would need to play a different, even longer and more calculated game.

Towards the end of January 1302, Robert left his scarred and battle-worn lands of Carrick and rode to Sir John de St John and surrendered to the English king. It was a risk, and one that could have worked against him given the treatment of some of the Scottish nobility following their defeat at Dunbar in 1296. Yet Robert must have banked on the simple belief that he was significant enough to Edward to warrant a respectable welcome should he surrender. He guessed right. The King of England promptly allowed him back into the English fold, declaring that he and his earldom of Carrick were to be 'unharmed in life and limb, and in lands and tenements, and free from imprisonment' on account of his father's loyalty and the loyalty that Robert swore to undertake in future.[42]

While neither Edward nor Robert trusted each other, by crossing over to the English camp Bruce was able to receive a number of benefits. Firstly, during the harsh winter of 1301/2, he could secure English loans and food from south of the border and from his lands in Ireland, which gave his vassals in Carrick a chance of survival. That same year, he was granted the lucrative wardship of the young Earl of Mar, which meant control of lands in the north-east of the Scottish kingdom bordering the Comyn estates, bolstering his income. Three years later he would also secure the forfeited lands of Ingram de Umfraville, formerly a Guardian.[43] Robert's change in allegiance also helped the rest of his family. One of his brothers, Edward, entered into the household of Edward of Caernarvon, while Alexander Bruce was provided by Edward I the living of Kirkinner, near Wigtown. This helped Alexander's career, as the Cambridge scholar became Deacon of Glasgow in 1306.[44]

But perhaps the most important event of 1302 for Robert on a personal level was his ability to secure a lucrative second marriage. With the King of England's blessing, at the age of twenty-eight he married the thirteen-year-old Elizabeth de Burgh, daughter of Richard de Burgh, Earl of Ulster. Where is uncertain, but Canterbury or somewhere near his father's land in Writtle may have been appropriate.[45] From here on in, Robert was once again a husband, and his hope must have been to father more children as soon as possible to secure his lands and titles, having so far Marjorie as his only child and heir. It also meant he had secured a useful ally and made further connections in Ireland where his mother's family had been influential and he retained lands. Whether his conscience allowed him to enjoy his new-found position is altogether another matter.

The year 1302 was also one of great political change on the European stage, which directly impacted the Scottish position. Pope Boniface VIII, now at odds with the French king over his rights to claim authority over temporal rulers, moved to outright opposition. Suddenly facing a French firestorm, Boniface desperately sought allies, and having found Edward I he had little choice but to forgo the Scots. *Scimus Fili* was suddenly a dead letter, and to drive the point home the pontiff issued an edict demanding the Scots show obedience to their *rightful* overlord, the King of England. The forthright patriot Robert Wishart, Bishop of Glasgow, was accused directly by the Holy Father of inciting conflict between the two nations.[46] It was a bitter blow.

The French position had also altered, with war erupting in Flanders. What followed was a devastating defeat for Philip IV's army at Courtrai on 11 July that year, in which, much like at Stirling Bridge, his mounted cavalry was decimated by the enemy's infantry. The traditional rules of warfare were changing, and with some rapidity. In the same year, the citizens of Bordeaux, chafing under French occupation, rebelled. Philip was mindful that it was now in his best interests to turn the truce with England into something of a permanent peace.[47] The turning of the tide had only one outcome for the patriot Scots. Without the King of France or the Pope to call on for aid, their leverage against Edward I was suddenly redundant. Fearing the worst, the Scots sent a desperate delegation which included bishops Lamberton and Crambeth, as well as the Earl of Buchan, James Stewart and Ingram de Umfraville, in a bid to keep French support. Despite their pleas, Philip needed peace with England more, and a peace settlement was ratified on 30 May 1303 in which Philip's only daughter, Isabella, was set to marry Edward of Caernarvon.[48] The Scots were now firmly out in the cold.

As the year drew to a close, at Michaelmas, Robert Bruce attended an English parliament at Westminster where he was privy to the King of England's preparations for another campaign to subjugate Robert's homeland.[49] With international pressure now abated, Edward had free rein to attack Scotland with impunity. The muster was ordered to meet at Roxburgh for Whitsun 1303.[50] In April, Robert to was ordered to assemble 1,000 infantry and as many mounted men-at-arms as he could find from his lands in Carrick and Galloway to support the king's army. The now twenty-nine-year-old Robert was to be drawn into the retinue of the nineteen-year-old Prince of Wales, who had set off from London on 13 March. Robert's father-in-law, the Earl of Ulster, dispatched 3,457 men in 173 ships to aid an attack on the Isle of Bute, which saw the capture of Rothesay Castle and neighbouring Inverkip on the mainland. Robert, who was there during the fighting, was accompanied by Aymer de Valence, the future Earl of Pembroke. Their campaign was a success. Following the capture of Ayr, Bruce was given custody of the castle in December 1303 as well as the lucrative sheriffdom of Lanarkshire in January 1304, valued at £494.[51] In fighting his compatriots, Robert was at least securing his financial future, if attacking his countrymen with surely mixed feelings.

Edward I had been successful as well. Marching along the north-east, he avoided the distraction of Stirling Castle, instead crossing the Firth of Forth on three floating bridges which he had constructed and shipped from King's Lynn in Norfolk at a cost of £938.[52] Taking Brechin Castle in August, he marched north via Aberdeen, Banff and Elgin, before reaching Kinloss Abbey by 13 September. His march had been designed to overwhelm, and it is no coincidence that it followed his past victory progresses through the country. The symbolism could not have been plainer. The Scots could reclaim their castles, but Edward would take them back again with impunity. Resistance was futile. With his enemy in retreat, he swept south again, making for Dunfermline Abbey, where he decided to settle for the winter, hoping his presence in Scotland would drive greater fear into the hearts of his enemies.[53]

With Lamberton, James Stewart, John de Soules and the Scots delegates in France, the acting Guardian of the realm was John Comyn, Lord of Badenoch. Lamberton, sensing the worst, wrote to William Wallace ordering him to raise the common army, backing up his demands by offering the patriot knight financial aid from his revenues in Scotland.[54] Wallace duly obliged, and along with Simon Fraser began a campaign to harass the English in and around Selkirk Forest. But this was not enough against such a well-devised campaign. With significant English successes secured, and without the hope of aid from the King of France or the Pope, the Scots were overwhelmed and unable to resist in any sustainable way. As Edward bedded down at Dunfermline, Scottish lords began to seek terms of surrender. By 9 February 1304, the acting Guardian of Scotland formally surrendered, submitting to Edward I at Strathord, near Perth.[55] Those still in France were not ignored either, Edward demanding Wishart face three years in exile, while the Guardian John de Soules preferred perpetual exile despite being given a safe-conduct to return. James Stewart and Sir Ingram de Umfraville were also given leave to return into the English king's peace, which they begrudgingly accepted.[56]

Yet, for William Wallace, Edward I reserved the greatest and most personal distaste. In orders to his son and English representatives, the king declared that 'no words of peace are to be held out to William Wallace in any circumstances.'[57] With Wallace still an outlaw and seeking shelter in the dense cloak of Selkirk Forest, the King of England sought to test the new-found loyalty of those Scots who had surrendered, sending out Simon Fraser, recently an ally of Wallace, with John Comyn to capture him. The man who exerted himself the most, Edward declared, could expect the greatest of rewards. Comyn and Fraser of course failed to find their quarry, perhaps reluctant to actually seek out and capture him. In February, Robert Bruce was ordered, along with Sir John de Segrave, to finish the job. Despite forest skirmishes, Wallace and his men escaped the attempt.[58] The king, overjoyed to hear that Wallace was now on the retreat, wrote to Bruce and his pursuers congratulating them and urged them to complete the job: 'As the cloak is well made, also to make the hood.'[59]

In March, Robert Bruce VI, Lord of Annandale, died in England. His mortal remains were transferred to the Cistercian abbey of Holm Cultram in Cumberland, no doubt in a ceremony attended by the leading members of his family. With Annandale now gone, Robert Bruce finally came into his father's patrimony, but rather more significantly, he also inherited his father's claim to the Scottish throne. Although he was far from able to act directly upon his desires at this point, he suddenly had the impetus and status to improve the chances of realising his ambition. Bruce temporarily left Edward's campaign with the king's leave to enter into the lands newly bequeathed to him by his dead father. In April, the King of England wrote to Robert requesting more troops and siege engines for the king's planned attack on Stirling Castle. Bruce replied that while he was trying to raise horses and armour, he was struggling, as he had received no rents from his new lands at Writtle, Tottenham and Hatfield Regis.[60] Edward went on to complain that Robert had sent siege engines but had omitted to send a vital rod with which to operate them.[61] It may well be that during this delicate time Bruce began to operate with more subtle resistance in order to assuage his guilt in attacking Scotland.

When Robert turned north again, he reached the siege of Stirling Castle in May. The castle was defended by Sir William Oliphant, who had been appointed by the late Guardian Sir John de Soules to hold it in the name of John Balliol. Oliphant, realising the King of Scots was not coming with a French army after all, instead chose to defend it on behalf of the lion, the Scottish royal sigil.[62] Edward I, using his siege engines, bombarded the castle for twelve weeks until the garrison surrendered unconditionally.[63] Annoyed that he had not yet been able to deploy his largest siege engine, aptly named War Wolf, and possibly smarting at being grazed by a crossbow bolt which had embedded itself in his armour while riding too close to the battlements, the king ordered the defeated garrison back into the castle until he could try out the weapon. Watching the scene were the Queen of England, Marguerite, and Edward of Caernarvon, along with other Scots now in the camp of the English. After a sustained bombardment, the garrison were finally allowed to leave in procession, barefoot, and with cruciform ashes on their furrowed brows, as the custom dictated.[64]

During this military hiatus, the King of England and those in the English army had failed to notice the Earl of Carrick slip out of camp. Robert, it seemed, had his own dangerous game to play, and he now rolled the dice – with life-changing consequences.

6

A Champion Arises

Robert Bruce arrived discreetly for his surreptitious meeting with Bishop Lamberton of St Andrews at the abbey of Cambuskenneth, a mile or so from Stirling Castle. Their rendezvous had been pre-planned. There must have been an air of nervousness as the two men began talking in hushed terms about the future, in fear of being caught or overheard by those who may have followed. The details of their conversation are not entirely known, but they surely must have discussed the failing health of England's soon-to-be sixty-five-year-old monarch, which had been rapidly declining in the last year. Robert's claim, now more than ever, hung in the balance, and if he was to make a bid for the Scottish throne then he needed both unflinching support from the Church and perfect timing. The death of Edward would provide such an occasion.

Lamberton, a supporter of Bruce, listened intently, and by the end of the discussion the two men agreed to mutual support. Together they sealed an indenture which bound them, promising to help one another in all their businesses and affairs, to warn each other of danger, as well as acting to avert it. They would be each other's eyes and ears. To underline their commitment, they each pledged a crippling fine of £10,000 should either fail to adhere to its clauses.[1] The terms of the indenture are vague, a necessity if either man was caught, but with Bishop Lamberton now by his side, at least in secret, Robert could begin a discreet campaign to build a following for when the time would come to reach out and take the crown of Scotland.

With the Stirling garrison pounded into submission, Edward I had won. Returning to England, the king focussed his mind on the future government of Scotland. This time, the old leopard had learnt from his previous mistakes, offering a consultative role to the Scots so they could have a say in how their country ought to be governed. The velvet glove, off the royal hand since Norham in 1291, was back on for now. In late February, the king appointed Robert Bruce, Bishop Wishart of Glasgow and Sir John de Mowbray – an earl, a bishop and a baron – to represent the Scottish Community of the Realm, and to take time to discuss and proffer ideas on how future government should be settled.[2] They soon recommended that the community should be given the opportunity to elect ten of their body, who in turn could attend a future English parliament where the final details could be debated. Edward I agreed.

On 28 May 1305, a Scots parliament was held at Perth where two bishops, two abbots, two earls and two barons were elected, along with one representative of the community north of the Forth, and one from the south. The latter two positions went to Sir John Inchmartin and Sir Adam Gordon, but Robert was not elected, nor indeed was Bishop Wishart.[3] This may have been procedural, rather than a sign that the two men were being closed out of the political arena, for shortly after, at the English parliament at Westminster on 15 September, Bruce would find a seat on the twenty-two-strong Scots Council, created to advise the new Lieutenant of Scotland. Bishops Lamberton and Crambeth, the earls of Buchan, Dunbar, Ross and Atholl, along with barons Alexander MacDougall, John Comyn of Badenoch and John Mowbray, all found seats.[4]

The 'Ordinance for the Government of the land of Scotland' was Edward's agreed Scottish settlement, creating a blueprint for proposed governance.[5] The reference to a kingdom was promptly erased, and Scotland was instead relegated to the legal status of a land, in effect subordinated and amalgamated into the Kingdom of England. Edward was cautious enough to offer all the key positions to English representatives, who in turn had power to remove any of those beneath them, that is, anyone who would later pose a threat to newfound peace or the English regime. The new office of Lieutenant of Scotland, imbued with extensive powers of jurisdiction, went to Edward's nephew John of Brittany, Earl of Richmond, who was the younger brother of Duke Arthur II of Brittany, the latter now married to Queen Yolande, widow of Alexander III, late King of Scots.[6] Reporting to him was the Chancellor, William de Bevercotes; the Chamberlain, John Sandale;

and the Chamberlain Comptroller, Robert Heron.[7] When it came to the administration of law and order, eight justices were appointed in four regions: Galloway, Lothian, south of the Mounth and north of it. In each region, one justice would be Scottish and one English, to ensure a careful application of the law. The sheriffs too were replaced, and Englishmen were appointed to Edinburgh, Jedburgh, Linlithgow and Peebles.[8] Control of key castles mostly remained in English hands. Despite having a voice in their government, many Scots magnates must have found that the royal velvet glove was rather threadbare.

At the time the settlement was being debated, the Scots themselves were all too aware of a much greater horror unfolding nearby that can only have helped focus the mind – Robert's in particular. After Bishop Lamberton's plea in early 1304, William Wallace had continued to fight a guerrilla campaign to harass English forces in and around Selkirk Forest. His luck eventually ran out that year when Wallace was defeated on the banks of the River Earn and as a result spent the remaining year carrying out hit-and-run raids as a fugitive, appearing and disappearing like a shadow in the forest. On 3 August 1305, near Glasgow, he was outmanoeuvred and taken by men in the service of John Stewart of Menteith, keeper of Dumbarton Castle and son of the late Earl of Menteith who died in 1294. Menteith was granted lands of £100 by a grateful king, while the sum of 40 marks was gifted to the man who had physically captured Wallace, possibly Robert Rae or Jack Short, with another 60 marks granted to those in his employ during the dramatic event.[9]

Wallace was tied to a horse and dispatched to London, arriving on 22 August, and was housed overnight in the home of William de Leyre, alderman of Baynard Castle Ward in the parish of Fenchurch. The following day, he was hauled through the bustling streets and jeering crowds of London to Westminster for a mock trial, his sentence a forgone conclusion. Wearing a crown of laurel leaves, on account that he had once allegedly boasted that he would sit in Westminster wearing a crown, his trial was carefully crafted to provide maximum humiliation and a theatrical spectacle for all assembled, both within and without Westminster Hall. There he was accused of treason, his long list of crimes read aloud, and a traitor's sentence duly passed. Wallace flared up, denying that he could be adjudged a traitor given he had never sworn an oath of allegiance to the King of England. His judges, John de Segrave,

Peter Malore, Ralph of Sandwich, John Bakewell and the Mayor of London, refused to listen.

Taken out from the Hall, there would be no respite between his sentence and execution. Bound to a hurdle, he was dragged east, re-entering the capital, which was then separate from Westminster, and hauled to the Tower of London and back again to Aldgate, finally coming to a halt at Smithfield. There he was hanged on a gibbet, but not to death. Cut down, he was castrated, disembowelled and eventually decapitated. His body parts were taken by one of his judges, John de Segrave, who was paid 15 shillings for the task of distributing them. Wallace's head was set on London Bridge, the right arm sent to be displayed on the bridge at Newcastle-upon-Tyne, his left arm to Berwick. His right foot went to Perth while his left foot was most likely sent to Stirling, the place of his greatest victory over the English in 1297, and not Aberdeen, as some chroniclers suggested.[10]

This was a grim and powerful symbolic gesture, designed to overawe any remaining would-be renegades and remind them of the futility of opposition to the King of England. It was certainly unjust, as Wallace, under the letter of the law, was no traitor and therefore should not have met the penalty of a traitor's death. His crimes, like those of his peers, had warranted imprisonment rather than a mutilation designed for very specific breaches of fealty. To the English, the death of William Wallace was jubilantly celebrated, with songs written to mark the occasion, whereas in Scotland his brutal execution shocked, sickened and made the man into a martyr. It would be one of Edward I's greatest errors of judgement, and far from overawing, it focussed the mind towards the need to re-establish Scottish sovereignty rather than live under the yoke of increasingly violent English oppression.

It certainly focussed Robert Bruce, albeit we do not know his exact reaction to the execution at Smithfield. Since his surreptitious meeting with Lamberton, Robert may well have been building discreet coalitions to shore up a foundation on which to launch a bid for the Scottish throne. Yet, however successful he may have been at this juncture, there remained a significant contingent of men who would probably not support him, in particular the Balliols and Comyns and their adherents, who still held out for the return of King John or the accession of his heir, Edward Balliol, the latter still in English captivity. Just because Bruce wanted to champion his right did not mean Scotland would unite behind his cause. His greatest challenge now rested with John 'the Red' Comyn, Lord of Badenoch, who had assumed the leadership of the Comyn family. He was nephew to King John, cousin to the Comyn Earl of Buchan, and brother-in-law to the English Aymer de Valance, soon to be Earl of Pembroke. If Bruce was to secure the crown, he needed to reconcile Comyn to his cause one way or another. What happened next tested the limits of Bruce's personal ambition, and has gone down in the annals of history.

What is certain is that, on a cold night on 10 February 1306, Robert and John Comyn met at the Church of the Greyfriars in Dumfries. Comyn had been resident at his nearby castle at Dalswinton, not far from Bruce's family home of Lochmaben. The two men, who had a history of bitter rivalry and had clashed violently at Peebles during the summer gathering near Selkirk Forest in 1299, could guarantee a safe, violence-free meeting constrained by their choice of location. Spilling blood in a church was sacrilegious and warranted excommunication, the gravest of punishments.

Bruce and Comyn met at the high altar, and a discussion ensued in which Robert most likely made it clear that he intended to secure the crown as Edward I would likely die soon due to ill health. He may even have offered Comyn a substantial bribe: support Bruce and be rewarded with great land and office, perhaps even his own earldom of Carrick, which would provide a much-needed incentive to change John's natural sense of allegiance to the Balliol kingship. Whatever the detail of this private conversation, what is clear is that tempers soon began to flare, voices were raised, and the debate became over-heated. Something snapped. Perhaps insults flew, and one or both grew physical, but in the ensuing argument Robert lashed out with a dagger and plunged it into Comyn, wounding him. Bruce's men, possibly including his brother-in-law Christopher Seton and Sir James Lindsay, and possibly his brothers Thomas and Neil, who may have been with him either inside or immediately outside the church, ran to Bruce's defence and finished Comyn off, along with John's uncle Robert.[11] Bruce had murdered his principal rival in cold blood.

Or at least, this is the most likely narrative of events from the facts that we can best distinguish. The murder of John Comyn at the hands of Robert Bruce has, somewhat unsurprisingly, entered into the deep realms of myth and legend, and even near-contemporaries struggled to report on the action, given the suddenness of the crime, not to mention its spectacular nature and location. Chroniclers like the author of the Scalacronica, written in the mid-1350s, and John Barbour, author of the somewhat whimsical yet epic poem *The Bruce*, composed in the 1370s, increasingly embellish the story, as does the *Flores Historiarum* and John Fordun.[12] The best account, and one written closest to the actual events, was that of Walter of Guisborough, but he too was writing from a monastic house, whose foundation was that of the Bruces. Whatever the accounts noted, the broader motives are clear; if Bruce didn't have Comyn's support to rule, an internal civil war would break out once he had taken the crown. But even here, the evidence is murky. Some chroniclers suggest it was Robert who had made an offer to Comyn, while others suggest it was Comyn who first offered Bruce a choice to be king or a key official in a Comyn government. Opinions are divided.

The pro-Bruce medieval writer John Barbour, as well as the author of the Scotichronicon, written over a century later in the 1440s, claimed Bruce and Comyn had met previously, and in that earlier meeting went so far as to create an indenture, similar to that between Bruce and Lamberton, setting out their agreement, albeit perhaps in somewhat vague terms for risk of the document falling into the wrong hands.[13] Only afterwards, Comyn, feeling devious and duplicitous, handed his half to King Edward, thereby breaking his faith with Robert. If this were true, it certainly cast the Earl of Carrick in the better light, but such an argument feels heavily contrived with the benefit of hindsight and works to rehabilitate Robert's actions from a distance.

Edward, so the alternative stories go, determined to prevent a reopening of the war, summoned Bruce to attend him at Westminster to scrutinise the vague terms of the indenture at a winter parliament.[14] Robert dutifully attended, although at this stage unsure why he had been summoned, and was subjected to a public interrogation by an irate king. Given a reprieve of an evening to find his seal, which would authenticate the Comyn portion of the document, Bruce fled Westminster. Fordun, another chronicler, suggested that he had been warned by his friend at court, the titular Earl of Gloucester, Ralph de Monthermer, who had heard that evening that the king had decided to put Robert to death.[15] On receiving twelve pieces of silver and a set of spurs, the Earl of Carrick got the message loud and clear. The silver represented biblical betrayal and the spurs suggested flight.

Having fled before he could be arrested the next day, on the road north Robert and a friend intercepted a messenger who happened to be carrying a letter from John Comyn to Edward I, suggesting that Bruce should be imprisoned and executed for his crimes against the king's peace. Robert, now fully exposed by Comyn's betrayal, sought vengeance and with nothing else to lose, arranged through his brothers Thomas and Neil a meeting with John Comyn at the Church of the Greyfriars in order to confront him. In his heightened temper, Robert challenged Comyn, declaring that he lied after the latter feigned ignorance, and subsequently lashed out, killing his rival.

This later version, built up by successive chroniclers, is often the story people know today, seeking as it does to rehabilitate Robert's tarnished reputation as a devious murderer, which sits at odds with his later legacy. Yet, while there may be grains of truth in it, many of its assertions can be simply discounted. There is no evidence that Bruce was at Westminster in winter, nor did Edward I hold any English parliament at such a time. Furthermore, when news reached the king in England that Comyn had been killed, there was no certainty recorded in the government archive, or from Edward himself, that Robert Bruce was behind it. If Edward had indeed interrogated the Earl of Carrick before his alleged flight, as later stories would suggest, the king can only have had a sudden lapse of memory in this situation; while he might have been ill at the time, this seems very unlikely indeed. These colourful later additions, while adding further drama to an already dramatic tale, must be discounted as they do not corroborate.

It seems, therefore, that Bruce's meeting with Comyn at the church in Dumfries was probably the first of its kind between the two men and was designed to discuss Robert's claim to the throne, backed up with some kind of offer of support that was significant enough to coax Comyn over to his side, or at least to begin to consider the possibility. Robert's offer needed to be compelling. Comyn resisted the idea. As tempers flared, John was murdered by Bruce and his men.

Only one question remains: did Robert Bruce intend to kill John Comyn before he had entered the church? Was his action at the high altar one of passion, provoked by a man who failed to take the bait and suddenly threatened Robert with exposure by informing the king and therefore jeopardising Bruce's plan, or had Robert entered the church knowing that if he could not win Comyn over he would have no choice but to kill him and remove his principal rival? We can never be truly certain, but given that Robert was determined to secure the crown and knew his best chance was in the weeks and months following the future death of Edward I, which looked increasingly imminent, time would be against him. Robert Bruce must also have known that winning over the Comyns, let alone the Balliols, was unlikely to come through diplomacy. The last eight years had taught him that. But still he needed to try.

In killing Comyn, who carried his own claim to the throne, Bruce certainly made the Comyns, Balliols and their supporters his bitterest enemies, now bound together by a blood feud, but was this enough to stop him? Probably not. For Robert was astute enough to realise that his path to the Scottish throne would be bloody either way, be it fighting the English or his own countrymen. Perhaps by February 1306 Bruce had an inkling of the wider support he could expect, as later events and the speed of his actions and plans following Comyn's murder would indicate. With this in mind, as Bruce entered that church on a cold night on 10 February, he must surely have expected to leave either with Comyn at his side or, the more likely, alone with blood on his hands.

During the next six weeks, Robert enacted the plans he had been working up after his meeting with Lamberton at Cambuskenneth in the summer of 1304. Murdering Comyn came with a significant price, not just to his political ambitions but also to his immortal soul. Hastening to Glasgow, he fell on the mercy of Bishop Wishart, seeking to make penance for the spilling of blood in God's holy church, which endangered him spiritually. In an age when purgatory and hell were as real to most as Stirling Castle, Bruce's actions would have weighed heavily on his conscience. He was all too aware that he faced the threat of excommunication, debarring him from taking the holy sacrament and forfeiting his right to such things as a Christian burial, a necessity if he was to rise again on Judgement Day. If the pope denounced him as an excommunicate before his inauguration, his bid to secure the throne would be greatly hindered spiritually and politically. Many would refuse to follow him. Bishop Wishart, a long-time Bruce supporter, greeted his friend, heard the earl's desperate confession and absolved him of his crime.

Afterwards, Wishart offered Bruce his public support in return for a guarantee that Robert as king would protect and obey the Church of Scotland, and more importantly, reclaim the sovereignty of the kingdom, not establishing a kingship subordinate to that of the crown of England.[16] Robert accepted, possibly over relics including St Thomas Becket's shirt and comb and the tomb of St Kentigern, and at that Wishart went rummaging through his treasury and brought out the royal standard of Scotland, the Lion Rampant, which he had been hiding from Edward's officials.[17] He also passed to Bruce rich robes that were to be worn at the forthcoming inauguration. With Wishart and Lamberton both now firmly behind him, Robert could be confident that he had the Church's backing. For the Balliol kingship, this was a turning point. To underline his promises, Robert wrote to Edward I demanding recognition of his right to rule as King of Scots, the implication being that he would do so as a sovereign king, not under Edward's tutelage. Edward responded in contemptuous fashion, simply demanding that Bruce return the castles taken from him. Robert hit back, informing the King of England that he would continue to take castles as he saw fit, and that if Edward did not recognise his right to rule he would defend himself 'with the longest stick he had'.[18] That stick was already poking a hornet's nest.

Before Bruce could make his way to Scone, and indicated by Edward's pointed response, Robert invested time and energy in calling out his supporters and securing key strategic castles to prevent being outmanoeuvred in the immediate future by the Balliols, the Comyns and the English. His own castles, including Lochmaben and Loch Doon, were provisioned from stores seized from the castles his men took. He marched to Tibbers, which fell on 22 February, while also securing Comyn's castle of Dalswinton.

On 3 March, the castle of Dumfries was swiftly taken by Bruce when its custodian, Sir Richard Girard, handed over the keys. Inside were the two justices of Galloway, who were holding session in the Great Hall. During the tumult, they barricaded themselves in. They were eventually forced out after threats were made to torch the castle, and were given safe conduct to travel to the border with England.[19]

Ayr Castle fell, as did Dunaverty, which was handed to Robert by Malcolm Macquillan. Rothesay on the Isle of Bute was captured around the same time when Robert Boyd of Kilmarnock, a close supporter and friend of Bruce, sailed ships to the island and overcame the garrison there by threats, and then travelled on to attack the castle at Inverkip.[20] Thus Robert secured the seas between his lands in the west and Antrim on the coast of Northern Ireland, keeping lines open with his supporters, which included

James Stewart and the MacDonalds and MacRuaridhs, who were opponents of the MacDougalls, Balliol-Comyn men who had become increasingly powerful in the region. Despite the gains, Robert did suffer setbacks, especially when Sir John de Menteith refused to give Alexander Lindsay and Walter Logon the castle of Dumbarton, which sat strategically guarding the Clyde.[21] Wider support across Scotland was, after all, far from guaranteed and Bruce knew it.

As he headed to Scone to prepare for his inauguration, Robert and his party were stopped on the road near the Hill of Ericstone by an enigmatic man who would soon become the scourge of the English and one of Bruce's closest friends and allies. Dismounting, he knelt on the road and introduced himself as James Douglas, the son of William Douglas 'Le Hardi' of Douglasdale, who had fought alongside Wallace and had subsequently died in English custody in 1299. James Douglas, disinherited as his father's estate had been attained, proffered his homage and fealty to Robert, who gladly accepted him into his service.[22] Others had flocked to Robert's banner since February, including Gilbert de Cattay, Neil Campbell of Lochawe, husband of Bruce's sister Mary. Thomas Randolph, his nephew, and the earls of Atholl, Lennox and Menteith also came out in support.

Nonetheless, a considerable number remained opposed to Bruce, such as the earls of Ross, Angus, Sutherland and Strathearn, mostly tied by blood-feud to the Balliol-Comyns, who were sworn to enact revenge for Bruce's killing of the Lord of Badenoch, and others including Ingram de Umfraville, Alexander de Abernethy, John Mowbray and David of Brechin.[23] Some felt their best chances lay with the English. Moving around Scotland would therefore be dangerous for Bruce given his mixed support, especially in Berwickshire, the Lothians, western Galloway, a sizeable area of Perthshire and Fife, the far north east, Invernessshire, Rossshire, Argyll and Lorn.[24] Bruce knew it was only a matter of time before the English mobilised. He needed to continue at his current breakneck speed.

On 25 March 1306, the Feast of the Annunciation of the Virgin, ten years to the day since Robert Bruce and his father had begrudgingly bent the knee to Edward I at Wark during the Great Cause, Robert came to his inauguration, that most sacred and symbolic moment of Scots kingmaking.[25] It can only have been made more sanctified by the date, falling within the octave of

Passion Week, which venerated the Resurrection.[26] It was a moment to pause, and despite the great risk of capture, due ceremony was observed, adding important legitimacy to the moment. Robert, elegantly robed, was escorted to the place of enthronement by the Countess of Buchan – despite the absence of the Stone of Destiny, which had been confiscated by Edward I a decade earlier – who placed a gold circlet on his head in absence of the royal crown of Scotland.[27] According to ancient tradition, this moment was always undertaken by the premier earl in Scotland, the Earl of Fife, but given he was a child and in the ward of England, his aunt, from that ancient family, made the remarkable decision to courageously leave her husband, the Comyn Earl of Buchan, to perform the ritual herself. Buchan was in England, but his wife was residing nearby, perhaps for this purpose, at her manor of Balmullo, and rode one of her husband's destriers to Scone.[28] For the countess, it was a brave decision; in addition to the risk she now faced, she also knew that she could never return to her husband.

With Bruce thus enthroned, the inauguration was overseen by bishops Wishart, Lamberton and David de Morovia of Moray, and must have included attendees such as the abbots of Scone and Inchaffray, the earls of Lennox, Atholl, Menteith and most likely the young Earl of Mar, who was in Bruce's wardship. With them were also the bishops of Dunkeld, Brechin and lords and barons including James Stewart and his eldest son, Andrew; Sir Christopher Seton and his brother John; Alexander Scrymgeour, the royal standard bearer; and Bruce's four brothers, Edward, Neil, Thomas and Alexander, and two of his sisters, Mary and Christian, along with his ten-year-old daughter Marjorie.[29] Robert's wife Elizabeth, daughter of the Earl of Ulster, was also crowned alongside him. Two days later, on 27 March, Bishop Lamberton of St Andrews celebrated High Mass for the new king, now styled Robert I, King of Scots, and paid homage and swore fealty to him for his temporalities.[30] Over the two days, all assembled would have done the same. It is also possible that Robert may have knighted men in his service to further bind the ties of loyalty to him.

Edward I had first heard of the murder of John Comyn on 23 February 1306. The news was confused and fragmentary. The following day he had one of his clerks pen a letter to the recently elected Pope Clement V, formerly known as Bertrand de Got, who was previously Archbishop of Bordeaux and, as a result of his Gascon birth, a former subject of the King of England as Duke of

Aquitaine. To the pope Edward simply noted that 'some people … are doing their utmost to trouble [the] peace and quiet of the realm of Scotland.'[31] At this juncture he did not know that Robert Bruce was the culprit and was charging around Galloway enacting plans to seize the Scottish throne. To clarify the situation, the king ordered two Oxford friars north of the border to inquire for further details.[32] The news he got back exasperated him beyond measure. Once more the Kingdom of Scotland, which he believed to be conquered, was falling through his grasp.

The English war machine began to spring into action. Castles along the northern march, including Carlisle and Berwick, were reinforced and provisioned. On 5 April, Edward appointed Aymer de Valence to command English forces in the east while Henry Percy was to command the west. Ships from the Cinque Ports were ordered to sail north and harbour at Skinburness near the Solway Firth, and orders for a feudal muster were sent out with a view to assemble for 8 July.[33] Valence and Percy were given a clear brief to 'strip and burn the lands, goods and gardens of any rebel' and execute any found complicit in Comyn's murder or aiding Robert Bruce.[34] More to the point, the king gave the rare command to raise the dragon banner, a symbolic act that temporarily suspended the established rules of chivalry and traditional conventions of war. With the rules in abeyance, anyone caught on the wrong side of Edward's wrath could be put to death with impunity, being regarded as outside the law.[35] Those velvet gloves were off once more, only this time, angry, ill and utterly furious at the need to ride north yet again, Edward no longer had an appetite for mercy.

Before he left the south, the king gave an early proclamation that he intended to knight his son and heir, Edward of Caernarvon, and anyone of the right degree wishing to be knighted should also attend him at Westminster on the Feast of Pentecost on 22 May. In all, 297 men responded and made their way to receive the expensive honour. A month before, on 7 April, Edward made his son Duke of Aquitaine to increase his status prior to his marriage to Isabella of France.[36] On the morning of the knighting ceremony, Edward, flanked by the earls of Lincoln and Hereford, dubbed his son a knight in the chapel of St Stephen, where the prince was girded and received his belt of knighthood. Afterwards, they walked the short distance to Westminster Abbey where the Prince of Wales dubbed the remaining 297 men.[37]

The culmination of the day was an elaborate feast held in Westminster Hall, where at the height of the service two swans were brought into the chamber, either golden cast swans or living swans kept in two golden cages; the evidence is not altogether clear. Here, over these two birds, the King of England made a solemn vow to avenge the death of John Comyn and thereafter to go on Crusade. His son was next, swearing never to sleep two nights in one place until he had reached Scotland.[38] Other oaths were most likely taken that night but remain unrecorded. The Feast of Swans, as it became known, was Edward I's symbolic attempt at binding men to a single national cause, in which as a band of brothers they would bring Scotland, and Robert Bruce in particular, to heel. It was also the beginning of the king's preparations for passing on the crown of England to his eldest surviving son.

By early June, Aymer de Valence had raised 300 knights and 1,300 infantry, including an additional thirty men-at-arms and eight hobelars from Carlisle who had responded to the king's muster of the feudal host.[39] King Robert was in the north-east attempting to recruit further support from the Garioch, but his recruitment was becoming difficult in this region, where his elevation remained highly controversial and divisive. In the far north, David de Morovia of Moray preached to his diocese that those taking up arms to support King Robert would receive God's grace as if they had taken up arms and fought in the Holy Land.[40] It was a compelling offer but emphasises the great lengths to which Robert's adherents went to drum up support for him.

While Robert was in the north-east, Valence advanced to Perth and quickly occupied the town and castle there, but not before he took Cupar Castle near Fife, capturing Bishop Wishart of Glasgow on the way. Lamberton was captured at Scotlandwell, Kinrossshire, but not before he had ordered his tenants to flee and join Bruce's army. That indenture of 1304 and the bishop's subsequent unswerving support remained true even when facing the greatest of dangers. Wishart and Lamberton, along with the captured abbot of Scone, were dispatched south to England, the former two being gaoled at Winchester and Portchester castles respectively on the English south-coast, and the abbot at the castle of Mere.[41]

News reached Robert that Valence had taken Perth. He decided to send Elizabeth, his queen, and the ladies of the court, including his sisters Christian and Mary, his daughter Marjorie and the Countess of Buchan, north under the protection of his brother Neil to Kildrummy Castle in the hopes that they would remain free from harm. This done, he turned his attention and his small army towards Perth, riding up to its gates on 18 June and demanding that Valence either give up the castle or fight. Valence, listening to the counsel of Ingram de Umfraville, who was a Comyn partisan, agreed to accept Bruce's terms to give battle the following day but instead made secret alternative plans to attack Robert's camp that night, which would be an unexpected breach of their agreed terms.[42] After all, with the dragon banner raised, the conventional rules of chivalry were set aside, and Valence and Umfraville exploited that fact to their advantage. Thinking he had mutually agreed terms, King Robert and his men retired 6 miles from Perth to a place known as Methven.

As dawn broke on 19 June, the Translation of the Feast of St Margaret, Valence assembled his forces and lined up at the border of the woods at Methven.[43] As the command was given, Aymer's forces rushed headlong into Bruce's camp, catching the occupants entirely by surprise. The fighting was fierce and at close quarters, brought about by the relatively constrained space. Bruce was almost captured when Philip Mowbray reached out and caught the king's reins, but Robert's brother-in-law, Christopher Seton, was able to help him.[44] In a desperate situation, Robert and his men had no chance to regroup, and in the ensuing chaos began to scatter, fleeing for their lives. In the devastation, Bruce and his brothers, James Douglas, the earls of Atholl and Lennox, Gilbert de la Haye and Neil Campbell were able to escape, but many more were taken prisoner or killed. Thomas Randolph, later earl of Moray, and Alexander Scrymgeour, Robert's standard bearer, were just two of the many bound by the English and escorted south.[45] The Battle of Methven was a disaster for Robert I, coming only three months after his inauguration. With the few men he had, he fled to the Mounth in the north-east to regroup with any of the survivors who had managed to get away. In all, he had as few as 500 men. His small army had been reduced to a war band, and things were set to get much tougher.

With King Robert now a fugitive, the castles he had spent time occupying through February and March were quickly falling back into English hands. Dumfries, Tibbers and Dalswinton were recaptured, as was Loch Doon in August. Edward of Caernarvon reached Scotland in early July, arriving at Bruce's family castle of Lochmaben on the 11th, the day on which it fell to the English. He then moved to Perth, setting the countryside, towns and villages along his route ablaze. His actions were condemned by his father, who wrote to him ordering Edward to spare the poor and be less indiscriminate.[46] Valence too was ordered to show more leniency. It was unusual that under the dragon banner it was the highest levels of society who were to be targeted rather than the common folk who had for years faced the unforgiving brunt of war.

This time, the penalty meted out to those who had joined Robert and shown their defiance for English rule was ruthless. Sir John Seton, captured at the fall of Tibbers Castle, was executed at Newcastle on 4 August.[47] In the same town, Alexander Scrymgeour, captured at Methven, was hanged along with fourteen others.[48] Sir Christopher Seton, husband of Bruce's sister Mary, was taken at the fall of Loch Doon. He was summarily executed at Dumfries.[49] Simon Fraser, like William Wallace the year before, was taken to London and, wearing a crown of periwinkle, paraded through the city and hanged, drawn and quartered. His head was soon spiked next to that of Wallace on London Bridge.[50] The bloodletting was uncommonly savage, and Robert must have borne that fact with a heavy heart. His bid for the throne was costing many men their lives, some of them his friends.

He needed to regroup. After his loss at Methven, and realising that only a few men were reaching him after being scattered by the battle, Robert sent word to his brother Neil to escort the queen and her ladies south to rendezvous with him somewhere in the foothills of the Mounth. It is unlikely that he made it as far north-east as Aberdeen to greet them, but once they were reunited they travelled west and in some haste towards the shores of Loch Lomond. As they reached the shrine of St Fillan of Glenlochart, whose Celtic feast day was 20 June, the day after Methven, Bruce gave an offering and venerated the relic, a pastoral staff, and received further absolution from Abbot Maurice of Inchaffray before his followers.[51] He clearly felt the weight of judgement upon him, and perhaps wrestled with the terrible notion that God may not have been on his side after all. On 5 June, two weeks before his defeat, the Archbishop of Canterbury and the Bishop of Carlisle had pronounced Pope Clement V's judgement of excommunication on Bruce.[52] News of this must have reached him before the battle. A fugitive king, with Wishart and Lamberton beyond his help on the way to English gaols, Robert I needed all the spiritual support he could muster.

As Robert and his gathering moved into Lorn sometime in late July, he knew he was entering hostile territory. They reached Dalry near Tyndrum, and there encountered the forces of John MacDougall of Lorn, son-in-law of the murdered John Comyn, Lord of Badenoch. As King Robert and his party attempted to pass, MacDougall's men swept down the hillside and attacked, injuring James Douglas and Gilbert de la Haye and many others.[53] Robert managed to regroup his forces but the ensuing skirmish was significant enough to greatly reduce his numbers. Eventually overcoming MacDougall's forces, Robert realised that, with the queen and her ladies in his party, and his forces dwindling fast, he could not keep everyone safe.

He took a fateful decision to send Elizabeth, his sisters Mary and Christian, his daughter Marjorie and the Countess of Buchan back to Kildrummy again under the protection of his brother Neil Bruce, in the hope that they would make it up to Orkney where they might yet take ship and sail to Norway, seeking a safe refuge with Bruce's sister Isabel, who was now dowager queen of that country.[54] To bolster their escort, Alexander Lindsay and his son David, as well as the Earl of Atholl, went with them.[55] Robert was left with a small contingent of men, which included James Douglas, Neil Campbell of Lochawe and Gilbert de la Haye.

Robert and his queen knew the risks they were taking in separating. Having left the fleeing party, Neil Bruce led his charges to Kildrummy, successfully avoiding capture. However, Edward of Caernarvon had teamed up with Aymer de Valence and began to lay siege to the castle, not realising that Elizabeth and her party, along with Atholl, had already escaped further north. After a short siege, Kildrummy fell to the prince. Captured inside were Neil Bruce, the young Donald, Earl of Mar, and Robert Boyd along with Alexander and David Lindsay.[56] The queen made it as far as Tain on the southern shore of the Dornach Firth, where they sought sanctuary at the Garth of St Duthac's Shrine. Ignoring the rules of sanctuary, William, Earl of Ross approached and seized the royal party.[57]

The fates of those captured were ultimately cruel and designed to make a statement. John of Strathbogie, Earl of Atholl, was taken to London, and irrespective of his status and kinship to Edward I, being of illegitimate descent from Edward's grandfather King John of England, he was sentenced to hang. Despite the intercession of Queen Marguerite, the king, very ill and of short temper, refused to listen and instead ordered that Atholl's gibbet be erected considerably higher than those around him to mark him out for his treachery. He was then decapitated, the head arranged next to that of Wallace and Fraser.[58] Robert's brother could expect no clemency either. Sent by Edward of Caernarvon to Berwick to await the command of the king, who was residing at Lanercost Priory, too ill to march into Scotland himself, Neil Bruce was to be hanged, drawn and quartered at Berwick, a sentence that was duly carried out.[59] In a moment when the traditional conventions of war were suspended, very few were safe from the wrath of the English king.

The women captured at St Duthac's shrine would not face a traitor's sentence, but were nonetheless subjected to grave horrors.[60] Elizabeth, the queen, was sent south and imprisoned at the royal manor of Burstwick-in-Holderness.[61] On a meagre daily income, she was fed and watched over by two women, especially chosen for being grim and without humour. No one was permitted to talk to her or use her title, and the queen was forced to complain to Edward I that she had 'neither attire for her person or head nor a bed, nor furniture for her saving only three garments a year'.[62] Edward and his son were unmoved. Bruce's sister Christian, whose husband Christopher Seton had been executed at Dumfries, was sent to Sixhills in Lincolnshire to enter into a Gilbertine convent.[63]

The worst punishments were meted out to Isobel, Countess of Buchan and Mary Bruce. The king reserved a particular dislike for both women, Isobel because she had crowned Robert as king. As punishment, they were to be kept for four years in purposely designed cages big enough to house a small privy, which provided their only means of privacy. There is much myth and creative storytelling surrounding the subject of these cages, first prompted by some chroniclers who suggested they were positioned on or suspended over the walls of Berwick and Roxburgh, with Isobel at the former and Mary the latter. However, Edward I's memorandum explicitly orders the cages to be set inside the castle towers, and this

114

is also supported by the author of the Scalacronica, who states the same and was writing some fifty years after events.[64] It would not have been possible to survive exposure to all weathers – snow, rain, howling gales and biting northern winds – for the next four years, even with the limited shelter of a privy. These cages were most certainly cruelly created, but were set up inside tower rooms as the king's command suggested.

Although they were free from the weather, Isobel and Mary were not free from public gaze, the cages deliberately constructed with 'sparred sides that all might look in from curiosity'.[65] To ensure they could not be spirited away, the king was careful that they would only ever be served their ration of food by Englishwomen, Englishmen being prohibited in case they grew too attached.[66] The ten-year-old Marjorie Bruce, Robert's daughter, was spared a cage although Edward I had initially requested one to be made for her proposed captivity at the Tower of London; instead he had the young girl transferred to the Gilbertine convent at Walton in Yorkshire.[67] Only in June 1310, as Robert was beginning to make significant gains in Scotland and threatening the English in England, were Mary and Isobel treated with more dignity. Isobel was transferred to the Carmelite convent of Berwick in the same town in which she had been held since 1306, while Mary was eventually freed from her cage at Roxburgh and sent for further, more genial captivity at Newcastle.[68]

Robert's whereabouts after Dalry become increasingly difficult to chart, demonstrating the speed of his flight to regroup and avoid capture. He certainly headed across Loch Lomond and travelled south-west through Lennox, where he met up with the titular earl, who had managed to escape with some of his men from Methven. Nearing the shore, they took ship and sailed past the Isle of Bute, down the Firth of Clyde around Arran to the Mull of Kintyre.[69] There they met up with Angus Og MacDonald of Islay, keeper of Dunaverty Castle. The MacDonalds, supporters of Bruce and opponents to the MacDougalls, continued to hold to King Robert's cause and acknowledged him as their king. Robert later rewarded Angus Og with the lordships of Morven, Duror, Glencoe and Lochaber.[70]

Bruce, however, was still dangerously exposed, especially when news arrived that an English fleet under the command of John Menteith and John de Botetourt was heading to Kintyre, having sailed from Skinburness. The English arrived on 22 September and began laying siege to Angus Og's castle at Dunaverty, believing Bruce to be there, but did not find him; he had already melted away, either to the island of Rathlin or somewhere along the Antrim coast, where he and his father-in-law held lands and knew many noble families who would support him in times of great need.[71] For the next four and half months, King Robert and his men simply disappear entirely. Rather than sitting idly by, however, Robert was using this chance to recover, regroup and gather both men and arms to him. If King Robert was a fugitive in his own fractured kingdom, he certainly had no intention of staying that way for long.

PART TWO

Honour & Glory

Rejoice and laugh with me, for the Lord is my helper and
I shall fear no more what men can do to me. The Lord is
my helper, and I shall see the downfall of my enemies.

Scotichronicon

7

The Turn of the Tide

If Robert was to regain his kingdom and establish his rule, he needed more men, more money and a dose of exceptional good fortune to change his current position. It is at this moment, the darkest of his personal life and his political career, that King Robert I came into his own like never before. With his winter planning beginning in earnest, it is most likely that he used the time to travel between Rathlin Island, the Isles and Antrim seeking support for his forthcoming endeavour. The fact that even as a fugitive on the run he was able to raise men to his banner is testament to his persuasiveness. He certainly drew recruits from his Antrim lands in Olderfleet, Glenarn and his estates near Coleraine and Port Stewart. James Stewart had his own lands, at Roe on Loch Foyle, by virtue of his marriage to Egudie de Burgh. Robert could also count on his own de Burgh alliance, owing to his marriage to Elizabeth. De Burgh, while superficially loyal to Edward I, was willing to offer a degree of support to help his troubled son-in-law.[1] Bruce wasted no time falling back on the common ancestry of the peoples of Ireland and Scotland, possibly sending his brothers Thomas and Alexander to tour the northern parts of Ireland armed with a letter exhorting the people to join him and together recover their ancient liberties in the face of an oppressive neighbour. Such passionate words were bound to excite many.[2]

As king, Robert proved to be an enigmatic figure. One of his most essential supporters at this time was Christiana MacRuarie, otherwise known as Christiana of Mar on account of her marriage to the brother of the Earl of Mar. Christiana was the only surviving daughter and heir of Alan MacRuarie of Garmoran and she held extensive lands throughout the Isles including Moidart, Knoydart, Rum, Eigg, Uist, Barra, Gigha and Arisaig.[3] It was Christiana, according to the Scotichronicon, who provided King Robert with ships, men and money to tour the Isles and recruit men-at-arms. It paid off. His numbers began to build, thanks to her support and that of the MacDonalds, the Bissets of Antrim, O'Neills of Tyrone, O'Connors of Connaught and the O'Donnells of Donegal.[4]

Bruce's confidence grew with his numbers, and in November 1306, despite his estates being under English occupation, he sent men back to his earldom of Carrick to secretly collect his Martinmas rents, due on the 11th of that month, in order to pay his new recruits.[5] Yet he was not given complete respite to regroup. Edward I, now gravely ill at Lanercost Priory, continued to send out urgent and frustrated correspondence to his men, urging them to close the net on this perceived Scottish renegade whom the King of England believed was 'lurking' in those parts. Hugh Bisset was ordered to raise a fleet on 4 January, but, perhaps because of conflicted loyalty, failed to set sail until 2 May, which proved far too late to be effective.[6] By the end of January, Robert was ready, physically and mentally, to launch his campaign.

He settled on a simple plan and chose to divide his forces, taking the larger group to Carrick via Arran while his younger brothers, Thomas and Alexander, sailed to Galloway to counter the threat of the MacDoualls. Thomas and Alexander set sail, accompanied by Sir Reginald de Crawford, Malcolm MacQuillan, a chieftain of Kintyre and others. They reached Loch Ryan on 10 February, and upon landing were met with resistance from a significant force mustered and commanded by Dougall MacDouall. The fighting on the beach was ferocious and bloody, and in the ensuing skirmish, Thomas, Alexander and Reginald Crawford were captured, while the defeated MacQuillan and an Irish knight were beheaded on the foreshore, their heads being sent to Edward I, who promptly dispatched them to Carlisle.

The bloodletting did not end there. The captives were transferred to Edward of Caernarvon at Wetheral Priory, where they arrived on 19 February. The prince instructed they be sent to Carlisle for sentencing, and once they arrived, Thomas, despite being badly wounded, was drawn through the streets by horses and beheaded. Crawford and Alexander Bruce, the latter of whom should have been protected as a man of the cloth, were hanged. The heads of these three men, along with that of Malcolm MacQuillan, were then fixed to the three gates of the town, while Thomas's was displayed on the parapet of the great keep.[7] Despite the winter respite, the personal and political stakes remained as high as before.

Unaware of the horror unfolding in Galloway, Robert set sail for Carrick, landing on Arran. James Douglas had already made a pre-emptive journey and secured arms and provisions in advance of Bruce's landing to support his growing need for both. Here the king met Robert Boyd, who had been at Kildrummy at the time of its fall. He had escaped when the castle was captured so knew that the queen and her ladies had fled north, but was so far unaware of their fate, or that of Neil Bruce. That sad news was yet to reach him.

Landing in Carrick, Bruce turned his attention to Turnberry, now under the command of Sir Henry Percy with a strong English garrison of 100 men. Given the size of their unit, many of the men were billeted in cottages and tents beyond the castle walls, and whether they set a watch or not, Robert took the decision to attack in the dead of night. In the ensuing slaughter, the confused garrison were unable to defend themselves, being caught by surprise and therefore starved of any real discipline. As the ambush unfolded, the men on the castle walls were unable to help, Henry Percy refusing to advance out beyond the gates because he could not gauge the size of the hostile opposition in the dark. Robert was being tactically astute, using the cover of a moonless night to mask his small numbers and amplify the threat, which worked to devastating effect.[8] The Scots remained in the vicinity of Turnberry for three days and nights, swelling their provisions and taking what they needed by plunder.

In his first strike back, Robert had ultimately succeeded. But his gain was comparatively small. The English had tightened their hold over Carrick in his absence, and their reign of fear kept Bruce's tenants in line. With no sizeable army in tow, Robert struggled to convince his tenants to openly support their king. He resorted to propaganda to spread the word of his return, and this, coupled with further successes, began to turn the tide of opinion.

Sometime after Turnberry, Christian of Carrick, a possible kinswoman of Bruce, and certainly his lover – she bore him two of his six illegitimate children, named Nigel and Christian – arrived with forty men-at-arms.[9] It was Christian who, no doubt with some reluctance, sat him down and told him of the news of the death of Thomas and Alexander Bruce, and also that of his brother Neil after the fall of Kildrummy. She had more to tell him, including the cruel incarceration of his wife, his daughter and their ladies in religious houses or, worse still, in cages. The list of the dead would have been long, and how Bruce received the news can only be guessed at, as no evidence survives to tell us. It must have come as a bitter blow, and one that would have eaten into his confidence and conviction in the short term. All those who had lost their lives or were now facing great hardship did so as a result of his actions. In killing John Comyn, Lord of Badenoch, Robert must have thought that he had indeed incurred the wrath of God, which in a highly spiritual age would have sat incredibly heavy on his conscience.

It is at this moment that the great myth of Robert Bruce and the spider is positioned in folklore. There are no contemporary or near-contemporary mentions of it, and it is most likely a post-Reformation addition to the Bruce legend that took off in the centuries following his death. According to the tale, when all seemed lost, Robert sought solitude to contemplate his misfortune, finding a cave among the remote hinterlands of Carrick. Lying there, looking up at the ceiling of his chosen hideaway, as he debated abandoning his cause in order to save his friends, he noticed a spider attempting to spin its web. Six times it tried to cast a line between the jagged rocks, and six times it was thwarted. Yet it never gave up. On the seventh the spider was able to make its mark and build its web as if from nothing. Bruce had been given a sign, and from there on he knew that to abandon his struggle would be to fail those who had given their freedom or their lives to make it at all possible. After this lesson in perseverance, he would emerge from the cave with a determination that now there would be no turning back.

However unlikely this tale is, it certainly comes at a moment when Robert had to make the critical decision to go on or disappear. To stop now would be to abandon his people, his friends and ultimately his kingdom. The loss of his brothers and the incarceration of his wife and daughter had a deep effect on him. He now understood that in order to even the odds he needed to forgo the lifelong conventions that he had been tutored in since childhood. The code of chivalry was the bedrock of his way of life. It was what governed the rules of war, society and position.

Yet as Edward I had chosen to put aside its conventions by raising the dragon banner, so Bruce now had to do the same. It sounds simple enough with the benefit of hindsight, yet to forgo the knightly code, so interwoven into the psychology of those of his social class at the start of the fourteenth century, was a giant leap to make. In his darkest hour, Robert had the courage, foresight and unwavering ambition to set aside his belief in order to achieve success.

Robert's ability to rethink and to reconfigure himself at a time of greatest need was applied with pinpoint precision. It was a great quality in a leader, and is one reason why so many people would join and follow him when so much would be set against them as a result. They believed in him. His change of tactics would prove simple and highly effective. No more pitched battles and large engagements. Instead, King Robert would become the commander of a guerrilla war, using hit-and-run tactics to surprise and pick off his enemies. They would move fast across difficult terrain, using their knowledge of the land, forests and woods to exaggerate their numbers so the enemy never knew the full scale of their war effort. They would dismantle and slight castles, and poison the wells to prevent the fortifications from being retaken, securing the Bruce effort as a result. Lastly, and with great effect, they would apply scorched-earth tactics to starve their enemy into retreat while they themselves remained well provisioned.[10] This was the antithesis to chivalry, but its effects were to be extraordinary.

Edward I grew increasingly irascible and restless, sensing King Robert was beginning to win back ground. Writing to Aymer de Valence, who held command of the Scottish campaign and who had at his disposal 2,000 men, the king goaded and chastised him. Accusing Valence of hiding bad reports from the king dented the pride of the young man who was soon to be Earl of Pembroke.[11] Valence took the bait. His forces had the region of Carrick and Galloway well garrisoned. Ingram de Umfraville and John de Menteith held Ayr, and they were soon joined by John MacDougal of Lorn. Sir Dougal MacDouall, having been recently knighted by the King of England for defeating Thomas and Alexander Bruce, rode through the south-west of Carrick. Robert Clifford kept watch over the fords across the River Cree while John Botetourt moved around Nithsdale.[12] They were a formidable opposition, and Valence knew they were well placed to repulse any Bruce advance. He just needed to be sure of Robert's whereabouts.

News came swiftly in April, as King Robert moved his men into the valley of Glen Trool. The glen is long and steep-sided, with a narrow track that hugs the loch along the banks. Aymer, sensing an opportunity to track and capture Robert, dispatched a cohort under the joint command of Henry Clifford and John de Vaux. They marched their men into the valley without hesitation, but Bruce, who had anticipated their move, was able to ambush them as the English travelled along the narrow track, having positioned his men above their line higher up the valley side. With the advantage of height, the Scots were able to rain down rocks and employ their archers, showering their enemy with a deadly hailstorm. English discipline quickly fell apart and their ranks disintegrated. Although Glen Trool was a skirmish only, its impact on Robert and his men can only have been electrifying, breaking the perceived sense of English invincibility. From this action, confidence would quickly grow.

In early May, King Robert, now with nearly 600 men under his command, moved a few miles east of Kilmarnock. He challenged Valence to combat, selecting the advantageous position at Loudoun Hill, where he positioned his men on the side of the valley below a jagged, tooth-like crag of rock that dominated the area.[13] He was using his knowledge of the terrain to his best advantage, for below his position, on either side of the hill, the land was boggy, negating the possibility of a cavalry charge aimed at encircling his men. If the English were to reach him, Robert having no cavalry himself, the English horse would have to narrow their charge and funnel into the Scottish lines in order to avoid becoming swamped in the marshy ground – if they knew it was marshy at all. It was a shrewd move. To further combat the cavalry risk, Robert and his captains ordered that three trenches be dug and covered over, while they themselves would muster their men just behind these lines to act as bait.

They did not have to wait long. When Valence arrived and deployed his cavalry in the expected way, their horses floundered in the marshes and the trenches, allowing the Scots to pile in and slaughter them. Seeing the unfolding massacre of the vanguard, the rear lines took flight, depriving Valence of the opportunity to regroup. He had no alternative but to flee himself, heading for the safety of Bothwell Castle, leaving up to 100 knights dead in the field.[14] Through strategic planning and knowledge of the terrain, King Robert and his men had secured a telling victory. When, three days later, he struck hard at the unsuspecting Ralph de Monthermer, Earl of Gloucester, and his contingent, he was able to chase the earl to the walls of Ayr Castle.[15]

Once more, the tide appeared to be turning. It had a galvanising effect. Five days after the battle at Loudoun Hill, a pro-English Scot, possibly Alexander de Abernethy, who was based at Forfar in the foothills of the Mounth, wrote to English officials:

> I hear that Bruce never had the good will of his own followers or of the people generally so much with him as now. It appears that God is with him, for he has destroyed King Edward's power both among English and Scots. The people believe that Bruce will carry all before him, exhorted by 'false preachers' from Bruce's army. Men who have previously been charged before the justices for advocating war and have been released on bail, but are now behaving worse than ever. I fully believe, as I have heard from Reginald Cheyne, Duncan of Frendraught and Gilbert of Glencarnie, who keep the peace beyond the Mounth and on this side, that if Bruce can get away in this direction or towards parts of Ross he will find the people all ready at his will more entirely than ever, unless King Edward can send more troops for there are many people living loyally in his peace so long as the English are in power. May it please God to prolong King Edward's life, for men say openly that when he is gone the victory will go to Bruce. For these preachers have told the people that they have found a prophecy of Merlin, that after the death of 'le Roy Coveytous' the people of Scotland and the Welsh shall band together and have full lordship and live in peace together to the end of the world.[16]

Robert had taken time, along with his supporters, to realise that to win would mean an assault on the hearts and minds of the people as well as the army of English. The application of carefully selected preachers ensured that King Robert was able to spread the message that he was Scotland's champion, come back to reclaim the kingdom and overthrow the oppressive English occupation. Bolstered by a succession of apparently God-given victories, he began to look like the champion he was promising to be. Falling back on the prophesies of Merlin, well understood by the common folk of the time, was a means of adding legitimacy to his actions. His preachers spoke of hope, and after years of civil strife, this was just what was needed. The Bruce myth, which would build over the next seven hundred years, began here.

With news of the English defeat reaching the ears of Edward I, the king convinced himself that the only man capable of bringing an end to Robert's advance was Edward I. In June he was still too ill to move from Carlisle, having transferred there from Lanercost Priory in March. On 3 July, despite suffering from dysentery, he had strength enough to ride out of the castle at the head of an army. But his illness was inescapable, and for the next three days they progressed barely 2 miles a day. On 6 July, they encamped at Burgh-by-Sands, and on the following morning, as the king was lifted up in his bed, he died in the arms of his servants.[17] The death of the king was kept secret as news was dispatched south to London to his son, Edward of Caernarvon, who now became Edward II, King of England.

The new king headed north, arriving at Burgh-by-Sands on 19 July to view his father's body and lift the veil of secrecy. From there, Edward travelled to Dumfries to accept the homages of the Scottish lords who were still loyal to England.[18] By the end of August, having ventured into Galloway and finding no resistance, he turned south, leaving Scotland, having appointed Aymer de Valence as Lieutenant. The new king needed to bury his father, secure his reign, undertake his coronation and marry his intended wife, Isabella, daughter of Philip IV, King of France. With such pressing needs, it was not long before Edward needed Valence, now Earl of Pembroke and already a well-polished veteran of the French court, to complete the delicate and complex royal marriage negotiations in France. In his place, on 13 September 1307, the king appointed his cousin John of Brittany, Earl of Richmond, as Lieutenant of Scotland, a position he took up in late October.[19] Richmond had already undertaken the role as far back as 1305, but unfortunately for England he was a notoriously indecisive commander. For King Robert, this sudden change in fortune would prove most welcome.

With the English threat reduced, Robert was now free to alter his approach and undertake the second part of his well-devised strategy. If he was to secure his rule, it was not just the English that he had to overcome but also his enemies within his own kingdom. In 1307 he counted four in particular: the MacDoualls in the south-west, who had slaughtered his brothers Alexander and Thomas at the start of the year; the MacDougalls in the western Highlands, who attacked him and his men at Dalry in 1306; William, Earl of Ross, based in the north with great influence and land holdings, who had captured his queen and her ladies in breach of the sacred rules of sanctuary in the Garth of St Duthac's shrine; and, most important of all, in the north-east, John Comyn, Earl of Buchan, a relative of the murdered John Comyn, Lord of Badenoch, and holder of a strong claim to Robert's throne. If Bruce had any chance of gaining control of his kingdom, he needed to prevent his enemies from uniting under a common banner and pooling their resources, which would, together, far outstrip his own.

In September, once Edward II had withdrawn to England, Robert marched his forces into Galloway, laying waste to lands, dwellings and estates great and small, leaving devastation in his wake. The MacDoualls were unable to stop him, and before long a stream of refugees flooded south across the border into England, seeking shelter in places such as the Cumbrian forest of Inglewood.[20] Those who were brave enough to remain were forced to pay fines guaranteeing their good behaviour, giving King Robert the confidence that, at least initially, the area was somewhat subdued. The money raised swelled his coffers, bolstered provisions and also secured further weaponry. Deciding to keep the pressure on the region, the king left James Douglas with a small contingent to defend his authority and ultimately extend it beyond the immediate region. While Robert was absent over the next eleven months, Douglas continued the campaign with relish, taking of over Douglasdale, upper Clydeside and the great forest as far east as Jedburgh.[21] Marching through Selkirk Forest, he captured the king's nephew Thomas Randolph, who had been fighting for the English. Randolph would eventually, after some initial resistance, change sides in favour of his uncle.

James Douglas's most celebrated victory at this time, as noted by Barbour, was his capture and recapture of his ancestral castle of Douglas. On Palm Sunday, 17 April 1308, as the garrison left the safety of the castle walls to hear Mass in the nearby church, Douglas and his small band of men attacked the garrison in church to cries of 'Douglas, Douglas, Douglas'. With much of the garrison butchered, James and his men took the undefended castle, feasting on the Palm Sunday meal in the hall that had been prepared for the garrison. Before leaving, they decapitated the prisoners, including the cook and a porter, burnt the bodies on a great pyre and stripped the provisions from the castle to feed the men. The infamous incident would become known as 'the Douglas larder'.[22] The castle however, was soon reoccupied by the English and subsequently attacked two more times by Douglas, who razed it on the second occasion. Episodes such as this built for James a formidable reputation among the fearful English, who nicknamed him the 'the Black Douglas' on account of his perceived savagery and skilful guerrilla tactics. To the Scots, he was and remains the 'the Good Lord James'.[23]

Much as the author of the letter written at Forfar on 15 May 1307 predicted, Robert Bruce marched north into the western Highlands with his brother Edward and key loyal supporters including the Earl of Lennox, Neil Campbell, Gilbert de Cattaye and Robert Boyd. At this juncture, with battle success under his belt, Robert's ranks had swelled to approximately 3,000 men. As he marched, his movements were supported by a small fleet under the command of his man Angus Og.[24] The MacDougalls were within his sight. John of Lorn's victory at Dalry had almost broken Robert and his men, and now the king was determined to see the tables turned. John himself had fallen ill, and was therefore unable to stem the tide of Bruce's advance; he had no choice but to seek a truce. Robert magnanimously agreed, offering John terms that would last until the following year. In a stroke of strategic genius, the king had temporarily silenced one of his four enemies, allowing him to deploy his men to capture even greater prizes: the Earl of Ross and John Comyn, Earl of Buchan. The MacDougalls were humiliated, and John of Lorn wrote to Edward II in the intervening months, desperately explaining his actions and embellishing the facts in order to seek the king's help and save his skin from the inevitable:

> I have received your last letter [dated] March 11th, for whose contents I express my deep gratitude to your majesty. When it arrived I was confined to my bed with illness, and have been for six months past. Robert Bruce approached these parts by land and sea with 10,000 men, they say, or 15,000. I have no more than 800 men... The barons of Argyll give me no aid. Yet Bruce asked for a truce, which I granted him for a short space, and I have got a similar truce until you send me help. I have heard, my lord, that when Bruce came he was boasting and claiming that I had come to his peace, in order to inflate his own reputation so that others would rise more readily in his support.

May God forbid this; I certainly do not wish it, and if you hear this from others you are not to believe it; for I shall always be ready to carry out your orders with all my power, wherever and whenever you wish... I am not sure of my neighbours in any direction. As soon as you or your army come, then, if my health permits, I shall not be found wanting where lands, ships or anything else is concerned, but will come to your service. But if sickness should prevent me I will send my son to serve you with my forces.[25]

It was an almost pitiful plea. John clearly feared King Robert's retribution, and rightly so. Leaving the western Highlands, Robert moved north-east, leading his army through the Great Glen, but not before capturing the Comyn castle of Inverlochy near Lochaber in October. He quickly secured Castle Urquhart on the northern shore of Loch Ness too. As he emerged from the Great Glen, Robert was reunited with one of his ardent ecclesiastical supporters, Bishop David de Moravia of Moray, along with others including David de Barclay and William Wiseman. Swelling his forces yet further, the royal army was able to capture Inverness and then Nairn, razing any captured castles to prevent reoccupation or the need for the king to garrison them.

With some success achieved in the north, Robert was now prepared to turn and challenge the powerful Earl of Ross. William held great influence in the region, his earldom stretching through a considerable swath of northern Scotland. His reach was extended further due to the neighbouring Earl of Sutherland being a minor and in wardship to Ross, meaning the latter had control and access to Sutherland's lands, castles and revenues.

Robert was in a conundrum. If he took on Ross, he might struggle to overcome him decisively, yet he could ill afford a defeat before he met and challenged Comyn, his principal rival for the throne.

But the fortunes were in Robert's favour. Earl William, fearing that his own numbers of 3,000 would not be sufficient to fend off the king, given they were spread across his borders of Ross, Sutherland and Caithness, put out feelers for both parties to agree to a truce. Robert was eager to accept, and so it was agreed that neither party would attack the other until after the truce expired on 2 June 1308.[26]

At the start of November, Bruce was now free to take his army and launch a frontal attack on his main rival, John Comyn, in the earl's own backyard. Before reaching John's estates, Robert tried his luck and led a surprise attack on the English-held castle at Elgin, which was able to drive him off. Undeterred, Robert marched from there into his own lands of the Garioch to find more men who would flock to his banner. The Garioch would also prove a strong place from which to launch an attack on Comyn, the lands sharing a border. It was just at this moment, when King Robert was most ready to strike, that he suddenly fell gravely ill at Inverurie. His sickness was so profound and incapacitating that his supporters feared he would die.[27] With the king now dangerously exposed, his brother Edward Bruce took the decision to move him on a litter with the army to an inaccessible, defensible marsh known as the Slioch near Huntly. Suddenly, everything hung in the balance.

John Comyn wasted no time in taking the initiative. The Earl of Buchan mustered his forces and joined his allies, including David Strathbogie, the new Earl of Atholl, who did not share his late father's allegiance, which had seen him executed for supporting Robert in 1306. They were also joined by John de Mowbray; Reginald Cheyne, Warden of Moray; and Duncan Frendraught, Sheriff of Banff.[28] Through December, the king showed no sign of recovery. On Christmas Day 1307, after a night of heavy snow, Comyn and his forces reached the Slioch and set their archers to work. The king's men, under the command of Edward Bruce, fired back, and the skirmish was sufficient to spook Comyn, who withdrew his forces, possibly unsure how to attack the Slioch without losing too many of his men.[29] He returned a week later on 31 December with greater numbers of infantry, but to his amazement, before he could deploy his troops, Edward Bruce marched out in full battle array, his men carrying and protecting the king in a litter. Their appearance was formidable, enough for Buchan to lose confidence and slink away a second time. Edward Bruce moved the army on. After a short stay at Strathbogie, the royal party made its way back to Inverurie, the chief town of the Garioch.

Comyn must have been somewhat frustrated that his last two attempts to capture or kill a sick and vulnerable enemy had been thwarted. Yet, with his numbers bolstered by the arrival of David of Brechin from Angus and further English troops, Comyn gathered his forces and marched to Old Meldrum. There, in late January or early February, he dispatched a small contingent to attack the king's men guarding the periphery of their camp at Inverurie. Sensing that the net was finally closing in on him, Robert summoned enough energy to gingerly mount his horse with assistance, and there led his troops out in battle formation. He was in no fit state to fight, needing to be held upright, but by this juncture the myth of Robert Bruce had captured the imagination of many. His successes since 1306 had been exceptional, and for those who now faced him he appeared to be blessed with a higher protection.

The enemy thought their adversary was close to death, yet as they saw him ride out with his men, their conviction evaporated. Perhaps they had been misinformed. Perhaps God had a plan for this king. In any event, whatever Comyn's men thought, they began to take flight, and in the ensuing chaos of retreat the king's men were able to give chase, turning Inverurie into less of a battle and more of an unqualified rout.[30] Without lifting a sword himself, Robert had secured a victory and defeated his greatest rival simply by his presence on the battlefield. It was nothing short of a miracle that only added to his enigma. Shortly afterwards, his men went harrying Comyn's extensive lordship, putting his tenements to the torch with such savagery that it entered into folklore and was referred to as the 'herschip (plundering) of Buchan'.[31] It marked the extermination of Comyn power in Scotland. Buchan had no choice but to flee all the way to England, where he died a broken man before the end of 1308.

In early spring, Robert recovered from the mysterious illness that had almost incapacitated him for three to four months. Resuming command of his forces, he and his brother Edward marched around the north-east consolidating, and then advancing, their gains. Comyn castles were quickly overrun, including Tarradale in the Black Isle and the castles of Dundarg, Kelly, Balveni, Rottray and others. Reginald Cheyne's castle of Duffus was taken, as was Skelbo near Dornoch, which fell to William Wiseman.[32] On Palm Sunday, as James Douglas seized Castle Douglas in the south, Bruce and his men attempted to take the castle of Elgin again from the English, narrowly avoiding victory when John de Mowbray arrived with reinforcements to stave off the attack. By May, however, on the third attempt, the king was able to gain his coveted prize. Elgin fell to his men as English morale in the north-east began to disintegrate.[33]

Aberdeen fell to the Scots when the disgruntled townsfolk revolted against their English occupiers, first offering the town to the king and with the castle falling soon afterwards. It was a much-needed strategic gain, for Aberdeen's port opened the possibility of trade with continental Europe and Scandinavia. It was soon used to trade in weapons and other arms, and not just with the continent but also with English medieval arms dealers who had no scruples in trading with their king's enemy north of the English border. Despite Edward II's attempts to prohibit these commercial exchanges, weapons were still traded.[34]

By the end of 1308, between the River Tay and the Moray Firth, the English hold on north-eastern Scotland was greatly diminished. Only four towns remained under Edward II's control: Perth, Dundee, Forfar and, way up on the north coast, Banff. Before the year was out, Forfar would be retaken by the Scots thanks to the cunning of Phillip the Forester, Keeper of the Forest of Platar, who led a small cohort of men up and over the walls at night, overcoming the defending garrison.[35] In keeping with his now successful policy, King Robert ordered that these castles be razed lest they be retaken by his enemies.

With Comyn defeated, and the truce agreed with John of Lorn and the MacDougalls about to expire, Robert needed to finish the job. Marching west, he sent a message to James Douglas to meet him at Tyndrum near Dalry, that fateful place where both men had narrowly escaped with their lives two years earlier. On their march to Lorn, the royal army passed through the Pass of Brander, where, much like at Glen Trool, a narrow pass navigated the side of Loch Awe, with a steep drop into the cold, dark waters below. Robert sensed a potential ambush lined up by his enemy. However, the king was aware of the terrain, and, possibly expecting John of Lorn to apply similar tactics to those he used at Dalry, where he attacked from above, Robert sent Douglas ahead to reach even higher ground.

Just as expected, the MacDougalls waited for the king's men to pass along the track, ready to roll boulders and shoot arrows down upon them. As the advanced guard descended into the pass, the skirmish got underway; but as MacDougall's men began to engage, James Douglas and his contingent let loose their arrows from a greater height. John had been outmanoeuvred by his enemies' application of his own strategy. Douglas's men then charged down the steep-sided loch, committing to hand-to-hand fighting. The MacDougalls, stricken by panic, fled and headed for the small bridge across the River Awe, attempting to bring it down after they had crossed to prevent the king's men giving chase. So quick and energetic was the pursuit that James Douglas and his cohort were able to cross and chase their quarry before the bridge could come crashing down.[36]

After a short time holed up in his castle of Inchchonnell, John of Lorn fled to Edward II and the English court.[37] After the victory at the Pass of Brander sometime between 15 and 23 August, Robert I and his men advanced on the castle of Dunstaffnage, which was surrendered to him by John's ageing father, Alexander MacDougall of Argyll. In return for hostages, Alexander recognised Robert as his legitimate king, but the change of allegiance was hollow, and within a year MacDougall too fled to England to re-join his defeated son at the court of the English king.[38] Much like with the Comyns, the MacDougall power in the western Highlands was broken.

To further consolidate his position, Robert did not neglect the need to bring Galloway under his control. While he and James Douglas were fighting the MacDougalls, the king ordered his trusted brother Edward Bruce, along with Robert Boyd and Alexander Lindsay, to head south to attack the MacDoualls. Dougal MacDouall, who had remained in the area after Douglas had laid waste to the region the year earlier, remained a threat. Dougall, expecting to defend himself after the expiry of a truce with Robert, had sought and received the help of Ingram de Umfraville and Aymer de St John.

Marching their forces through Galloway, they met Edward Bruce and his army at the crossing of the River Cree, near to the castle of Buittle. There battle was joined, and Edward's forces prevailed but were unable to capture MacDouall.[39] He continued to fight for the English, becoming custodian of Dumfries Castle, despite his family seeking refuge in England as Edward Bruce continued to lay waste to Galloway. Despite their best efforts, while Edward Bruce could claim to control the countryside, there remained a number of strategic castles in the hands of the English, namely Caerlaverock, Lochmaben, Buittle, Tibbers and Dalswinton in addition to Dumfries. His efforts would be rewarded by his brother the following year when Robert made him Lord of Galloway.[40]

With three of his four enemies now overcome, the king returned to the Earl of Ross. Before he met him in the autumn, Robert travelled back through the north-east where he began to conduct the government of his kingdom. It was a small but symbolic note. On 28 September he was at Inchmahome Priory, and by 5 October he was at Dunkeld, where he issued a charter to Coupar Agnus Abbey to help determine the election of a new abbot in defiance of Edward II's preferred appointee. Robert's choice was William Sinclair of Roslin.[41] If Bruce was to secure his kingship, defiance would not just be needed on the battlefield or in the taking of castles, but also in his appointments, lay and ecclesiastical, which he used to reward those loyal to him. By 14 October he had arrived in the neighbourhood of Perth, still held by the English. On the 31st of that month he finally met up again with William, Earl of Ross at Auldearn near Nairn.

Following the expiry of their truce, the earl had watched from his estates as Robert had won victory after victory. He had even escaped the jaws of death by overcoming his mysterious illness. With no relieving army seemingly forthcoming from England, and surrounded on his southern and eastern borders, Ross understood the benefit of capitulation. Robert understood the need for clemency, and when to offer it. Therefore, without the desire for war, and against a backdrop of great pomp and ceremony, the Earl of Ross bent the knee and gave his homage and fealty to the King of Scots, forfeiting his lands. Robert in turn immediately re-granted them to the earl and exercised his royal patronage, granting William the lands of Dingwall and Ferincrosky in the sheriffdom of Sutherland. To ensure he would remain loyal, William offered as surety the bishops of Moray and Dundee.[42] The bond would be set strong, and in 1315, the earl's heir, Hugh, would marry Robert's sister Maud, who had not shared the fate of those at Kildrummy – who had, of course, been captured by Hugh's father. In securing the loyalty of Ross, the king had also ensured the loyalty of the Earl of Sutherland, the former's ward, as well as the north as a whole.

By the autumn of 1308, King Robert had achieved a breath-taking turnaround in his fortunes. Having been forced to flee into relative obscurity, he had since won the hearts and support of many. Galvanising his men once more, he had landed back in his ancestral heartland and fought a bitter guerrilla war to overcome his principal enemies, sometimes at great personal loss. With the application of a well-considered strategy and a stroke of good fortune following the death of Edward I in July 1307, he was able to capitalise on his gains, promulgate his propaganda and swell his ranks with those who either wanted change or believed in his cause. In overcoming the Comyns so completely Robert had removed his major rival, and in coming to terms with others, most notably the Earl of Ross, he had banished many of his most pressing concerns. The tide had turned in his favour. Yet Robert's battle to secure his kingship was far from over, and he was set to face many challenges in the years to come. King Robert I was just beginning his rule.

8

A Kingdom Reclaimed

At the beginning of 1309, King Robert welcomed English and papal envoys into his kingdom. After his successes in the previous year, it was clear to both Edward II and Pope Clement V that the King of Scots meant to keep on going until he achieved full recognition of his status and with it the independence of Scotland. With Edward II currently facing an internal crisis at home among his own magnates, a temporary respite in hostilities with his Scottish neighbour was welcomed, meaning both parties were ready to agree the terms of a temporary truce. Despite the devil in the detail, the complexities were ironed out, although the King of England refused to acknowledge Robert I as King of Scots, and Bruce would accept nothing less in the long term. They may have temporarily set aside their differences, but if the future was ever to be permanently settled, one or both would have to compromise. On 2 February, the deal was sealed; the truce was set to last until 1 November that year.[1]

Robert wasted no time in capitalising on his good fortune. He sent out a summons ordering his first parliament to assemble the week before Easter at St Andrews, a well-chosen location, given the saint's significance to the country. It set the tone for what was to come. This was the first time the king was able to demonstrate how far he had come; he was no longer a mere war captain but a king, judiciously exercising the administrative affairs of his office after years of war. Parliament was well attended. Malcolm, Earl of Lennox was accompanied by William, Earl of Ross and William, Earl of Sutherland. The holders of the five earldoms of Fife, Mar, Buchan, Caithness and Menteith, too young to attend in person, their titles being held in wardship, sent officials from their communities to ensure their presence was noted. Edward Bruce was there in his capacity as Lord of Galloway, along with the king's nephew Thomas Randolph, baron of Morton, who was the son of the king's half-sister. It was at this parliament that Robert began to hand out rewards to his supporters, and Randolph received the Lordship of Nithsdale, which comprised lands running north to south through Dumfriesshire.[2]

The list of barons was comprehensive, including James Douglas, Angus MacDonald of Islay, and – most likely under duress – Alexander MacDougall of Argyll. The list of knights included Neil Campbell, David de Barclay, William Wiseman, Alexander Fraser, John Fenton and Edward Keith, as well as the ever-loyal Robert Boyd and Alexander Lindsay. Some of the king's more recent supporters included Hugh, son of the Earl of Ross, now betrothed to the king's sister; Alexander Stewart of Bonhill, James Stewart's nephew; William de Vipont, who had been a close adherent of William Wallace and who was from English-held Berwickshire; and John de Menteith.[3] The king could also count on much wider ecclesiastical support, shown by the presence of the bishops of Ross, Brechin, Dunblane, Dunkeld and Moray. The incoming Abbot of Arbroath, Bernard, who was also Chancellor of Scotland, was present too. Bishop Lamberton of St Andrews, captured and incarcerated by Edward I in 1306, was temporarily released from English captivity and sent north by Edward II to attend, acting as an intermediary between the two kingdoms. Bishop Wishart of Glasgow remained in England under the close supervision of the Bishop of Poitiers, but was nevertheless represented by a nominee from his diocese.[4] Gilbert de la Haye, who had been beside Robert since before Methven and had endured the hardship of a fugitive's life, formally took up his role as Constable of Scotland. James Stewart, the High Steward of Scotland, and Sir Robert Keith, the Marischal, were also present.

The parliament had simple goals: give full public recognition of Robert's kingship, reinforce the bonds with those attending and send out a clear message to the people of Robert's kingdom that there was no doubt as to who truly ruled Scotland. Proceedings began with Robert laying before his audience a letter from Philip IV, King of France. In it, the French monarch expressed his support for the King of Scots, and was quick to remind him of the old alliance between their two kingdoms. It was Philip's express wish that Robert and his people join him in a forthcoming Crusade.

This was the first time Robert had been addressed as King of Scots by a foreign power, but this in itself, like many things associated with the King of France, was not entirely as it first appeared. As any message had to go through England first, Philip, in an attempt to avoid a political faux pas with his son-in-law Edward II, had taken the precaution of drafting two identical letters, one addressing Robert as king while the other, an open letter, referred to him as Earl of Carrick.[5] Philip IV's gesture was welcome among the Scots and could be played up, but was nevertheless something of a hollow gesture. Robert asked his parliament to respond on his behalf, the body of men doing so, thanking Philip for his affection towards their king but also reminding him of the devastation that had been wrought in recent years at the hands of the English in Robert's kingdom. They stated that only after 'the tempests of war having been quelled and secure peace being granted' would they be in a position to readily join the Crusade.[6] It was a somewhat pointed reply.

The second and perhaps most important piece of business at the parliament came initially from the clergy. On 17 March, they gathered together and made a significant declaration that was designed to underpin the legitimacy of their king's right to the throne. Describing themselves as 'the bishops, abbots, priors and others of the clergy duly constituted in the realm of Scotland', the Declaration of the Clergy set out, in unequivocal terms, to rationalise the events of the last twenty years. They declared that the king's grandfather Robert V, Lord of Annandale, had been the rightful successor of the late Alexander III, and that the appointment of John Balliol as king had been induced by threats and fear. His subsequent deposition and the ensuing years of war were 'great evils that had befallen the kingdom', and as such the people of Scotland, now wishing to bring an end to the bloodshed and calamity, had taken 'by divine providence' Robert VII, Earl of Carrick as their king; in turn, 'through Christ's mercy [Robert] recovered and restored the kingdom'.

In offering this declaration, the clergy were making it clear that Robert, and Robert alone, had the legitimate right of succession, as the nearest male heir to the deceased Alexander III and Robert Bruce V. Secondly, to reinforce the point, the declaration determined that the Community of the Realm had chosen their king also, so both hereditary right and public interest were working in harmony. Lastly, Bruce, through his actions in securing the kingdom –inasmuch as he had secured it – had so far delivered on his promises, and in the medieval mind, success in war was attributed to an act of God. God, it seemed, offered divine approval of Robert's accession. Combining these three points together, Robert's rule was considered indisputable.

It was a well-crafted document.[7] As if to pre-empt the response of those in opposition, including supporters of the deposed John Balliol still residing in Picardy, the clergy ensured that the declaration included a clause stipulating that if anyone should claim a right to the Scottish kingdom 'by means of documents sealed in the past and containing the consent of the people', these were only agreed under duress and coercion and therefore could not be upheld as valid. It was therefore a declaration that came with a built-in insurance policy.[8]

The success of this document cannot be underestimated, as indeed was King Robert's intention. To reinforce the point that the clerics' view was held by the Community of the Realm, the lay magnates at parliament, including six earls and Edward Bruce as Lord of Galloway, also attached their seals to an equivalent identical document.[9] Both lay and ecclesiastical representatives presented a united front.

Yet this does not entirely reflect the facts of the event. Not all members of the Community of the Realm were counted, including the earls of Dunbar, Strathearn, Angus and Atholl, still absent supporting Edward II in England, as were Alexander de Abernethey, John de Mowbray, Adam Gordon, David of Brechin and many others. Robert still only possessed two-thirds of his kingdom, which would have been acutely apparent to all those at the assembly. Nevertheless, simplified versions of the declaration were soon passed down to the clergy to preach from their pulpits during the daily services, to ensure the people of Scotland in areas reclaimed by Bruce also sung from the same hymn sheet. The following year, at the Scots annual convocation of the clergy in February, the prelates reissued the document in preparation for its presentation before the General Council of the Church, which was held in Vienna under the auspices of Pope Clement V. The pope had a grand vision and wished to unite all the kingdoms of Christian Europe together so as to refocus their minds on Crusade and recovering the Holy Land. Robert and his prelates could only seek to build on this.

As the parliament drew to a close, Robert moved to the royal mausoleum at Dunfermline Abbey on 20 March with his entourage, most likely with the intention of making devotions and marking the obsequies of Alexander III, who had perished on 19 March 1286. As the proclaimed heir to the late king, it was another public act designed to reinforce Robert I's kingship, highlighting the natural continuity between the two men.[10] By mid-spring he was touring his kingdom, his progress taking him down the west coast of Scotland from as far north as Loch Broom to Dunstaffnage in Argyll. In June, Robert ordered David de Barclay, now the sheriff of Forres, not to impede the Cistercians at Kinloss Abbey in their plans to divert a watercourse to their precincts. A month later, Bruce reached Cromarty; it was the farthest north he would travel in his reign.[11]

In August, Robert's royal progress and exercise of his royal prerogative saw him issue a charter on the 8th to William Thane of Cawdor at Loch Boon which converted the thanage into an annual rent of 12 marks. The charter was witnessed by Malcolm, Earl of Lennox, John Menteith and others still in the king's company. On 20 October, Robert reached Dunstaffnage, the former seat of the MacDougalls, where he granted a second charter, this time bequeathing to William de Vinpoint three baronies in Lothian and Berwickshire.[12]

During his travels along the Western Isles, Robert had the support of the fleet of Angus MacDonald of Islay. To the communities living in these parts, Robert's new-found security as king would have been in stark contrast to his earlier ventures there in the previous three years. Yet in areas that also had the potential to erupt into violent opposition given their wary loyalty, which had been bought through defeat, the king was able to use his progress to cement and reinforce ties of loyalty by showing his authority and administrative dedication. No one was left in doubt as to who now wore the crown. On 2 November, King Robert completed his progress, having arrived at St Andrews on the east coast, where he appointed the ever-loyal Earl of Lennox as Sheriff of Clackmannan.[13]

As the end of the year appoached, the truces agreed ten months earlier between Scotland and its southern neighbour were due to expire. Edward II, however, was still facing great political difficulty in England. Following his departure from Scotland in August 1307, the king had spent the intervening years in conflict with his magnates, who were chomping at the bit for political reforms denied to them since the closing years of the reign of Edward I. Edward II had no intention of granting them. In part as a result of vast inherited war debts to the tune of £200,000, the King of England was constantly short of money, and with corruption in his administration – charges of which were most notably levied at former Treasurer Bishop Langton, who had been arrested and imprisoned – the king had limited options or time to raise an army and go north of the border.[14]

To make matters worse, the king's lover, Piers Gaveston, had been elevated to the royal earldom of Cornwall, receiving extensive gifts of patronage and having taken on the role of *custos regni*, or regent, in the king's absence during a short trip to France when he married Isabella, daughter of the King of France, in January 1308. Gaveston by virtue of his new status began to alienate his jealous peers.[15] When the Earl of Cornwall took on the lead role at the coronation in February that year, carrying the crown of St Edward the Confessor and fastening the left spur onto the king's foot, Piers had broken the established rules of courtly conduct; he was, in essence, too much the *nouveau riche* or arriviste for the traditional earls to tolerate.[16] Held in contempt, opposition to Edward II's lover intensified and spilled over into a highly charged parliament held on 28 April 1308, which eventually ended with Gaveston exiled to Ireland on 25 June, the king appointing him lieutenant of that country, where he excelled in the job.[17]

During the latter part of 1308 and the first half of 1309, the King of England had been focussed on bringing about the return of his lover, which he achieved that June, but resentment still seethed at court. As the year drew to a close, Edward was still fundamentally at odds with his disgruntled magnates and in no position to resume the Anglo-Scottish conflict.[18] Despite the appetite, the means were simply not there. In November, he sent instructions to the commanders of his garrisons at Berwick and Carlisle to engage in separate talks with the Scots to bargain for truces until the middle of January. Robert obliged, realising that an extended peace would only allow him to further consolidate his gains and win people over to his cause while the English king was preoccupied with domestic affairs. In December, truces were sealed with the garrisons of the English-held castles Banff, Dundee, Perth and Ayr, these agreements later merging into a general truce between the two countries that was set to last until 7 June 1310.[19] Robert had been given more breathing space.

The King of Scots was all too aware, however, that his good fortune at Edward's expense could only last so long. On 16 June 1309, Robert's opponents had taken the opportunity during an audience with Edward II to plead with the king to raise an army to defend English positions in Scotland, warning him that the remainder of the Scottish kingdom would be lost 'by reason of our default and laxity'.[20] Among the petitioners were Alexander de Abernethey, the Umfravilles and the MacDougalls. Coupled with this, Edward had also received a stinging criticism from his own English earls, who in a recent parliament accused him of having 'lost Scotland'. With intense opposition to Gaveston again mounting at court, the king had been forced to appoint a commission of Lords Ordainers to look into reforming the government of the kingdom as well as prying into the running of Edward's royal household as a means of placating the earls. Edward did not need further incentive to seek out a solution to his mounting problems. Sending out writs of summons, the king decided that heading north would put a healthy distance between him and his detractors while at the same time protecting Gaveston, who would hopefully achieve a great victory against Robert Bruce and therefore improve his reputation back at home. In the king's mind, it was a win-win situation.

Edward's army assembled at Berwick on 8 September 1310, but, possibly to his disappointment, it was small. Only three earls – Cornwall, Warenne and Gloucester – attended the king's summons with their respective retinues, while others like Pembroke, Lancaster and Warwick sent their minimal feudal obligations. At least the king could rely on old stalwart fighters such as Robert Clifford, Henry Percy, John de St John and John de Segrave, along with at least fifty of his own household knights. The City of London offered up 100 crossbowmen for the specific defence of Berwick, which in turn freed up that garrison to join the king's ranks. In support of the cavalry were 3,000 infantry, mainly made up of Welsh conscripts. To help feed the war machine, forty-two English ports offered ships to provision English-held ports in Scotland, including Berwick and elsewhere.[21] The king's strategy was to look to invade from both east and west, sending a smaller force under the command of John MacSween west of Berwick with the intention of capturing Knapdale, which Edward had recently granted to MacSween on condition that he could wrest it from the pro-Bruce John de Menteith. To help bolster his position, the King of England summoned John of Lorn and Richard de Burgh, Earl of Ulster, Robert's father-in-law, and their men. John was to land in his ancestral heartlands of Argyll, while de Burgh was to reach Ayr, bordering Bruce's earldom of Carrick.[22]

Robert had learned over the last three years that his best bet was to avoid a pitched battle with the English, whatever the temptation. His forces, however loyal they had become, did not have the resources to meet Edward in the field. Besides, with no son to succeed him, Robert could not risk death or capture. Despite his gains, he was ultimately still vulnerable when faced with an English aggressor. Robert therefore deployed his now preferred *modus operandi*, resorting to guerrilla tactics in order to harry his enemy, eating away at their resolve. He took his men into the hills and forests, only to reappear in lightning raids on English contingents before disappearing again as quickly. As ever, it was a well-deployed strategy.[23]

Without an opposition to fight, Edward II was forced to tour the south-east and Clyde valley, visiting English-held castles to restock them and hopefully inspire the garrisons to continue in their struggle. He reached Biggar at the end of September, expecting Bruce to challenge him, but King Robert did not appear. Edward then marched to Bothwell Castle, held for the Earl of Hereford by Walter FitzGilbert, to reinforce the garrison before moving on through the Clyde valley to Renfrew. He learnt soon after that the expected Irish contingents had not set sail on account of the unseasonable weather, and with little promise of a good fight the king turned his army around and headed back east to Falkirk, before pausing at Linlithgow at the end of October. His hope that John MacSween would open a front by winning Knapdale was thwarted when John de Menteith swept in and decisively defeated his enemy. The following month, disappointed and probably somewhat frustrated, the King of England retired to Berwick, where he remained for most of the next six months.[24]

Robert had bided his time. As soon as the English army had retreated to the far south-east, the King of Scots swept through

Lothian, inflicting damage on those who remained loyal to Edward II.[25] The exact details of Robert's movements during these months are sketchy, the Scottish evidence no longer surviving. But the contemporary English chronicler of the *Vita Edwardi Secundi*, who was most likely John Walwyn, and who was present with the king's army during the campaign, wrote an eyewitness account of one of Robert's raids during this time:

> One day, when some English and Welsh, always ready for plunder, had gone out on a raid, accompanied for protection by many horsemen from the army, Robert Bruce's men, who had been concealed in caves and in the woodlands, made serious attack on our men. Our horsemen, seeing that they could not help the infantry, returned to the main force with a frightful uproar; all immediately leapt to arms and hastened with one accord to the help of those who had been left amongst the enemy. But assistance came too late to prevent the slaughter of our men ... Before our knights arrived, up to three hundred Welsh and English had been slaughtered, and the enemy returned to their caves. From such ambushes our men suffered heavy losses. For Robert Bruce, knowing himself unequal to the King of England in strength or fortune, decided it would be better to resist our king by secret warfare rather than to dispute his right in open battle. Indeed I might be tempted to sound the praise of Sir Robert Bruce did not the guilt of homicide and the dark stain of treachery bid me keep silent; for a criminal conviction [murder of John Comyn, Lord of Badenoch] involves the loss of all honour.[26]

Robert's strategy was clearly paying off, and although the figure of 300 men killed during this particular skirmish may have been exaggerated for added dramatic effect, it shows the psychological impact that King Robert's tactics were having on the enemy. Edward was not gaining ground, and even the chronicler himself had to acknowledge the impressive skill in Robert's cleverly designed approach. With the raids becoming increasingly aggressive and successful, the King of England temporarily ventured out from Berwick in an attempt to meet Robert head on, but the King of Scots 'always as the [English] army approached ... kept to trackless boggy mountain places whither such an army could not easily penetrate'.[27] Edward had no choice but to retire again to Berwick.

If Robert was to be overcome, the King of England knew he needed to change strategy himself. With the infantry now back in England, their forty-day feudal service completed, the king's numbers were dwindling. On 17 December, Robert met with Robert Clifford and Robert FitzPain near Selkirk. Discussions for a truce were outlined, and Robert, encouraged but still wary, agreed to a further meeting at a designated place somewhere near Melrose, this time with the young Gilbert, Earl of Gloucester, and Piers Gaveston, Earl of Cornwall. Just before the rendezvous could take place, Robert was informed either by a spy or someone who switched sides that the earls planned to seize him, breaking their promise of parley.[28] The King of Scots had been given a lucky escape, but the whole event highlights that Edward II was growing increasingly frustrated at not being able to win in Scotland and that Bruce was right to be cautious even in his pursuit of peace on his terms.

To add to the threat, Robert did nothing to quell rumours that he had gathered a fleet from the Western Isles with the intention of invading the English-held Isle of Man, strategically important to the south-west coast of Scotland and with established and lucrative trading routes to Ireland. The rumour proved unfounded, but it was enough to make the English jumpy. When another emerged that Robert was now in Galloway and then attempting to raise men in the north-east to come to the defence of his kingdom, Edward sent Piers Gaveston, who had overwintered at Roxburgh, with 200 men-at-arms to Perth via Dundee, with the aim of cutting off any channels of communication between the two regions. The Earl of Cornwall remained at Perth until 14 April and the Easter celebrations.[29]

The King of England's determination to gain a victory only intensified. In late February, he sent out writs ordering sixty ships to transport John of Lorn and a force of 4,000 men-at-arms, including 500 hobelar horsemen, to land at Ayr and Argyll, a resumption of his plan from the previous year.[30] When news arrived on 15 February that the Earl of Lincoln had died, Edward II sent the Earl of Gloucester south to act in his place. Lincoln's son-in-law, the overmighty Thomas of Lancaster, who was also Edward II's cousin, was set to inherit the earl's titles of Lincoln and Salisbury, and soon arrived just south of the Scottish border with an entourage of 100 knights to do homage for his inheritance. But Lancaster, cantankerous and stubborn, refused to offer his oath in

Berwick, demanding that the king venture onto English soil lest his right to the earldoms be challenged in future. Edward refused and a standoff ensued, which Lancaster eventually won. Travelling out of Scotland to meet his cousin, the earl bent the knee and Edward granted him his titles, adding them to his other earldoms of Lancaster, Leicester and Derby, making him the richest and most powerful English earl at this time. During the ceremony, Thomas, as a committed Lord Ordainer working on reform back in London during the king's absence, refused to acknowledge Piers Gaveston.[31] The possibility of confrontation when Edward returned to England was looking more and more certain, which only made the king less likely to give up in Scotland and head home.

Angered by Lancaster's impertinence, Edward tried to galvanise the campaign once more. In mid-May the king paid out of his own reserves the cost for 600 infantrymen to be sent from Northumberland. He also ordered Piers Gaveston to ride out to Dundee while Henry Percy and the Earl of Angus were to hold Perth in his absence, responding to a rumour that Robert was again in the area.[32] Yet the Irish contingents again failed to sail. A week later, the king controversially went one step further, ordering a general feudal levy without the necessary parliamentary sanction. It won him no favours with the Lords Ordainers, and when it became apparent that the number of people responding to the summons was meagre, the king abandoned the levy altogether on 5 July.[33] With an elusive King Robert refusing to meet him in the field, Edward was hamstrung. With limited resources and no way for him to raise the necessary troops, fighting a campaign was futile. On 16 June, he reluctantly summoned an English parliament to meet him at Westminster for 8 August, and at the end of July 1311 Edward broke his camp at Berwick and marched back home to meet his fractious and openly hostile magnates.

The campaign of 1310–11 had one unintended outcome. In failing to gain a decisive victory, the English had exposed their limitations. Robert, for the first time, had taken the initiative against the English, and he was now determined to exploit it. As soon as the King of England was far south, Bruce launched a campaign to harry the northern counties of England. For the first time in twenty years of English aggression, the hunter became the hunted. King Robert planned two chevauchées, or lightning raids, the first setting out on 12 August and lasting for eight days. With his men moving fast, they burnt all of the lands belonging to the lordship of Gilsland, turning next to the town of Haltwhistle, which had formerly been in the possession of the Bruce family, before attacking the greater part of Tynedale. On their march, they burnt and pillaged, taking whatever resources they thought to be useful as well as prisoners for ransoming.[34]

A second attack came a month later, beginning on 8 September and this time lasting until the 23rd of that month. Bruce headed to Northumberland, deploying the same scare tactics at Harbottle and Holystone before moving onto Redesdale, burning the district around Corbridge and the Earl of Angus' lands at Ovingham. The English, prepared after the previous chevauchée, put up a greater resistance, and as a result more of them were killed than previously. Robert and his men then turned to the valleys of the north and south Tyne, laying them to waste.[35] The chronicler of Lanercost reported that due to their numbers, 'nor could the wardens whom the King of England had stationed on the marches oppose so great a force of Scots as [Robert] brought with him'.[36] Despite the destruction, the numbers of those killed remained significantly fewer than expected. Nevertheless, the shock tactics paid off. Those communities directly affected in Northumbria sent envoys to Robert after he had returned to Scotland, begging him to accept a local truce to prevent further attacks, which rumour suggested was likely. The Scots king, sensing an opportunity, accepted the truce, which was to last until 2 February 1312, but not before extracting the enormous sum of £2,000 for the privilege.[37]

This protection money gave him an idea. If he was to win back the remaining part of his kingdom, then carrying on with a policy of raids into the marches could prove more lucrative than was first apparent. The strategy did not just have to focus on England, either. At the end of September, Robert either raided or at least threatened to raid the Scottish lands of Patrick, the pro-English Earl of Dunbar, whose estates in Lothian were ripe for the picking. Just like the Northumbrians, the earl's tenants, desperate to avoid calamity, paid for a truce to last until 2 February the following year. In 1313, they renewed the terms of their desperate negotiations again, this time offering 1,000 quarters of corn in lieu of coin.[38] As his coffers began to swell, Robert was able to use his English revenues – twice what the lands under truce would have normally paid to Edward II's treasury – to fund a campaign to recapture English-held castles in his own kingdom. There was a palpable irony in such an ingenious strategy.

As 1312 unfolded, Robert may have initially anticipated the return of Edward II's war machine. However, Edward had found himself hindered by a drama altogether more personal back in England. After his return from Scotland, the Lords Ordainers had forced upon the king the Ordinances, a set of laws which greatly hindered the king's royal prerogative, extracted reform and demanded the permanent exile of Piers Gaveston. Outmanoeuvred, Edward was forced to accept the political reality and the Earl of Cornwall, stripped of his title, went into his third and final exile. The King of England refused to give him up, though, and by January 1312 Gaveston was back, sheltering at York with the king, the queen and Gaveston's wife Margaret, with their new-born daughter, Joan. The English nobility, led by Thomas of Lancaster and based in London, gathered many of the earls and sought to bring in Gaveston.

In the coming months, a game of cat and mouse ensued in which Edward and Gaveston moved further north, spending some time at Newcastle while Piers recovered from a serious bout of illness. Rumours abounded that the King of England was making overtures to King Robert to take Gaveston into custody, keeping him safe from the English earls in return for recognition of Bruce's kingship of Scotland. This is most certainly the invention of hostile or uncertain English chroniclers reacting to the confusion of the situation, and is not mentioned in any of the Scottish evidence of this time or in the century thereafter.[39] Even the colourful Barbour makes no mention of it in his famous poem *The Bruce*. Nor would Robert have been likely to accept such an offer, understanding that a political deal made under such dubious terms would never be supported by the English magnates in England. It gave him no long-term assurances. Edward himself, throughout his nineteen-and-a-half-year reign, would never give up his belief that he, and not Robert, had the right to rule over Scotland, so this piece of hearsay seems to be just that.

In the end, Gaveston was captured at Scarborough Castle after being separated from the king. On 19 June, despite a deal agreed to keep him in safe custody until the next parliament, he was murdered on the orders of Lancaster, Warwick, Hereford and others at Blacklow Hill just outside the town of Warwick. His dramatic and unprecedented death while ostensibly under the protection of the king almost caused civil war in England, only narrowly averted by an arduous eighteen-month negotiation led by the remaining non-complicit earls, and neutral envoys from both Philip IV of France and Pope Clement V.

With Edward II highly distracted, Robert had been given yet another advantage.[40] In August 1312, two months after Gaveston's murder, Bruce launched another strike on northern England, pillaging Northumberland, particularly Hexham and Corbridge. He attacked Norham, removing cattle and taking prisoners, whom he could later ransom to bolster his finances even more.[41] During the raid, he took temporary possession of Lanercost Priory, where he stayed for three days with his men, imprisoning the canons, whom he released when he left, and doing 'an infinity of injuries' which the chronicler of that religious house fervently noted.[42] Seeing the strength of King Robert's position and his relaxed nature in carrying out his harrying clearly had a profound impact on Lanercost's chronicler, for it is the first time in his writing that he acknowledges Robert as King of Scots. This was no scribal error.

With the success of another raid, Bruce set his sights on the lucrative bishopric of Durham. Sending another chevauchée under the command of Edward Bruce and James Douglas to the prosperous town, the band arrived on market day while Bishop Richard Kellaw was absent in the south nurturing a fragile peace between Edward II and his magnates. Edward Bruce and Douglas stripped the town of its possessions and much of it was put to the torch. The cathedral itself was at least spared the flames.[43] After such an attack, the townsfolk later offered their Scottish enemy £2,000 for a truce which was arranged to last until the Nativity of St John the Baptist, 24 June 1314. So strong was Robert's position that he only accepted the terms on condition that he could continue to march his men on future raids through the diocese if he wished to strike further south into England. With little alternative, and perhaps some relief, the townsfolk accepted.[44]

Further truces were extracted for similar sums from Westmoreland, Copland and Cumberland, but where they sometimes struggled to find the capital, offered up hostages for ransoming instead.[45] Those failing to pay altogether could expect a visit from the heavies, and when Cumberland's payment faltered in April 1314, Robert sent his brother across the border to temporarily occupy Rose Castle, belonging to the Bishop of Carlisle, as well as burning two churches and many towns, and driving off cattle from Inglewood Forest while securing another batch of prisoners for ransoming.

Robert made certain those who were taken prisoner were kept safe and well. If he was going to keep seeking payments, he needed to stay true to his word and ensure people would hand over further hostages in the future. This policy was not only financially viable but also highlights something of Robert's character. He did not take life without just cause, and was magnanimous when he needed to be. He was also thinking long term. Keeping with his plans, Robert repurposed the money, applying it to building up his numbers and amassing arms through trading – mostly with the Irish, who had bought the weapons from the English.

Robert slowly began to reclaim castles, Banff having fallen to the Scots as early as 1310. Nine smaller castles also came to him by mid-1311, including Dalswinton, Dirleton, Loch Doon, Luffness, Kirkintilloch, Muchkart, Selkirk and Yester. Ayr, on the northern border of his earldom of Carrick, fell from English control at the end of that year.[46] In April 1312, he was using money from his northern raids to fund the siege at Dundee, which was captured only after a three-month siege.[47] The lesson of this latest venture was to prove decisive. Given the significant number of castles still in English possession, King Robert knew he had neither the time nor the resources to take each one back by sitting out a protracted siege. Even though Edward II was distracted, he could not rely upon that forever. He needed to apply the tactics of 1306 again, knowing as he did that English possession of a third of Scotland was only possible because they could guarantee safe havens in the form of these castles when they crossed the border into his kingdom. If Robert could reclaim them, then he could effectively deprive the English of their lifeline in Scotland. Edward II's campaign of 1310–11 had proved the point, with the English king only able to move from castle to castle, never to venture further afield in order to recapture lands lost to Robert since 1307.

Before his venture into northern England that year, Robert held the second parliament of his reign at Ayr in July, but no evidence survives to indicate what business was done.[48] Another parliament followed the king's return, at Inverness in October. Here he was attended by David Strathbogie, Earl of Atholl, who had sensed the limitations of English ambition and switched allegiance. For Robert, the arrival of Atholl was a welcome but nevertheless suspicious turn of events. The earl, whose wife, Joan, was daughter of the murdered John Comyn, Lord of Badenoch, needed to be treated with care. The king was also aware that Atholl was greatly indebted to the King of England, and therefore his motivations for switching sides were financial rather than ideological.[49] Extending the hand of forgiveness, at Inverness Robert confirmed David in possession of his earldom of Atholl, an important prerequisite underpinned by oaths of fealty and homage. Perhaps to counter his power, the King of Scots turned to his young nephew Thomas Randolph, Lord of Nithsdale, and elevated him to the ancient but somewhat moribund earldom of Moray, which included a large and powerful conglomeration of lands and estates in the north of Scotland, which abutted those of Atholl and other earls. Randolph's new earldom also absorbed the forfeited lands of John Comyn of Badenoch. It was a shrewd and calculated move that bound one supporter closer to the king while keeping another firmly in check.

The second item of parliamentary business focussed on international affairs. Robert gave an audience to the envoys of King Haakon V of Norway, who were seeking to reaffirm the long-standing relationship between the two countries and also overcome some recent difficulties which were diplomatically sensitive. For Robert, the fact that his sister was now the Dowager Queen of Norway and sister-in-law to King Haakon must have added some gravitas to proceedings. On 29 October, he formally ratified a treaty that was essentially a re-run of the Treaty of Perth, agreed in 1266 by Alexander III. It was witnessed by the Chancellor of Scotland, Bernard, Abbot of Arbroath, and the bishops of Moray, Ross, Aberdeen and Caithness as well as the earls of Ross, Atholl and the newly elevated Moray.[50] The annual perpetual payment for possession of the Western Isles had lapsed during the last few decades, and Robert now agreed to resume it; the balance of any former missed payments was written off.

Incidents of Scottish and Norwegian piracy were also addressed. 600 marks were paid in compensation by the Scots for the illegal seizure of the Seneschal of Orkney, taken by Scottish pirates while he was transporting Norwegian taxes; the taxes had been appropriated too. The Scots had previously claimed the Seneschal had in turn allowed the imprisonment and dispossession of one of their merchants, Patrick Mowat, who had been beaten and generally maltreated as a consequence. It was all a bit of an ugly affair, resulting in tit-for-tat exchanges, but at Inverness promises were made to investigate Mowat's plight.[51] It was a satisfactory end to the discussion, and made even more agreeable to Robert because

Haakon had acknowledged him publicly in the wording of the treaty as being 'by the Grace of God King of Scots'.[52]

With the parliament concluded, Robert could focus his energies on the next stage of his campaign to reclaim the remainder of his kingdom. On 6 December, he and a band of men moved to Berwick, where they fixed their newly engineered ladders to the walls of the castle and attempted to scale them on a moonless night. The garrison had not spotted them, but as they reached nearer the parapet their plot was discovered when a dog, sensing the danger, began to bark uncontrollably. Robert and his men were forced to climb back down and flee before the garrison could let loose their arrows, leaving their ladders, which were displayed at the pillory the next day, no doubt receiving much attention from the somewhat relieved townsfolk.[53] Not accepting failure, Robert then moved his men north to Perth. The town had become increasingly vulnerable since the fall of Dundee, which had hindered the passage of English provisions along the River Tay.

Perth was not an easy target to take, the town surrounded by walls and towers built by Edward I. On one side the River Tay acted as a natural barrier, while an artificial moat had been dug on the remaining three sides. Robert set up camp outside the walls as if to begin a siege. Over the coming weeks, nothing much happened except for a few precarious soundings to find a crossing over the watery fortifications. Then, suddenly and quite unexpectedly, the Scots broke camp and disappeared, the garrison believing that they had left the area altogether. In fact, King Robert had marched just a few miles away to lurk in the local woodland. Days passed.

With the townsfolk relaxed after the threat of siege had apparently passed, the king and his men returned on another dark night. Having discovered a place to cross the moat from their earlier reconnaissance, they were able to throw up their rope ladders and scale the walls unchallenged. Pouring into the town, Robert's men quickly overcame the garrison and the surprised townsfolk. It was all over before they really knew what had hit them.[54] Perth's defender, William Oliphant, who had previously held Stirling Castle in 1304 against Edward I, was taken into captivity and for his insistence in holding out against the new king was imprisoned in the Western Isles.[55] The bigger prize, however, was the capture of Malise, Earl of Strathearn. The somewhat aged earl was taken to the king by Strathearn's own son, who had been fighting that night for Robert and pleaded for forgiveness, which Robert duly gave.

The king, not wanting to inflict injustice, permitted the garrison to depart while the castle of Perth was subsequently demolished.[56]

Perth was a precious acquisition for King Robert; now he held all the castles along the east coast except Dunbar. This opened up much greater control of the ports, expanding his ability to trade with continental Europe. Along with international commerce, there was a marked increase in Scottish piracy, with crews spying out and often attacking English ships in the North Sea.[57] With Perth under his control, Robert decided to divert his focus and resources to permanently securing the south-west, ensuring that his brother Edward could now fully exert his influence as Lord of Galloway. Three castles in the region still held out in 1313: Buittle, Caerlaverock and Dumfries. Robert began to lay siege to the latter, which capitulated on 7 February. The commander of the castle, Dougal MacDouall, Bruce's long-standing enemy and the man responsible for the execution of his brothers Alexander and Thomas, could expect little in the way of leniency. However, despite his better judgement Robert allowed MacDouall to go free, and the man soon fled to the Isle of Man, being given office there by Edward II.[58] Within quick succession, Buittle and Caerlaverock were also overcome.[59] The south-west was finally his.

Robert now turned his attention to another strategic prize. As far back as 1310, he had been rumoured to be planning an invasion of the Isle of Man, raising a fleet in the Western Isles for such a purpose, only for nothing to come to fruition. Now, some three years later, he was ready. With the English contained to small pockets in the south-east and Lothian, and Edward II still preoccupied with his magnates and now overseas in France for the knighting of his brothers-in-law, the King of Scots had the freedom to risk venturing out of his kingdom by sea and launching the much-anticipated campaign. He wasted no time.

On 18 May, Robert and his army were ferried across the Irish Sea to the Isle of Man, landing at Ramsey, where over the next two days he marched across the small but strategically important island. After staying overnight at the nunnery of Douglas, he set up camp and laid siege to Rushen Castle on the 21st.[60] Following a three-week siege, the garrison surrendered on 12 June, worn down and knowing full well that little support would be forthcoming from England in helping to overcome their current predicament. Satisfied with his success, the victory must have been all the more sweet for Robert when surrendering to him for a second time in as many months was Dougal MacDouall. Once more, against his better judgement, Robert exercised clemency and allowed MacDouall safe passage to Ireland, where he fled by boat, remaining in English service right up until his death in 1327.

The Isle of Man was strategically too important for its annexation to remain unchallenged. Since 1311 in the possession of Henry de Beaumont, a close friend of Edward II and Isabella of France, the island was recovered by the English in 1315 when John of Lorn launched an invasion and held it until he was evicted by Robert's nephew Thomas Randolph, Earl of Moray, in 1317. After another sixteen years in Scottish hands, it was eventually wrested back again by Edward III in 1333, and it has remained under English control ever since.[61]

Over the next ten months, Robert's efforts would be similarly rewarded. In September 1313, the castle of Linlithgow fell to William Bannock, a farmer who was supported or coerced into helping a cohort of Robert's men-at-arms. Bannock, who regularly sold his hay to the garrison, was able to hide soldiers in his hay wain. On gaining entrance to the castle, he stopped his wagon in the gateway, preventing the great wooden oak doors from closing, allowing the Scots to jump out and attack. Those waiting in the nearby woods soon swarmed in, Bannock himself killing the gatehouse porter.[62] In a short space of time, Linlithgow was theirs. There was more to come.

On Shrove Tuesday, 12 February 1314, James Douglas and a group of men approached the border castle of Roxburgh on another moonless night while dressed in heavy black cloaks. The garrison mistakenly thought they were stray cattle moving slowly out on the grassland. Given it was Shrove Tuesday and the last evening before the start of Lent, the majority of the guard and townsfolk were inside feasting before the start of the forty-day fast. Hooking up their ladders as before, Douglas and his men were up and over in no time, opening up the gate and overpowering the guards. When those in the hall realised what was taking place, the Gascon commander of the castle, Sir Guillemin de Fiennes, was able to hole up in one of the castle towers with a few of his men. The standoff only came to an end when de Fiennes took an arrow in the face while on the parapet the next day. With no hope of holding out, the wounded commander gave permission to surrender, and Douglas allowed him and his men safe conduct to travel back to England where de Fiennes died of his injuries shortly afterwards.[63] It was yet another impressive victory achieved with a prudent application of limited forces.

The next castle to fall the following month was Edinburgh, perched at the top of the volcanic rock that dominates that town. Thomas, Earl of Moray, having laid siege to the fortification without success, eventually procured the help of a local inhabitant named William Francis, who informed the earl of a perilous but hidden route up the side of the volcanic rock which he had used when he lived inside and had to creep out discreetly to visit his lover in the town below. With a guide, suddenly the impossible became possible. After their ascent, they flung over their now well-used ladders, mounted the walls and surprised the unsuspecting garrison, who believed they were out of harm's reach. The castle gates were eventually opened, the men waiting outside swept in and together they overcame the castle guard. The Gascon governor, Sir Piers Liband, whom the author of the *Vita Edwardi Secundi* believed was a cousin of the late Piers Gaveston, had no option but to capitulate.[64] He offered to change allegiance, perhaps to buy himself time, though he later turned renegade and was recaptured and executed as a traitor. William Francis was given a handsome reward by a very grateful King Robert, who granted him lands in Roxburghshire.[65] Keeping with his policy, Robert ordered the castle defences demolished. The chapel of St Margaret of Scotland, the royal saint, was to be left untouched.

Since the outset of 1309, King Robert had worked tirelessly to reclaim his kingdom. Now, by the start of spring 1314, he had almost achieved that. Only the castles of Berwick, Dunbar, Jedburgh, Bothwell and the mighty Stirling remained in English possession. He had secured the south-west, captured the Isle of Man, brought men back into his fold, including the earls of Atholl and Strathearn, and had rewarded his followers with great gifts of land, none more so than his nephew Thomas Randolph. In the exercising of his patronage, the king was both wise and judicious, ensuring the grants would help to bind men to his cause, and also to act as a counterweight to those whose loyalty was as of yet dubious and relatively untested. He played the political game well, deploying a carefully crafted strategy whereby he avoided open confrontation with the King of England on the battlefield, taking the initiative in the war against his overmighty neighbour following the departure of Edward II from Scotland in 1311. By pursuing military action in the northern counties of England, Robert had both secured the resources to fight at home, but also to strike fear into the hearts of his enemies. He may have been ridiculed as King Hob by some of the English, but those in the north knew him for what he was – no longer a fugitive on the run, but a king whose wrath could be brought to bear, yet whose word given in truces was to be relied upon.[66]

Robert had also been careful not to focus his energies exclusively on war. He took the time to exercise the administration of his kingdom, holding at least three parliaments between 1309 and 1312, conducted foreign correspondence with the kings of France and Norway and had been recognised as King of Scots by both of them, even if Philip IV had done so only cautiously and without much sincerity. As the spring of 1314 approached, Robert was looking secure in his kingship, yet just at that moment he was all too aware that Edward II, now reconciled with his magnates and with the Ordinances temporarily set aside, was assembling one of the largest armies seen since his father had marched to Falkirk and inflicted a devastating blow on the Scots, overcoming the patriot Sir William Wallace in 1298. None could be sure what might follow, but there was every chance it would challenge Robert's kingship like never before. Once more, his crown was directly under threat. Once more, he was called upon to defend it.

9

Divine Providence

The year 1314 would be defined by the outcomes of war, and so would King Robert and Edward II. In response to Robert's successive achievements, the King of England had been bombarded with criticism about his apparent failure to stem the tide of Bruce's resurgence. English rule in Scotland was now thinner than ever. In November 1313, Patrick, the pro-English Earl of Dunbar, along with Sir Adam Gordon, Justiciar of Lothian, had taken the liberty of penning a desperate letter to the king, speaking on behalf of the community of Scotland's south-east, who had suffered greatly in recent years at the hands of King Robert's raiders. They implored Edward to ride north with a great host to win back control and ultimately defeat what they saw as the scourge of this self-proclaimed Scottish king.

At the same time, news arrived in England that King Robert had laid down a different kind of gauntlet, announcing that any Scottish landholder who withheld their allegiance to him as King of Scots had but one year to proffer it. Should they hold land in both England and Scotland, then if they wanted to keep their Scottish lands they would have to forgo their English properties as part of the deal. It was meant as a final rallying call to separate the wheat from the chaff once and for all. Scottish nobles still in opposition to Robert had been given a stark choice. They were either with the new king or against him, their estates to be confiscated by an indignant ruler if the latter. This placed Edward II in a predicament; he feared further loss of support at a time when possession of the remaining English-held Scottish castles was dwindling.

With the shackles of political opposition somewhat loosened in England, in the November parliament Edward II attempted to countermand King Robert's decree. Shortly afterward, he wrote back to the Earl of Dunbar and others, assuring them that he intended to be at Berwick before the following midsummer.[1] War was now inevitable.

In December, writs were sent out across England summoning subjects for military service and ordering the army to assemble at Berwick for 10 June to 'suppress the wicked rebellion of Robert Bruce and his accomplices in the king's land of Scotland'. Like his father before him, Edward was asserting what he considered to be his birthright, as Scotland was once more referred to as a land. Eighty-seven barons and all of England's earls were expected to turn out.[2] The earls of Hereford, Gloucester and Pembroke responded, as did the Scottish Earl of Angus and his brother Ingram de Umfraville. Also heeding the call was the king's brother-in-law Ralph de Monthermer, who had been titular Earl of Gloucester until his stepson came of age. The veterans of the previous Scottish campaigns were quick to come to Edward's call, including Giles d'Argentan, who at the time was considered the third greatest knight of the age.[3] Marmaduke de Tweng and John Comyn, son of the murdered John Comyn of Badenoch, could not resist the opportunity, nor could many knights from all over Europe who had also been invited to join the campaign.[4] The King of England, it appeared, wanted the flower of chivalry to join him to stand witness when he finally overcame his greatest adversary.

But not all of England's earls were so eager to see their king succeed. Despite the fragile peace that had been forged over the last eighteen months following the murder of Piers Gaveston, the earls of Lancaster and Warwick, both ardent critics of the king, refused to come, sending instead their minimal feudal obligation. The earls of Arundel and Warenne found further excuses; Warenne, who was attempting to annul his marriage to the king's niece, felt it appropriate to stay away from his somewhat irked master. Together, the four earls contributed perhaps as few as sixty knights and men-at-arms.[5]

Their obstinacy mattered little. In all, Edward II managed to raise approximately 20,000 men, the largest army deployed since Edward I's Falkirk campaign in 1298. It would be a force gathered with a single purpose: the destruction of Robert Bruce and his adherents. Some 2,000 cavalry were drawn from the retinues of the earls and barons, with the king himself providing eighty-nine knights, seventy of whom had been recruited purposely for the campaign, along with thirty-two of Edward's bannerets.[6] There were 5,000 infantrymen from north and south Wales, and archers too, including 100 crossbowmen from Bristol.[7] On 24 March, writs were issued ordering the muster of 16,000 infantrymen from thirteen English counties, while 4,000 men were conscripted from Ireland under the command of Richard de Burgh, Earl of Ulster. John of Lorn was given the responsibility of raising a fleet to transport them across the narrow Irish Sea.[8] Edward may have hoped to raise nearer 25,000, but this had not been possible, and as with all campaigns in the medieval period, desertion was certainly a feature.

To support his great war machine, the king commissioned sixty ships from English ports around the country to transport provisions by sea so the army could be fed. Following their journey out of Berwick, the enormous baggage train of 106 four-horse carts and 110 eight-oxen wagons stretched an impressive 4 miles in length.[9] It is unsurprising that the author of the *Vita* commented, 'Never in our time has such an army gone forth from England.'[10] Edward meant to win.

As preparations got underway in England, Edward Bruce resumed the siege of Stirling Castle begun the year before. Stirling was a mighty fortress which sat atop a steep, rocky outcrop overlooking a valley, marking the gateway between the Scottish Lowlands and the Highlands. Its value for whoever held it was as much in its symbolism as its strategic importance. Having been under English control since Edward I had unleashed his War Wolf in 1304, Stirling's garrison had been spooked by the fall of Edinburgh, Linlithgow and Roxburgh. When Edward Bruce resumed his siege, the constable of the castle, Philip de Mowbray, fearing the worst and knowing that Edward II was already on the march north, agreed in mid-May 1314 to surrender the castle to the Scots if the King of England did not appear in sight of its walls before Midsummer's Day, 24 June.[11] Edward Bruce accepted the terms, even if he did not discuss them first with his brother the king. It would make little difference, for Robert would have known full well that even if Edward II arrived in time and regarrisoned, his guerrilla army could disappear into Lennox and elsewhere, eluding the English forces in the difficult terrain, only to attack the castle again within a year when the King of England inevitably headed south once more. It was a strategy that Bruce had employed in 1311 when invading the northern counties of England and Lothian.

On 26 May, the English king arrived at Newminster, having left London on 21 April, travelling via York and Durham. It was at Newminster that word arrived via messenger that Philip de Mowbray had come to terms with Bruce during the recent two-month siege.[12] Such a challenge immediately galvanised the army and forced the king to speed up his plans. The following day, 27 May, Edward ordered the infantry to march in haste, the effect of which the *Vita* described: 'Short were the halts for sleep, shorter still were those for food, hence horses, horsemen and infantry were worn out with toil and hunger.'[13] It would be a gruelling 50-mile march from Berwick if Edward was to reach Stirling on the 24th, which he simply had to do. Perhaps this was part of the Bruce strategy all along. If Robert could not challenge the king in battle because of superior numbers and the great risks he and his men would be exposed to, he could grind down his opposition through fatigue, making them vulnerable to lightning Scottish raids as they travelled around the country.

The benefit of Mowbray's offer was that King Robert knew exactly where Edward II and his army were heading as they crossed into his kingdom. As a result, the King of Scots summoned his army to muster at Tor Wood for the end of April, which lay south and in sight of Stirling Castle.[14] As before, his army was quite different in character to his opponent's, most notably in the absence of heavy cavalry, the arm having been key to winning medieval battles over the last two centuries. Although this had been challenged in 1302 at the Battle of Courtrai between the Flemish and the French, where the Flemish infantry had won a stunning victory, decimating the stunned French cavalry. Years of guerrilla fighting meant that Robert's army needed to be lightly equipped in order to hit, run and hide, moving with great agility across tough terrain. In preparing to harry the English there was little need for the large destriers, the knights' war horses; such horses needed to be imported to Scotland and had not been for some years. Open-field warfare was just not their way anymore.[15]

Instead, Robert's army was composed of infantry, highly skilled archers from Selkirk Forest and 500 light horsemen who were commanded by Robert Keith, the Marischal.[16] He divided them initially into four divisions, which would later become three. His own division was made up of men from Carrick, Bute,

Kintyre, Argyll and the Isles, supported by Angus MacDonald of Islay.[17] Thomas Randolph, Earl of Moray, was given command of a second division made up of the men of Moray and the north. Edward Bruce, who by now had been made Earl of Carrick, made up the third, which was likely composed of the men of his Lordship of Galloway, while the remaining division was commanded by James Douglas, who had the men of the Borders, Renfrew and the Stewarty, given that their lord, Walter Stewart, could not command in person, being a minor. Walter had succeeded his father, the late James Stewart, who had died on 16 July 1309.[18] Following the demise of his long-standing ally, King Robert had travelled to the Cistercian abbey of Paisley to oversee his funeral, the last gesture between two great friends.[19]

In all, Robert's army of 1314 was approximately less than one-third of Edward II's, numbering around 6,000, each division made up of about 1,500 men.[20] The king now awaited the arrival of David Strathbogie, Earl of Atholl, whose loyalty he could still not entirely guarantee. He was in for a long wait.

In the third week of June, King Robert sent James Douglas and Sir Robert Keith with a few horsemen to reconnoitre in order to gauge the size of the approaching army.[21] On the 22nd, hearing that Edward had now reached Edinburgh and was travelling up the Roman road towards Stirling, King Robert moved out of Tor Wood into his preferred position of the New Park, on the west side of the valley, which was covered by a dense woodland, much larger than is seen there today.[22] It was a perfect spot to oversee the valley and launch a hit-and-run raid on the much larger English lines as they passed.

Stirling Castle, perched on its rocky outcrop, sat to the north. To the south, just beyond Tor Wood, was a river called the Bannock Burn, which in most parts was steep-sided and flowed east to join the tidal River Forth, which itself flowed into the much larger Firth of Forth. To the east of the valley, opposite Bruce and his men in the woods of New Park, was the Carse, an expanse of mixed ground, some areas more dry and stable while others, especially further north and east, were marsh-like, becoming waterlogged according to the tides.[23] A series of wet summers over recent years had no doubt affected the water table, making it higher than in a typical year, which meant the Bannock Burn could still be fast-flowing and deep in places even at the height of summer.[24] Therefore, between the Bannock Burn and Stirling Castle, the valley was a relatively

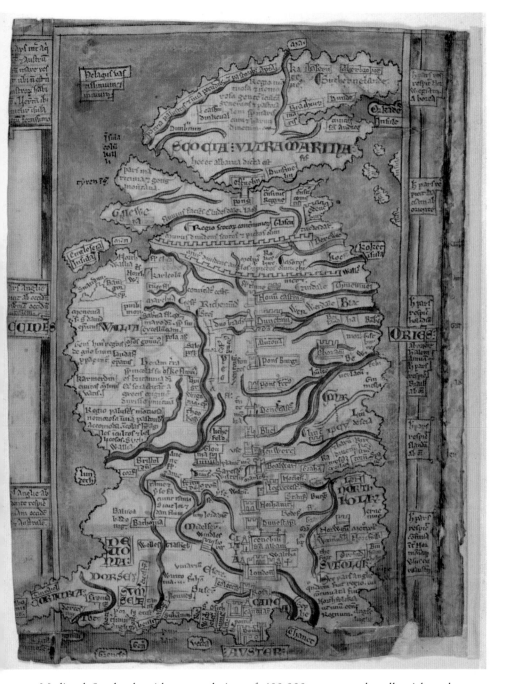

Medieval Scotland, with a population of 400,000, was a culturally rich and vibrant kingdom ruled over by the royal House of Dunkeld until 1290. The complex and delicate relationship between the kingdoms of Scotland and England was punctuated by points of contention, none more hotly contested than the claim of English suzerainty, which in Robert's lifetime resulted in a bitter war.

There are no contemporary extant records of what Robert Bruce looked like, yet this facial reconstruction by Liverpool John Moores University Face Lab, based on a plaster cast of his skull, goes some way in enabling us to see him once again. Born on 11 July 1274, Robert descended from an illustrious house of Norman lords who arrived in Scotland in 1124 under the patronage of King David I of Scotland. As a descendant of the royal House of Dunkeld, he pursued his grandfather's claim to the throne of Scotland, which he took in 1306.

Right: Edward I, King of England, spent sixteen years invested in the affairs of Scotland, invading and seizing control of the kingdom despite promises to the contrary. His determination to reduce Scotland to a mere appendage of England, rather than a continued independent kingdom, resulted in the First Scottish War of Independence.

Below left: Alexander III, King of Scots, sat crowned and robed on the left of this manuscript illumination, had a congenial friendship with his brother-in-law Edward I, King of England. During his reign, Alexander carefully rebuffed the claims of English overlordship, maintaining Scotland's independence from her neighbour.

Below right: The curse of St Malachy, Archbishop of Armagh, hung heavy over the Bruce family ever since their ancestor Robert de Brus had allegedly offended him during the archbishop's pilgrimage through Scotland in 1140. King Robert, and his father and grandfather, often made votives to appease the wrath of the saint; over a century later, Malachy's intercession was still thought to bring continued misfortune upon their powerful dynasty.

On 18 March 1286, Alexander III, King of Scots, was riding along a narrow coastal road enveloped in dense fog during the depths of an inhospitable night. Detached from his guard, the king's horse stumbled, throwing him off the cliff to his untimely death. This memorial near Kinghorn marks the spot. His demise, leaving only a young granddaughter to succeed him, proved calamitous for Scotland.

King John Balliol of Scotland kneels to give homage to Edward I on 26 December 1292, once again giving up Scotland's independence. With John having been chosen to rule as a result of the arbitration of the Great Cause, the Bruce and Balliol families remained bitter rivals. Balliol's rule, weak and ineffective, would prove disastrous.

Above: By 1296, a defiant King John Balliol and his Scottish magnates fought back against the continued provocation of Edward I. The King of England promptly raised an army and marched to war, laying siege to the town and castle of Berwick at Easter 1296. So shocking was the massacre that took place that men, women and children were said to 'fall like autumn leaves'. To this day, the Siege of Berwick is remembered as one of the bloodiest acts to unfold on British soil.

Right: Facing the overwhelming might of a full English invasion, the rule of King John collapsed. In July 1296, Edward I stripped Balliol of his crown and imprisoned him. His tabard on his surcoat, bearing the Lion Rampant of Scotland, was torn from him during a humiliating deposition ceremony. From this act alone he is remembered to history as '*Twme Tabart*' or '*Toom Tabard*'.

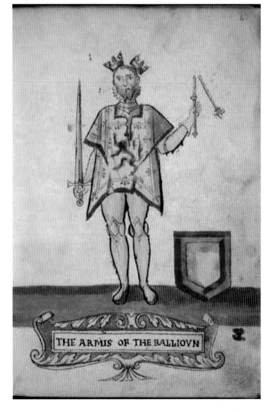

THE ARMIS OF THE BALLIOVN

In September 1297, the Scots gave battle at Stirling Bridge. Under the joint command of William Wallace and Andrew Murray, their army attempted to overcome the aggressive imposition of English imperial ambition. As battle raged, a contingent of Scots with their great Lochaber axes was dispatched to bring down the bridge which the English army was still crossing. It proved decisive. The Scots victory did much to bolster their resolve until their subsequent defeat at the hands of Edward I less than a year later at the Battle of Falkirk.

The murder of John Comyn, Lord of Badenoch, at the Kirk of the Grey Friars in Dumfries on 10 February 1306 cleared the way for Robert's accession to the crown of Scotland. Comyn, lured to the church by his rival under the pretence of peace talks, was stabbed to death during a heated debate. His murder shocked Christendom and stained Robert's reputation for the rest of his life.

Right: In great haste, Robert was inaugurated as King of Scots on 25 March 1306 at Scone Abbey. In the absence of the Earl of Fife, whose hereditary role was to crown Scottish kings, the earl's aunt, the Countess of Buchan, performed this rite. She would later be imprisoned for her action and kept in a cage by an enraged Edward I.

Below: There are many myths associated with Robert Bruce, and this one of the spider is perhaps the best of those that still abound today. Facing unprecedented odds and on the verge of abject defeat in early 1307, it was at this moment, according to legend, that Robert learned the lessons of perseverance and fortitude, watching a spider tirelessly rebuild its web. The intervention of spiders in caves is a common tool of medieval folklore, and can be found in other heroic tales, like David's flight from Saul, and Mohammed and the Coreishites. While this story is just a myth, it does tell us a lot about how Robert came to be viewed.

Above: The skirmish at Glen Trool in April 1307 was the first of many victories that King Robert and his followers could claim. It had the catalytic effect of galvanising wider support for the king and broke the perception of English invincibility in Scotland.

Below: In May 1307, with six hundred men under his command, King Robert engaged Aymer de Valence in battle at Loudoun Hill, below a jagged-tooth crag of volcanic rock surrounded by marshy terrain. Having chosen the location with care, Robert and his men dug camouflaged trenches, luring the English cavalry to their deaths, while many others would flounder in the fetlock-deep marsh. The Scots, having broken the vanguard and forced the English to retreat, were victorious.

Above: From 1307, Edward II, King of England, was doggedly determined to uphold his inherited rights to Scottish overlordship. Even after his major defeat at the Battle of Bannockburn in 1314, Edward secured international condemnation against the King of Scots, which resulted in Bruce's excommunication while Scotland was placed under the hard papal censure of interdict. Only with Edward II's deposition in 1327 was Robert's rule formally recognised in England by Queen Isabella and her regime.

Below: By the end of 1308, after overcoming the enemies within his kingdom, Robert was able to focus some of his energy on governing his realm. He would spend years redistributing lands, titles and gifts through the careful exercise of royal patronage. This seal, one of many, was used to authenticate his royal deeds.

From 1310, Robert's guerrilla tactics paid off as he slowly reclaimed Scottish castles previously under the command of Edward II's English garrisons. Under the cover of darkness in March 1314, Thomas Randolph, Earl of Moray, and a handful of his men scaled the seemingly impenetrable volcanic rock foundations of Edinburgh Castle. Once over the castle walls they were able to open the gates, allowing the Scots to pour in and quickly overcome the garrison, including its commander, Sir Piers Liband.

The Battle of Bannockburn, fought on 23–24 June 1314, was a defining moment for King Robert's legacy. It did much to solidify his reputation and legitimacy as king, his victory appearing to be an act of divine providence. Yet it would take Robert another fourteen years to secure a permanent peace with England, so determined was Edward II to prevent it.

The Great Famine of 1315–17 devastated Western Europe. During these years there was a great scarcity of food, widespread pestilence and cattle murrain, and the population of Britain was reduced by approximately one-tenth. To contemporaries it felt like the apocalypse had come, as this contemporary manuscript, the *Biblia Pauperum*, illustrates. Death sits astride a lion whose long tail ends in a ball of flame depicting Hell itself. Famine points to her hungry mouth. It is a chilling reminder of the vulnerability of the population at the time.

Frustrated by ongoing English resistance to his rule, King Robert took the fight to the English. In 1315 he laid siege to Carlisle, deploying great siege engines on the town walls. Carlisle was well defended by Sir Andrew Harclay, who unleashed his springalds, as captured here in a contemporary manuscript. Robert was forced to retreat, according to the Chronicle of Lanercost 'marching off in confusion'.

In May 1315, Robert's brother Edward Bruce, following the invitation from Domnal O'Neill, King of Tyrone, launched a campaign to secure the High Kingship of Ireland and challenge Edward II's authority as overlord of that kingdom, whose English power was centred on Dublin. Upon landing in Antrim, Edward Bruce began to lay siege to Carrickfergus Castle, which stubbornly held out for over a year. The Bruce campaign failed when Edward was killed at the Battle of Faughart near Dundalk in October 1318.

In 1320, in a bid to win the support of Pope John XXII, overturn papal censures against him and win recognition of his status as king, Robert, his clergy and his lay magnates each sealed letters composed in beautiful rhythmic Latin setting out their arguments. Only the letter from the lay magnates survives, remembered to history as the Declaration of Arbroath.

Above: In 1322, King Robert, having faced off an English invasion under the command of Edward II, took the fight to the English. Launching a sizeable raiding party of Highlanders and Islesmen into England, Robert sought to capture Edward II, who was in residence at Rievaulx Abbey in Yorkshire. News arrived at breakfast that the Scots were closing in; fearing capture Edward narrowly escaped, leaving his baggage train and great seal behind in his haste. Although thwarted, King Robert had emphasised the futility of continuing to oppose his Scottish rule.

Right: Robert was conventionally pious and throughout his life went on pilgrimages, making votives in memory of lost friends and relatives. As his health rapidly deteriorated in 1328, his last pilgrimage was to St Ninian's Cave at Whithorn in Galloway. Perhaps on nearing death he sought forgiveness for the murder of his rival John Comyn, whom he killed not far away in 1306 at the Kirk of the Grey Friars, Dumfries.

Left: At the point of death, Robert retreated to his newly built manor at Cardross. There, lying in bed, he made his final gifts of patronage and was attended by many of those who had supported him during his life and reign, including James Douglas, Thomas Randolph, Gilbert de la Haye and Robert Keith the Marischal. Bernard, Bishop of the Isles most likely acted as his final confessor before he slipped quietly away on 7 June 1329 at the age of fifty-four.

Below: Dunfermline Abbey had over the centuries become a royal mausoleum for successive Scottish kings. Robert had been careful to make regular provision for his interment there, ensuring his final choice of resting place was both symbolic and fitting for the life of a man who was determined to uphold and enshrine his status as Scotland's rightful king.

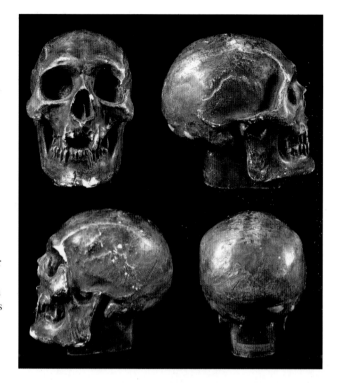

The royal mausoleum of Dunfermline Abbey was subject to desecration during the Reformation. In 1818, King Robert's tomb was rediscovered and opened, and a plaster cast was made of his skull. From this, the team at Liverpool John Moores University Face Lab were able to generate their facial reconstruction of the deceased king.

James Douglas proffers support to King Alfonso XI of Castile, committing to battle at Tebas de Ardales in Spain against the Islamic Prince of Granada in an act of Holy War. During the battle, Douglas wears the embalmed heart of King Robert, posthumously fulfilling the late king's oath to take up arms against the common enemy of Christendom. The battle would cost Douglas his life.

Above: King Robert's legacy would be tested soon after his death. By 1334, many of his leading supporters were dead and his infant son King David II was forced to flee into exile in France. In 1346, having returned to Scotland five years earlier, David was captured at the Battle of Neville's Cross and imprisoned for eleven years in England. Here he is seen proffering to Edward III homage for his Scottish kingdom, recognising English overlordship in return for his freedom, in spite of his father's years of campaigning for independence.

Left: A brass rubbing of King Robert's later tomb stone at Dunfermline Abbey. In the seven hundred years since his death, Robert remains a man shrouded in myth and legend, his deeds still resonating with people around the world. In life he was Scotland's champion, and he has continued to maintain an exalted place in the history of kings.

constricted horseshoe shape, bordered by rivers and woods. In order to reach the castle in the north, Edward's army had to ford the Bannock Burn as they emerged from Tor Wood to continue their journey up the old Roman road.[25]

King Robert ordered his men take up their positions. The Earl of Moray was sent with his division towards the north east of the park, setting up his moveable and highly flexible schiltron overlooking the kirkton of St Ninian's. Edward Bruce and James Douglas positioned themselves along the edge of the wood at New Park, hidden from view. Robert himself decided to lead the vanguard, and took his 1,500 men to the most south-westerly point of New Park on the edge of the wood, closest to the Roman road and the traditional ford of the Bannock Burn, again hidden and ready to pounce when he so chose.[26] The small Scottish baggage train was installed a very safe distance away beside Camsbuskenneth Abbey, and guarded by William of Airth.

As morning broke around 4.30 a.m., the Scots army rose and broke their fast on the Vigil of St John the Baptist with prayers and bread and water. All they had to do was wait for the King of England's army to appear. As Edward II's great host snaked its way through Tor Wood on that morning, the king and his counsellors were met by Philip de Mowbray, constable of Stirling Castle, whom Robert had given safe conduct to ride out and meet with the English king. Mowbray confirmed that Edward was in view of the walls of the mighty fortress, fulfilling the pledge that the constable had made with Edward Bruce. The English king had won this round.

Having marched so far and so hard in so few days, Edward still needed to head to the castle to set up camp and regroup before setting out again to secure the remaining Scottish castles in his possession, and to reclaim more. Given the last campaign in 1310–11, the king did not expect that Robert and his army would commit to a battle any time soon, if at all. Mowbray informed him that Robert and his men had taken up position in the New Park, waiting to ambush his men if he chose to pass that way. He also made Edward aware that over the last month, Bruce and his men had dug deep pits filled with upturned stakes either side of the road, then covered them up, much like they had done at the Battle of Loudoun Hill in 1307.[27] Anyone walking over them, especially the cavalry, would founder, and thus a march north would restrict the army to a narrow column. This was typical Scottish guerrilla tactics, designed to pick off as many men as they could without a pitched battle before the English army moved on. It was now clear that the English needed to move north but away from the Roman road, in a space that was less constricted for an army of its size.[28]

It was late afternoon on 23 June when Edward II's great army finally began to emerge from Tor Wood. The vanguard was comprised of mounted knights and men-at-arms. But all was not well. Command of the vanguard was disputed between the young Earl of Gloucester who claimed his family had always held the privilege, and Edward's brother-in-law Humphrey de Bohun, Earl of Hereford, who was the hereditary Constable of England. This office gave Hereford key responsibilities during times of war, and so the two men were at loggerheads.[29] Such matters of family pride and honour would not help when the army came into open conflict with the Scots.

The vanguard began to ford the Bannock Burn further downstream on the earlier advice of Mowbray. As they crossed, Gloucester and Hereford saw a small contingent of men down on the slopes below the woods of the New Park nearest to them and King Robert's banner flying. Among the group was the distinctive figure of a man on horseback wearing armour, his helmet covered by a leather crest surmounted by a high crown. It was too good an opportunity to miss: the King of Scots detached from the main bloc of his army. Without direction from Edward, who had not yet emerged from Tor Wood, some of the vanguard led by its competing earls simply charged in mixed battle array. Hereford's nephew Henry de Bohun reached the relatively isolated Bruce first. Robert saw the attack coming and had time to prepare himself. Pulling himself out of the path of the oncoming lance, he raised himself up in his stirrups, pivoted, and as Henry de Bohun levelled with the side of the king, Robert brought down his axe with an almighty thud, splitting de Bohun's head in two.[30] He was the first casualty of the campaign. The king's remaining guard then met the oncoming members of the disorganised English line, with some of Bruce's other men emerging from the woods to join the battle.

In the ensuing skirmish, the Scots were able to drive the horses and their riders back, only this time towards the traditional ford of the Bannock Burn and the aforementioned pits. It had been Robert's plan all along. He was not going to let his traps go to waste, given they were a key part of his harrying strategy. In the confusion of the mêlée that followed, the Earl of Gloucester was thrown from his horse while others plunged into the camouflaged pits. The fighting was both fierce and chaotic. With the first skirmish quickly turning against them, Hereford, Gloucester and the vanguard beat a hasty retreat.[31] Robert had his first victory of the day.

The second was not long in coming. This time, Robert Clifford and Henry de Beaumont, the latter the dispossessed holder of the Isle of Man, had been able to surreptitiously cross the Bannock Burn further downstream near the hamlet of Bannock, and were now successfully traversing the Carse, making for the Roman road near the kirkton of St Ninian's with a force of knights some 300 strong. Thomas Randolph prepared to meet them head on. In the absence of horses, his men formed up into a moveable circular or square schiltron, a shield wall of 15-foot spears much like a hedgehog with a hollow centre, which made it difficult for the oncoming cavalry to penetrate.

As the two contingents came into contact, the impact was great. Sir William Deyncourt was killed immediately, and many others, including Sir Thomas Grey, the father of the author of the Scalacronica, was unhorsed and taken captive by the Scots, who were able to pull prisoners into the centre of their protective formation. The frustrated knights, trying hard to break through the deadly walls of spears, started to throw axes, maces and even swords, but failed to make any impact.[32] Without much hope of success, Beaumont and Clifford gave the order to retreat. Randolph and his men, through grit, determination and a good dose of courage, had repelled the much stronger English cavalry force. It was yet another Scottish victory. The English party returned to the rest of the army, where morale quickly began to plummet.[33]

The English reconnaissance attempt did prove more fruitful in other ways, as Clifford and Beaumont had identified that there was sufficient hard ground to travel north to Stirling without having to take the narrow Roman road. This allowed Edward the possibility of moving his army without falling into Bruce's pits a second time. The king and his counsellors decided the bulk of his cavalry and men-at-arms would ford the Bannock Burn and set up camp on the drier areas of the Carse to the east side of the Roman road. The king's harbingers had discovered that there was sufficient hard standing for a camp that could accommodate at least the cavalry and the archers. The infantry was to cross in the early morning, camping instead for now on the south side of the burn due to limited space. It would prove to be a fateful decision.[34] The Scots had not committed to an open battle for seven years, so there was the feeling that this manoeuvre, while risky, was not entirely reckless.

Robert must have been highly satisfied with the events of the day. Using caution, effective deployment and the use of the land to his advantage, he and his nephew Randolph had secured two victories. Yet it was also clear to him that the significant size of Edward's army, 20,000 strong and camped on both sides of the Bannock Burn, made his job almost impossible. At best they could consider sweeping into the outer reaches of the camp on the Carse during the night, to harry and raid before disappearing into the shadow of the night prior to a total retreat. The author of the Scalacronica suggests that Robert was determined to withdraw that evening and head into Lennox.[35] It was certainly in keeping with his tactics to date; he had achieved so much over the last eight years by doing the same. Fighting a battle against these numbers did not make sense, and Robert was acutely aware of it. With his wife, Queen Elizabeth, still in English captivity, along with his only daughter, Marjorie, he still had no direct legitimate male heir. Nor did his only surviving brother, Edward Bruce, and as Edward was stationed with Robert, everything that had been gained since those early desperate years of his reign could be lost in a day should they be killed or captured.[36] It was too much to risk, both for Robert himself and more broadly for the Kingdom of Scotland.

What happened next changed everything. Alexander Seton of Seton, a Scottish landholder, had previously been a supporter of Robert at the time of his accession in 1306 but had submitted to Edward I in the defeat following Methven. Despite temporarily re-joining Bruce in 1309, Seton had found it increasingly difficult to maintain his support for the King of Scots, with his lands held in Lothian and his neighbours all pro-English.[37] With an attuned ambivalence, he once more ended up in English employ, and was close enough to the commanders of Edward's army to know of and be privy to the king's planned movements. Witnessing the events of the first day, and hearing of angry disputes between Edward II's military counsellors, Seton took the opportunity to switch sides, discreetly walking between the two camps during the night.

Seton was quick to gain an audience with the King of Scots, and after professing his loyalty once more was able to inform Robert that Edward II meant to move to Stirling first thing in the morning. More importantly, he explained that the king intended to move the cavalry first, leaving the infantry on the south side of the Bannock Burn, with the aim of regrouping at Stirling. He also reported that the English commanders were hotly divided, the Earl of Gloucester and Ingram de Umfraville, the brother of the Earl of Angus, wishing to remain on the Carse for a day so the exhausted army, the infantry in particular, could recover from their forced march. Edward, the Earl of Pembroke and the veteran Sir Giles d'Argentan preferred to march to Stirling, securing the castle and bringing the army together on better ground.[38] As tempers flared, the king somewhat rashly accused Gloucester of cowardice and treachery, and in the arguments that followed, discipline at the top began to fray.[39]

With Seton's switch of allegiance, Robert had been given an insight into Edward's plans. The tables were beginning to turn. He knew the King of England would move his 2,000 cavalry and contingent of archers first, which meant that Robert's divisions, 6,000 strong, would have the superior numbers on this side of the burn. If he was to risk a direct assault, so long as the English infantry were unable to cross in time, he would have a small but real chance of winning in an open confrontation. Given his men were well trained in the use of the schiltron, which had proved so effective on the first day against two cavalry assaults, this looked even more likely, encouraging him to think he could inflict a real blow. The opportunity must have seemed almost like an act of divine providence, a gut-wrenching temptation that Robert and his commanders simply could not ignore. If Robert were to break with his long-term strategy and commit to a pitched battle despite his better judgement, it would need to be executed with absolute precision and unprecedented determination. Robert decided to stand and fight.

As dawn broke in the early hours of Midsummer's Day, Robert made his confession to Maurice, Abbot of Inchaffray, who celebrated Mass before the army in the woods of New Park.[40] The king's host was well attended by ecclesiastical representatives, many of whom had been careful to bring a collection of well-preserved Holy relics in a bid to invoke Holy intercession during the campaign. There were the proud banners of St Andrew and also St Kentigern from

Glasgow, as well as the banner of St Thomas Becket from Arbroath, a saint whom King Robert particularly venerated. Abbot Maurice had brought the relics of St Fillan, and the Abbot of Arbroath also transported the reliquary casket of St Columba, known as the Brecbennoch.[41] In all it was quite the collection, and as Robert prepared to plunge into the unknown, those Holy relics seemed to offer reassurance. The calm before the storm must have felt somehow spiritual or otherworldly in itself. To mark the solemnity of the moment, the King of Scots knighted some of his principal men who had yet to receive the honour. This included the young Walter Stewart, and his now loyal and long-standing friend James Douglas.[42] With the ceremony complete, the king then turned to his men and gave an address, which survives, having been recorded for posterity by the Abbot of Arbroath, who was present:

My lords, my people, accustomed to enjoy that full freedom for which in times gone by the kings of Scotland have fought many a battle. For eight years or more I have struggled with much labour for my right to the kingdom and for honourable liberty. I have lost brothers, friends and kinsmen. Your own kinsmen have been made captive, and bishops and priests are locked in prison. Our country's nobility has poured forth its blood in war. These barons you can see before you, clad in mail, are bent upon destroying me and obliterating my kingdom, nay, our whole nation. They do not believe we can survive. They glory in their warhorses and equipment. For us, the name of the Lord must be our hope of victory in battle. This is a day of rejoicing: the birthday of John the Baptist. With our Lord Jesus as commander, St Andrew and the martyr St Thomas shall fight today with the saints of Scotland for the honour of their country and their nation. If you heartily repent for your sins you will be victorious under God's command. As for offences committed against the Crown, I proclaim a pardon, by virtue of my royal power, to all those who fight manfully for the kingdom of our fathers.[43]

The words, so personal to both Robert and his audience, could not have failed to inspire. All that now remained was for the King of Scots to order his men into position in three divisions under the cover of the woods of New Park: Edward Bruce to the south, Thomas Randolph in the centre along with James Douglas very close to Randolph on the northern end of the line. Robert would take the rearguard and commit to wherever he was most needed.[44]

As planned, Edward II, Pembroke and the king's forces on the Carse formed up and faced north towards Stirling. The battalions of cavalry were behind the vanguard, and the archers were positioned eider side of the left and right flanks. The English considered it a strong formation. Should the Scots repeat what they had done the day before to Clifford and Beaumont near the kirkton of St Ninian's, both sets of archers were well placed to shoot from left and right and decimate the schiltrons without the need for injury to the English cavalry. Arrows were a schiltron's only real weakness. Barbour records that the English advance looked like it had formed one single column, which is accurate from the view point of the Scots standing in the woods at New Park looking to the east.[45] However, it was not. From the English perspective, the deployment was well thought out and had been tried and tested. Moreover, in their minds it was likely that King Robert had already disappeared overnight, no attack having come during the evening.[46] As they set out, no one in the English ranks could have expected what happened next.

King Robert's army came out from the woods of the New Park and formed up to the English army's left flank. Led by the Abbot of Inchaffray, carrying in front of him a crucifix, all knelt and began to pray, reciting the *Pater Noster*. Edward II, amazed, thought initially that they were kneeling in submission but soon realised his mistake.[47] Turning the army about to face west as a single entity was difficult in terms of repositioning the divisions in such limited space. The archers on the flanks were suddenly in the wrong place, effectively right at the front of the army, ahead of the vanguard, while the right flank of archers had become stuck at the back. In a stroke, Robert had ensured that his schiltrons, at least immediately, were safe so long as Edward's archers were blocked behind extensive numbers of mounted men. As the Scots took up their formations uphill from the English, the archers could not respond effectively and were forced out of the way as the vanguard under Gloucester and Hereford charged the Scottish lines.[48]

The result was the same as in Clifford and Beaumont's efforts the day before. Medieval mounted knights at this time had almost always seen lines of infantry break and run during a full-scale cavalry charge. Holding nerve and standing in situ was a likely death sentence, and mounted men would simply have ridden over those standing still. But horses would not run into a schiltron; they would instead seek to leap over it or swerve out of the way altogether. With all these things in mind, as the Earl of Gloucester led the charge moments ahead of the main vanguard with the Earl of Hereford behind him, he fell victim to the discipline of the well-trained Scots. Rather than buckle, the schiltron walls stood firm and Gloucester, with the front line of knights, ploughed headlong into a wall of spears as Robert's men stood their ground. The twenty-three-year-old Earl of Gloucester, who was not wearing his surcoat because he did not think he would be fighting in a battle that morning, was impaled or unhorsed and killed.[49] Hereford and the remainder of the vanguard arrived seconds later to plough into the same wall, now filled with the dying bodies of knights and horses. In the tightly packed space, Edward II's steward Edmund Mauley, John Comyn, Pain Tiptoft and Robert Clifford were all killed.[50] The vanguard was broken up, scattered in confusion or impaled, and without hope of reforming for a second charge due to very limited space.[51]

Edward Bruce's division had taken the brunt of the attack but was still holding up. James Douglas and Thomas Randolph, along with the king's brother, then advanced towards the remaining English lines, reducing the space the English army had for manoeuvre. The 17,000 English infantry, still on the south side of the Bannock Burn, could do nothing but watch the horror unfold. The English cavalry were penned in. Edward's remaining men charged to meet their oncoming assailants. 'When both armies engaged,' wrote the chronicler of Lanercost, 'and the great horses of the English charged the pikes of the Scots, as it were into a dense forest, there arose a great and terrible crash of spears broken and of destriers wounded to death.'[52]

As the fighting grew thick and intense, the Welsh archers, now regrouped into some semblance of formation following the charge of the vanguard, began to loose their arrows, aiming for the schiltron commanded by Douglas on the left, inflicting heavy casualties on his 1,500 men. Robert, having the advantage of oversight at the rear, was able to command Robert Keith the Marischal to attack with his 500 light horsemen, who were able to cut down and scatter the archers before their onslaught impacted on Robert's ever-increasing advantage.[53] The King of Scots now committed his own division, supporting one of the other cohorts who needed most support, possibly closing off the northernmost escape route towards Stirling Castle. With both sides fighting fiercely, and the English columns too jammed together to be effective, Robert and his army began to enclose them and, step by step, began slowly pushing the English back towards the Bannock Burn.[54] The battle was becoming a bloodletting.

Edward's army began to panic. With no breathing space, and the wall of spears pressing in on them from almost every side, they were unable to strike out. For many, their only chance remained in flight, heading back across the Bannock Burn to reach the infantry on the south side where King Robert's men would not follow. In desperation, some of the soldiers towards the back began to break ranks and run, but the panicked determination to re-cross created a crush of men laden with heavy armour. The steep-sided banks of the burn became a quagmire, and 'many nobles and others fell into [the burn] with their horses in the crush while others escaped with much more difficulty ... many were never able to extricate themselves from the ditch'.[55] Men were treading on each other, drowning or crushing others in a bid to escape. Barbour noted that the Bannock Burn became so choked with corpses that eventually some of the men were able to cross over dry-shod on the drowned bodies of others.[56] Desperate fugitives seeking to flee across the Forth also drowned.

In the thick of the fighting, Edward II's horse was killed. He was immediately remounted, but only after his shield bearer, Roger Northburgh, was captured. Despite the king fighting fearlessly, 'like a lioness deprived of her cubs', the Earl of Pembroke seized Edward's reins and gathered around them 500 mounted men, who hacked their way through the crush and took the king from the field for his own safety.[57] Edward protested, wanting to keep fighting, but Pembroke and Giles d'Argentan knew that his capture would be catastrophic for the English and bring about the end of all hope of winning in Scotland. They forced themselves through the carnage, Edward himself killing men with his mace as he left, and headed initially around King Robert's schiltron to the castle at Stirling.[58] There, Phillip Mowbray rightly told the king to flee rather than be held hostage behind the walls of the castle and so the king, with Pembroke and his 500-strong guard, rode in haste around the base of the rocky outcrop and took the road to Linlithgow, heading for Dunbar.[59]

Robert watched furiously as Edward II and his men fought their way out of the unfolding carnage and fled past his cohort to Stirling. While he had probably never thought it possible to take the king hostage, as the morning unfolded, he had come exceedingly close. He now had a stark choice. He could send Robert Keith with his light horsemen in hot pursuit as they were almost even in number to the King of England's guard, but they were considerably less well armoured. Keen to keep his army together until he could be certain that the flower of English knighthood was devastated on the field, Robert had little choice but to stay put. Only as the battle drew to its bloody close later in the day did he allow James Douglas to take off in hot pursuit with a small contingent of sixty light horsemen.[60]

As James travelled through Tor Wood, he met Sir Laurence Abernethy, a pro-English Scot who was only now bringing a contingent of men to fight for the King of England. When he heard of the disaster, he immediately switched sides, and joined Douglas in the pursuit of the royal bodyguard with apparent gusto. Snapping at Edward II's heels, they followed the king and his men to the gates of Dunbar, picking off stragglers.[61] Once in the safety of the castle, Patrick, Earl of Dunbar sent away his servants to ensure no treachery could take place by which the King of England might fall into the hands of the Scots. Shortly after, Edward and a small group of his men commandeered a ship and sailed from Dunbar to Berwick, bringing the campaign in Scotland to an abrupt and bloody conclusion. It was an inglorious end to an inglorious battle.

With Edward free of danger, the Earl of Dunbar and Phillip Mowbray, realising that they could not hold out any longer, surrendered their castles to the King of Scots.[62] Stirling was then slighted. King Robert was shortly to receive Bothwell Castle too. The Earl of Hereford, along with Robert de Umfraville, Earl of Angus, his brother Ingram, Maurice de Berkeley, John de Segrave, Anthony de Lucy and others, escaped the battle as well, riding to the walls of Hereford's castle. Once admitted by his constable, the fugitives were promptly imprisoned and handed over to King Robert along with the fortification.[63] With such a devastating defeat, the constables of the few remaining English castles knew which way the wind was blowing.

The Scots had suffered very few casualties among the senior members of their cohort. Two knights of note, William de Vinpont and Walter Ross, the younger son of the Earl of Ross, were killed,[64] as was William of Airth, whose order had been to protect the Scottish baggage train at Camsbuskenneth. The Earl of Atholl, whose loyalty to Robert had always sat uneasily, had failed to turn up at the New Park, instead deciding to join Edward II by attacking Robert's baggage train. His betrayal may have been caused by a simple act of jealousy, reminiscent of that between Gloucester and Hereford, as Robert had appointed Gilbert de la Haye as constable of his host, a role which Atholl claimed by hereditary right. Atholl was also aggrieved by the king's brother, who had seduced the earl's sister only to abandon her in favour of the daughter of the Earl of Ross. With his sister's reputation impugned and his hereditary rights undermined, Atholl felt he was being ridiculed and promptly changed sides.[65] In response, King Robert forfeited all Atholl's lands and banished him to England, a sentence the earl was only too happy to accept.

Those on the English side suffered a great deal more. The death toll is impossible to determine, given that the muster roll was captured by the Scots, but what is certain is that the Earl of Gloucester perished, as did the third greatest knight in Christendom, Sir Giles d'Argentan. So too did William, Lord of Hingham, Edmund Hastings and at least forty knights, many hundreds of archers and other men-at-arms. Pembroke's nephew John Comyn, son and namesake of the murdered John Comyn, Lord of Badenoch, was also dead, as was one of his Comyn cousins. Ralph de Monthermer had been captured along with John de Clavering and many others, now great prizes fit for lucrative ransoms. The good fortune did not stop there. Edward II's extensive baggage train, which had previously stretched for 4 miles, was looted and the king's royal seal, his instrument of government and authority, was captured along with his shield when Roger Northburgh was taken. For Robert, the victory on the battlefield was a gift that kept on giving.

The king, though, was magnanimous as ever in victory. He spent the evening of the second day of the battle watching over the bodies of Robert Clifford and his own second cousin the Earl of Gloucester, who was related to him through the king's grandmother.[66] When he emerged in the morning, the king was greeted by Sir Marmaduke de Tweng, who fell to his knees and offered himself up as a prisoner, having previously hidden his surcoat and armour while in the king's camp overnight. Robert duly accepted. In a gesture of goodwill, before negotiations and discussions of prisoner exchanges could really begin, Robert sent the bodies of Clifford and Gloucester back to England along with the chivalrous Marmaduke de Tweng and

Edward's brother-in-law Ralph de Monthermer, who took with him Edward II's royal seal.[67] The king did not request the payment of a ransom for either man, although each would have brought a hefty price. In showing magnanimity to a defeated enemy, Robert wished to stretch out the hand of peace, hoping that he could now capitalise on this profound and seemingly divine victory.

This battle, which would be known to posterity as the Battle of Bannockburn, was something that neither Robert Bruce nor Edward II predicted. In mustering his 6,000 men to harry the English as they marched in force around the Kingdom of Scotland, it was the best outcome that Robert could have hoped for. Seton's betrayal and support for the King of Scots was an act of divine providence, one which the spiritual and superstitious Robert felt compelled to act upon. While the English held their infantry on the south side of the Bannock Burn, Robert took a chance that his superior numbers on the Carse, if wisely deployed, could prevail over the English cavalry. It was a deadly game of chance, and one that Robert himself had not thought to employ until the early hours of the morning of the second day of battle.

In winning this great victory, Robert had cemented his kingship in the eyes of the Scots. God, after all the uncertainty, once more appeared to favour him. But everything would now ultimately rest on how a humiliated and defeated Edward II would respond. More than this, there was the matter of whether the repercussions of King Robert's great victory would resonate with any of the European royal houses, including the spiritual leader of the Christian world, the pope, who thus far had failed to recognise the legitimacy of Robert's rule. All the King of Scots could do was wait.

10

Brothers, Kings, Countrymen

King Robert understood his opponent. In the grip of such a humiliating defeat, Edward II, facing deep political hostility in England from men such as his overmighty cousin Thomas of Lancaster, had little space to manoeuvre. As a result, the English king would make himself impervious to any overtures of peace from Scotland, holding on to his belief that it remained his by right of inheritance. If Robert was to win recognition of his status and the independence of his kingdom, he would have to press home the strength of his position.

On 1 August 1314, King Robert ordered his brother Edward, along with James Douglas and William de Soules, Lord of Liddesdale, once again to raid into northern England, this time with an impressively large army. Bypassing the English-held town of Berwick, they laid waste to swathes of Northumberland while those who could defend the county walled themselves up behind the parapets of their northern castles. The people of the bishopric of Durham, the honour of Penrith and Copeland all parted with more racket money to the tune of 800 marks to avoid the pillaging as Robert's army applied their now well-established tactics of collecting booty, driving off cattle and ransoming prisoners.[1] Edward II responded, ordering Sir Andrew Harclay, Governor of Carlisle, into the area in an attempt to push the Scots back, but at Rerecross-on-Stanemoor his smaller force of hobelars was simply swept aside. Once more, the people of the marches were left defenceless against the strength of a focussed Scottish army.

Moving further south into the county of Richmond, just 50 miles from where the King of England was holding parliament at

York, Edward Bruce and his men reached as far south as the River Tees before turning back to Scotland via the north-west by way of Swaledale, Cumberland and Liddesdale.[2] As his army crossed back into Scotland, the King of Scots penned a letter to his English counterpart, expressing his desire for a permanent peace settlement, a communication timed to perfection, having made it abundantly clear to all that the English were unable to defend their northern homeland, their position dangerously exposed.[3]

Peace talks opened at Durham on 20 October, headed by the English under the watchful eye of John Botetourt, underpinned by a temporary truce agreed between the two countries at the request of Philip IV of France.[4] Robert sent his procurators Gilbert de la Haye, Robert Keith the Marischal, Neil Campbell and Roger Kirkpatrick to represent the Scots. In their first mission, the Scots got off to a good start, reaching agreement on the release of Robert's wife, sisters and daughter Marjorie, along with the now old and blind Robert Wishart, Bishop of Glasgow, who, like the others, had remained in English captivity for the last eight years. In the autumn, writs were sent out to move the prisoners to York in anticipation of their release over the coming winter.[5] In exchange, Robert would release Edward II's brother-in-law Humphrey de Bohun, Earl of Hereford, and any remaining English prisoners. But now the talks quickly became bogged down, the English representatives pointedly refusing to recognise the legitimacy of Robert as King of Scots or the independence of the Scottish kingdom. Try as they might, the Scottish delegation could not find a way to break through the deadlock, Edward II himself having made strict assertions that on no account would he move on the notion. Without the possibility of a permanent peace, the talks soon collapsed.[6]

A frustrated King Robert summoned parliament to meet at Camsbuskenneth for 6 November. Very few records survive, but it is clear that Robert followed up on his earlier proclamation of October 1313:

> It was finally agreed, adjudged and decreed by the counsel and assent of the bishops and other prelates, earls, barons, and other nobles of the Kingdom of Scotland, and also all the community of the aforesaid kingdom, that all who died outside the faith and peace of the said Lord King in the war or otherwise, or who had not

come to his peace and faith on the said day [1 November 1314], although they had been often summoned and lawfully expected, should be disinherited perpetually of lands and tenements and all other title within the Kingdom of Scotland.[7]

It was a move designed to reinforce Robert's position within his realm. He was a man of his word, after all, and more importantly was in a position to back himself up with action. Those who had failed to cross the line and join him were now excluded from his beneficence. Those who had supported him, meanwhile, especially his long-standing adherents from the uncertain years of 1306-8, could expect reward for sustained personal loyalty. Gilbert de la Haye was restored to the important office of Constable on 12 November, following the defection of the Earl of Atholl at Bannockburn. Neil Campbell, husband to Robert's sister Mary, was given custody of Atholl's former lands, which elevated him to the highest of noble ranks.[8] But Robert was conscious of the partisan divisions that had prevailed among his subjects since 1286 and caused dangerous political tensions during the Great Cause. He was therefore keen to exercise caution in his gift-giving, ensuring a balanced distribution of lands that did not solely favour his closest followers. It was a wise strategy that bound the broadest group of men to him as they saw universal opportunities for advancement, fostering a culture of continuous loyalty. Those who had received lands since 1308 were able to have their gifts reconfirmed in times of peace, which gave the holders more security in their lucrative titles and estates.

The king instructed the courts throughout the remainder of 1314 and into the summer of 1315 to undertake a royal inquiry into landownership and dues among the lay families, churches and within the burghs, to clarify and settle the greater changes that had taken place in landholding since the king had come to the throne. With the absence of many historical records, especially royal charters, which supported or confirmed these earlier land grants following the confiscation of these documents by Edward I in 1304, this royal inquiry was well timed and highly significant, for it provided clarification and political and social stability.[9] For Robert, it drew a line in the sand, marking the full restoration and reorganisation of his kingdom. News of the death of John Balliol on 25 November 1314, at the age of sixty-four, in Picardy, seemed to be propitious; his claim to the throne passed to his son Edward, who was Robert's junior by eleven years. The king was on a winning streak.

As the parliament drew to a close, the king moved to Dunfermline Abbey where on 16 November, during the Feast of St Margaret of Scotland, he issued a charter in favour of William Lamberton, Bishop of St Andrews, confirming his earlier grants of churches to Dunfermline which provided patronage and revenue to support the provision of the king's own mausoleum, which was commissioned next to that of Scotland's previous royal monarchs.[10] Even in victory, the king was looking to his afterlife and legacy. He had only turned forty the month after the Battle of Bannockburn.

Frustrated by lack of progress with the English, Robert was determined to force Edward back to the negotiating table. Marching at the head of his army, he crossed the border into England on 30 November, St Andrew's Day, and headed to the honour of Tynedale, which had previously been held by Alexander III of Scotland. The overwhelmed inhabitants, exhausted by years of attrition and not expecting English relief, willingly offered up their homage and fealty to the King of Scots.[11] To prove their new-found loyalty, they took it upon themselves to attack their pro-English neighbours.

As an act of further defiance, Robert granted the manor of Wark-on-Tyne to William de Soules and land in North Tynedale to Philip de Mowbray. It was without doubt aggressive posturing designed to irk Edward II into realising that further resistance to a permanent peace settlement would only further erode his royal dignity, being unable to raise an English army to defend the north owing to his internal political problems.[12]

The move appeared to have some effect, for talks were temporarily reopened with the English at Dumfries as the year drew to a close. However, they collapsed again shortly before Christmas, with the King of England still refusing to recognise Robert as king. What Robert was thinking at this moment can only be guessed at, but surely he was deeply frustrated. He had practically won back the whole of his kingdom except for Berwick, defeating the English in open battle despite unprecedented odds. He had successively invaded the north of England, regularly extracting tribute, prisoners and goods, grinding down the resolve and loyalty of its inhabitants. Yet his ultimate prize still eluded him. In deep despair, he took himself west on pilgrimage to Withorn in Galloway to venerate the shrine of St Ninian before he paused to celebrate the Christmas festivities.

As the new year began, Edward II was not to be found idle. The King of England wrote to his brother-in-law Louis X of France, who had recently succeeded to the Capetian throne following the premature death of his father Philip IV in a hunting accident on 29 November. The English king requested that Edward Balliol remain in England in his brother's household, sending a proxy to perform homage for the late John Balliol's lands in Picardy. Edward was forming plans for the Balliol heir. With Bruce's threat to disinherit his opponents in Scotland now enforced, those disaffected and still in England could be rallied under a Balliol banner; Edward Balliol's family cause could be reignited.

At the same time, Edward II ordered John of Lorn to invade the Isle of Man, which he did quickly and successfully. With the strategically important island taken, the Solway coast, which gave direct access to the former Balliol lordship of Galloway under the control of Edward Bruce, was once again open to attack. In March, John of Lorn was ordered to command a fleet of sixty ships with the purpose of transporting 10,000 men to invade his former lands in the Western Isles. Sir John Botetourt was created admiral of a fleet of ships on the east coast with orders to capture Scottish privateers as well as to blockade Flemish ships transporting supplies to Scottish shores.[13] If the King of England could not raise an army himself due to lack of funds, he could work behind the scenes to build a unified opposition to Bruce's growing hegemony.

By mid-February, however, keeping to the terms agreed in the autumn, the Scottish prisoners were finally exchanged for the Earl of Hereford and the remaining English captives. Their return marked a high point in Robert's reign, but it must have been a strange as well emotional occasion for them all, having not seen one another for eight years. The Lady Marjorie was now an adult, Queen Elizabeth almost a stranger to her husband and vice versa. Nor is it clear what burdens these women brought back with them, especially Mary Bruce, who had been caged at Roxburgh for some years. Isobel of Fife, who had crowned King Robert at Scone, did not return, having died some years earlier in misery.

After her release from her cage at Berwick in 1310, she had been forced to retire to the Carmelite convent in that town. Three years later she had passed into the custody of Henry de Beaumont, at which point she disappears from the record. It is highly unlikely that Robert would have abandoned her in his negotiations, and so it is safe to believe that she had died, achieving a different kind of freedom altogether.

With these women came Bishop Wishart of Glasgow, Andrew Murray of Avoch and Bothwell and Thomas Morham.[14] Disappointingly for the king, his nephew Donald, Earl of Mar, refused to come home, preferring to stay in England where he had built up a close relationship with the King of England. But Mar's absence was soon forgotten when the young Earl of Fife finally returned home of his own accord in the summer of 1315. As the premier earl of Scotland, whose chief role included crowning the King of Scots, his return was a boon for King Robert. To ensure that this awkward situation could not repeat itself, Fife surrendered his earldom to the king, who promptly restored it under an additional tailzie, or entail, which gave the king the legitimate right to assign the earldom to a new heir should the holder die childless. Robert was effectively ensuring that an Earl of Fife would always be present to crown any future king – all the more important because Edward II had allowed Fife to return on condition that his wife remained at the English court.[15] Ingram de Umfraville and David of Brechin also crossed the line to join King Robert.

On 25 February, the king was at Dumbarton, where he decided to remain for the next month. Here he oversaw the fitting out of a fleet of ships which was to be used for his next military venture. On 3 March, he granted to Walter Fitz Gilbert, the man responsible for the previous capture of the Earl of Hereford and others, the barony of Cadzow in Lanarkshire and adjacent lands, in return for twenty-two chalders of corn and six chalders of meat annually. (A chalder was a Scottish dry measure of about 3.5 cubic metres, depending on the material measured.) The king was in good company, for the charter was witnessed by Edward Bruce, Thomas Randolph, Abbot Bernard of Arbroath, Walter Stewart, John Menteith, James Douglas and James Lindsay of Barnweill.[16] Gilbert de la Haye, Robert Keith the Marischal, Alexander Fraser and Malcolm Fleming of Biggar were also at court.

Robert may have moved to St Andrews thereafter to spend time with his queen, hoping all the while to reconstitute a relationship that was fundamental to his longer-term hopes. He had held the throne for nine long, difficult years, but with Elizabeth's absence he had been unable to father any legitimate children to succeed him. He had one daughter, Marjorie, but the threat of female succession hung heavy in the minds of many following the calamity that had engulfed Scotland after the death of Margaret, the young Maid of Norway. Without the birth of a male heir, all of Robert's gains hung in the balance and his long-term legacy remained precariously uncertain, especially with Edward II attempting to promote the interests of Edward Balliol from England.

In April, the King of Scots summoned the nobles and leading ecclesiastical figures to parliament at Ayr. It was to be an important gathering, for there he decided to set down the royal succession, removing any doubt as to what should happen in the event of his death. The succession grant was given in favour of his male heirs yet to be born, followed by his brother Edward Bruce and any of Edward's sons thereafter. If both male lines should fail, then Marjorie was to inherit. The wording of his tailzie was geared towards the nearness of male degree, which was the very legal justification that had underpinned the Bruce claim to the throne first deployed by Robert Bruce V, Lord of Annandale, during the Great Cause.[17] It also placed emphasis on worthiness and strength, inasmuch as Edward Bruce was fit and able to secure the crown at a time when power would be carefully transferred from one man to another.[18] This reasoning was no doubt drawn from the Declaration of the Clergy in 1309–10, which had used such a point to strengthen Robert's own claim to the Kingdom of Scotland. In the unfortunate event that a minor should succeed, it was also decreed that Robert's nephew Thomas Randolph, Earl of Moray, should act as Guardian of the Realm and safeguard the adolescent king. Robert clearly placed great personal trust in Moray, who was now the leading figure at court alongside Edward Bruce.

Nevertheless, the settlement exposed a very clear vulnerability. Neither Robert or Edward had legitimate male heirs, and Marjorie, now nineteen, was without a husband. It is therefore no surprise that at the same parliament a marriage was arranged between Marjorie Bruce and Walter Stewart, High Steward of Scotland. The royal couple were given the valuable baronies of Bathgate and Ratho in Lothian as wedding gifts from a proud and loving father.[19] While no one could have known at the time, this marriage would bring Marjorie's son and the House of Stewart to the throne of Scotland towards the latter part of the fourteenth century. Two hundred years after that, their descendant James Stewart would become James VI of Scotland and James I of England.

Robert Bruce's sisters and their male heirs were not considered in the succession settlement, perhaps for fear of gifting a claim to other men not of the Bruce family lineage, at a time when Robert needed no internal rivals. At this juncture, Mary was married to Robert's long-standing supporter Neil Campbell. Maud Bruce, meanwhile, had married Hugh, son of the Earl of Ross, whose father had come over to Robert in October 1308; their first son and heir, William, was born in 1315. Christiana Bruce, married for the third time, was wife to Robert's other long-term ally Andrew Murray, who had also been in captivity in England until his recent release, at the same time as his wife. They would shortly receive the Garioch, a gift of land that had previously belonged to Robert when he himself was but Earl of Carrick.[20] The king, close to his family, made sure his sisters were well provided for, most certainly conscious of all they had gone through for supporting his cause.

In April, Robert was free to launch the next part of his strategy aimed at applying yet more pressure to Edward II to recognise Scotland's sovereignty. Ireland, off the western coast of England and Wales, was of strategic importance. Under the nominal rule of the King of England since 1170, English power was centred around Dublin. On too many occasions in the last three decades, had Anglo-Irish troops in the pay of English lords played a key role in successive invasions of Scotland. After all, John of Lorn had only just taken the Isle of Man with the help of the Bissets of Antrim. The broader Irishry, however, had much more in common with the Scots through their shared ancient Gaelic ancestry.

Robert and Edward Bruce between them saw the benefit of now focussing their ambitions and energies on Ireland with the aim to draw together a successful Hiberno-Scottish coalition, underpinned by the figureheads of two kings. Brotherhood, kingship and shared cultural identity were to become the new weapons of war. The High Kingship of Ireland had remained vacant for many years, so the plan was that Edward Bruce would land in Ireland with promises of liberation to secure it, uniting the Irish under one banner and together with Scotland posing a significant and very real threat to the King of England. The parliament at Ayr approved the Bruce brothers' adventure, and by the start of May the fleet was ready to sail. Robert oversaw the feasts of the Trinity on 18 May and Corpus Christi on the 22nd before the invasion was launched under the command of his brother. The King of Scots was to remain in Scotland for now.

The records are hazy, but in all it is likely that Edward Bruce's forces numbered between 4,000 to 6,000 men who were perhaps raised from the common levy, which meant they served for forty days. He could also count upon the support of Domnal O'Neill, King of Tyrone, whose lands were concentrated around Ulster and who may have been connected to Edward at the time of his fosterage with other Gaelic families during his childhood.[21] It is no surprise that when Edward first landed he focussed his energies on cultivating support from the areas around Ulster, Leinster and Thomond, where it is possible priests had been softening up the populace by preaching the benefits of the Scots' arrival.[22] It was O'Neill who had written to King Robert extending the initial invitation to claim the High Kingship after his success at the Battle of Bannockburn. The temptation to open another front that would threaten the King of England and free up some of his natural Irish supporters may also have been partly encouraged by previous obligations which Robert and his brother may have made during his winter months in exile as far back as 1306.[23] If this were true, Robert now had the opportunity to thank and repay the support he perhaps garnered during his darkest hours. Taking with him Thomas Randolph, Philip de Mowbray, John Stewart, Fergus of Ardrossan and many other knights, Edward Bruce set sail, landing at Glendun in Antrim on 26 May.[24] The army then headed to the English-held castle of Carrickfergus and began to lay siege to it in June.

On 6 June, Edward, under the watchful eye of his principal supporter Domnal O'Neill, was crowned High King of Ireland.[25] It must have been the pinnacle of Edward's career, and for the Bruce family, which now boasted two kings, it was a defining moment in their long history. From there, while the siege of Carrickfergus was still underway, Edward attacked the forces of Richard de

Burgh, Earl of Ulster and father to Queen Elizabeth, Robert's
wife, at Connor-in-Down on 1 September. De Burgh was routed
and subsequently fled into the west of Ireland. Roger Mortimer of
Wigmore, Edward II's contingency, was resoundingly defeated in
battle at Kells in Meath in December and forced to retreat.[26] The
Bruce brothers' campaign had been rewarded with great success so
far, but there was much to do before any real and tangible gains
could be proclaimed.

For Edward II, the Bruce invasion into Ireland was provocative
and very threatening. Rumours soon began to circulate that Robert
and his brother sought to build support among the Welsh, allowing
them the opportunity to invade England through Wales, which the
author of the *Vita* saw as a dangerous development, 'for these two
races [Welsh and Irish] are easily roused to rebellion'.[27] Rumour
became fact when a Bruce agent was caught by English officials
in Wales and found to be carrying letters addressed to the people
of that principality which were designed to be copied and widely
circulated. The content was damning:

> Since each Christian man is obliged to assist his neighbour
> in every difficulty, so also should those who proceed from a
> common root, who share the same race, ancestors, and country
> of origin. On that account we have now and for a long time
> been overwhelmed by sympathy with you in your servitude and
> oppression. Affronted by the vexations of the English, we are
> bound to attend to your plight, and, with the help of the Most
> High, to expel from the borders of your land with all force the
> unnatural and barbaric servitude imposed by the English, so that,
> as from earliest times, the Albanic and British people having
> expelled their enemies, should become one in perpetuity. Since no
> enemy is dispersed willingly or easily, and since the English yoke
> bears so heavily upon you as it did recently depress the Scottish
> people, we intend by your own efforts and with our irresistible
> assistance, you will be able to recover your full rights and to
> possess peacefully your prosperity and inheritance.[28]

At least one letter made it through, for the Steward of Cardiganshire,
Gruffydd Llwyd, responded, claiming that if Edward Bruce were to
come to Wales or send a representative in his place then Wales
would rise up for his cause.[29] To add to the growing hysteria,
Thomas Dun, a Scottish privateer, prowled the Irish Sea preying

on vulnerable ships as well as passing messages between Irish and Welsh clerics.[30] Edward II, without the finances to raise an army during a period of growing famine, and increasingly concerned by the very real possibility of an uprising in Wales, decided to regarrison his mighty Welsh strongholds, many built by Master James of St George following Edward I's conquest there in the 1280s. Armour for 100 crossbowmen and twenty footmen was sent from London to Beaumaris on the Isle of Anglesey alone.[31]

But war in 1315 came at a very real cost for all parties. At the start of that year most of western Europe was subject to heavy rainfall, which devastated crops and led to widespread starvation of the European populace. England and Wales were badly affected. Following the winter of 1315–16, Scotland and Ireland would fare no better when the cold, withered hands of famine reached into these lands during successive crop failures over the next two years. As the dearth grew worse in England in 1315, Robert was able to appropriate and redirect Irish exports of grain and revenue bound for England to Scotland instead, which meant Edward II found it increasingly difficult to supply his castles of Carlisle, Newcastle and Berwick. They suffered greatly as starvation weakened their respective garrisons.

In mid-September, Thomas Randolph returned briefly to Scotland, bringing with him five ships 'full of goods of the earth of Ireland', albeit it one of the vessels sank en route. On his return journey he ferried back 500 Scottish reinforcements to bolster Edward Bruce's campaign.[32]

At Berwick, Scottish privateers also preyed on English ships. On 30 October, Berwick-bound supply vessels were forced to throw stores of corn overboard to escape their Scottish pursuers.[33] Both natural disaster and Scottish pirates made Robert's future raids into the northern march all the more targeted and devastating. By the autumn of 1315, the price of victuals and wheat in England soared to unsustainable levels.[34] When famine struck in Scotland, Robert's people were also faced with severe hardship, but may have weathered it better than their English neighbours as they grew hardier oats, which may have been less affected by the vicious weather.[35]

Having watched his brother sail away at the end of May, King Robert turned his attention to the growing threat of John of Lorn, a man who seemed intent on being a persistent thorn in the king's side. After safely depositing Edward Bruce and his army on the

Antrim coast, the ships were sent back to Robert at Ayr. There, the king, along with his now son-in-law Walter Stewart, sailed the fleet up the Sound of Bute to the mouth of Loch Fyne and into East Loch Tarbert. Making use of well-known folklore, Robert was determined to enact prophecy:

> The Man that sails from shore to shore
> At Tarbert with his ships of war
> Shall grasp the Isles in his hand
> By force of arms none shall withstand.[36]

Cutting down trees, he rolled his ships across the Isthmus, a stretch of land that divides Loch Tarbert from east and west leading to the sea. According to the playful account in Barbour, the wind was with him, allowing the ships to roll easily over the logs as intended. Whether true or not, Bruce successfully crossed Loch Tarbert and fulfilled the prophecy. In an age of superstition, this was all that was required to bring to heel any recalcitrant chieftain who was thinking of challenging his overlord and joining the king's enemies. To hammer home his royal authority and reinforce his control in the region, the king created the sheriffdom of Argyll, with its seat at Tarbert, which developed into a royal burgh and prosperous castle port.[37] Following this achievement, Robert may have been tempted to focus next on recapturing the Isle of Man, but most likely lacked the necessary numbers to risk leaving Scotland and launching an attack. He instead left the job to his nephew Thomas Randolph who had been granted the island: Randolph eventually succeeded two years later.

With the Western Isles secured again, Robert could once more turn his attention towards northern England. With his brother opening up a front in Ireland, and the King of England increasingly burdened in times of growing famine, Robert was given free rein to raid again. Accompanied by James Douglas, Robert marched into the bishopric of Durham, and while King Robert remained at Chester-Le-Street, Douglas raided into Hartlepool. There, with his usual efficiency, Douglas put fear into the hearts of his opponents, many of whom fled on boats out into the sea to await his retreat. Those left behind, including many burgesses and their wives, were taken prisoner for ransoming. The people of the bishopric, exhausted by never-ending wartime attrition made worse by the breakdown of local law and order, bought yet another truce, this one running for two years and costing 1,600 marks.[38] The Scots, riding high, returned home.

The victory gave Robert an insatiable appetite. Three weeks later, he crossed the border again and made for Carlisle, where he and his father before him had been governor of the castle, providing a useful familiarity with the area. Carlisle was the main depot for incoming Irish supplies and so was ripe for the taking. Departing from their usual surprise tactics, Robert had decided to undertake a traditional siege, the reasons for which are not entirely apparent. Perhaps this was a cultivated attempt to highlight the futility of Edward II's position and ongoing opposition to the Scots king. James Douglas was set to work gathering provisions for the Scottish army by raiding the local suburbs and surrounding villages, while Robert oversaw the start of the siege by surrounding the walls and overseeing the assault on the city gates.

For five successive days they relentlessly assailed the walls, and on the fifth day deployed a siege weapon, possibly a stone-throwing trebuchet, which was unleashed on the Caldew Gate. Unfortunately for Robert, the castle and town were defended by Sir Andrew Harclay, who, predicting the Scottish attack, had ensured that Carlisle was well provisioned, not just in arms but in expensive war machines. The most devastating were the springalds on the parapets, used for discharging long arrows which could kill several men with a single shot.[39]

As the days wore on, the frustrated Scots resorted to their siege ladders at night, but the garrison were too alert for this approach to succeed. Robert attempted a deception by leading a very large cohort of his men to an assault of the eastern gate, hoping to draw the defenders from the far reaches of the town walls, freeing James Douglas and his small troop of men to scale a particularly high section of abandoned wall. Again, the deception proved futile, the lessons of the fall of Edinburgh, Roxburgh and elsewhere having been learnt by the English. On 1 August, after ten days of assault, Robert had achieved very little and with gritted teeth called off the siege, 'marching off in confusion' according to the chronicler of Lanercost.[40]

The failure to capture Carlisle appeared to mark a subtle change in the king's fortunes. Until now he had rarely tasted failure since regaining the greater part of his kingdom. In the late summer, after returning from the borders, he spent time at Inverkeithing with his queen, who may have recently miscarried or delivered a stillborn child.[41] The need for an heir was cruelly brought home to him and his wife. On 1 November, Robert was at Ayr granting lands in the barony of Kincardineshire to Alexander Fraser, who was soon to marry Robert's sister Mary, widowed earlier in the year following the death of her husband Neil Campbell. On 5 and 7 December respectively, he granted the sheriffdom and burgh of Cromarty to his brother-in-law Hugh Ross, husband to his sister Maud.[42] The year drew to a close at the abbey of Dunfermline, where King Robert held his Christmas court and brooded over his next move.

In January, the king took James Douglas into Lothian and there attempted a surprise attack on the town walls of Berwick, the last English-occupied castle in Robert's kingdom. A two-pronged attack was planned for a cloudy night, Robert moving by land, Douglas by sea. As they began their assault, the aim being to surreptitiously scale the walls, the skies suddenly cleared and both cohorts of men were quickly discovered and repulsed, Douglas himself narrowly avoiding capture. Despite their failure, King Robert opted to maintain pressure on the Berwick garrison. Utilising Scottish privateers, he blockaded the port, preventing supplies reaching a much-beleaguered garrison now under the command of Maurice de Berkeley.[43] The dearth of provisions, coupled with the growing onslaught of widespread famine, soon began to bite.

In February, one of their men, Edmund de Caillau, a kinsman of the murdered Piers Gaveston, left the castle with a force of 300 men in search of food by raiding into Teviotdale, although only fifty were fully armed and in good health. Before long, they were met by the much smaller force of James Douglas, where the two parties engaged in close hand-to-hand fighting. Douglas again narrowly escaped with his life, but in the ensuing conflict de Caillau was killed.[44] When the men returned to Berwick, the garrison sought vengeance, and one of their party, Robert Neville, threw down the gauntlet and invited Douglas and a band of men to meet him and others outside the walls of the town for a fight to the death. James accepted, and in the mêlée that followed, Neville, his brother Ralph and other English knights were killed. From this incident alone Douglas added to his fierce English reputation as 'the Black Douglas' and the more poetic and equally demonic 'foul devil of hell'.[45] Even so, Berwick remained in the hands of the English.

Robert's run of bad luck continued. Sometime in the spring of 1316, his daughter Marjorie Bruce unexpectedly died at the age of twenty. The stories of her demise differ, but one included a sudden illness shortly after the birth of her only child, a boy named Robert. According to another version, while heavily pregnant and out riding, Marjorie was thrown from her horse and killed instantly. To save her unborn child, a possible heir for her father, a rough caesarean was carried out on the roadside and the child was saved. Whatever the truth of it, Marjorie, married for just over a year, did not live to see her son grow up. No evidence survives to capture the king's reaction, but the loss of his only legitimate child must have proved devastating on both a personal as well as a political level.

Robert held parliament at Lent in Edinburgh, but little is known of proceedings for none of the records survive. Low-key talks with English envoys also appear to have been undertaken in the early months of 1316, but they, like so many before, proved abortive, for any short-term truce that had been agreed was over by 30 May.[46] Once more, a permanent peace looked as unachievable as ever. Robert must have despaired. While the king was at Melrose Abbey on 24 June, the second anniversary of the Battle of Bannockburn, he ordered the dispatch of Scottish forces back into England, which were mustered initially at the Park of Duns. The Scottish force travelled to Tynedale and through the much-beleaguered bishopric of Durham, which handed the payment promised a year before, guaranteeing them immunity from the savage marauding. Heading much further south, the Scottish force crossed the River Tees and there divided into three separate cohorts.

The first headed north-west and laid waste to Penrith and Carleton.[47] The second advanced into Richmond, where they received further payments to stave off destruction. The final cohort made for and subsequently burnt West Witton in Wensleydale, before crossing into Lancashire. Here their numbers were swelled by the second force, who had joined them after Richmond. From there they travelled to Furness and burnt the local villages, capturing large quantities of iron which they took with them back to Scotland by way of Copeland, which suffered similar treatment.[48]

During many of these successive raids, the lands of Thomas, Earl of Lancaster remained untouched, which led many in England to claim that Edward II's cousin was in league with Robert Bruce. These rumours failed to dissipate, and, as later events would show, were grounded in fact, although it is unclear precisely when the collusion first started between the two men. Perhaps to avoid further speculation, Robert's forces raided the lands of the earl for the first time. In response, the duplicitous Lancaster made a show of raising men with a view to bringing the marauding Scots to heel. It was the first time he showed an appetite for it. By the end of September, Thomas had gathered a sizeable force at Newcastle, where he anticipated that his cousin the king would join him. But Edward chose not to arrive, still seeking revenge for the death of his lover Piers Gaveston, who had been murdered in 1312 at the hands of his powerful relation. With both sides unable to overcome the other through strength of arms, the tensions between them overrode everything at this time, which destabilised the English government and burdened the country with political turmoil. Civil war could erupt at any time.[49] Without further support, Lancaster disbanded his forces, perhaps knowing all along that his gesture was nothing more than that, a gesture.

In September, Edward Bruce achieved a breakthrough in Ireland with the fall of Carrickfergus Castle after a prolonged siege in a country now deeply affected by famine. He had thus gained a strong foothold, allowing him to exercise control over the greater part of Ulster, giving him control of the Antrim coast. Returning to Scotland, on 30 September he met Robert at Cupar in Fife, where, during a council of prelates, earls and barons, the increasingly fractious relationship between himself and Thomas Randolph was settled. As Robert's heir and now High King of Ireland, Edward was increasingly jealous of the special relationship between his brother and Randolph, and may have felt that the Isle of Man, previously granted to Thomas, ought to come to him instead as his brother's lawful heir.

The island at this time was still under the control of John of Lorn, but to settle the issue Robert made his view perfectly clear. The island was to remain in the hands of his nephew Thomas, and to this effect a re-grant was made by charter and was witnessed by Edward as High King of Ireland.[50] In return, Edward expected and probably negotiated much-needed reinforcements, his own troops greatly weakened by widespread pestilence. His rule in Ireland had so far not been widely acknowledged despite his title, with the Irish clans often at war with one another over competing local interests. Many held deeply divided opinions on the Bruce landing. Some felt Edward was no different to the English occupiers, while others saw him as a fellow countryman bound to them by ancestry and deserving of their loyalty. Yet in times of great hardship, with scarcely any food to eat, the presence of an occupying force in the Irish midst was a burden many found unwelcome and poorly timed. As a result, Edward Bruce was far from popular.

In early autumn, the threat of an English army heading into Scotland abated. Edward II had ordered a muster to Newcastle for 8 July, but few had responded to the summons, so it was delayed until 10 August and then again to 6 October. Eventually, realising that a muster was simply unachievable when so many were starving and malnourished, the muster was abandoned altogether. The timing was right, for 9 October saw the death of the Bishop of Durham, Richard Kellaw, which resulted in growing tension between the King of England and his cousin, who both proffered candidates for Kellaw's replacement. In the end, Queen Isabella promoted her own candidate, Louis de Beaumont, to the vacant see.[51] Meanwhile, English envoys were sent to broker a peace with the King of Scots while Edward II appointed the Earl of Arundel as Warden of the Scottish March on 19 November and Roger Mortimer as Lieutenant of Ireland on 23rd.[52]

On the 21st, the royal envoys arrived at the border town of Jedburgh while Robert resided at Melrose. The King of Scots appointed representatives to negotiate on his behalf, including John Menteith and Thomas Randolph, who, after initial discussions, were granted safe-conducts to travel to York to complete the temporary peace settlement, which was duly agreed. This agreement between England and Scotland gave Robert the opportunity to join his brother in Ireland, where he could help to shore up Edward's failing campaign. This was not what Edward II had hoped to achieve. As preparations were made, Robert rode to Glasgow on 26 November for the funeral of his long-time friend and mentor Bishop Wishart of Glasgow, who had finally succumbed to old age. He then saw out Christmas at Coupar Angus Abbey with his wife, Queen Elizabeth.

As January dawned, the king joined Thomas Randolph at Loch Ryan and took ship with his army for Larne in Ireland, leaving James Douglas behind as Lieutenant of Scotland with the support of Walter Stewart. From there the royal party rode to meet Edward Bruce at the recently captured Carrickfergus, where he was holding court. With his brother's campaign stalled by infighting among the Irish chieftains, Robert, well aware of the powerful application of prophecy and symbolism, encouraged Edward to ride out and make the traditional progress of the High King through the five provinces of Ulster, Meath, Leinster, Munster and Connaught. It was a move designed to show the strength and capability of Ireland's new king and demonstrate the alternative to English rule. It would also have the potential to draw the Anglo-Irish out to battle under the command of Edmund Butler.

The journey south began well enough. Accompanied by Randolph and Domnal O'Neill, King of Tyrone, they attacked the lands of pro-English lords, and by mid-February had reached Slane in Meath. The host must have been approximately 3,000 to 4,000 strong, for when they reached the manor of the Earl of Ulster at Ratoath, Richard de Burgh fled to the walled town of Dublin rather than stand and fight his son-in-law and the king's brother.[53] Familial bonds were not enough to guarantee support, but nevertheless, as the joint Bruce army advanced towards the villages beyond the town walls of Dublin, the threat of a siege was enough to convince the mayor to seize and imprison the Earl of Ulster lest he have a change of heart and find a way to let the Scots into the town.[54]

Edward II's supporters were clearly feeling suspicious, having thus far failed to achieve any victory against the Bruces' Irish endeavour. The imprisonment of the Earl of Ulster mattered little anyway, for both Robert and Edward were focussed on the royal progress and their aim to unite the Irish clans, not a protracted siege of a substantial town that would take months or years to overcome. They rode south-west into Leinster and Munster, shadowed by a smaller force commanded by Edmund Butler, Edward II's Justiciar of Ireland, who had as few as 220 men-at-arms, 300 light horse and 400 foot.[55] Neither side committed to any meaningful battle.

News arrived in the Scots camp that the chief of O'Brien clan had promised the High King and his party Gaelic Irish support should they sweep west. Buoyed by the potential to gain further men for his cause, Edward and Robert with their joint army headed west to rendezvous with O'Brien and his clan at the bank of the River Shannon. However, they were to be bitterly disappointed, for in the weeks between the letter arriving and their march, the clan chief had been defeated in battle by his rival, Muirchertach O'Brien, who then took up position at the river with a force of arms hostile to the Bruces.[56] Without hope of unity, the High King withdrew, the campaign beginning to falter as food and provisions began to run out, especially while they were in the south-west, the most hard-hit region during the ongoing famine.

Limping to Limerick, they were denied entry, and as starvation and dysentery set in, swathes of the Bruce army began to grow sick. In the clutches of catastrophe, there was little option but to turn north and beat a gruelling march back to Ulster. On the way, at Leinster, they skirmished with the forces of Edmund Butler, who must have accurately judged the poor condition of the Scots army. During the retreat, many more died of hunger while the rest, according to the chronicler Fordun, slaughtered their horses for sustenance, so desperate had their situation become.[57] To make matters worse, news reached the army that Roger Mortimer of Wigmore, now Lieutenant of Ireland, had landed with fresh reinforcements on 7 April at Youghal, having sailed from Bristol. The threat he posed was now a very real one, given the poor condition of the Bruce army.

Nor had the progress achieved its goals. In the Annals of Connacht, the author captured the mood of the populace, many of whom went so far as to identify the presence of the Bruce brothers and their army as the very cause of the famine itself, given they had stripped the land bare of what little could be found as they had marched from place to place.[58] Failing to unite the Gaelic Irish clans under his banner, and without any significant gain over the Anglo-Irish, the Bruce Irish endeavour was looking highly compromised and ineffective. Robert had failed to help his brother consolidate his position. Without much opportunity to help him further because of dwindling forces, and with news arriving from home that skirmishes had taken place on the northern march, Robert knew he needed to head back to Scotland, which he did at Pentecost on 22 May.[59]

During his absence, the Earl of Arundel, appointed by the King of England as Lieutenant of the Scottish March, had crossed into Scotland on 23 April with a large enough force to harry the surrounding area of Liddesdale. Arundel appointed Thomas Richmond, who led a cohort of men hoping to capture James Douglas at Lintalee near Jedburgh, but, true to form, Douglas got wind of the oncoming raiding party and was able to set a trap. The English walked into the ambush, and in the fighting that followed Thomas Richmond was killed.[60] With this minor Scots victory, Arundel lost his nerve and beat a hasty retreat back into England.

In the week before Robert set sail from Ireland, a much more serious invasion had unfolded on the Scottish east coast. The townsfolk of Humberside, thoroughly disenchanted and irked by the Scots' annual raids, grouped together and sailed their enterprise up the Firth of Forth towards Fife. As they glided up river, the Earl of Fife and his sheriff cautiously followed their progress from the banks with a Scots force, readying the defence for when the English party would land, which they did at Inverkeithing. As the invaders disembarked, the Scots soon realised that they were in fact outnumbered – many of the English most likely had been hidden below deck – and had little choice but to retreat inland.[61] There the defending Scots met up with William Sinclair, Bishop of Dunkeld, who was advancing to rendezvous with them with a force of sixty horsemen. With their numbers bolstered, the earl, bishop and sheriff returned and routed the men of Humberside, who were either cut down during their retreat or drowned as they fled. Only a handful made it back to England alive.[62]

As Robert landed back in Scotland to hear of the raid into Fife, he was soon to receive altogether more disturbing news from the continent, initially arriving at his court as unofficial hearsay and latterly from his Scottish supporters at Avignon. On 28 March 1317, with the encouragement of Edward II, Pope John XXII issued a bull of excommunication levelled at King Robert and his brother, Edward, citing their invasion into Ireland and ongoing skirmishes into northern England, as well as their refusal to acknowledge Edward II's rights in Scotland, as just cause for the papal censure.[63] It was a devastating pronouncement which placed both men beyond the reach of the Church, barring them from taking the Sacrament and being buried in holy ground. To mitigate the damage, Robert forbade the publication of the papal decree in Scotland, perhaps in fear that his subjects, quick to forget the success of Bannockburn, may attribute famine, failed recognition of Scottish independence and increasing failure in Ireland as God's judgement on himself.

To make matters worse, Robert's chosen candidate to replace the recently departed Robert Wishart as Bishop of Glasgow,

Stephen de Donydover, was turned away from the papal palace at Avignon, his title remaining unconfirmed when he died some months later while still abroad. Papal relations were now more than frosty.[64] Shortly afterwards, John XXII imposed a truce between the Scots and the English. The Holy Father no longer favoured Robert and his subjects, believing their actions were the reason preventing the King of England from taking up the papal call to Crusade in the Holy Land. The English diplomatic machine had been working overtime.

The summer of 1317 saw a lull in activity at Robert's court. The weather improved greatly, and for the first time in two years the harvest looked promising. On 1 June, the King of Scots was at Scone along with Thomas Randolph, who had returned from Ireland. Along with James Douglas, Randolph witnessed the king's gift of Skene in Aberdeenshire to Robert Skene.[65] Two weeks later, he was still there attending either a meeting of his council or parliament, the records being somewhat unclear.[66] Shortly afterwards, a papal dispensation was received at court, granting Edward Bruce the right to marry Isabel, daughter of William, Earl of Ross, dated to 1 June, given that the two were too closely related under Canonical law. Such permission gave Robert hope that in the absence of a male heir of his own, at least Edward had the chance to fill the gap. Leaving Scone, the king ventured to Arbroath where he stayed until at least 7 July. By the 24th, he had moved on to Melrose Abbey along with James Douglas, Randolph, Walter Stewart, Robert Keith the Marischal, Patrick, Earl of Dunbar as well as the bishops of St Andrews and Dunblane.[67] Here they awaited the arrival of the pope's official envoys, who carried the formal papal letters of excommunication.

When they arrived, Robert immediately resorted to delaying tactics, keeping them waiting for weeks until late August. The letters, given their content, were not addressed to him as King of Scots, but rather his lesser, previous titles, which gave the king the opportunity to refuse to read them for fear of undermining his own position. In doing so, he temporarily avoided both the formal pronouncement of his excommunication and also the papal truce detailed in the documents. This was fully intended, for Robert was still fixed on overcoming the garrison at Berwick, with the town still blockaded by Scottish privateers. Before embarking for war, the king called a parliament at Edinburgh on

16 and 17 September where the papal letters were discussed. It was agreed that the earls, prelates and barons would pen a letter to the pope outlining their advice to their king, which was that he should not read the papal decrees given they had not properly addressed him as King of Scots and were therefore prejudicial to him. The letter was sealed and accompanied by a second letter from Robert himself.[68]

At the same time, and probably in concert with one another, Domnal O'Neill, King of Tyrone, and other Irish supporters drew up the Remonstrance of the Irish Princes, a document that was timed to reach Avignon at the same moment as the Scottish letters. The Remonstrance warned the pope against English slanders and went into great detail assuring him of Edward Bruce's right to the High Kingship of Ireland through a line of 197 ancient kings starting with Brutus himself that was only broken with the invasion of the English in 1170. This invasion, the Remonstrance made clear, had brought terrible atrocities on the people of Ireland, atrocities that were also inflicted on the Irish Church. Worn down and desperate for salvation, the Irish princes had elected a head of their own, and so Edward Bruce, and he alone, had the right to rule Ireland.[69] It was compelling propaganda, and designed to outmanoeuvre Edward II's envoys at Avignon and turn the tide of papal censure away from the Bruces. While it did not have an immediate effect, it certainly sowed the seeds for a weakening of papal anathema.

In October, Robert began to tighten his hold over the town of Berwick by intensifying the blockade. The garrison was now greatly worn down and in dire health. At the same time, in the autumn, Thomas Randolph was in a position to lead a force of men to the Isle of Man, where he quickly ejected John of Lorn, who fled, dying a year later. At Christmas, the king was at Newbattle Abbey, a daughter house of Melrose Abbey, where he used the Christmas period to hand out further gifts of patronage to knights loyal to him. In late January 1318, he confirmed Nicholas Scrymgeour, son of Alexander III's former standard bearer, as keeper of Dundee Castle, and on 10 February further lands were gifted to him which had previously belonged to the Balliols.[70] On 26 February, while at Clackmannan, the king may well have received an exciting and much-needed fillip in the guise of a secret offer from a man and his wife within Berwick, promising to betray the town to the Scots. Considering this an unmissable opportunity, Robert set plans into motion.

The letter had come from Peter of Spalding, who had apparently been a victim of xenophobic harassment because he had married a Scotswoman. Losing patience with his neighbours, Spalding took a great personal risk and penned a letter which he got out to Robert Keith the Marischal, who in turn passed it on to King Robert. As the living conditions at Berwick had steadily deteriorated, tensions had mounted between the townsfolk and the military garrison, who used their strength to the disadvantage of the general populace. As the rapacity of the garrison grew and provisions quickly dwindled, the people complained to Edward II, who responded, giving them command of the town walls while the garrison retained control of the castle. Spalding promised Robert that on the night when he was scheduled to guard a section of the wall he would allow entry to the Scots should they come.

Robert did not hesitate. On 1 April, the Scots massed at the Park of Duns and silently approached the town. As agreed, under the cover of darkness they scaled the section of wall left clear by Spalding. Once they were over, hard fighting broke out. The garrison, unable to fend off the Scots, retreated behind the walls of the castle, leaving their enemy in possession of the much-prized town. Eleven days later, on the 12th, King Robert himself rode to Berwick to see the siege first hand, bringing with him an army from Teviotdale, Lothian and Mease. Thomas Randolph was tasked with completing the job, which was expected to take some time.

Leaving a Scottish division to carry on the siege, the rest of the army then headed into northern England to raid, both to commandeer provisions for the besiegers and also to stave off any English relief force sent north to break the Scottish siege lines. The Scots were at Harbottle on 21 May before moving to Wark and Mitford, raiding as far south as Newcastle.[71] During a separate chevauchée, James Douglas and Thomas Randolph together raided into Yorkshire, burning Northallerton and Boroughbridge on 28 May, later extracting protection money of £1,000 from the townsfolk of Ripon. Given the large sum, which the people of the town could not immediately muster, six hostages among the burgesses were taken prisoner. Two years later, the wives of these men petitioned the King of England for help as the townsfolk had failed to raise the promised money and the Scots therefore refused to return their husbands. In response to the immediate threat in 1318, and again without hope of raising an army to fend off the Scots, the King of England ordered the lords and burgesses of Yorkshire to raise what men they could to defend the north.[72] It was an ineffective defence. Fuelled by their successes, Douglas and Randolph went on to burn Knaresborough and Skipton-in-Craven before heading back to Berwick.[73]

By the start of June, two months after the fall of the town, the castle garrison at Berwick, led by Roger Horsley, looked close to surrender. King Robert returned on 5 June to oversee the capitulation on the 18th, which was driven largely by starvation. The capture of the castle was strategically significant. For the first time in his twelve-year reign, King Robert had regained the entirety of the Kingdom of Scotland as had belonged to Alexander III, who had died in 1286. It had not been easy, as shown by the Berwick garrison's determination to hold out until the bitter end. To show his gratitude, a much-relieved king rewarded Peter of Spalding with lands previously belonging to the Earl of Angus, including a role as Keeper of the Forest of Kilgarie.[74]

Given the energy required over the last few years to win Berwick, Robert broke with his traditional strategy of slighting castles, and ordered that the fortifications be improved, overseen by the Flemish engineer John Crab, and created his son-in-law Walter Stewart as Governor. To bolster his royal authority in the region, he appointed either Alexander Seton or Robert Lauder as Sheriff of Berwickshire. Lastly, the king was careful to provision the town and castle to last for a year's siege, knowing all too well that Edward II would intend to march north to retake it.[75]

Robert's defiance in taking Berwick and sacking northern England was not well received at the papal court at Avignon. Enraged by the King of Scots' actions, the pope responded by placing the whole of Scotland under interdict in June. The bull did not merely prohibit Robert and his brother Edward from access to the Church, but also applied the same rules to all subjects of the Kingdom of Scotland. Church services were prohibited, and the pope absolved all Scottish subjects of their oaths of allegiance to their king. It was a dangerous moment, which could have so easily worked against him; but Robert, sensing the need to keep control of the situation, simply ignored the papal declaration and ordered his subjects to continue in their religious observations as normal. It did nothing to endear him to the heir of St Peter. The same bull was read aloud in England that September, with the intention of reminding the people of King Edward's just cause in refusing to acknowledge Robert as King of Scots.[76] The war of words would rumble on.

Ignoring papal anathema, King Robert headed to the cathedral of St Andrews on 5 July to preside over the dedication ceremony. The cathedral, which had been under construction since the twelfth century, had been ready some years earlier, but now was the right time to conduct the ceremony. Accompanied in a show of unity by seven bishops, fifteen abbots and nearly all the nobles and barons of Scotland, Robert's ceremony went off without a hitch.[77] Six days later, Robert celebrated his forty-fourth birthday. But as the heady days of summer began to wane, so too did the king's recent good fortune.

Desperate news arrived in late October that his brother Edward, recently reinforced by a great army of Scots, had marched out of Ulster and engaged John de Bermingham in battle at Faughart near Dundalk, close to where Edward had been inaugurated as High King of Ireland years earlier. With a Scots force of approximately 3,000, the battle had grown fierce, and in the intense fighting Edward Bruce had been killed. His corpse was mutilated, his head being sent to Edward II in a bucket of salt. His limbs were separated for display across Ireland as the usual warning to would-be renegades.[78] For his efforts, a very grateful King of England rewarded Bermingham with the earldom of Louth in May the following year.

For Robert, the loss of his last surviving brother, who died without a legitimate heir, was devastating. The horror of his end was made all the more real as the king knew his brother had died an excommunicate and was therefore unable to receive salvation in death. In a deeply spiritual age, and with a conventional piety expressed throughout his life, Robert must have been deeply affected. On the political side, the succession hung in the balance once more, for the king's only living heir was his two-year-old grandson and namesake, Robert Stewart.

By the autumn of 1318, the King of Scots also knew that the years of carte blanche to harry the English were coming to an end. Since the victory at Bannockburn, Edward II's preoccupation with domestic affairs, especially his conflicts with his cousin Thomas of Lancaster, had brought English politics almost to breaking point. But as 1318 unfolded, the King of England and his overmighty earl had been urged by a desperate nobility to seek some form of peace, however hollow. On 7 August, they exchanged the kiss of peace before the papal cardinals Gaucelin d'Eauze and Luke Fieschi, and on 9 August the Treaty of Leake was agreed, a formal indenture designed to settle their differences. As part of that process, there was a general agreement that now united them: Edward II could once more turn his attention towards Scotland. At an English parliament at York on 20 October, the English king, having just received the head of Edward Bruce in a basket, summoned his forces to a general muster at Newcastle for 10 June 1319. Hearing of the staggering £53,062 raised for the English war effort, Robert knew that Edward intended the kind of full-scale invasion not seen in four years.[79] Once more, he would be called upon to defend his title and the independence of his kingdom.

PART THREE

Perseverance & Victory

For as long as but a hundred of us remain alive, never will
we under any conditions be brought under English rule.
It is in truth not for glory, nor riches, nor honours that
we are fighting, but for freedom – for that alone, which no
honest man gives up but with life itself.

The Declaration of Arbroath, 1320

11

United We Stand

Facing the threat of yet another mass confrontation with the English, and only too aware of the personal losses he and the Bruce family had endured since 1306, Robert's anxieties got the better of him. With his brother Edward dead, and his only daughter also in the grave, the succession settlement of 1315 required urgent revision. With the number of candidates who could follow him to the throne swiftly dwindling, Robert's kingship was once more vulnerable, for if he fell in battle his only living heir was his sole grandson, Robert Stewart. The succession of a two-year-old boy could unravel everything. Years of struggle and sacrifice to secure the crown could be undone in the blink of an eye.

On 3 December 1318, Robert and his magnates, lay and ecclesiastic, made their way to Scone for parliament. The order of business was varied, including the ongoing work of codifying laws and settling complex land disputes, but the central theme rested on securing the succession and, by default, the Bruce family legacy. Building on the settlement of three years prior, a further tailzie was drawn up which stipulated that if Robert died without male issue the crown would pass to his grandson, Robert, the only living heir of Marjorie and her husband, Walter Stewart. Should this precious child come to the throne while still underage, he and the realm were to be watched over by a nominated guardian, specified as Thomas Randolph, Earl of Moray. If Moray himself was called to an early grave, the guardianship would then pass to the next best man, James Douglas, laying down something of a royal insurance policy.[1] In the circumstance that Robert

Stewart himself died without any male issue, either before or after King Robert I, then and only then would the claim of any living daughters of Robert Bruce or the heirs of Robert's sisters be upheld.

Perhaps somewhat short-sightedly, the act failed to specify any order of seniority in this situation; although precedents could be applied, this was a major oversight. With the details discussed and agreed, Robert insisted that the assembly swear an oath to uphold the succession settlement, and the king and his son-in-law, Walter Stewart, took their vow on the gospels and relics found at Scone Abbey.[2] For all involved, it was a carefully devised ceremony, designed to extract a visible and solemn expression of loyalty both to King Robert himself but also to his family's future fortunes, thereby guaranteeing at least in theory, the future security of the Scottish kingdom. To ensure adherence, Robert had the settlement proclaimed throughout his kingdom via the sheriffs, and copies of the act were made by dutiful clerics who kept them safe in various chanceries. Anyone who sought to undermine the settlement was to be branded a traitor and suffer the full penalty of the law.[3]

With part of his anxiety allayed, Robert's attention turned back to war. At the same parliament, a sheriff's 'wappinschaw' or general inspection was decreed, set for 15 April 1319, in preparation for the forthcoming conflict with the English. As part of it, all laymen holding lands worth £10 or more and who were legally obliged to maintain a lance or a sword needed to be ready to have their weapons inspected. So too did lesser men worth the equivalent of a cow or more, whose responsibility it was to maintain either a lance or a bow with twenty-four arrows.[4] As war preparations got underway, the king spent Christmas at either Arbroath or Berwick, and in January sent Randolph and possibly Douglas into the marches to collect the tribute that had previously been promised from various English towns in the last year or more. On 25th of that month, the Earl of Moray was at Lochmaben Castle, where he received representatives from the communities of Cumberland and Westmoreland, who had come to settle their extracted tribute of 600 marks.[5]

Every penny they could gather could only help fund the Scottish war effort and reduce the English war chest. The king may have led a small force himself across the border to Dunstanburgh in Northumberland to attack and disrupt the erection of a small castle by Thomas, Earl of Lancaster. Whether Lancaster and Bruce were in wider collusion at this point is not exactly clear, but the construction of a fortification so close to the Scottish border was unwelcome at any rate, a point that Robert made all too clear by his successful chevauchée.

Yet, for all the action undertaken in the last few months, the king himself must have still been dogged by anxiety and nagging uncertainty. His failure to secure wider recognition of the legitimacy of his rule was a predicament that continued to undermine him. It was a constant thorn in his side. Until he had achieved it, there would be no rest in a long-standing conflict that still had no end in sight. He was getting older, and his health, never robust, could at times fail him dangerously. He was also painfully aware of the many people he had lost along the way. As his brooding grew deeper and perhaps melancholic over the late winter, Robert's fears focussed on that centuries-old Bruce family curse that had appeared to haunt them for generations.

On 8 February, the king made his way to the Cistercian abbey of Coupar Angus and made votive offerings to the dead St Malachy O'Moore. His offering was not just a simple candle lit while in kneeled prayer; like his grandfather before him, the king offered a lamp that could burn perpetually at the saint's altar. To further support the gift, Robert granted lands in Perthshire to fund the scheme, which also ensured prayers should be given by the monks on his behalf during their daily services. He must have hoped that his spiritual care for St Malachy would ultimately be rewarded by the saint's holy intercession. It was a powerful gesture, and while Robert espoused a conventional piety, it seems most likely that the very personal losses he and his family had endured were never far from his mind. Kneeling in prayer was the accepted way of dealing with grief. The recent death of his last brother, Edward, was yet another reminder of how precarious life could be.

Throughout the spring, the King of Scots remained in Lothian, ensuring that the defences of Berwick were robust enough to stave off the imminent threat heading their way. On 25 March, the king, together with the Bishop of St Andrews, the earls Fife and Moray, as well as Walter Stewart and James Douglas, granted lands at Tranent near Haddington and Elphinstone, Gogar and Dundas to Alexander Seton, the man who had betrayed the English on the first night of the Battle of Bannockburn.[6] On 1 May, in high spirits and careful as ever to remember those who had supported him when he needed it most, Robert awarded Peter of Spalding lands in Angus. Satisfied that the defence of Berwick had been well planned and prepared, the king turned his attention to the western part of the march, heading into his ancestral homeland, where at Lochmaben he awarded Thomas and Simon Kirkpatrick lands which had been previously forfeited to the Crown.[7] Their father had been a companion of Robert's during the deadly encounter with John Comyn in 1306 in the church of the Greyfriars at Dumfries which had set Bruce on his fateful play for the crown. The king clearly had a long memory.

In England, now that Edward II and Thomas, Earl of Lancaster had secured a somewhat fragile peace between them, the King of England turned his attention back to Scotland. Focussing the start of his campaign on Berwick made strategic sense, given that the English no longer held castles beyond the border in which to centre themselves before going on the offensive through Lothian and elsewhere. Orders given at York for a muster at Newcastle for 10 June were extended to 22 July, allowing time for the necessary men, equipment and supplies to be assembled.[8] Writs of summons went out and by July approximately 10,000 men had mustered: 1,400 cavalry, 1,200 hobelars and 7,500 foot soldiers and other men-at-arms.[9] Edward expected to be in the north for more than a season, so he ordered the royal administration, the Chancery and the Exchequer, to relocate from Westminster to York. Queen Isabella and her ladies also accompanied her husband, taking up residence in a manor house outside the town walls of York while the king travelled on to Newcastle to meet his troops in June. From there Edward headed into Scotland.

The King of England's forces, with the earls of Lancaster, Hereford, Pembroke, Surrey, Arundel and the newly styled Earl of Norfolk, who was the king's half-brother Thomas of Brotherton, arrived below the walls of Berwick on 8 September. They promptly began their assault despite the immediate absence of siege engines which had not yet arrived.[10] King Robert, not present for the risk of being cornered at Berwick was too great, left the defence of the town and castle to his captains Alexander Seton, Robert Keith, Adam Gordon, Walter Stewart and Patrick, Earl of Dunbar, who each responded to the King of England's assault from land and sea with a stout defence. The assembled English navy of seventy-seven vessels under the command of Simon Driby, which cost £1,725, was immediately put to good use. In an attempt to scale the walls before the siege engines could be called up, a small boat was somehow fixed to the mast of a ship and, when filled with men, hoisted up to the level height of the town walls with the aim of lowering a ramp or bridge over the parapet. This endeavour, creative as it was, failed when the ship ran aground, and the Scots garrison promptly attacked it and set it alight.[11]

After fierce fighting on both sides, a five-day respite ensued while Edward II and his war council called up the necessary siege engines from nearby Bamburgh and further afield. While the men sat idle, news arrived in camp that the Scots had crossed the border and were harrying villages around Carlisle, hoping to draw the English away from Berwick. In response, Edward II sent 1,200 hobelars under the command of Sir Andrew Harclay to track them down while the siege continued.[12] Fighting resumed on 13 September, and the garrison was nearly overcome, but in the end the English were beaten back again. The Scots had taken so long to capture the town; they were certainly not going to give it up without a real fight. However, just before a third assault could take place, disturbing news arrived at the English camp – news King Robert had hoped would cause division.

Sir Andrew Harclay had failed to capture his quarry.[13] Instead, the Scots contingent under the command of Thomas Randolph, Earl of Moray, and James Douglas had slipped south of Carlisle and marched through County Durham into Yorkshire, heading under the cover of darkness each night towards York. Perhaps on a tip-off from turncoat Edmund Darel, an English royal household knight, the Scots appeared to have one mission in mind: the abduction of Queen Isabella.[14] The plot was prematurely sprung when a spy, possibly Darel, was caught at York and placed under interrogation, confessing to William Melton, Archbishop of York, and Lord Chancellor John de Hothum, Bishop of Ely. With the cream of the York garrison fighting with the king at Berwick, the queen was brought behind the safety of the town walls, but it was quickly decided to send her further south, by way of the rivers Ouse and Trent, to the relative safety of Nottingham Castle.[15] Isabella had a lucky escape. If Robert had succeeded in capturing her, he most certainly would have been in a position to dictate the terms of the queen's release, giving him his ultimate prize: recognition of his status and the independence of his kingdom.[16] To have lost his quarry must have come as a bitter disappointment, yet the presence of his men so far behind the English lines could still be played to his advantage.

With the queen safely dispatched to the south, it fell to the Archbishop of York, the Lord Chancellor and the town mayor, Nicholas Fleming, to raise what men they could find among the clergy and the peasantry to head off the advancing cohort of Scots led by Randolph and Douglas on 12 September. The brave but doomed English militia found the heavily armed and well-trained Scots 12 miles beyond the town at Myton, near Boroughbridge. The subsequent clash quickly turned into a massacre as the militia were slaughtered, with the mayor cut down and dismembered, while Melton and Hothum narrowly escaped back to York.[17] Such was the carnage that the whole event became known as the 'Chapter of Myton' on account of the large number of clergymen killed defending their town. For Douglas, his deep-rooted reputation with the English as the 'black dog' would only have been reinforced by these events.

The massacre at Myton threw Edward and his war council at Berwick into confusion, with divisions immediately opening up about what to do next, perhaps as King Robert had intended. Lancaster had already grown intolerant of his cousin. With the Scots at large in England and York without a strong garrison to defend the walls of this major town, many northern magnates – including Lancaster, who held considerable northern estates which were now vulnerable to attack – wanted to break the siege and head south to defend their property from Randolph and Douglas. The remaining war council, led by the king and made up of mostly southern lords, wanted to continue the siege, Edward himself suggesting that they divide their forces, one continuing at Berwick while the other should hunt down the Scots as they returned to their homeland. Debates became heated, tempers flared, and Lancaster promptly packed up and left with his men, approximately one-third of the army, returning to their estates without Edward's permission.[18] Incensed, Edward II had no choice but to break his siege lines and return to England, retreating from Berwick for Newminster Abbey in Northumberland. As he moved south, he hoped to meet the retreating Scots, but Randolph and Douglas, perhaps expecting this, made a withdrawal back across the Pennines, before sweeping through the northern march, burning and pillaging in their wake.[19]

No sooner had the siege of Berwick dispersed than rumours of Lancaster's collusion with King Robert began to resurface. Hugh Despenser the Younger, increasingly a dangerous favourite of Edward II and now his chamberlain, wrote on 21 September to the sheriff of Glamorgan, who was looking after Despenser's affairs. He went so far as to claim that the Earl of Lancaster was in league with the King of Scots, and that together they had orchestrated the recent events at York. It soon became clear that this feeling was widely shared. Rumours abounded that the earl had allowed Randolph, Douglas and their men through his lines unmolested, having taken a bribe of £40,000 from the King of Scots to help bring about the end of the English campaign.[20] An increasingly despondent and frustrated English army failed to understand why the campaign had ended before it really began. Even the chroniclers felt there was truth behind the rumours, the *Vita* lamenting, 'O noble earl, why do you not recall to mind the chosen generation, the royal stock which you disgrace ... how great a charge is the crime of broken faith!'[21]

Lancaster, desperate to curb the gossip, hit back: 'I cannot stop up the mouths of men, but I can offer to clear myself either by the decision of a good man, or if it be necessary, by the white-hot iron, or if an accuser shall appear and wish to put himself on record, I shall offer my innocence by legal process.[22] No accuser dared come forward and in the end Lancaster was able to purge himself on oath alone rather than through trial by ordeal. Whatever the truth of it, for at this juncture there is no surviving evidence that Robert ever paid Lancaster any bribe, the King of Scots had succeeded in throwing the English into confusion by sending his men to York, and as a result had staved off another serious threat to his kingdom. He had outmanoeuvred the English again, giving the impression of one favoured by God, and broken the spell of bad luck which had haunted him during the previous three years. Perhaps St Malachy was listening after all.

With his chances of winning in Scotland somewhat reduced, Edward II was quick to reach out in the hope of arranging a truce. To this effect he appointed Robert Baldock as his representative and sent him via Newcastle to Berwick to encourage King Robert to engage.[23] Simultaneously, keeping with tradition, Robert did what he always had done in the last decade when he knew the King of England was at a disadvantage, and ordered James Douglas and Thomas Randolph back across the border on All Saints' Day, 1 November and, as before, they commandeered cattle, provisions and equipment from the harassed populace.[24]

Peace negotiations opened shortly afterward. Robert was represented by William de Soules, Hereditary Seneschal of Scotland, and his deputy, Alexander Seton. Along with them were also Robert Keith the Marischal, Roger Kirkpatrick, William Mowat, James Bren and the canon of Glasgow Cathedral, Walter de Twynham.[25] On the English side, Edward II appointed Aymer de Valence, Earl of Pembroke, the commander who had won the Battle of Methven in 1306, and Hugh Despenser the Younger, his chamberlain.

The discussions proved productive, and a two-year truce was agreed on 21 December, coming into effect eight days later on the Feast day of St Thomas Becket and set to last until Christmas 1321. At the same time, other compromises were reached. Berwick's fishing rights were fully restored, improving trade and sources of revenue, and the content of English ships wrecked on the Scottish coast would be returned to the King of England. More importantly, Harbottle Castle in Northumberland, recently captured by the Scots, would be handed over in custody to nominated English ambassadors. These terms were duly satisfied eight days after the talks concluded, and were held to until the end of the truce. According to the terms agreed, if no permanent peace settlement had been reached between Robert and Edward by Christmas 1321, then Harbottle would be destroyed, which in any event happened after the Earl of Hereford received instruction from Edward II on 25 August 1321 to do just that.[26] With the terms drawn up and sent north, Thomas Randolph agreed to them on King Robert's behalf.[27]

The presence of a fresh truce provided a pleasant and much-needed break in hostilities between the two countries after a decade of war and attrition. While the years of poor harvests had temporarily abated, 1318 and 1319 saw the outbreak of the lethal virus rinderpest among cattle, its human equivalent being measles. This virus charged across northern Europe, arriving in England in 1318. As the English army had advanced north in the summer of 1319, bringing with them cattle and oxen, the virus had also travelled, and was taken into Scotland by the raids of Douglas and Randolph, who had captured infected livestock as part of their lucrative booty. This panzootic, with a mortality rate of 50 per cent in bulls and oxen and 80 per cent in cows, afflicted both countries greatly until the end of 1322. It hit hardest in Scotland, however, which relied more heavily than England on a pastoral economy.[28]

Yet, despite a temporary cessation in hostilities, King Robert still faced ongoing papal censure, remaining both an excommunicate and also a leader of a nation under interdict. On 18 November, Pope John XXII, frustrated that his ruling had been flouted by the King of Scots, issued letters summoning the king and William Lamberton, Bishop of St Andrews; Henry Cheyne, Bishop of Aberdeen; William Sinclair, Bishop of Dunkeld; and David de Moravia, Bishop of Moray, to attend him at Avignon to account for their ongoing disobedience. They had until 1 May the following year to present themselves. On 6 January 1320, the pope upped the ante once more and reissued his sentence of excommunication against Robert, focussing on his murder of John Comyn in 1306 as the just cause, and instructed both his cardinal envoys and the prelates of Scotland to absolve King Robert's subjects of their oaths of allegiance to him.[29] The pope was running out of patience, and Robert, fearful that his people may not keep faith with an excommunicate king, knew he could not hold back the tide of papal censure indefinitely.

In March, Robert ordered a meeting of the Great Council at the Cistercian abbey of Newbattle near Edinburgh, the business to be divided around the Easter week, which fell on 30 March.[30] Here the pope's recent letter was hotly debated, and it was agreed that no representation in person should be sent, but instead a series of letters should be drafted setting out their position. The first letter would come from Robert himself, the second from the prelates and the third from the magnates of Scotland. The letters were indeed written, and sealed at Arbroath on 6 April. Only the third survives, and it has been remembered to history since the nineteenth century as the Declaration of Arbroath. The Declaration was an expertly crafted document, designed to appeal to the pope and written in the rhythmic Latin used by the Papal Curia, designed to be read aloud in front of a full papal court. Its form, written by an eloquent Latinist – perhaps Bernard, Abbot of Arbroath or Alexander Kinninmonth, who would later become the Bishop of Aberdeen – goes to the heart of Robert's, and indeed Scotland's, determination to assert and defend its independence from England.[31]

More concise and creatively constructed than the recent Remonstrance of the Irish Princes, the Declaration set out a version of Scots prehistory which made clear to the intended audience that its people had come from Greater Scythia, occupying Scotland, withstanding the Romans, the Danes and the English over a period in which they had been ruled by 113 successive kings, a great line which had until recently remained unbroken. Before arriving in Scotland, it claimed, the people had been converted to Christianity by St Andrew, and as a consequence the papacy had always extended to the Scottish people its special protection in veneration of the martyred saint. The document went on to describe how Scotland's liberties and independence had been threatened by the advances of Edward I, who, despite being invited to help as a respected friend, had turned enemy, pillaging the nation.[32] From there, and perhaps most importantly, the author sets out the justification for Robert's kingship:

But from these countless evils we have been set free, by the help of Him who though He afflicts yet heals and restores, by our most tireless Prince, King and Lord, the Lord Robert. He, that his people and his heritage might be delivered out of the hands of our enemies, met toil and fatigue, hunger and peril, like another Maccabeus or Joshua and bore them cheerfully. Him, too, divine providence, his right of succession according to our laws and customs which we shall maintain to the death, and the due consent and assent of all of us, have made our Prince and King. To him, as to the man by whom salvation has been brought into our people, we are bound both by law and by his merits that our freedom may still be maintained, and by him, come what may, we mean to stand.[33]

The assembly at Newbattle Abbey were making it very clear to the pope that they both had the right to appoint Robert and had faith in him as their king. Following in the tradition of his ancestors, Robert had been, and remained, their champion. Given they claimed they would stand by him, the authors of the Declaration were effectively rebuffing the pope's recent proclamation to the cardinals and prelates to absolve Scottish subjects of their allegiance to their king. Whatever the papal censure, the people of Scotland would stand by Robert just as he stood by them. They went on:

> Yet if he should give up what he has begun, and agree to make us or our kingdom subject to the King of England or the English, we should exert ourselves at once to drive him out as our enemy and a subverter of his own rights and ours, and make some other man who was well able to defend us our King; for, as long as but a hundred of us remain alive, never will we under any conditions be brought under English rule. It is in truth not for glory, nor riches, nor honours that we are fighting, but for freedom – for that alone, which no honest man gives up but with life itself.[34]

The passion of this document makes it clear that the Scots were bound by a simple determination to reassert themselves, and that they viewed Robert as the man to lead them. However, the document also warned of outside interference in the royal succession, perhaps a targeted nod, making it clear that Scotland would vehemently reject any attempt by either Edward II or the pope to bring Edward Balliol to the Scottish throne. Balliol was Edward's man, not theirs. They would not have him, especially if he was under the tutelage of an English king.

The letter ended by entreating the Holy Father to admonish Edward II for his interference in Scotland and for the English king to be content with his own dominions. The Scots took the pain to state that they would joyously go on Holy Crusade if they were free of their enemies at home, but if the pope persisted in believing the English version of events as daily outlined by Edward's envoys at Avignon, then he alone would be to blame for the continued carnage and destruction of Christian souls in Scotland.[35] The Declaration was dignified in its arguments yet bold and provocative where it needed to be in reminding the Vicar of Christ of his role as an impartial leader of Christendom.[36]

King Robert's own letter, which is only known because of the papal reply, complained that the Holy Father still failed to address him by his royal title. He also sought to have his sentence of excommunication revoked, and probably took the opportunity to highlight his commitment to crusade. The second letter, composed by the prelates, probably reflected many of the points set out by the king and the barons.[37]

The Declaration itself was issued in the names of eight earls, thirty-one barons and all the 'freeholders and whole community of the realm of Scotland'. Despite absent seals from lords in the Western Isles or the south-west, excepting Fergus of Ardrossan, the letters were handed over to three envoys, among them Alexander Kinninmonth, whose task it was to safely deliver them to the Curia. They arrived at the end of June 1320,[38] but that was a week short of the pope's excommunication of the four Scottish bishops who had been summoned to attend him by 1 May and who had failed to arrive.

With the letters sent, Robert and his council as an insurance policy wrote to King Philip V of France in the hope of gaining his assistance both at Avignon and in his upcoming meeting with his brother-in-law Edward II, who was due to arrive at Amiens to perform homage for the English-held duchy of Aquitaine and Ponthieu. It is telling that Philip made Odard de Maubission, his papal envoy, available to the Scots. However, Edward II, shrewd as ever on the diplomatic stage, was quick to respond, instructing his envoys in Paris to apply pressure on the King of France to proclaim Robert's excommunication throughout his French kingdom.[39] Despite the truce, war could still be fought in the realm of diplomacy and in the corridors of power.

The King of Scots may also have written a letter to Edward II at this time, a copy of which would have likely been included in the same bundle sent to the Papal Court to highlight to the pope Robert's commitment to a reasonable peace and therefore a focus on crusade.[40] Although undated and written in Latin, the letter expressed Robert's desire for a permanent peace:

> Since while kindly peace prevails the minds of the faithful are at rest, the Christian way of life is furthered and all the affairs of Holy Mother Church and of all kingdoms are everywhere carried on more prosperously, we in our humility have judged it right to entreat of your highness most earnestly that having before your eyes the righteousness you owe to God and to the people, you desist from persecuting us and disturbing the people of our realm, so that there may be an end of slaughter and shedding of Christian blood. Everything that we ourselves and our people by their bodily service and contributions of wealth can do, we are now and shall be prepared to do sincerely and honourably for the

sake of good peace and to earn perpetual grace for our souls. If it should be agreeable to your will to hold negotiations with us upon these matters, let your royal will be communicated to us in a letter by the hand of the bearer of the present letter.[41]

With this attempt to create a broad canvas of support now complete, Robert could only wait for the pope's response, hoping all the while that he may have engineered some kind of breakthrough.

While he waited, King Robert turned his attention to further rewarding those closest to him. Since Bannockburn, either through gifts of individual patronage or through successive parliaments and petitions, the king had been working to engender a period of stability among the landed nobility and thus create bonds of loyalty to him that underpinned his rule and his dynasty. In the medieval world, where land equalled power, the distribution of royal patronage was both significant and highly political. On 1 April, Robert, while staying at Berwick, granted the barony of Staplegarden to his long-time friend James Douglas, which as part of the gift included the castle and various smaller land parcels in and around Jedburgh Forest. It was a lucrative grant, and one possibly designed to lead Douglas into the role of Warden of the West and Middle March. Douglas also received the sheriffdom of Roxburghshire, which gave him extensive control over much of Teviotdale, including land previously under the influence of the de Soules family.[42] A few months later, the king felt it appropriate to reward his illegitimate son and namesake, Robert, with the barony of Sprouston in Roxburghshire.

With such grants, it was clear that Robert was favouring both James Douglas, his own family and his son-in-law Walter Stewart, who also received lands in the area. Established families like the de Soules maintained their existing lands but did not appear to procure any additional favour. While Robert was careful in his application of patronage, it nevertheless created a simmering resentment among some of his subjects, who, having once fought for the English and eventually come over to his banner, now found themselves out of favour, or with limited influence at Robert's royal court. This bitterness soon spilled over into outward conspiracy and plotting.

Robert may have been aware of the growing tensions and restlessness among some of his lesser nobility, and he may also have known that something more sinister was afoot. But as yet he sat back to watch events unfold. At the previous Great Council meeting at Newbattle Abbey, the king may well have used the occasion as a test of loyalty, carefully noting who came to seal the declaration documents that set out to justify, reinforce and uphold his right to rule. At some point in the months that followed, a plot to kill the king was uncovered and formally made public. The contemporary evidence is highly contradictory, but what is clear is someone, possibly Patrick, Earl of Dunbar, or Agnes, Countess of Strathearn, or the Countess of Atholl, approached the king and let him know that his life was in danger. Another chronicler suggested it may have been Murdoch of Menteith.[43] The aim of the alleged plotters was the murder of the king and his replacement by William de Soules, Lord of Liddesdale.

William de Soules was the Hereditary Seneschal of Scotland, and could boast a claim, albeit a very weak one, to the crown of Scotland. His father had been one of the minor competitors during the Great Cause but had quickly been ruled out by Edward I and the jury as he was descended from an illegitimate daughter of King Alexander II. William, by right of his mother, was connected to the former Comyn earls of Buchan, and his maternal aunt was the Countess of Strathearn. Why he felt he had a backable claim to the throne in 1319 is not altogether clear, but he had certainly watched from the side lines as James Douglas, Walter Stewart and others profited from lands in and around his own estates in Roxburghshire. Resentment, and perhaps the encouragement of his mother and other Comyn relatives now in exile, was enough to push him into action.

De Soules gathered about him a number of co-conspirators. At least eleven men were accused, although in the ensuing trials five were acquitted. Robert and his immediate council were quick to act to cut off some of the the heads of this Hydra before it could overcome them. The plotters were arrested, and on 4 August the king assembled a parliament at Scone to hear the testimony of the would-be assassins before his justices pronounced sentence. William de Soules confessed to his crimes, but in an act of clemency, Robert had him sent to Dumbarton Castle, where he was to be perpetually incarcerated, and where he subsequently died.[44] The Countess of Strathearn, perhaps not the informer at all but rather a co-conspirator, also met the same punishment. Three of the men – Gilbert de Malherbe, John Logie and a squire, Richard Broun – were to face the ultimate sanction, being drawn at the tails of horses before their public hanging and beheading.[45] Malherbe was a baron of Stirlingshire who had been loyal to John Balliol before 1306 and had in recent years coveted Jedburgh Forest, lands which the king had lately bequeathed to James Douglas. Logie had been a ward of the sixth, but not contemporary, Earl of Strathearn, while Richard Broun had fought for Edward I against Robert Bruce and his brother Edward in Galloway, and was in the English garrison at Stirling Castle two years before it fell to Robert following Bannockburn.[46] All three men had received little favour from the king since they had joined his side.

Roger de Mowbray and his brother attempted to flee once they knew the conspiracy had been sprung, but both were killed during their flight. Roger's body was brought to Scone and presented to Parliament on a litter; his corpse was found guilty and condemned to the hangman's noose and the headsman's axe. Robert, never one for excessive violence and perhaps mindful of the horror inflicted on his own brothers at the hands of Edward I, commuted the sentence and allowed Mowbray's body to be buried without mutilation.[47]

The last known conspirator was David de Brechin, who under interrogation claimed he had been made aware of the plot only after his peers had first sworn him to secrecy. Although he did not wish to participate in it, because of his oath he felt he was unable to inform the king of what was afoot. It was a poor defence which found little sympathy among his peers. To make matters worse, if Robert had been using the Declaration of Arbroath as a test of loyalty, he may have remembered that de Brechin, whose family had previously been Comyn devotees, had failed to attach his own seal to the letter, instead using that of his wife, Mary Ramsey.[48] With the evidence stacked against him, David de Brechin was condemned to death on the basis that he more than anyone had endangered Robert's life by withholding vital information. Consequently, he was dragged through the streets behind a horse, hanged and beheaded.[49] His death more than any of the others was noted engendered great pity, for he, according to Barbour, was the 'flower of Christian knighthood', a reputation he had acquired while fighting in the Holy Land.[50] The deaths of these men and the dark deeds that arose as a result of conspiracy led to this gathering being known to history as Robert's 'Black Parliament'.

Yet the king himself had shown a degree of mercy. He had been severe with those who had endangered his life, no doubt sending out a message to warn others who felt empowered to challenge his right to rule, but he had also spared the lives of others, most notably William de Soules himself.

Five others were acquitted: Patrick Graham, Eustace Maxwell, Walter de Barclay, Eustace de Rattray and Hamelin de Troupe. Graham had previously been a supporter of John Balliol. Maxwell had held Caerlaverock Castle for Edward II until as late as 1313, when it fell to the king's late brother. De Barclay had joined Robert as early as 1306, while Rattray had a more chequered history of loyalty as a landowner in Gowrie, having joined the king in 1306 only to defect again, fighting for Edward II in the garrison of Perth Castle prior to its fall in 1311. Hamelin de Troupe, Sherriff of Banffshire, had long supported Bruce, but he may have lost out in the patronage game to the Earl of Ross and his son, Hugh, the king's brother-in-law.[51] Each man had a dubious past, and possibly some connection with the conspirators, yet sufficient evidence was not found or recorded to prove their guilt. Either way, they had aroused sufficient suspicion to be interrogated, which nevertheless tainted their reputations in Scotland.

For the following two months, an air of suspicion hung heavy over the kingdom as people were further interrogated and the plot was finally expunged. Ingram de Umfraville fell under the watchful eye of the king's men. He had been a long-time supporter of Edward II and had served the English king as Warden of the West in March 1308. He was eventually captured by King Robert at Bannockburn and subsequently ransomed.[52] After gaining his freedom, Ingram remained in Scotland, but outside of the royal sphere of influence. He was a close friend of David de Brechin, who, like de Umfraville, received little patronage from his king despite being a prominent Angus baron.[53] According to Barbour, Ingram sought King Robert's permission to leave Scotland, having given up his lands in the kingdom on account of his friend's execution, which the king rather chivalrously granted.[54] However, it is more likely that Ingram fled, the interrogators closing in on him after the Black Parliament. His later dealings at the court of Edward II indicate that Ingram was perhaps in league with Edward Balliol, who was still serving in the household of the King of England's half-brother the Earl of Norfolk. Ingram would not be the only defector in the coming months.

Yet, despite the number of people involved, the conspirators were not drawn from the higher end of Scottish noble society. No great lords or office holders were involved beyond William de Soules himself as Hereditary Seneschal. While the plotters had been well connected, they were nevertheless part of the lesser nobility, men at the fringes of the royal court. It was their limited access to the king, and their failure to broker any real power or patronage, that led these men with their dubious loyalties into a desperate act.

The fact that the chroniclers are so confused about who informed the king is proof enough that Robert could still command the loyalty of the most influential members of Scottish society. The Scots were, in the main, united behind him. Nor did the plot change the way he granted his patronage, continuing as he did to provide gifts to family and close friends, along with religious institutions and the royal mausoleum at Dunfermline Abbey.[55]

With the plot behind him, the King of Scots could focus on the papal reply. He must have waited in great anticipation since April to hear the pope's response, and on 28 August the wait finally came to an end. The Holy Father had listened attentively to the beautifully crafted Declaration read out in his papal court by Alexander Kinninmonth, and had to some degree been moved. In his response, Pope John XXII began his address by saluting Bruce as 'that illustrious man Robert, who assumes the title and position of King of Scots'. While still not an affirmation, it was a step in the right direction and a gesture that Robert was glad to accept.[56] The pope expressed his personal commitment to exhorting the King of England to make peace with Robert and his realm, and to that effect would send envoys to Scotland including the Archbishop of Vienne, and also encourage the King of France to do the same.

The papal and French envoys arrived months later, joining the Scottish and English negotiators, and peace talks took place at Newcastle, Berwick and Bamburgh between January and April 1321. But like so many times before, Edward II refused to relinquish his right to Scottish overlordship, which the Scots vehemently opposed, and so without the possibility of securing the permanent independence of Scotland, the talks broke down without meaningful resolution. The Declaration of Arbroath was as good as a dead letter. Yet again, at a critical moment, Robert had been unable to engineer the outcome that he most desired. However, his relationship with the papacy at Avignon was beginning to soften. Exasperated by the doggedness of Edward II, Robert could only comfort himself with the knowledge that the two-year truce between the two countries still held.

12

Towards Peace

With an Anglo-Scottish truce in place and the recent conspiracy crushed, Robert turned his attention back to the distribution of royal patronage. The king was at Scone on 18 November when he called for the examination of Alexander II's royal charter to Melrose Abbey. Business as usual was the order of the day. No records survive to indicate where Robert and his court observed the Christmas festivities, the king only re-emerging in the historical record in mid-January 1321 when he granted £10 per annum from the lords of Buittle to the Cumbrian Cistercian abbey of Holm Cultram.[1]

Robert was making a statement with this grant. Holm Cultram was the daughter house of Melrose Abbey, and his patronage was an ongoing reminder that the King of Scots formerly held historic lordship in parts of northern England, even if they had been forfeited since the time of Edward I. At the same time, he also gifted to one of his illegitimate sons the former Soules lordship of Liddesdale. Robert, still without legitimate sons of his own, had always been careful to recognise his bastards and see them cared for, which could not be said for many other lords.[2] Later in the month, he moved to Berwick and took up residence in the castle where he would remain until sometime in April.

Robert had plenty to think about as he wrestled with the shortcomings of the current truce with England. If he was to gain recognition of his status then he needed to engineer the current cessation of hostilities into something far more prolonged, or, better still, a permanent peace. Only the month before, tensions had begun to mount when Scottish ships had been wrecked along the English east coast and a garrison at nearby York had ridden out and arrested the Scots, along with their German and Flemish shipmates. The temporary peace could still be fractious.

Whether through a diplomatic intervention or both parties seeing the benefit of a longer armistice, on 19 January Edward II ordered a delegation to assemble at Newcastle in the coming months, being represented by the Earl of Pembroke and the Archbishop of York. Papal envoys still in England were to chair the meeting, while Robert was to choose representatives of his own.[3] Their initial meeting was in any event delayed by the prolonged absence of the Earl of Pembroke, who was currently in France on other business. While the wait continued, King Robert added yet more lands to those held by his close companion James Douglas, granting him half of the forfeited barony of Westerker in Dumfriesshire, which had previously belonged to the traitor William de Soules. It was another fitting gift to a man of steadfast loyalty.

In early April, the Earl of Pembroke returned and made his way north. Robert appointed William, Archdeacon of Lothian and Alexander de Kinninmonth and sent them to Newcastle to negotiate. As in all previous encounters, the English presented their long-standing argument, articulated by that storyteller Geoffrey of Monmouth, that the kings of England held dominance in the British Isles by virtue of ancient tradition and circumstance. The Scots employed their arguments set out in the Declaration of Arbroath, which, as usual, highlighted the long line of 113 Scots kings who had ruled the kingdom without external English interference. With such polarised debates it was all too clear that neither party was yet ready to compromise, and with the English again refusing to budge on the issue of Robert's status or the independence of the Scottish kingdom, the talks began to unravel. The suggestion that the truce be extended for twenty-six years was discussed and thrown out, leaving the current truce intact until Epiphany 1322. Permanent peace was most certainly not on the cards.

The notion that Robert was prepared to agree to a twenty-six-year term was a clever stratagem. Since 1314 he had laboured tirelessly to bring about his aims, yet each time Edward II had doggedly refused to comply. Even in the face of defeat, the King of England held fast. As the years wore on and Robert continued to suffer bouts of ill health, he must have grown increasingly tired and deeply frustrated at the prospect that England's king, ten years Robert's junior, could continue to hold on to his entrenched political position for decades to come. If a long truce was the only possibility he could secure, then the King of Scots could use this respite to consolidate his gains. His people needed time to recover from years of war, and many estates across Scotland were still extensively damaged. With time to heal, the Scots could achieve a much stronger position for any future negotiation or conflict. If Robert was not alive when that extended truce expired, then any future heir, be it his grandson Robert or sons yet to be born, then they too would be grown men by the time a renewed conflict was required. It gave the Scottish cause hope and removed the risk of future military confrontation with England under the rule of a minor. A long truce was all the more relevant at this time: Robert's wife, Queen Elizabeth, was pregnant.

In the absence of any records, the queen's pregnancy is glimpsed only through the very specific gifts of patronage that Robert offered up in 1321. In July, the king granted the forfeited lands of Inverkeithing and Queensferry, formerly owned by Roger Mowbray, to the royal abbey at Dunfermline to cover the cost of a candle to burn perpetually in the choir of the royal mausoleum in honour of the Virgin Mary and before the shrine of St Margaret for the souls of Robert, his ancestors and successors.[4] It was a pointed gesture, for St Margaret was often called upon for protection during child labour. It is highly likely that Elizabeth gave birth to a daughter, Matilda, in 1321. Another daughter would be named Margaret. For Robert and his wife, the birth of a child after years without must have been an incredibly joyous moment, though tinged with some disappointment. The need for a male heir became more pressing as each year passed, and so the uncertainty of Robert's royal legacy looked set to continue.

On 8 July, the king opened a parliament at Scone. The failed negotiations with the English were discussed, and further gifts of patronage were awarded. The young Malcolm, Earl of Lennox was likely confirmed in his earldom and the Sheriffdom of Dumbarton.[5] In August, Robert moved north through his kingdom, arriving on the 4th at Cullen in Banff along with others in his retinue which included William Oliphant, Gilbert de la Hay and Edward Keith.[6] Even at this late stage he was still in pursuit of rebels connected to the previous year's conspiracy, in particular the traitor Alexander Broun, who had so far avoided capture. While in the region Robert used his presence as much as his patronage through September to remind the local, previously pro-Comyn populace of his power and authority. Loyalty was the king's price for peace, and it had come at a great cost over the years. Robert never forgot those who had stood by him and had fallen in consequence. He granted £20 to pay for six chaplains to say Masses in the chapel of the Bishop of Ross at Tain for the souls of the late king Alexander III and his former ally John Strathbogie, Earl of Atholl, remembering that the latter had been executed by Edward I in 1306 for his part in supporting Bruce and attempting to spirit Queen Elizabeth and Robert's family to Norway.[7] The King of Scots had a long memory and a deep soul.

While Robert had been kept busy in the north of Scotland from midsummer until the end of the year, in England Edward II had been battling with his overmighty vassals. Since 1319, the King of England had favoured Hugh Despenser the Younger, a man who was both rapacious and predatory. As Despenser's confidence grew and his carefully crafted manipulation of Edward intensified, the royal favourite went on a landgrab in the Welsh Marches. His actions threatened the long-established ancient families who held extensive estates in that region, among them the king's brother-in-law the Earl of Hereford and his cousin Thomas of Lancaster, ensuring bitter resentment spilled over in the royal court and into open confrontation.

What followed was a brief war where the Contrariant rebels, as they became known, rose up and demanded the permanent exile of both Hugh Despenser the Younger and his father, also named Hugh. Edward, facing outright civil war and threatened with deposition, was temporarily forced to banish the Despensers at the parliament of August 1321. Vengeful and determined to reassert his royal sovereignty thereafter, Edward fought back, and by the end of that year, with help from his wife Isabella of France and a growing contingent of magnates who flocked to his side, the king took the fight to the unsuspecting Contrariants, catching them off guard. Sweeping west and then up into the Welsh Marches, he and his growing army were able to take the war to his enemies, and he began to win victory after victory. However, he was unable to capture his key target, Thomas, Earl of Lancaster, who had been responsible for the murder of Edward's lover Piers Gaveston in 1312. Nevertheless, buoyed by his successes, and sensing a turn of the tide, Edward focussed his sights north to Lancaster, who held out at his favourite castle of Pontefract. Sensing the danger, Lancaster eventually threw in his lot with the Contrariants and doomed himself in the process.

On 6 January 1322, as war erupted in England, the Anglo-Scottish truce expired at Epiphany. The next day, Robert, aware of the growing divisions south of his border, seized the opportunity and sent Thomas Randolph, James Douglas and Walter Stewart on a two-week raiding mission through County Durham, Hartlepool, Cleveland and Richmond.[8] As the raids harried northern England, Andrew Harclay left Carlisle and rode south to plead for help from his king, who was then waging war with the rebels at Gloucester. Harclay informed his king of Robert's raid, although the King of Scots was not leading the raiding party himself, being too ill to ride.[9] As Edward was on something of a winning streak in the Welsh Marches, he was not mindful to ride north until he had overcome his disgruntled vassals. Instead he sent Harclay north to raise a defence and negotiate a temporary truce with Robert.[10]

Harclay was right to be worried, for only a month before, and unbeknown to the Sheriff of Cumberland, Thomas of Lancaster had reached out to the King of Scots for aid. Using the pseudonym 'Roi Arthur' or King Arthur, Lancaster and his allies John Mowbray and Robert Clifford were corresponding directly with Thomas Randolph and James Douglas from 6 December. It was suggested that in return for offering Robert the recognition in Scotland that he so craved, the King of Scots should ride south and support the rebel earl and his co-conspirators in depriving Edward II of his throne. Robert was wary of the idea, declaring, 'How will a man who cannot keep faith with his own lord keep faith with me?'[11] Yet, despite offering Lancaster no clear assurance, the king instructed James Douglas and his nephew Randolph to continue to engage with the English rebels, perhaps offering false hope, all the while playing a cautious game to see how this latest situation may yet unfold, offering Robert something of an opportunistic advantage.

The evidence for Lancaster's complicity quickly began to surface. In January, as Harclay met Edward at Gloucester, a group of northern men marched south to Thomas of Lancaster who was still at Pontefract. They begged the earl to take up arms to beat off the raiding Scots who had crossed the border and were attacking their homes, but Lancaster feigned an excuse. 'And no wonder,' exclaimed the chronicler of Lanercost, 'seeing that he cared not to take up arms in the cause of a king who was ready to attack him.'[12] On 10 January, Thomas fatefully played his hand and began to lay siege to Edward II's castle at Tickhill. While the earl was bombarding the royal fortification, the Contrariant rebels in the Welsh March collapsed under the weight of Edward's advance, leaving the Earl of Hereford to flee north to meet up with Lancaster. As Edward sent out writs of summons for levies which amounted up to 15,000 infantry to assemble at Coventry for the start of March, Thomas's luck ran out.

As February drew to a close, Edward heard via William Melton, Archbishop of York, that letters had come into the archbishop's possession written in the name of 'Roi Arthur'.[13] It was, of course, political dynamite. Lancaster's Scottish dealings were promptly exposed, giving Edward the evidence he had required for so long to prove his cousin's treachery and King Robert's interference in English affairs of state. The king immediately published the letters across England, and in doing so the populace, including Lancaster's powerful retainers such as Fulk Lestrange and Peter de Mauley, quickly turned their backs on the mighty earl. Once Edward found a way to cross the river at Burton-on-Trent, the earl's hope of sustained resistance was lost and he fled north along with the Earl of Hereford and others, only to be cornered at Boroughbridge by Andrew Harclay and 4,000 northern levies.[14] Trapped, the Earl of Hereford was killed attempting to cross the bridge on the first morning of battle. By the second, Lancaster was captured and promptly taken to his castle at Pontefract, where Edward caught up with him and there had his cousin tried before his peers, including the recently returned Despensers, ultimately in revenge for the earl's murder of Piers Gaveston ten years earlier.

An indenture found on the body of the Earl of Hereford promising Scottish aid further implicated Lancaster and others. Thomas was promptly sentenced to death, his mock trial similar to that of Gaveston's, where afterwards he was immediately taken out of the castle to a nearby hill, faced north as a pointed reminder of his dealings with the Scots, and beheaded with two or three strokes of a sword.[15] In return for his efforts and decisive action, Andrew Harclay was awarded the Earldom of Carlisle at the subsequent parliament at York by a very grateful English king.

His lukewarm flirtation with Thomas of Lancaster had given Edward II a reason to march against Robert. The indenture found on Hereford's body made it clear that Robert, too ill to meet Lancaster in person, would send Randolph, Douglas and Stewart to his defence if needed.[16] The English king, in high spirits since his stunning victory, was determined now more than ever to overcome his long-standing Scottish enemy and recover the kingdom that had been gradually lost since his accession in 1307. On 25 March, he ordered a staggering and unrealistic muster of 40,000 men from his territories in England, Ireland, Wales and Gascony, who were to assemble for 24 July at Newcastle.[17] In the end, approximately 20,000 men, 2,100 hobelars and 1,250 cavalry arrived for the forthcoming campaign.[18]

In an attempt to distract the mustering forces, King Robert, now recovered from his illness, raised his own army and marched into England on 17 June along the west coast, raiding into Cumberland and Lancashire. He plundered heavily, attacking Holm Cultram, which only the year before he had granted gifts, and despite his father's body being buried there. When Robert needed to be ruthless, he could be. He marched on into Copeland, where he accepted a ransom payment from the abbot to spare the district. Unrelenting and forever needing to hamper the English, Robert continued to march beyond the sands of Leven to Cartmel, burning and harrying the town of Lancaster.[19] When further raiding parties led by Thomas Randolph and James Douglas met up with the king, they ventured into Preston together and headed 15 miles further south before deciding their lines were potentially overstretched, with a large English army forming to the east at Newcastle. With men, money and foodstuffs in abundance, the Scots turned north and crossed the border back into Scotland by 24 July, 'trampling and destroying as much of the crops [at Carlisle] as they could'.[20]

It had been a prudent strategy, and the captured provisions would only aid Robert's next move. He certainly had no intention of meeting Edward II in the field as he had done at Bannockburn eight years earlier; that victory had been unexpected, a result of good fortune and a sudden impromptu change to his military planning, aided by Seton's treachery. To take such a risk a second time would be foolhardy, and Robert knew it. Instead, he ordered the evacuation of Lothian and more widely the south-east of Scotland, while the English were mustering to its south. As the populace moved north into the heart of Scotland, they purposefully took with them cattle, sheep and food supplies while destroying everything else left behind, leaving the district devoid of sustenance for the marauding army that was yet to pass through it. Before his march south, Robert had spent time in May at Berwick, personally overseeing its defence.[21] On no account was he prepared to lose the jewel in his crown, having spent so many years trying to capture it. By the end of July, the king and his people were as ready as they could be to see off Edward II's large army. The Scots now had no choice but to stand.

The campaign in Scotland in 1322 was to be Edward II's last. Leaving Newcastle on 10 August, the king led the army with ten earls in train, including the pro-English Scottish earls of Angus and Atholl, through Lothian to reach the outskirts of Edinburgh on the 19th. With the absence of any English-held castle north of the border, the army was forced to keep on the move without a central base. Edward had apparently pre-empted the logistical challenge and ordered approximately thirty-six ships under the command of Robert Bataille to bring supplies up the northern coast, expecting them to put in at the port of Leith.[22] However, harried by storms out in the North Sea and dogged by Flemish mercenaries aiding the King of Scots, the majority of the English ships failed to make it through. As a result, the army, 20,000 strong, quickly began to starve, being unable to find sustenance from the land as a result of Robert's scorched-earth policy.[23] The army sent out foraging parties. Contemporary chroniclers claim they found very little, although Barbour creatively recounts one cohort discovering a lame cow near Tranent. When it was brought into camp, Earl Warenne exclaimed that it was the dearest beast that he ever saw and would have cost more than £1,000 to procure.[24]

Facing such desperate privation, Edward II and his war council knew there was little alternative but to retreat to England as the men in the army were dying of starvation and dysentery. Leaving Edinburgh, the English army sacked Holyrood Abbey in frustration, and before they crossed over the border they set fire to Dryburgh Abbey and Melrose. At the latter, James Douglas emerged from the forest and beat off the attack, chasing the weakened and malnourished army further south to the border.[25] At the same time, another force led by King Robert and Thomas Randolph emerged to shadow the enemy. By the end of August, only three weeks after their initial departure to Scotland, the army was back at Newcastle and subsequently disbanded.[26]

Edward II's run of good fortune was coming to an end. Once back in England, the king headed to Durham and from there at the end of September sent writs to the keepers of Bamburgh, Dunstanburgh and Alnwick, reproaching them for their failure to resist the Scots, who were now focussing their energy on besieging the mighty castle of Norham.[27] In growing frustration, he moved further south to Yorkshire in a bid to raise reinforcements, and on 2 October summoned his northern magnates to meet him at Blackhow Moor in the hills of Cleveland.[28] The new Earl of Carlisle, Andrew Harclay, was unable to respond, as his 4,000 men deployed at Boroughbridge had since gone home, having completed their feudal service. In order to meet Edward's summons, Harclay headed further south to raise men in Lancashire.[29]

During September, while Edward sought to protect the north, Robert moved his army west in order to bolster his forces, calling upon the men of Argyll and the isles of Arran and Bute. On 30 September, he crossed the Solway and raided once more into the district around Carlisle, and was in Cumberland when he heard the news of Edward's attempted muster at Blackhow Moor. Robert felt he had been touched by the hand of fortune yet again, and decided that if he was ever to break the unrelenting opposition to his crown, he had to act decisively. He would do the unthinkable and march east in an attempt to capture the King of England. On 13 October, he and his fleet-footed army had reached Northallerton, not far from Edward's camp, which had been moved south of Blackhow Moor to Old Byland near Rievaulx Abbey.[30] Robert was closing in. All that remained was to navigate Scawton Moor and, rather more impressively, the large rocky escarpment that dominated the edge of it. Robert and his army could either go around it or scale it; the former would add considerable time to their journey, potentially allowing Edward the possibility of escape if word of their advance reached him prematurely.[31] Robert knew that if his plan was to succeed there was only one choice.

On discovering the Scots' advance toward Edward II, the English army under the command of John of Brittany, Earl of Richmond, advanced across Scawton Moor and took up position on top of the rocky escarpment at Sutton Bank.[32] It was a commanding position, and one that the Earl considered advantageous, but Richmond had failed to recognise the determination of his adversary. Moreover, he should have taken heed of the reputation 'the Black Douglas' had deservedly earned over the last decade or more. Scaling the rocky outcrop under a hail of rocks thrown down on them by the English, James Douglas, Thomas Randolph and their men made the difficult climb in a bid to reach the English.[33]

While Douglas and his men climbed, unbeknown to Richmond and his men, including the Earl of Pembroke, who arrived with reinforcements, Robert deployed a force of Highlanders and Islesmen he had recruited on his sojourn in the west to scale this natural wall further along the escarpment, which they duly managed. Once at the top, they rounded and hit the English army in the flank just at the very moment Douglas, Randolph and their men made it to the summit after their gruelling climb. Facing enclosure front and back, the English were suddenly outmanoeuvred. Fighting was fierce on both sides, and panic began to set it in among the English ranks as the inevitability of the outcome became clear to all. 'The Scots were so fierce and their chiefs so daring and the English so badly cowed,' wrote Thomas Grey, the English author of the Scalacronica, 'that it was no otherwise between them than a hare before greyhounds.'[34] The English broke ranks, fleeing across Scawton Moor with the Scots in pursuit. Pembroke made it back to the comparative safety of York, but the Earl of Richmond was captured amid the chaos, as were Henry de Sully, Butler of France, and the renowned Roger de Cobham, considered the best knight in England until this mishap.[35]

With another stunning victory added to his name, Robert immediately ordered Walter Stewart on toward Rievaulx Abbey, determined to capture Edward II. As the King of England was having breakfast with Hugh Despenser the Younger, news arrived of the English defeat and the threat that was now bearing down upon them. Edward had no choice but to flee, leaving behind his household items, vast sums of money and, worst of all, his privy seal, which had been lost once before to the Scots at the Battle of Bannockburn. In a later act of generosity, King Robert sent it back to the humiliated king, who had been made a fugitive within his own kingdom.[36] Edward made for York via Burstwick-in-Holderness and remained there for some time.

In all the confusion, Queen Isabella, who had been placed in the safety of Tynemouth Priory, now found herself cut off behind enemy lines, the English countryside around her teeming with the Scots, who began to raid, perhaps aware of her presence. Isabella, with Despenser's wife, Eleanor de Clare, and her retinue, was forced to make a break for it, first by commandeering a ship in waters full of Flemish pirates, and then by horse. The retreat itself may have been dramatic and quite possibly subject to Scottish attack, as one of Isabella's ladies was allegedly killed while another went into premature labour, dying shortly afterwards.[37] Isabella would never forgive nor forget this traumatic event; it marked the beginning of the end for her marriage to Edward II.

With his principal prize now out of reach, Robert had nevertheless secured another symbolic victory. He had made his enemy a fugitive in his own country and emphasised Edward's vulnerability in protecting northern England. Remaining at Rievaulx Abbey, the King of Scots had his prisoners brought to him. John of Brittany, who was argumentative and offensive, remained a Scottish prisoner for two years, only being released after an enormous ransom of £20,000 had been settled. Robert, however, was more gracious with his French captives, all too aware that he needed the continued support of the French crown. Henry de Sully and other French knights were invited to remain with Robert as his guests for as long as they wished but were also allowed their freedom to return to France without ransom.

Such acts of chivalry had the desired effect, for the release of the French prisoners was positively received by Charles IV, King of France. As a gift to James Douglas, who had been cheated out of a ransom for his prisoner de Sully, Robert promised compensation. Two years later, he awarded Douglas extensive powers in his lands across the northern marches with England, and in the charter which enshrined these rights he was given the token of an emerald ring, marking the king's special favour. Such a gift was a very personal mark of friendship and to history this is remembered as the Emerald Charter.[38] Leaving Rievaulx, the Scots broke up into small raiding parties and harried east Yorkshire before meeting back up again on 22 October and turning north, crossing back into Scotland on All Soul's Day, 2 November.[39] Robert would go on to celebrate Christmas the following month with great revelry, possibly at Arbroath.[40]

Andrew Harclay, Earl of Carlisle, soon heard news of Edward's retreat to York. Having raised levies from Lancashire, he met up with the king, who was 'all in confusion and no army mustered', so he had no choice but to disband his men.[41] With the king unable to raise an army to make war with Scotland so soon after his defeat, Harclay grew increasingly impatient. Earlier in the year, when he had met Edward at Gloucester, he had been granted the authority to treat with the Scots in order to reach a new truce, marked in letters patent issued on 9 February.[42] This was before Edward had beaten his rivals in England, executed his cousin and twenty-two other rebels and marched north to Scotland. Harclay, however, still felt empowered to take up the king's original command and began subtle negotiations with Robert, which the earl hoped to sell to Edward. New to his elevated position, the Earl of Carlisle clearly did not understand the king to whom he had sworn an oath of homage and fealty. Edward would be unmoved, and Harclay was acting beyond his remit. Nevertheless, the ambitious and perhaps realistic earl knew that years of stalemate between the two kings was unlikely to end in English victory. On 3 January 1323, he took it upon himself and rode to Lochmaben Castle, where Robert was in residence, and there laid out his hopes for a permanent peace.[43] These actions alone were treasonable.

For Robert to engage, he must have been told by Harclay that he had been empowered by Edward to negotiate – a likely possibility given Edward's recent humiliation. Discussions deepened, and an agreement was drawn up which was to form the basis of a treaty. In it, the terms acknowledged that both kingdoms had prospered when ruled by two separate kings and that it was therefore to the common profit that Robert should hold Scotland 'free, entirely and in liberty' for him and his heirs. There was to be a commission of twelve representatives, six nominated by each king, to bring about the peace. Harclay would then work to convince Edward II of the merits of the deal, and if Edward agreed within a year, the King of Scots, in return for recognition of his status and the independence of his kingdom, would found an abbey in Scotland with a rent of 500 marks for the souls of those slain in war.

Robert would pay the sum of 40,000 marks over ten years as tribute, and, importantly, would give Edward II the choice to appoint from within his own family a wife for Robert's grandson and heir, Robert Stewart. The marriage would help to unite the two countries and restore the ties that had once existed between these great kingdoms under the reigns of Alexander II and his son, Alexander III. At the same time, it was set out that neither king would be obliged to receive in his realm any of the men who had previously been disloyal to him. This was an important term, for if any of the Scottish or English nobles returned to Scotland having been dispossessed of their lands and chattels as a result of their continued opposition to Robert since 1314, then the King of Scots' extensive programme of land resettlement through gifts of patronage would surely be jeopardised. The treaty also made provision should Edward could not be persuaded by Harclay to agree to its terms; if so, Robert would not be bound by any of it.[44] Harclay was given a year to bring Edward on side. For the Earl of Carlisle, and Robert too, it was a pragmatic deal that worked for the benefit of both sides.

For Edward, it was treason. On 8 January, the King of England got wind that something was afoot, having been informed that the Earl of Carlisle had entered Scotland without his royal licence. Edward clearly understood the situation and dispatched direct orders that on no account should a truce be brokered with Robert Bruce. Harclay was to present himself to the king and report on his actions. On 13 January, the king ordered William Airmyn, Keeper of the Chancery Rolls, to search with some urgency through recent records to establish whether Harclay had in fact been given an earlier commission to treat with the enemy.[45] Angry at this perceived undermining of his authority, Edward II ran out of patience and issued orders for Harclay's arrest. The earl went into hiding, but was eventually cornered at Carlisle Castle by Anthony de Lucy, who arrived at the fortress in the guise of a friend, only to reveal his true intention. There Andrew was promptly seized, and five days later he stood trial for treason.[46] The outcome by this juncture was a forgone conclusion. On 3 March, having been sentenced to death, he was hanged, drawn and quartered for his crimes. His dismembered body was displayed on the gates of Carlisle, Newcastle, York and Shrewsbury, while his head was sent south and exhibited at the Tower of London.[47]

With Harclay gone, Edward knew that the north-west was now vulnerable to attack. Given that he would be unable to raise an army until the following year at the earliest, the king gave his permission for negotiations to open with the Scots, only this time on his own terms and with his royal dignity intact. Henry de Sully was sent to act as mediator, a fitting appointment given recent events, and in the ensuing talks a thirteen-year truce was finally agreed upon at Bishopthorpe near York on 30 May 1323. Despite falling short of a permanent peace, the treaty was ratified by King Robert at Berwick eight days later.[48]

The details set out a practical agreement. No new fortifications were to be built along the border, while English and Scottish wardens would be appointed to keep watch on the crossings, settle disputes and refer complicated matters to the two kings for judgement. Perhaps more important for Robert, ships bringing goods to Scotland would not be targeted by the English. It was a vital clause, for the King of England had been close to shutting down wartime naval supply of both goods and men, mainly coming from Flanders, which had helped bolster Robert's activities.

The Scottish king also had ambitions to see Berwick's lucrative wool trade re-established, which would furnish him with highly profitable customs levied on domestic and overseas traders.[49] Lastly, the King of England agreed not to oppose the Scots in approaching Pope John XXII in a bid to overturn the excommunication and interdict that remained in force against Robert and his people. In all, the thirteen-year truce, which looked towards the possibility of a permanent peace, gave Robert time to consolidate and gave his heir the chance to grow into adulthood. The terms were certainly to the advantage of the Scots, which is unsurprising given their victories the previous year. Robert could feel some satisfaction with the outcome.

The king then called a parliament at Scone. Despite limited records, it is likely that the terms of the treaty were discussed at length. It may be that envoys were dispatched to Flanders to promote trade now that English ships were no longer a risk, and others sent to Paris and Avignon to garner support for the lifting of the papal censures. Edward II soon granted safe-conducts for forty knights, including Thomas Randolph, Earl of Moray, to travel through England on their way to treat with the Papal Curia, arriving by mid-January 1324.[50] While at Scone, the king awarded a new chapel dedicated to the Virgin of the Carmelite Order in Banff, grants of lands designed to fund bread, wine and wax for Masses said for his soul and those of his ancestors and successors. It is a suggestive donation which hints that Queen Elizabeth was once again pregnant, for not only was the gift a possible dedication imploring divine intercession and protection during pregnancy but it was granted to a chapel in an area that Elizabeth herself appeared to strongly favour.[51]

The royal family soon moved to Dunfermline Abbey, where the refectory was undergoing extensive refurbishment. It was a suitable place in which to wait out her pregnancy, and symbolic too, for there, during labour, the queen would be able to wear the birthing serk of St Margaret, a relic that Robert felt would protect his wife and result in the arrival of a much-needed direct male heir.[52] While in residence, the king may have attended the tomb of Alexander III, as well as progressing with his own funerary monument, which had been commissioned as early as November 1314.[53] Content with their location, the court does not seem to have moved away from Dunfermline for some time, observing the Christmas festivities there in December.

By the middle of January 1324, however, Robert had been compelled to leave his heavily pregnant wife and head north. By the middle of February he was at Aberdeen, possibly as a result of growing hostility in the north-east, which was a former Comyn territory. While the exact reasons remain unclear, it may well be that his brother-in-law Hugh Ross, who had assumed the earldom of Ross following the death of his late father on 28 January 1323, was rightfully asserting his claim of overlordship to the former Coymn lands of Buchan.[54] Adam Gordon may have been doing the same in the lordship of Strathbogie. Robert's presence, like his last appearance in the north only three years earlier, had the same effect, calming any growing hostilities and reaffirming his royal sovereignty as well as the position of those he had appointed to rule these northern lands in his name. The king was not prepared to suffer any challenges to his rule. He had headed south by the beginning of April, granting lands in Aberdeen to Alexander Seton.[55]

Before he had the chance to finish his trip south to Dunfermline, news reached Robert that, on 5 March, Queen Elizabeth had safely delivered not just one male heir, but two.[56] After all these years of waiting, in what must have seemed a miracle, the queen gave birth to male twins. Robert, only months shy of fifty, had an heir and a spare.

The first was named John, possibly in reference to Pope John XXII, whom Robert was courting through Thomas Randolph at this very moment. Such a dedication might be enough to soften papal resolve entirely. Equally, the name John, not one to appear in the canon of Bruce family history, may also have marked Robert's greatest victory at Bannockburn, fought on the feast day of St John the Baptist, 24 June. The second twin was baptised David; the interdict placed over Scotland did not prohibit new-born innocents from entering into God's holy protection by baptism. The name David may have been chosen in honour of the great Scots King David I, founder of Dunfermline Abbey. Another suggestion is David, Earl of Huntingdon, through whom Robert claimed lineal descent and therefore the crown of Scotland. Protecting their children now became Robert and Elizabeth's principal task, for at last the Bruce family, and all Robert had sought to achieve, suddenly had the real possibility of longevity. The Bruce family legacy would continue after all.

In late April, following his return from the north, Robert heard of the outcome of his nephew's mission at Avignon as well as the rapid deterioration in the relationship between Edward II and his brother-in-law Charles IV, King of France, which seemed to edge the two kings closer to an Anglo-French war over English territories in Gascony. Thomas Randolph, accompanied by Henry de Sully, had gained an audience with the Holy Father on 1 January 1324, and there set out his argument seeking the lifting of papal censures against Robert and his people.[57] A theatrical discussion got underway, in which Randolph claimed he was there to seek permission to join the planned crusade. Pope John XXII thanked the earl for his offer but reminded him he could not become a crusader as he was an excommunicate, though he could seek absolution if he did all in his power to aid Robert's reconciliation and that of his kingdom with the papacy. Randolph agreed to do so. He then informed the pope that, better still, Robert himself wished to join the crusade, and that if the King of France did not wish to lead it then Robert himself would undertake the task. The pope again reminded the earl that his king was an excommunicate, and so could not participate unless peace was reached with England and Scotland reconciled to the Church.

Thomas then made his calculated move, no doubt with a great degree of satisfaction. He made it abundantly clear to the Holy Father that if he would explain all this to Robert in a letter, addressing him simply as King of Scots, his liege lord would receive the pope's letter favourably and begin to enact what he asked. The pope, lured in by Randolph, who was manipulating his desire to see a crusade fought to reclaim the Holy Land, left his audience believing that such a simple gift was a small price to pay to shift the never-ending deadlock among the English, the Scots and Avignon. After seeking holy direction, John XXII decided he had no choice but to issue a letter to Robert, finally addressing him as King of Scots and thereby recognising the man's right to the crown. Desperate not to lose the support of Edward II, the pope also sent a rather meek letter to the King of England in an attempt to reassure him that his actions fundamentally changed little:

I remember to have told you that my bestowing the title of king on Robert Bruce would neither strengthen his claim nor impair yours. My earnest desires are for reconciliation and peace; and you well know that my Bull, issued for attaining these salutary purposes, will never be received in Scotland, if I address it to Bruce under any other appellation but that of King; I therefore exhort you in royal wisdom that you would be pleased patiently to suffer me to give him that appellation.[58]

Enraged by what he read, the English king wrote back an angry letter in which he demanded that the penalty of excommunication and interdict remain in force across Scotland. He also claimed that no Scottish bishop should be elected to the role when vacancies occurred in Scotland, allowing only English candidates the right to election, an English stipulation in force since the time of the king's late father Edward I but ignored by Robert. The pope refused the latter demand, pointing out that if no English bishops were able to take up their temporalities and spiritual duties in Scotland because Robert refused them admission into his kingdom, then the people of Scotland would be left without spiritual guidance entirely, something he was not prepared to countenance. He did, however, accede to Edward's demand to keep his papal censures in place, claiming that he refused to withdraw them on account of King Robert's invasion and confiscation of Berwick despite earlier papal prohibition before he had acted. The pope declared that until Robert chose to give Berwick back to the English, he would remain an excommunicate and Scotland under interdict. The Scots simply accepted the latter.[59]

In his actions, Edward II had knowingly broken the terms of the thirteen-year truce, having meddled in Scottish negotiations with Avignon. However, from Robert's perspective this slight could be ignored, given he had achieved at least one highly significant symbolic victory. On the international stage, his rule was now publicly acknowledged by papal letter, a fact that Edward II was unable to ignore. The English king's continued opposition to King Robert would make him look isolated and out of step.

By summer 1324, despite Edward's ongoing opposition, feelers were put out for further negotiations to convert the thirteen-year truce into a permanent peace. Edward's erupting war in Saint Sardos in Gascony meant he could not afford conflict on two fronts. Bringing the Scots to the table allowed him to buy time and remove the temptation for Scottish action. Robert himself may have preferred not to interfere anyway, unless he could guarantee an opportunity in his favour.

At this juncture, Edward's international misfortunes were only just getting underway. On 15 July, the English king granted safe-conducts for Bishop Lamberton of St Andrews and the Earl of Moray to attend talks in England. These conducts were extended and reissued on 3 November, for in that month the Scots and English came together at York to open talks.

On the English side, Edward sent the Despensers to represent him. This time Robert, emboldened by his recent victory, instructed Randolph and Lamberton to be more aggressive in their demands. During the talks, the Scottish delegation requested the return of the ancient Stone of Destiny, confiscated by Edward I and housed at Westminster Abbey in a new coronation chair upon which Edward II himself had been crowned in 1308. Robert's daughter Margaret was offered in marriage to Edward's son and heir, Edward, Earl of Chester. The Bruces' former English-held manors of Writtle and Hatfield Regis in Essex should be restored to them, and the profits lost since their confiscation ought to be paid in full. Finally, and standard to all negotiations since 1306, the Scots demanded that Edward acknowledge Robert's title and forgo his claim to suzerainty over Scotland.[60]

Surprisingly, Edward's negotiators reported that the king was willing to hand back the Stone of Destiny but at present was unable to agree to the marriage between his heir and Robert's daughter. The phrasing of the reply suggested, perhaps somewhat coolly, that such a request could be considered in the future, although at this time Edward was putting out feelers in Castile and Aragon for a match for his son. As usual, he pointedly refused to acknowledge either Robert as king or the loss of his lands in Scotland, claiming that such an action would led to 'the manifest disinheritance of our royal crown'.[61] As to Writtle and Hatfield, Robert could look elsewhere.[62] Without the chance of agreement, the talks stalled and finally collapsed in December. Despite this, the thirteen-year truce held and no hostilities were resumed on either side of the border.

By the close of 1324, King Robert had experienced some good fortune. The birth of two daughters and twin sons had finally secured his dynasty. The continued loyalty of most of his subjects ensured his rule was stable. Domestic threats, most notably in the north-east, had been quickly dealt with. His continued raids into England up until 1323 had proved lucrative, and his strategic foresight in evacuating south-eastern Scotland during Edward II's campaign in 1322 ultimately saved his people. His invasion into England resulted in a major victory at Byland and the humiliation of the King of England. Securing a thirteen-year truce was a strategic move designed to allow his heir, who was then his grandson Robert Stewart, the chance to grow into manhood, while he himself continued to consolidate his power, complete the resettlement of lands by granting gifts of patronage to his supporters, and see his kingdom prosper again. Trade was once more unhindered following his agreement with England to prevent the loss of Scottish and Flemish ships, meaning his kingdom was open for business. He had even secured international recognition of his title and status as king.

At the dawn of 1325, as Robert looked into the future, he must have known he had achieved a great deal. But he was all too aware that he was growing older, and his health, threatened by bouts of mysterious illness since at least 1308, was increasingly failing. His most pressing task had not changed; he had to secure a permanent peace with England if he was to hand a secure kingdom to his son. Robert could not have known that English affairs over the next two years would suddenly bring this prize tantalizingly close.

13

Bruce Victorious

A period of sustained peace in Scotland after years of war was most welcome. For Robert and his court, it allowed considerable freedom to focus on the business of governing the realm. Yet, just at the very moment when the king was edging closer to a potential victory with England, his health deteriorated. By November 1324 he must have been in regular contact with his physician, for on the 20th of that month he gifted lands in Forfarshire, Carrick and Wigtown to Gille Pádraig Beaton, who held the office of chief physician to the king. This grant stipulated the provision to the royal household of a permanent surgeon-physician,[1] a sure sign that Robert was not getting any better.

Dogged since 1308 by recurring bouts of illness which often saw him incapacitated with an increasingly degenerative skin condition, Robert's periods of sickness seem to become more frequent from 1322. The loss of the king's exchequer rolls before 1327, which would have captured his daily expenses for medicines and healthcare, make it difficult to determine just how long each episode lasted. Between these events the king appeared healthy enough to live a normal life. The prognosis is not altogether clear. Nevertheless, from here on in, Robert himself grew increasingly aware that he was a very ill man whose hope for long life was dwindling. He was already fifty years old, an advanced age for a medieval man. On average, those within his social class could expect to live comfortably until their mid-sixties or beyond. The Bruce family could boast some longevity in their genes, as evidenced by Robert's illustrious grandfather Robert Bruce V, who died aged seventy-five. For Robert, however, time was running out.

In March 1325, the King of Scots was at Scone surrounded by his court, summoned to attend a parliament. No records survive to describe proceedings, but on the 26th the king made a grant of £2,000 worth of his Roxburgh feudal incidents for the fabric repairs to Melrose Abbey. James Douglas was given the task of collecting them.[2] This was not the first nor indeed the last gift to this religious establishment, a place Robert would later single out for a specified purpose when it came to his mortal remains. Melrose was close to his heart.

Parliament would certainly have debated Franco-Scottish relations, given that news must have arrived in Scotland that Edward II and his brother-in-law Charles IV, King of France, were now in open conflict with one another. Having ascended the throne in 1322, Charles demanded the King of England pay homage to him in Edward's capacity as Duke of Aquitaine, a necessity established since the mid-twelfth century, and fraught with peril for England's kings. While Edward II prevaricated, Charles rather provocatively determined to build a royal bastide in Agenais, imposing a threatening royal presence in Edward's territories. As tensions mounted, one of Charles's men was murdered, found hanging from a wooden post marking the spot of the proposed fortress. This turn of events, coupled with Edward's failure to offer homage, gave the King of France a pretext for war.

On 13 June 1324, Edward II sent Aymer de Valence, Earl of Pembroke, to France to advance diplomacy and avoid calamity, but en route Valence died, bringing to an end a distinguished career as a voice of moderation at court. With Pembroke gone, Charles summoned his army, 7,000 strong, and on 24 June formally confiscated the duchy. War erupted, and the inexperienced Earl of Kent, Edward II's half-brother, was appointed to raise a defence. Finding himself outnumbered, he chose instead to broker a temporary truce during the siege of La Réole. This gave an enraged Edward time to raise an army and head to France, but after much discussion in the opening months of 1325, the king, his council and Parliament agreed to Charles's offer of dispatching Queen Isabella, Edward's wife and Charles's sister, on a diplomatic mission to her brother's court to secure peace between the two countries. Shortly afterwards, Isabella set sail and reached Pontoise on 20 March to open negotiations.[3]

As these events unfolded, Thomas Randolph, Earl of Moray, and Robert Keith the Marischal were present at the French court, seeking Charles's aid to help convince the pope to lift the papal censures on Scotland. They certainly would have kept King Robert informed as dramatic events unfolded between England and France. For Robert and his parliament at Scone, conversations must have focussed on whether Charles IV would call upon the King of Scots for military aid against England during the dispute, given past Scottish promises; this was something Robert must have weighed in the balance. However, the French call did not come.

In the summer, Robert, James Douglas and the Bishop of St Andrews made their way into the west, and during their sojourn stayed at Tarbert Castle. The king and his retinue would have set sail from Cardross, the royal manor that he was now in the process of building. A beautiful location, Cardross sat on the northern shore of the Firth of Clyde, protected to the south-east by Dumbarton Castle and lodged firmly in the Gaelic-speaking area of Lennox. Robert would have felt at home. The lands did not fall within the royal demesne, so the king purchased them through a land exchange with the Earl of Lennox and David de Graham, the latter of whom he gave lands in Old Montrose in Angus in March 1326 as a mark of compensation.[4]

Given that Robert had slighted the majority of the country's royal castles during the first decade of his reign, many of which were still uninhabitable, the king appears to have consciously chosen a new greenfield site on which to build himself a defensive manor. He must have chosen the location simply because he liked it, and it also gave him easy access to the Clyde, which in turn offered coastal access to the west, the Antrim coast of Ireland and the Isle of Man. Inland, Cardross sat on the western fringe of central Scotland so again provided Robert with convenient access across his kingdom. The manor itself was modest in size, moated to offer much-needed protection, and originally included a hall, a king's chamber, a queen's chamber, a chapel, kitchen, larder, bakery and brew houses, a falcon mews and a medicinal garden. Beyond lay a royal park in which the king and his court could hunt, the park being maintained by keepers William, Gilchrist and Gillfillan. The garden was manicured by Gilbert, while the king's huntsman was, perhaps unsurprisingly, called Gillies.

By 1328, with Robert having settled into his new home, further buildings were added including the 'New Chamber' and the 'New Gate'.[5] Cardross was designed for luxury, and was certainly a place where Robert and his immediate family could settle and feel at home, having spent much of their time living at Scone Abbey. While all royal medieval courts were peripatetic by their nature, required to administer royal authority all over and be seen by the people, during the remaining few years of his life Robert would spend much of his time at Cardross, enjoying the comfort he had created for himself and others. He even kept a pet lion there for his own amusement.

Following his western tour to Tarbert, the king was at Scone on 12 October to confer further lands in Ayrshire upon William Oliphant, to whom he had previously granted the barony of Newtyle and Kinpurney in 1317.[6] On 1 November he was back at Melrose Abbey, one of Scotland's wealthiest monastic sites, perhaps to inspect the building works and remaining there to observe the Christmas festivities. In January 1326, however, the English had cause to believe that the Scots might be galvanising support to aid the King of France. Following Queen Isabella's diplomatic mission, peace had been restored in the summer of 1325 and her son, Edward, Earl of Chester, was made Duke of Aquitaine by his father, Edward II, and sent to perform homage for his lands, which he delivered at Vincennes on 24 September.

With peace achieved, Isabella, now in possession of her son and Edward II's heir, spectacularly refused to return home, declaring to a full French court that someone had come between herself and husband's marriage and that she would not return to England until that intruder was removed.[7] Isabella was referring to Edward II's lover and favourite Hugh Despenser the Younger. This airing of royal dirty laundry caused something of a European scandal and immediately threatened the King of England, who heard rumours in early 1326 that the King of France would aid his sister and invade southern England. If true, Edward and his counsellors feared King Robert would be called upon to break the peace treaty between them and march an army through northern England. Yet after enquiries were made, northern reports were quick to point out that 'the Scots are peaceful and wish to preserve the truce as most people say.'[8] Robert was also indisposed, having fallen ill once more.

On 10 January, the king issued a charter directing revenue from the customs of Berwick to pay for the monks of Melrose Abbey to partake in a daily king's dish of rice in almond milk or pea-water. If they were not consuming it, or there were any leftovers, these would be given as a paupers' pittance to help ease hunger among the neediest. In the same gift, the abbey was also instructed to clothe and shoe fifteen paupers a year.[9]

The choice of dish is telling, for in certain quarters from around this date, rice and almond milk was increasingly a meal prescribed to aid stomach cramps and intestinal complaints, and may be a marker of the regular diet the king was now directed to consume. His doctor, Paris University graduate Maino de Maineri from Milan, was already in correspondence with the king, even though he was still a few months from taking up his position. Rice was an expensive commodity, and among the first to use it in Europe were the Milanese, de Maineri's people. It is highly likely that this diet formed part of de Maineri's treatment for the king, and its effect was such that the king immediately thought to recommend it to others. From 1327, when the extant exchequer rolls begin, payments are recorded for the import of large quantities of rice and almonds.[10] Sadly for Robert, it was no cure.

At the start of March 1326, the king moved to Scone to hold council along with the bishops of Dunkeld and Dunblane, the abbots of Coupar Angus and Dunfermline; the earls of Fife, Strathearn, Dunbar and Ross, along with others including William Oliphant, David Barclay who was soon to become the steward of Prince David's household, and Robert's illegitimate son and namesake, Robert. There he inspected the charter of Malcom IV to the abbey of all its possessions, and also settled the outstanding land transfer in Angus to David de Graham in return for the lands in Lennox upon which Robert was building Cardross. More importantly, they discussed the recent approach by Charles IV's envoys to reaffirm the special relationship that existed between the two countries. As expected, the King of France sought assurances that if the English invaded his kingdom the Scots would invade England on his behalf, opening a second front. It repeated much of the agreement of 1295 drawn up between King John Balliol and Philip IV of France. In return, if Edward II and his armies invaded Scotland, the King of France would do what he could to repay the favour in some form or other, although it is not clear how. It was hardly a proposal of equal measure, but nevertheless the Scots engaged with the offer, and in early spring Robert dispatched Thomas Randolph and others to negotiate.

Agreement was reached and affirmed in the Treaty of Corbeil, which was concluded on 26 April and ratified by Robert at Stirling on or around 12 July.[11] His approach was thoroughly strategic.

As he had not yet acted upon its terms, he had not broken the peace treaty currently in place with England, but by formalising an agreement with England's enemy at a time of English vulnerability Robert hoped to persuade Edward II to come back to the negotiating table and offer a permanent peace with Scotland. True to form, Edward II was not yet convinced that the threat was significant enough to warrant capitulation over his lifelong claim to Scottish overlordship. Instead, he ordered his northern barons to improve the defences at Carlisle, Norham, Alnwick, Dunstanburgh and Wark.[12] In essence, he called Robert's bluff.

King Robert's good fortune now faltered. Towards the end of May, his eldest son and heir, John Bruce, perished aged two, the grip of King Death so very strong during medieval childrearing. He would be buried in the Augustinian priory of Restenneth. The second twin, David, was still in rude health, but John's death had reminded his father of the vulnerability of his situation. Calling a parliament at Camsbuskenneth on 15 July, Robert felt it immediately necessary to update the succession settlement last reviewed in December 1318 following the death of his brother Edward Bruce. A new talzie was produced in which David was declared the king's immediate heir, securing his precedence over Robert's grandson, Robert Stewart. In the event of a minority, James Douglas and Thomas Randolph would, as agreed before, assume the role of royal guardians of both the king and the realm. With the details drawn up, those assembled swore an oath of fealty to the young boy on the Gospels and other holy relics, binding them in loyalty to Scotland's future king.[13] To reinforce his status, David was also styled Earl of Carrick and given his own household by his father and sent to reside at Turnberry Castle, the seat of his father's lordship before 1306 and undergoing repairs at the time.[14] Robert was tying up all important loose ends.

From Camsbuskenneth, the king spent the summer and early autumn in the Scottish March, moving back and forth from Berwick in the east to Lochmaben in the west. Despite the peace holding, tensions were growing as political chaos began to unfold in England in the late summer. Robert attempted to oversee and offer justice in any breaches of the truce, highlighting to King Edward the complaints of Scottish merchants who had been attacked by Englishmen when they had put into ports along the north coast. On one occasion, nine Scottish merchants, sixteen pilgrims and thirteen women were robbed of £2,000 of cargo and then killed by English pirates at Whitby in Yorkshire. Their ships were subsequently set adrift.[15] In August, Edward II, himself facing a far greater danger of foreign invasion at home, wrote to Robert appointing Anthony de Lucy to work alongside the Scots on the upcoming arbitration to help maintain the peace and bring criminals to justice.[16] The last thing the English king could afford was Robert enacting the Treaty of Corbeil.

The King of England was right to keep the peace. After his queen had refused to return home at the end of 1325, Isabella had become a focus for opposition to the Despensers and Edward II's other unpopular advisers. Exiles and disgruntled members of court flocked to her banner, and in France the queen was united with the exiled and vengeful Roger Mortimer, Baron of Wigmore. They became lovers and subsequently attempted to raise an army with the help of the Count of Hainault in 1326, promising Isabella and Edward's son, Edward, Duke of Aquitaine in marriage to the Count's daughter Philippa. With a deal done in August, Isabella secured 132 ships, eight warships and up to 700 mercenaries, which gave her between 1,000 and 1,500 troops.

Setting sail on 21 September, her invasion fleet landed at Orwell in Suffolk on the 24th and promptly swept through the country from east to west, following in the wake of Edward II, the Despensers and his closest ministers. The speed at which everything was now moving meant Edward was unable to muster a substantial force to resist the queen's advance. At Bristol, Hugh Despenser the Elder and Donald, Earl of Mar, King Robert's nephew who remained loyal to Edward II throughout his life, hunkered down to hold the castle while Edward and his remaining party fled further west, taking ship from Chepstow, quite possibly heading for Ireland. The queen arrived at Bristol, and with a hostile town against the king's men, the castle fell and the sixty-five-year-old Despenser the Elder was dragged out, hanged, mutilated and beheaded; his body was fed to the dogs while his head was sent to Winchester, where he had been earl since 1322.[17]

Donald, Earl of Mar most likely escaped before the castle fell, and rode in all haste back to Scotland, hoping to convince King Robert to raise an army and come to Edward II's aid. Robert was overjoyed to see his nephew return, and immediately restored to him the earldom of Mar, which had formally been confiscated after 1314 following Mar's reluctance to acknowledge Robert's kingship. Accusations swirl in the official records, but the Lanercost chronicler believed that Mar was empowered by Edward II during the king's greatest need to broker peace terms:

> The king had been so ill-advised as to write to the Scots, freely giving up to them the land and realm of Scotland, to be held independently of any King of England, and, which was worse, bestowed upon them with Scotland a greater part of the northern lands of England lying next to them, on condition that they should assist him against the Queen, her son, and their confederates.[18]

The Lanercost report appears fanciful given the de-acquisition of Northumberland, and is probably simple hearsay, but it was quite possible that the offer of a permanent peace was something that Edward II was now willing to proffer if it meant saving his crown at the eleventh hour.

On 16 November, Edward, Hugh Despenser the Younger and a small band of men still loyal to the king were captured near Llantrisant in south Wales. The king was promptly taken to Monmouth Castle and then on to the mighty fortress of Kenilworth, where he was imprisoned, while Hugh Despenser the Younger was brutally put to death at Hereford. He was drawn through the streets, hanged to near-death on a 50-foot gallows and then castrated, his genitals being burnt in front of him. The executioner then cut him open and pulled his entrails out before, almost mercifully, the still-living Despenser was beheaded by his executioner. The Earl of Arundel, another loyal to Edward II, was executed the next day with a blunt sword that took twenty-two blows to part his head from his body.[19]

As the unprecedented bloodletting ravaged England, causing riots to break out around the country and the rule of law to collapse, Robert took the initiative. If Edward II could provide a permanent peace then he could explore that option. But given that the king was now a captive, and on 20 January 1327 deposed in favour of his fourteen-year-old son, Edward III, this looked unrealistic. It was not altogether out of the question, however, especially if Edward could be restored to his throne with King Robert's help. At the same time, the King of Scots could put pressure on the new ruling regime, headed up by Isabella and Roger Mortimer, who governed in Edward III's name, hoping to bring them to the table as they too would need peace to secure their fragile new rule. All Robert had to do was raise men, invade and wait to see who came out on top in England, at which point he could negotiate a permanent Anglo-Scottish peace deal. It therefore suited him to allow Donald of Mar to raise men in the Scottish March, as well as supporting his nephew's attempts to muster troops in Wales and Ireland to free Edward II from captivity.

On 2 February 1327, the day of Edward III's coronation at Westminster Abbey, King Robert's army formally broke the terms of the thirteen-year truce and began to lay siege to Norham Castle. While this attack was repulsed, Robert's men began a systematic campaign to attack many of the neighbouring castles in the Scottish March, hoping all the while to provoke further instability in England, which was to his immediate advantage.[20] Robert himself was taken ill again and probably stopped at Stirling. The chronicler of Lanercost proclaimed the king had leprosy, marking the first time this disease was attached to him. The diagnosis has since gone down in Bruce folklore, despite being unproven.[21] While the raids were unfolding, the king received news that one of his most loyal supporters, his son-in-law Walter Stewart, had suddenly fallen ill and died on 9 April. The funeral took place at Paisley Abbey, and Stewart's heir, Robert's grandson and namesake, most likely entered the royal household of the king's surviving son, David.[22]

Unable to take Norham or Alnwick, the king's army had instead gone raiding into Northumberland, causing enough devastation to prompt an English response.[23] Before the end of the month, the king ordered his men back across the Scottish border and waited. Queen Isabella and Roger Mortimer, having declared on 6 March their intention to maintain the peace with Scotland, appointed Henry Beaumont, Henry Percy and the Abbot of Rievaulx to discuss terms that continued to support the temporary truce; permanent peace was not on the agenda.[24]

With Robert's tendency to raid, however, the English government also began preparations for war. It suited Isabella and Mortimer to raise an army and head north to procure a victory against the Scots, something that the deposed Edward II had been unable to achieve. It would strengthen Edward III's right to rule and divert growing unease in England about the late king's forced deposition. Edward II was more popular than many first believed. Robert and his council simply prepared to meet the invaders.

Their strategy was a clever one. The king divided his Scottish army into three cohorts, headed up by James Douglas, Thomas Randolph and Donald, Earl of Mar. Robert himself, now recovered sufficiently to travel, was to head to Ireland. On 12 April, the king set sail from Cardross and crossed to Glendun on the Antrim coast. In 1326, his father-in-law, Richard de Burgh, Earl of Ulster, had died, leaving as heir his grandson William, who was in English wardship. Fearing for his nephew's patrimony, Robert set sail to secure it for him, all the while hoping to win support in Ulster to bolster his position and scare Isabella and Mortimer into coming to the table for talks; the threat of a united Hiberno-Scottish invasion restoring the imprisoned Edward II to his throne would have been compelling. There is evidence to suggest that in the weeks before he sailed, Robert had been in communication with Edward's former justiciar, John Darcy, and the de Lacys, who were mortal enemies of the Mortimers.[25] The Irish manoeuvre also somewhat nullified Mortimer himself, who held extensive lands in Ireland, stopping him from using Ulster as a launch pad for a second invasion into Scotland as Edward I and Edward II had done in previous campaigns.

By July, the King of Scots had negotiated an agreement with Henry de Mandeville, Steward of the de Burgh earldom, which supported his nephew's claim to its lordship as well as a truce with Robert until 1 August 1328. Buoyed by his success, he then sought to achieve the same with Dublin, the heart of English administration and power, but failed to do so. The Justiciar of Ireland, Thomas FitzJohn, Earl of Kildare, who was brother-in-law to Queen Elizabeth, Robert's wife, was loyal to Isabella and Mortimer, having proclaimed the rule of Edward III on 12 May. Just as these events were unfolding, Robert received news in August from Scotland that Douglas and Randolph had secured a victory in the war against the queen, her lover and Edward III.

Hot on the heels of their victory over Edward II, Isabella and Mortimer mustered an English army to York, the size of which does not survive in the records. What is certain is that the queen was joined by the forces of John of Hainault, who had accompanied Isabella to England during her invasion in September 1326. But their ongoing presence caused tension, the English military allegedly despising the Hainaulters more than they did the Scots. With division in the ranks, the army moved out from York on 10 July and made for Durham, followed in train by their vast war baggage.[26] As of yet they had no idea where the Scots army was located. Robert's divided forces, under the command of Douglas, Randolph and Mar, entered England by different routes, the latter two men possibly travelling by the Kielder Gap into the valley of the north Tyne.[27] On 12 July, Edward III's army received word that the Scots, possibly under the command of James Douglas, may have entered England via the west and headed in the direction of Carlisle or, better still, the English army. The reports conflicted. With their movements still unclear, the Scots were causing confusion.

The English were camped at Durham by 18 July, and soon saw smoke rising in the distance from the fires caused by the Scots attacking local villages. Encouraged into action, the English army moved along Weardale, but failed to locate their enemy, which was now at Cockdale burning the town.[28] Two days later the English cavalry camped at Haydon Bridge, having left behind their burdensome baggage train and opted to feed themselves from the land.[29] This was a grave error. For eight days the English remained encamped, and for eight days it rained heavily without respite. Provisions quickly began to run out, leading to a serious shortage of food and miserable living conditions. News of the Scots' whereabouts was still not forthcoming. Losing morale, Edward III and his counsellors, led by Mortimer, offered a substantial reward of £100 and a knighthood to any man who could locate the Scots. It was an incentive that was soon to prove fruitful, for shortly afterwards Thomas Rokeby, a squire who had been caught by the Scots and subsequently released, entered the camp and gave up their location. He was awarded his prize later in the year, on 28 September, by a thankful Edward III.[30]

On 1 August, armed with reliable information, the English forces broke camp and moved back to the River Wear and found the Scots encamped on the southern bank, positioned in a strategically defensive position on top of a hill. For days, the English would line up for battle in a bid to tempt their enemy, but on each occasion they failed to encourage the Scots to give up their stronger location and commit to battle. Overnight on 3 August, James Douglas ordered his men to break camp and instead took up position behind the walls of Stanhope, a hunting park belonging to the bishops of Durham.[31] It was a good move, placing the Scots in a much better location from which they could mount a lightning strike against the English camp.

On the night of 4 August, Douglas made his move. Under the cover of darkness, he led a contingent of his men in among the

English array of tents, intent on killing the enemy and capturing the young Edward III. Shouting 'Douglas, Douglas, Douglas!' they began cutting the tent ropes and slaughtering the men caught in the folds of the material. The English were caught off guard. In the chaos and confusion, the Scots managed to reach the large tent of the English king, cutting the ropes and collapsing it. Terrified, Edward III was pulled away by his household servants, his chaplain succumbing to the sword while trying to save his king. Edward was dragged to safety and his guard, now somewhat recovered from Douglas's shock-and-awe tactics, were soon able to offer protection. Seeing their chance had slipped out of reach, James and his men beat a hasty retreat.[32] The assault was over as quickly as it had begun, but as dawn broke, the extent of the Scottish attack became evident; the dead littering the encampment took the whole of the day to bury.

That evening, the Scots in Stanhope Park looked to be readying for a further engagement, as they blared their horns and lit great fires, but they in fact did the opposite, turning in the other direction and leaving the park altogether. The fourteen-year-old King of England, overwhelmed by the experience, 'shed tears of vexation'.[33] With the disappearance of Douglas and his men, and no sign of any other Scottish army, Edward III and Mortimer had no option but to disband their starving army. They may also have been made aware of a reserve contingent of approximately 5,000 Scots under the command of the earls of Dunbar and Angus who remained stationed along the march in case Douglas and Randolph had been unable to prevent an English advance.[34] Any chance of a glorious English victory was now gone, the cost of the campaign estimated at a staggering £70,000. Such a significant defeat, in line with the earlier Scots victories during the reign of Edward II, resulted in an immediate challenge for the rule of Isabella and Mortimer back in England.

News of the success was quickly dispatched to King Robert in Ireland, and he immediately returned to Scotland to capitalise upon the outcome. Joining forces with Randolph and Douglas, Robert and his men invaded Northumberland. Like before, the army was divided into three cohorts. The first, led by Robert, began to lay siege to Norham using great siege engines designed by engineer John Crab at Berwick. Douglas and Randolph headed to Alnwick and Warkworth, holding a great tournament outside the latter's walls as the siege drew on. With the assaults underway, Robert led further raids into the countryside, ravaging the see of Durham, Cumberland and Westmoreland. So bruising was the attack that the communities of Cleveland and Richmond both offered large sums of money for truces that would last until 22 May 1328.[35] To underpin his achievements, the king turned from raider to occupier, making public grants and gifts of Northumbrian land to his men, sending out a warning to the English in the process: Northumberland would fall, and Isabella and Mortimer would be powerless to stop it unless they opened talks for a permanent peace.

To add further pressure, Robert had allowed Donald, Earl of Mar to take a small force into the Welsh March in 1327 to help him raise further troops to support the earl's attempt to spring Edward II from his gaol at Berkeley Castle in Gloucestershire. At the same time, the Dunheved brothers, Stephen and Thomas, were working to free the king, possibly in tandem with the earl. Sometime in mid-summer, possibly late July, Edward II was dramatically sprung from his cell, and temporarily managed to escape, possibly beyond the castle walls. He was subsequently recaptured by the desperate castle garrison and sent back to his cell at Berkeley, and later transported from castle to castle, including Corfe and Bristol, to prevent his supporters from discovering his whereabouts.

Had Edward and the Dunheved brothers joined up with Mar and his Welsh supporters, as may have been intended, then it is highly likely that Donald would have taken Edward II to Scotland and to King Robert, to engineer an invasion of England by which to reclaim his crown and for Robert to secure his country's independence.[36] In the end, facing as many as three plots to free the deposed king in nine months, Isabella and Mortimer made their move. By 24 September, Edward III received news at Lincoln that his father had died of natural causes sometime on the 21st of that month.[37] It was all too convenient, and many at court felt a great sense of unease. But for now, the public declaration that Edward II was dead, whether true or false, was sufficient to end Mar's immediate hope of rescuing his patron and friend.[38]

In desperate need to re-galvanise their popularity, and facing the loss of Northumberland, Isabella and Mortimer attempted to raise a second Scottish campaign during the Lincoln parliament in September. However, seething from their recent defeat, parliament refused to vote the necessary funds needed to muster the men and equipment for such an effort. With no opportunity to meet King Robert in the field, Isabella had no alternative but to sue for peace. Only this time, she knew Robert would accept nothing short of full peace and a recognition of his status, long coveted and now impossible to withhold. On 9 October, the queen appointed two royal envoys, Henry Percy and William de Denum, to act as chief negotiators. They left and headed to the besieged castle of Norham to meet with the expectant King of Scots.

During their initial meeting on 18 October, Robert set out six terms that he felt were his red lines. Firstly, he was to possess the Kingdom of Scotland 'free, quit and entire' for himself and his heirs forever, without the rendering of any homage. This guaranteed not only recognition of his crown but also the independence of his kingdom. Secondly, it was laid down that his only son, David, should marry Edward III's youngest sister, Joan, born in 1321 at the Tower of London and known to history as Joan of the Tower. Through this marriage the two kingdoms would be united in peace and mutual harmony, as in the days of Alexander II and his son, Alexander III. Furthermore, the king demanded that no subject of the King of Scots should claim or hold lands in England, nor any subject of the King of England claim lands in Scotland, thereby protecting his land settlement since 1314. Robert would also give the King of England military aid, notwithstanding the Scots alliance with France, and England would return the favour. In addition, he set out that he was willing to pay £20,000 in compensation within three years of a conclusion of peace as a war reparation. Finally, and perhaps the point which was becoming most urgent in the face of the king's rapidly declining health, Edward III would agree to influencing Pope John XXII to lift all papal censures on Robert and his kingdom.[39]

The terms were similar in feature to those first drawn up by the English traitor Andrew Harclay when he met Robert in 1323. Saying that marriage was acceptable, as well as the fee of £20,000, the negotiators informed Robert on 30 October that Edward III would have to pass judgement on the rest before they could proceed. Further talks would be scheduled for the following month.

Talks resumed on 23 November at Newcastle, led by the Archbishop of York, and would run into early December while a temporary truce was in place, scheduled to last until 13 March 1328, giving both parties a deadline.[40] The Scots added further conditions to peace, including the return of all documents seized by Edward I in his campaigns as well as those in English archives that purported to claim England's suzerainty over Scotland in times past.[41] The Ragman Roll, detailing the Scottish submission in 1296, was especially singled out. As well as damning paperwork, Robert and his council sought the return of the Stone of Destiny, used at previous royal inaugurations and now kept at Westminster Abbey, as well as holy relics such as the Black Rood, pieces of the Holy Cross once belonging to St Margaret of Scotland. In some of these additional requests, despite their political position of strength, the Scots were to be sorely disappointed. But as talks progressed, for once they did not fail. The English, fully aware of the vulnerable situation they now found themselves in, could see they had little alternative. The talks closed as the Christmas season began.

In February 1328, Scottish representatives headed to York and there received the long-coveted letter patent of King Edward III, which set out in unambiguous terms a full agreement to the majority of the conditions laid down by King Robert and his counsellors. Finally, after twenty-two years of bitter campaigning by Robert and a further ten years before that since the Scots had been forced to submit themselves to Edward I in 1296, Robert was granted full recognition of his crown, and Scotland was free of England's claim to sovereign overlordship.

> To all Christ's faithful people who shall see these letters, Edward, by the grace of God King of England, Lord of Ireland, Duke of Aquitaine, greeting and peace everlasting in the Lord. Whereas we, and some of our predecessors, Kings of England, have endeavoured to establish rights of rule or dominion or superiority over the realm of Scotland, whence dire conflicts of wars waged have afflicted for a long time the Kingdoms of England and Scotland: we, having regard to the slaughter, disasters, crimes, destruction of churches and evils innumerable which in the course of such wars, have repeatedly befallen the subjects of both realms, and to the wealth with which each realm, if united by the assurance of perpetual peace, might abound to their mutual advantage, thereby rendering them more secure against the hurtful efforts of those conspiring to rebel or attack, whether from within or without; we will and grant by these present, for us, our heirs and successors whatsoever, with the common advice, assent and consent of the prelates, princes, earls, barons, and the commons of our realm in parliament, that the Kingdom

of Scotland within its own proper marches as they were held
and maintained in the time of King Alexander of Scotland, last
deceased, of good memory, shall belong to our dearest ally
and friend, the magnificent prince Lord Robert, by God's grace
illustrious King of Scotland, and to his heirs and successors,
separately in all things from the Kingdom of England, whole, free
and undisturbed in perpetuity, without any kind of subjection,
service, claim or demand. And by these present we denounce
and demit to the King of Scotland, his heirs and successors,
whatsoever right we or our predecessors have put forward in any
way in bygone times to the aforesaid Kingdom of Scotland. And,
for ourselves and our heirs and successors, we cancel wholly and
utterly all obligations, conventions and compacts, undertaken in
whatsoever manner with our predecessors, at whatsoever times,
by whatsoever kings or inhabitants, clergy or laity, of the same
Kingdom of Scotland, concerning the subjection of the realm
of Scotland and its inhabitants. And wheresoever any letters,
charters, deeds or instruments may be discovered bearing upon
obligations, conventions, or compacts of this nature, we will that
they be deemed cancelled, invalid, of no effect and void, and
of no value or moment. And for the full peaceful and faithful
observance of the foregoing, all and singular for all that we have
given full power and special command by our other letters patent
to our well-beloved and faithful Henry de Percy our kinsman and
William de la Zouche of Ashby and to either of them make oath
upon our soul. In testimony whereof we have caused these letters
patent to be executed.[42]

Robert was victorious. Not only had he received recognition and
secured a permanent peace as 'by God's grace illustrious King of
Scotland', the details of the letter implied he was the natural and
rightful successor to Alexander III, 'last deceased', removing at a
stroke the brief reign of John Balliol from the record. Furthermore,
Robert's highly symbolic prize of Berwick remained in his hands,
as it had during the reign of Alexander III. He also retained the Isle
of Man.

The king had, however, made one major concession. In order to
secure a wider peace, Robert had compromised in allowing Scots
and Englishmen alike to hold lands and reclaim lost inheritances on
both sides of the border. Isabella could not have given up the claims
of so many of her key supporters, and knew this was non-negotiable

for the English. The so-called 'disinherited' were now legally able to challenge Robert's land resettlement in an attempt to recover lands that had been lost to them during the long conflict. This included leading English magnates such as Henry Percy, William de la Zouche and Henry Beaumont, the latter claiming the Isle of Man, the former Comyn earldom of Buchan through right of his wife, Roxburgh Castle, the sheriffdom of Wigtown and the Crail barony of Fife, among other lands.

Not all claims were lodged by Englishmen. James Douglas was part of the disinherited too, lands he had claimed as part of his raids in northern England were lost to him as a permanent peace settlement was achieved, and so he, along with other Scots, could use the legal process to reclaim them.[43] This concession was a major one for Robert, as it threatened the very heart of his long-established policy of land redistribution, which had stabilised Scotland and bound men to his cause. He and his successors would now be open to years of significant legal challenges, jeopardising everything he had put in place with this policy. But Robert was working strategically. If this was the price to pay to secure peace and other major terms with England, then so be it. He could play a game too. While the greater terms were met and carried out, he could obfuscate the challenges, granting only key items of land to key English and Scottish players to appease more generally without really undermining his resettlement policy. In the years after that, he would mothball the remaining claims. It was a very risky approach, but one Robert seemed more than prepared to adopt.

During the peace negotiations, Robert fell gravely ill at Holyrood. On 10 March, the English delegates, the bishops of Lincoln and Norwich, Chief Justice Geoffrey le Scrope, Henry Percy and William de la Zouche arrived in Edinburgh and met Robert in his bedchamber on the 17th. The choice of venue lent its name to the resulting document, which became known in Scotland as the Treaty of Edinburgh. It was only a week before the twenty-second anniversary of Robert's inauguration at Scone. Propped up in bed, now disfigured and apparently incapable of moving much, the king met his English audience with a Scottish host. Around him stood the flower of Scotland, including James Douglas, Thomas Randolph, Gilbert de la Haye the Constable and Robert Keith the Marischal. Bishop Lamberton of St Andrews was there too, as was the king's chancellor, Bernard, Abbot of Arbroath. The earls of Fife, Dunbar, Ross, Mar and Menteith were present, as were a further six bishops and a number of barons, including Andrew Murray, who had lately married the king's widowed sister Christian. It must have been a sombre occasion given the king's health but nevertheless would have been celebrated with feasts.[44] Edward III ratified the treaty at Northampton during a parliament there on 4 May.[45] In England the agreement was called the Treaty of Northampton, though it was characterised as a capitulation and known by the epithet 'The Shameful Peace'.

One of the more immediate terms of the treaty was the royal marriage between David and Joan. Given their very young ages – Joan was seven and David four – the English were keen to see the marriage take place soon rather than allow Robert a future opportunity to renege on his commitment and perhaps seek a marriage with France given the Franco-Scottish treaty. As an insurance indemnity, Edward III had been quick to demand a £100,000 payment should the marriage fail to take place before Michaelmas 1338, when David reached the accepted age of consent at fourteen and was in theory able to make up his own mind. Joan's dower was to be provided by lands from the Scottish Crown up to a sum of £2,000 a year. Edward III offered no dowry, a telling sign that all was not as it seemed back in England.[46]

In the late spring of 1328, Robert began to recover again. Preparations for the royal wedding began in earnest, the ceremony scheduled to take place at Berwick in the month of July. For the king, such events may have been tinged with sadness, for his wife Elizabeth was no longer there to enjoy them. As negotiations had first opened back in October the year before, the queen had suddenly fallen ill and died at Cullen in Banffshire on the 26th, aged thirty-eight. The king was no doubt deeply affected by the loss of his second wife, who had been through so much and stood loyally by her husband throughout. Her body was lain beneath the choir at Dunfermline Abbey while her viscera were entombed in the Lady Kirk of Cullen. In honour of her memory and to help ease her passage through purgatory, Robert founded a chaplaincy in the Lady Kirk to pray for her soul.[47] This would not be the last time he made such a gesture.

Like any royal event, the marriage of Scotland's royal heir to the sister of the King of England was set to be a lavish affair. The king's exchequer rolls reveal that his royal coffers were heavily strained, in part due to alienation of lands he had gifted to men who had supported him over the years. The death of William Lamberton,

Bishop of St Andrews, on 20 May 1328 gave the king a sudden boost of income to the tune of £2,000, as the bishop's temporalities fell back into royal hands until Lamberton's successor could be consecrated in his new office.[48] At the beginning of July, Queen Isabella headed north with her daughter, accompanied by many magnates of England including the bishops of Lincoln, Ely and Norwich, as well as the young William de Burgh, Earl of Ulster.

Edward III, however, chafing under his mother's overbearing tutelage, refused to attend. To Edward the treaty was shameful, and as he grew in confidence and spirit he began to make his thoughts known in England and beyond. This was not a good omen for the future. King Robert clearly would have sensed the danger, as would the magnates of Scotland. To neutralise the immediate effect, Robert took the decision not to attend the wedding either, claiming illness, and so remained at Cardross.[49] Despite the tension, the wedding went ahead as planned. When Isabella departed with her retinue at the end of the festivities, she was escorted back to the border by James Douglas and Thomas Randolph, before they returned to Berwick and took the young couple to the king at Cardross. After a few days during which King Robert met his new daughter-in-law, David and Joan were transported to Turnberry Castle, the seat of David's earldom of Carrick.

When Isabella departed Scotland, she left behind William de Burgh, the young Earl of Ulster. An understanding had been reached between the queen and King Robert by which he would head to Antrim and install his nephew, building on his earlier work there the year before. Again, too ill to ride, Robert was transferred to his ship from Cardross in a litter and sailed with a retinue from Dumbarton to Larne, arriving there on 13 August. It would be his last venture outside his kingdom. True to his word, the King of Scots ensured his brief stay was sufficient to see his young nephew installed into his inheritance, which included possession of the great castle at Carrickfergus, before he sailed back home to Scotland. In light of his endeavours Robert must have hoped that William would thank him for his support by offering his own son, David, aid in the years ahead should Scotland's future king need it when he came into his own inheritance. Unfortunately for William, and David too, the earl was murdered five years later.[50]

Gravely ill again, Robert's thoughts turned towards death. Following peace with England, he had immediately sought to have the papal censures overturned. On 5 November, Pope John XXII, while not yet minded to grant the king his wish, nevertheless gave permission for Robert to receive plenary remission for his sins from a confessor who should be provided for the king in his last hours.[51] It was a rite that could be granted to any man living in a kingdom under interdict, giving Robert a lifeline for his immortal soul. His mood grew increasingly reflective. Throughout his final year, he continued to provide lands and patronage to his followers, shoring up support for his son. His gifts were also personal. On 16 October, during a royal sojourn in the north-east with his sister Christian, which included a stay at Cullen where his late wife had died, they both granted lands in Aberdeenshire to the hospital of Turriff to support a chaplaincy to say masses for the soul of their younger brother Neil Bruce, who had been executed on Edward I's orders in 1306.[52] Robert was clearly thinking over the deeds and events of his life, taking time to reflect deeply on those he had lost on the way, and who had sacrificed so much for him and his crown. At Cullen he founded another chaplaincy, only this time it was for the soul of Queen Elizabeth.

In the closing months of 1328, the king and his court moved west back to Tarbert. He was most likely accompanied by Bernard, no longer Abbot of Arbroath but Bishop of the Isles. He would stay for a month, giving one last show of royal will and authority in what had always been a troubled region since he first took the crown, taking the time to make final gifts of lands to long-term supporters like the Campbells.[53] As Christmas drew nearer, the king left Tarbert and sailed on his great ship to the Isle of Arran where he spent the Holy days with John Menteith. He once again fell ill and was briefly incapacitated, slowing his royal progress. His apothecary, John, was called for, who administered medicines and received payment of £18 for his tireless work to keep the king alive. In addition, he was awarded an extra gift of £14, Robert perhaps having grown close to a man he had needed frequently for some years. Before the festivities were over, he was well enough to be carried on a litter to his ship, which set sail for Turnberry. Robert arrived in January, staying with his son and daughter-in-law until at least 6 February. By now he likely knew that he was dying.

Back in the lands of his childhood, the king was determined to make a pilgrimage to the shrine of St Ninian, a cave on the coast of Galloway dedicated to a cult saint whose reputation was growing across Scotland. The journey from Turnberry to the cave just beyond Wigtown at Whithorn must have been a gruelling affair for a king in so much pain and discomfort. He had reached Carleton by 7 February, and on the 18th made it to Inchmichael, where the deathly grip of his illness once again took a firm hold, halting his progress for six weeks. On 21 March, he gifted to his grandson Robert Stewart the barony of Renfrew in Lanarkshire, and also made a gift to his nephew Donald, Earl of Mar. By 29 February, he had recovered enough to travel by litter to Glenluce Abbey, and two days later had made it to Monreith, only 7 miles from Wigtown. With the shrine in reach, he managed to make the short journey in a day, reaching the cave of St Ninian's on 1 April.

Robert most likely stayed at the shrine for the next three weeks, which included Holy Week, in penitential prayer. Such acts of spiritual devotion and the choice of location, in the heart of the former Balliol-Comyn heartland, must indicate that Robert's thoughts were given over to the murder of John Comyn, Lord of Badenoch, at Blackfriars Church in 1306, which he himself had perpetrated. The brutal killing of Comyn in a place of worship, not far from where Robert was now located, was not only sacrilegious but had fundamentally changed the king's fortunes forever. From there on in, there had been no going back for Robert, his family and his supporters. He could not have foreseen then the twenty-two-year journey that would follow to gain recognition of his authority. Perhaps this act of penance was acknowledgement at last that he had always intended to win Comyn over to his cause or end his life if he couldn't, as well as a time to pray for those who had died fighting in his name ever since.

By early May, Robert was back at Cardross. As his health began to fail once and for all, he made final awards of lands and gifts. Nearing death, he gave out orders to James Douglas and others there assembled that his heart was to be removed from his body after his death and taken on pilgrimage to the Holy Land. His remaining viscera were to be interred in the Chapel of St Serf in Cardross. His heart burial was a final act of penance that Robert believed would ease his soul's passage through purgatory.[54] On 11 May, he issued letters of protection to the Cistercian abbey of Melrose, where his heart would be interred after its return from pilgrimage. It was also the place where Alexander II's body lay in rest, while the abbey itself had been given an exemption from the papal interdict. With his plenary remission, the place of his heart's interment, and a symbolic posthumous pilgrimage to the Holy Land, Robert was creating an insurance policy for his eternal soul.

Some of his final bequests included gifts in return for the saying of perpetual Masses at Ayr and Berwick Blackfriars, as well as at Dunfermline, where his body was to be buried alongside Scotland's other royal monarchs.

In the end, death came quietly on 7 June 1329. Ensconced in his luxurious defensive manor at Cardross, he slipped away in his bedchamber in the company of those who had for so long supported him. James Douglas and Thomas Randolph were both by his side, as were Gilbert de la Haye, Robert Keith and others. Bernard, now Bishop of the Isles, was most likely his confessor, charged by Pope John XXII to hear his final confession before death came to take him. Against all odds, King Robert I had ruled in Scotland for over twenty-three years and departed this life just shy of his fifty-fifth birthday.[55]

14

Aftermath

The news of Robert's death was quickly dispatched across the kingdom, and the accession of his five-year-old son, David, now King David II, was proclaimed at the same time. The Bruce dynasty would go on, if not Robert's pure legacy, as events in the years to come would dramatically demonstrate. The late king's body was treated with care and respect and his dying wishes were soon enacted. The physicians got to work, opening up his mortal remains through an incision into his sternum, thereby removing the heart for its pilgrimage to the Holy Land. His viscera were also removed. With the job complete, his remains were embalmed, wrapped in a shroud of linen embroidered with delicate gold thread, and prepared for the final journey to Dunfermline Abbey, where Robert's body would be laid to rest next to that of his late wife Elizabeth, as was his wish. The heart was encased in a specially commissioned silver casket detailed with enamel. It was given to James Douglas, who would later wear it around his neck in battle to fulfil his vow to his friend and king.[1]

There is no surviving date marking when Robert's funeral took place. But what is known is that in the weeks following his demise his body was taken from Cardross on a carriage furnished in black, which set out east across central Scotland, passing the foot of Loch Lomond, stopping briefly at Dunipace and Camsbuskenneth Abbey before arriving in the town of Dunfermline. Either during its short journey from the west, or when it entered the town of his final resting place, the cortège was met by a file of mourners dressed in black, headed up by the late king's grandson, the twelve-year-old Robert Stewart, who then processed solemnly into the abbey with the coffin. During the ceremony, the church was lit by hundreds of candles, the exchequer rolls recording the payment for over 8,000 lbs of wax to fulfil this special purpose. Many of them would have been attached to the canopy chapel, which was made from imported Baltic wood and most likely, in keeping with other medieval royal funerals, adorned with carvings depicting Robert's heraldic coat of arms.[2]

With the smell of incense hanging heavy in the air, the nobility of Scotland, the majority of whom were Robert's closest allies and supporters, said their farewells as they transferred their loyalty to Robert's heir, David, King of Scots.

When the ceremony was complete, the coffin was interred within a stone vault beneath the floor of the choir, and in the months that followed was crowned by a beautifully commissioned box-canopied white-and-black Italian marble tomb, the materials having been purchased in Paris in June 1328. In the centre of this great monument would have lain a carved marble effigy of the king himself, colourfully painted, as was the custom of the time, and gilded to shimmer in the candlelight; 1,100 books of gold leaf that had been ordered from the town of York for the purpose. It would have been Robert's final testament to his royal power from beyond the grave. One of his closest friends and former advisers, Bernard, Bishop of the Isles and former Abbot of Arbroath, penned the inscription which adorned the top mantle of the canopy. It was a fitting epitaph:

> Here lies the invincible blessed King Robert. Whoever reads about his feats will repeat the many battles he fought. By his integrity he guided to liberty the Kingdom of the Scots. May he now live in Heaven.[3]

To support his soul's translation, in his last few years Robert had continued to gift considerable funds to religious institutions around Scotland to pay for Masses to be said both in his name and that of his family. There would have been a considerable number said in the first year of his death, with fewer thereafter on specified dates for many years ahead. For King Robert had always been acutely aware of his need to lead his soul through purgatory, especially given he remained an excommunicate.

It was fortunate timing, then, that within six days of his death, Pope John XXII in Avignon decreed Robert's excommunication lifted, along with the censure of interdict on Scotland. In another bull issued at the same time, the Holy Father went one step further, celebrating Scotland's return to the Church by granting its future kings the rite of holy unction in a full coronation, so long a missing feature of the Scottish inauguration ceremony but a key practice of the major monarchies of medieval Europe.[4] The letters arrived months after Robert's funeral, but with a retrospective application, and Robert's plenary remission allowing his confession prior to his death meant the people of Scotland never felt their king's soul was in peril. The right of future kings to a full coronation was a special recognition of Scotland's independence and sovereignty. It was the crowning moment in Robert's legacy.

In the years following his death, many of his relatives would also be buried alongside him in the choir at Dunfermline Abbey. His sisters Christian, Mary and Maud would be buried there, as was his daughter Margaret, sister to King David, who died in 1346 having previously married William, Earl of Sutherland. Her son was John Sutherland, who died in 1361. The company also extended to one of Robert's favourites, his nephew Thomas Randolph, Earl of Moray, and the king's brother-in-law Andrew Murray.[5] Each would have commissioned elaborate tombs throughout the choir near to their royal master to stand testament to the generations of people who came after them.

However, on 28 March 1560, during Scotland's Reformation, the abbey at Dunfermline, in particular the choir, belfry and nave, were razed by reformers, many of the tombs destroyed in an act of iconoclasm and left to the elements for years, excepting the nave, which was converted a few years later into a small parish chapel.[6] Scotland's royal monuments were left to the elements for centuries, until in 1818 work was commissioned to clear the centuries of rubble to make way for a larger Protestant church. During these activities, Robert's coffin, still secure in the stone vault beneath the choir floor, was unearthed and opened. There they found the body of a man whose sternum had been opened before being embalmed. It was quickly deduced to be that of King Robert I. Before the body was reinterred and the coffin brimmed with pitch, a plaster cast was taken of the skull, which survives today.

At the end of the twentieth century, with the modern advances of computer science, a facial reconstruction was created using the plaster cast to give us the first indication of what Robert may have looked like nearly seven hundred years after his death. The result revealed a thickset man, who would have had real presence in any audience. Unfortunately, there are no contemporary descriptions of Robert's appearance in any extant accounts. We have no idea of his height, build, skin tone, hair or eye colour. As a result, he remains primarily in the shadows, so the dressing of this facial reconstruction rests on assumption and our best guesses. Nevertheless, we at least have the shape of his face, which goes some way in helping us to picture the man.

But what was also noted from the plaster-cast skull of the king was a scar he must have sustained in conflict, for there was a deep blade cut to the jaw that must have healed in the months after battle, leaving him with a reminder of his efforts to secure the crown. There were also facial lesions which had left scars on the bone, supporting the view that in his lifetime, particularly sometime in the years prior to his death, Robert suffered from significant skin disfiguration to his face and perhaps his body.[7]

The cause of Robert's death has remained something of a mystery for nearly seven centuries. The physicians who directed the king's treatment in the last few years of his life failed to record his condition, perhaps because they could not diagnose it. If they did, their records do not survive. Only contemporary chroniclers, most of whom did not see Robert in person, went so far as to hazard a guess, the first being the chronicler of Lanercost, who claimed the king suffered from leprosy, which later chroniclers such as Froissart began to repeat.[8] This is unsurprising given their anti-Scottish bias, quick to sight the 'unclean sickness' as a fitting penance for a king who had murdered and, in their eyes, usurped his way to the crown.

So, is it true? Robert's symptoms, gleaned from surviving records, show ad hoc bouts of illness which appeared to start when on campaign in 1308. He suffered loss of appetite, problems with speech, and bouts of paralysis which, while temporary, could last for a number of months during different episodes throughout his adult life. Often these attacks came during intense periods of stress or when campaigning in the field. His skull confirms an advanced skin condition that was bad enough to damage bone. These are all symptoms of leprosy, which creates deep lesions that bore into the bone as well as leaving outwardly visible damage on the skin. It can also cause alopecia and problems with speech. Left untreated, it would have killed him; there was of course no known cure in the medieval world.

However, leprosy is an infectious bacterium, and those who were inflicted were isolated from society and forced to live outside their communities, as much for their own safety as for their neighbours. Medieval doctors may not have understood bacteria, but they were acutely aware that a person suffering from leprosy could pass it on to others. For a king whose personal rule was at the heart of government and expressed by his physical presence, it would have been impossible to carry out the daily functions of kingship as he did if Robert was a leper from 1308. A person inflicted with the disease would not be able to fight, father children, hold court and ride around his country consistently for over two decades without passing on the infection to some of those around him.[9] King Robert throughout his lifetime continued to perform these roles and was never isolated from his court.

Previous leper kings such as Baldwin IV, King of Jerusalem, who reigned at the end of the twelfth century, ruled through others from a distance before his premature death in 1185.[10] If Robert was indeed leprous, those supporters who remained close at hand put themselves at considerable risk. It seems, on the balance of probability, that leprosy was not the illness that inflicted the king, but that it was something equally unpleasant.

There have been many suggestions. Scrofula, today known as lymphadenopathy, is a well-known disease that causes lesions to develop around the lymph nodes, especially in the neck and groin. This would have scarred bone, had paralytic effects and caused great discomfort. Robert's condition could have been scrofula, but this would have been most unfortunate, for scrofula was a sickness traditionally cured only by the 'king's touch', especially in England. If Robert did indeed have the disease, it would have emphasised to his critics that in the eyes of God he was no king at all, for no king could be afflicted by a disease cured by the touch of a king.

Other suggestions have included tuberculosis, or consumption, which can lay dormant for years after infection in the body and flare up at key times, progressively weakening the individual after each attack. Alternatively, the king may have contracted syphilis, known at the time as venereal leprosy, a sickness that also produces skin disfiguration not too dissimilar to leprosy as well as cartilage loss and eroded joints. Robert, after all, had a string of illegitimate children and may well have had a number of sexual encounters with different women both during Elizabeth's long captivity in

England and after, as was typical of the period for a man of his status. There are even suggestions of successive strokes, from which he would slowly recover, but this seems unlikely.

Perhaps it was none of these. The writer Barbour suggests that Robert contracted his lifetime illness through his hard campaigning in 1306 and beyond, when he was forced into temporary exile and spent over a year living out in the wild, exposed to the elements, weakening his constitution.[11] He could easily have contracted an intestinal infection from bad water or poorly cooked food that caused serious internal organ damage.[12] This may be why Maino de Maineri often recommended the calming effects of rice cooked in either almond milk or pea-water to calm his gut. Equally, his condition could have been multiple, not just the result of a single diagnosis. With a lack of clear evidence, we will never know for sure what killed him. All that is certain is that from 1308 Robert was dogged by ill health which rapidly worsened after 1324, and which led to his death in June 1329.

One task remained before Robert's dying wishes were complete. James Douglas gathered about him a number of knights, including William Keith, Alan Cathcart, William de St Clair of Roslin, as well as Robert and Walter Logon and twenty-six squires. In early March, they left Scotland with the king's heart, their aim to take it into battle against the infidel. They travelled by sea, arriving at the port of Sluys, where they remained for twelve days according to Froissart. From there they sailed on, heading for Spain before anchoring on the south-western Spanish coast at Seville, not too far from the Strait of Gibraltar. After arrival, Douglas and his retinue headed to the court of King Alfonso XI of Castile and Léon, and presented a letter of safe conduct and an introduction from Edward III, who appeared to support their mission.[13] The timing could not have been better, for Alfonso was at war with the Prince of Granada. Spain at the time was a series of Christian kingdoms with an Islamic caliphate in the south.

On 25 March 1330, James Douglas agreed to fight for the King of Castile, and in command of his retinue rode out to battle at Tebas de Ardales, reinforced with a contingent of European knights who had also come to participate in Alfonso's forthcoming assault. In the fight that soon began, Douglas and his men charged ahead of the Castilian vanguard, seeing the enemy ranks apparently take flight in front of them. It was a grave mistake, for the tactics deployed were common among the

Moorish cavalry, who feigned flight to encourage their enemy to follow, only to swiftly turn their horses with great dexterity at the last moment and envelope the advancing pursuers. Aware of the imminent danger that Douglas now faced, and unable to intervene, Alfonso and his men left the Scottish and European knights to their own defence.[14] It was catastrophic. Flanked on all sides by the enemy, James and his comrades were trapped, and without the chance of recovery, were quickly overwhelmed. As men fell, Douglas attempted to save William de St Clair but both men were killed.[15] Only William Keith survived, having not taken part in the fighting due to a broken arm, and he was able to recover the king's heart that had been carried into battle around the neck of his friend who was now no more.

The death of James Douglas was as dramatic as many of his feats in life. His loss seemed an ill omen. Before returning home, William Keith arranged for Douglas's body to be boiled in the fashion of the Teutonic Knights, allowing the flesh to separate from the bone.[16] The flesh was collected up and buried in consecrated ground, while the bones were carefully packed up, allowing Keith to transport them, along with King Robert's heart, back to Scotland. On his return, Douglas's mortal remains were interred in the chapel of St Bride at Douglas and a tomb was erected to mark the spot, surviving to this day. Robert's heart, despite not making it to the Holy Land, had nevertheless taken part in a battle against the common enemy of Christendom, and so was sent to Melrose Abbey, the vow seemingly fulfilled, where it was subsequently interred with all due reverence.

The end of Douglas's life seemed to mark a downturn in the good fortunes of the Kingdom of Scotland and Robert's legacy. King David II came to his throne at the age of five, necessitating a long minority. He and his wife, Queen Joan, were crowned at Scone on 24 November 1331. At a time when kings were there to rule, not merely reign, a child king ultimately left the kingdom vulnerable. By 1332, Edward III, at the age of twenty, was secure in his kingship, having overthrown Mortimer and his mother two years prior in a coup d'état at Nottingham Castle. With his newfound independence, the King of England was quick to declare that the Treaty of Northampton was invalid, his allegedly forced acceptance of it being meaningless given that he had been a minor at the time. Backed by his subjects, who declared it a shameful peace, Edward encouraged Edward Balliol, the son of King John Balliol, to press his claim to the Scottish throne. Robert's legacy was once more in grave jeopardy.

Thomas Randolph, Earl of Moray, in accordance with King Robert's talzie of July 1326, had assumed the guardianship of both the young king and the realm. Facing the threat of an imminent Balliol invasion, preparations were made to defend the kingdom, only for Randolph's time to suddenly run out. Without warning he fell ill at Musselburgh on 20 July 1332 and died, with baseless accusations of poisoning levelled at the English. With Randolph dead, and Douglas too, the kingdom was dangerously exposed, encouraging Edward Balliol and many of the disinherited lords – led by Henry Beaumont, whom King Robert had promised some degree of restitution in 1328 – to set sail for Scotland. Panicked, an assembly of Scottish magnates, lay and ecclesiastical, elected Donald, Earl of Mar as Guardian at Perth on 2 August.

Just over a week later, Mar's forces, representing his young ward King David, engaged with Balliol's army at the Battle of Dupplin Moor. Balliol had gathered together a small force of approximately 2,000–3,000 men, and Mar, with far superior numbers, became complacent, failing to set adequate watches at night. During the small hours, Balliol's men crossed the river between the two armies undetected. This was a humiliating development, and one King David's magnates, especially King Robert's illegitimate son and namesake, immediately drove home, accusing Donald of treachery. The Scots always viewed Mar with suspicion, thinking he had been far too close to the English, and Edward II in particular. Some suggested he had been working for the English all along. In the battle that soon followed, Mar, indignant and defiant, charged his English enemy, as did the bastard Robert Bruce, both being killed in the ensuing action, in which the Scots were felled under a hail of English arrows and the crush of their own numbers, being restricted in a narrow space. Thomas Randolph's eldest son, also called Thomas, and Earl of Moray for less than a month, perished alongside his peers. The key figures of Robert's court were quickly falling from the pages of history.

Their deaths allowed Edward Balliol to march to Scone, where he was crowned as a rival King of Scots on 24 September 1332. King David now had a consecrated rival. But Balliol's gain was short-lived. Forces were raised under the command of John Randolph, second son to the late Thomas and now Earl of Moray; Robert Stewart, King Robert's grandson; Archibald Douglas, brother to

James Douglas; and Simon Fraser. On 16 December, while Balliol and some of his men were resting at Annan, this force made a surprise attack. In the chaos, known to history as the Camisade of Annan, Edward Balliol fled south, crossing the Scottish border into England. Victory suddenly looked possible, but once again fate was to deliver a bitter blow.

With Donald, Earl of Mar dead, King Robert's brother-in-law Andrew Murray was elected to assume his role as Guardian of the king and the realm. He was captured in action at Roxburgh by pro-Balliol supporters in April 1333 and was promptly replaced by an increasingly desperate Scottish assembly, who elected Archibald Douglas in his stead. In the same year, Edward Balliol returned from England with King Edward III, who was bent on recovering Berwick and nullifying the Treaty of Northampton. In the events that followed, which included a long siege of that town, Archibald Douglas mustered the Scottish forces to Halidon Hill, where Edward III had stationed his army. Much like in 1314, when Edward II was forced to race to Stirling Castle to relieve its besieged garrison, Archibald Douglas and his men were required to do the same to relieve Berwick, its commander having struck a deal with Edward III mirroring that of 1314. With the boot on the other foot, and the potential loss of Berwick, Douglas knew he needed a win in order for King David to survive.

The Battle of Halidon Hill, fought 2 miles outside the town of Berwick, is remembered as one of the most catastrophic defeats in Scottish history. On 19 July, the Scots were forced to attack Edward III's troops uphill, wading through marshy territory before a steep ascent under a hail of arrows that decimated their schiltrons. So dense was the fire, remarked a chronicler, that it was like battling 'into the sleet'. In the carnage, five pro-David earls were killed, including Hugh, Earl of Ross, who was King Robert's brother in law, as well as the earls of Atholl, Sutherland, Carrick and Lennox. The earldom of Carrick had been gifted to Alexander Bruce, an illegitimate son of Edward Bruce, High King of Ireland. Archibald Douglas also perished, Robert Stewart and John Murray escaped. Facing complete disaster, the infant King David and Queen Joan and their household were forced to flee to Dumbarton Castle. Holding out until the summer of the following year, they were then secretly shipped out of the kingdom to the Valois court of Philip VI, King of France, an ardent enemy of Edward III. In his absence, David II's magnates continued to fight for their infant king and the royal House of Bruce during what became known as the Second War of Scottish Independence.

In the end, Edward Balliol was defeated. On 2 June 1341, seven years after his flight, King David, now seventeen, returned to Scotland with his queen to assume direct rule. Five years later, as Edward III waged war in France, having opened the Hundred Years War in a bid to pursue his claim to the French throne, King Philip VI sought the help of King David in return for his years of protection. This debt, coupled with the long-standing agreements last noted in the Treaty of Corbeil in 1326, which promised Scottish aid to the French if attacked by England, meant David felt obliged to help.

Invading Edward III's kingdom, King David was eventually captured at the Battle of Neville's Cross, fought within sight of Durham Cathedral on 17 October. Initially held in the Tower of London, David was later transferred to Windsor Castle and then Odiham in Hampshire, where he spent the next eleven years in a relaxed confinement awaiting the payment of an extortionate ransom of 100,000 marks. He was eventually released in 1357, returning to Scotland to restore peace to the kingdom and reassert his royal authority. He died at Edinburgh without any male issue on 22 February 1371, bringing to an end the House of Bruce. He was succeeded by his fifty-four-year-old nephew, King Robert's grandson Robert Stewart, who ascended the throne as Robert II, the first of the Stewart kings of Scotland, and reigned until 19 April 1390. Robert Bruce's long-term legacy had not played out quite as he had envisaged.

Since his death, Robert Bruce has entered in to the realms of myth and legend. This is hardly surprising. Here was a man who almost lost everything, only to recover in the face of overwhelming adversity, overcoming innumerable obstacles and challenges, and dying in his bed having reigned for over twenty-three years. The chaos that followed after his death, reopening the bitterly divisive wars of Scottish independence, did much to polarise and romanticise subsequent opinion. King David's failure to rule like his father, and the resulting uncertainty and danger, perhaps saw King Robert's achievements – great as they were – exaggerated into something far more heroic and mythopoeic.

After peeling back nearly seven hundred years of myth to judge him for his actions and deeds alone, then, what is King Robert's real legacy? Without question, his greatest quality was his military prowess. His acute skill and strategic mind allowed him to see beyond the obvious and through the face of adversity. He was farsighted enough to meet Edward I's dragon banner with the same abandonment of chivalric customs, a lesson learned from the catastrophe of Methven. His subsequent guerrilla war, fought in the hills, mountains and boggy terrain of the Scottish landscape, ensured he and his small band of loyal followers were able to amplify their efforts and achieve unimaginable successes that would have been impossible under the conventional rules of war.

His self-awareness, charisma and emotional intelligence allowed him to take counsel; he inspired loyalty by offering his commanders a place at the table, and in return they gave him their lives and unstinting fellowship. His strategy to slight castles, depriving his enemy of fortresses and palaces to garrison, released his kingdom from a stranglehold that would otherwise have been nearly impossible to throw off. It was this lesson, which many kings before and since would fail to apply, which starved his enemy of a foothold in his kingdom and allowed him to focus his own energies on overcoming the enemy within. He was also lucky with the timing of Edward I's death and the domestic conflicts which prevented Edward II from launching a concerted campaign to bring down the Bruce regime in the early years of his rule. When his Scottish domestic enemies were defeated, he had the confidence, ability and strategic mind to take the fight to the English in order to apply pressure on the King of England in a bid to extract concessions from him that would secure Robert's ultimate prize: recognition of his rights and the sovereignty of his kingdom.

Robert was truly the champion of his nation, but he underestimated the stubbornness and determination of his enemy. Edward II, unafraid in war despite his later reputation, was as ruthless as his father, Edward I. The former's insistence on upholding his inherited rights to Scotland's overlordship caught Robert and his men by surprise, and the long wars of attrition that followed could have weakened Robert's perceived suitability to the Scottish crown. People can have short memories. Yet the hero of Bannockburn, a battle King Robert never would have planned to fight against such overwhelming odds, was one of his defining moments and continues to reverberate through history. His killing of Henry de Bohun on the first day gave him mythical status. His victory in 1314 ensured his people ultimately remained loyal to him, proving his God-given right to rule.

Robert's ability to be flexible, to act on a sudden advantage like Seton's betrayal of the English, allowed him to take the initiative. He dared, and he won. To some his actions were rash, for had he failed he would have compromised not just his crown and his life but possibly the very future of his nation. Yet he was often cautious, only committing to a fight if he knew he had a good chance of winning. His evacuation of Lothian and his retreat into central Scotland on various occasions was practical and representative of his ability to grasp the reality of a situation. He knew when to fight and when to run. His attempt to capture Edward II in 1322 was a courageous move born out of frustration, and although he failed to achieve it, he humiliated the English badly enough to engineer the thirteen-year truce that bought him and his heirs valuable time. Robert was a long-term player who understood the need for patience when it was most required in order to achieve his ultimate goals. His success in securing a permanent peace with England, or so he thought, was as much about his careful timing as anything, as he watched political chaos unfold in England and played it entirely to his own advantage.

Yet he could also overexert himself. The campaign in Ireland which saw his brother crowned as High King overstretched their forces, ultimately costing him dearly when Edward Bruce was killed in battle at Faughart in October 1318. The privation and near collapse of the joint Bruce army once again endangered Scotland at a time when neither brother had legitimate male heirs. Robert did not always play the political game well, either. During his early years, before he took the throne, his adolescent hot temper could get the better of him. His political isolation in the volatile years between 1296 and 1306 meant he was unpopular among his peers, especially his Balliol-Comyn rivals, unable to co-operate for a common cause.

His murder of John Comyn, Lord of Badenoch, has gone down in history as another incident where his temper got the better of him. Yet this feels too convenient. Having inherited his ancestors' failed claims to the Scottish throne, Robert knew he needed either to win over or remove his principal rival. As he entered Blackfriars Church in Dumfries in 1306, he knew there were only two ways to get what he wanted, and he was ready to employ either method. His ruthless action in seizing the crown was built on sacrilegious murder. In later life, particularly approaching the end, he seemed more penitential than ever as he weighed his earlier actions and perhaps felt himself wanting in the eyes of God. Yet it is unlikely he would have gone back and changed his course.

In his religious conviction, Robert was conventionally pious, shown by his frequent veneration of the Scottish royal St Margaret, as well as St Andrew, St Fillan, St Thomas Becket, St Serf and latterly St Ninian. He had to exhibit his piety publicly to fight back against papal censures that saw him excommunicated and his country laid under interdict. Yet he did not appear cynical. Nor would he be bullied into giving up what he had thus far achieved, irrespective of the international condemnation this could provoke. He called upon the intercession of these saints when he needed to be imbued with their holy power to achieve his aims. He also took care to endow the religious monasteries, abbeys and priories of his kingdom, many of which had been damaged during the long conflict with England. He gave gifts freely to many religious houses, including the newly consecrated cathedral of St Andrews, the building of which he oversaw in July 1318, and also the abbeys of Scone and Arbroath, Melrose and Holyrood, and of course the place of his royal burial and the royal mausoleum of the Kings of Scotland at Dunfermline.[17]

He took the time to remember those who had supported him, and those he had loved. His devotions in memory of his brothers, wives, sisters and supporters are noted throughout his reign. His piety no doubt won him respect from many of his prelates, who were some of his greatest advocates before and throughout his reign, and right up until his end. His closeness to leading clerics like Robert Wishart, William Lamberton, Bernard of Arbroath and Alexander Kinninmonth offered him core support that helped underpin his rule. Robert was careful to keep the symbiotic relationship between church and state robust, and this was ultimately to his advantage. The support of the churchmen in drafting both the Declaration of the Clergy in 1309 and the Declaration of Arbroath in 1320 helped to articulate his cause and offset Edward II's machinations among the Curia.

One of Robert's most notable qualities is his judicious exercise of patronage. Before 1314 he was cautious not to reward people too freely, but after Bannockburn his determination to disinherit those who failed to acknowledge his rightful kingship saw Robert set about securing his dynasty with the careful application of royal gifts and blandishments that would bind men and their families to him and his heirs. His strategy was carefully crafted and cleverly deployed. He exercised his gift-giving well, instinctively knowing when to give and when to take. His confirmation of the Earl of Ross and his heirs into their patrimony in 1308, and marriage within the royal family, helped turn an erstwhile enemy into an ardent supporter, winning him a key northern part of his kingdom. He gave many other enemies the chance to come over to his side and regain their lost lands in return for loyalty. Sometimes this worked, and other times it did not, most notably in the case of the Earl of Angus, who betrayed him once again at Bannockburn in 1314. His grants to Edward Bruce, Thomas Randolph, Walter Stewart, James Douglas and many others helped re-draw the map of Scotland in his family's favour.

His gift-giving often left him short of royal income and capital, having granted away full regalities and free baronies, but this rebinding of loyalty paid dividends in the following reign, which saw King David II retain his throne because Robert's patronage had engendered lasting loyalty to his royal house. Yet it could also provoke dissent. The Soules conspiracy was the work of nobles who had been kept out in the cold despite professing loyalty, and in acknowledging the disinherited in 1328 in return for a permanent peace with England, Robert did much to undermine his good work, arguably not foreseeing the risk this represented to his reign and that of his heir.

In his exercise of justice, a key marker of kingship, Robert was cautious and fair. He knew when to be hard and went to proffer clemency. His treatment of those caught up in the Soules conspiracy was balanced, perhaps a reflection of the lessons he had learnt at the hands of those who had been far less judicious. The systematic murder of his brothers and supporters at the hands of Edward I, dressed up as summary justice, must have left a deep scar on his conscience and made him acutely aware of the need to be different. He was also both sympathetic and responsive to the concerns of those who raised petitions and sought the application of his royal intervention.

He appeared genuinely close to his family, perhaps in part because he was only too aware of how much they had sacrificed to protect and further his own cause. His long absence without a male heir endangered the survival of his dynasty, yet he and his second wife Elizabeth never gave up hope and were rewarded for their efforts with two daughters as well as two sons. His closeness to his daughter from his first marriage, Marjorie, was clear from the outset when he refused to offer her up as a hostage during the conflict with Edward I. The premature death of his eldest legitimate daughter in 1317 must have devastated him. In all, Robert appeared to be a loving and protective husband, father and brother. He was also an inspiring and loyal friend to those who were closest to him, shown by their fierce commitment, which in many cases was lifelong.

In death, looking beyond the myth and the legends, Robert Bruce emerges as a man of exceptional qualities. While many of his deeds have been claimed by successive generations and adapted or romanticised for different ends, the real Robert Bruce, the man who became the King of Scots, deserves to be recognised for everything he achieved. His legacy today reminds us all that victory can be won in the face of adversity, and that anything is possible if you are truly determined. It is no surprise that, across the ages, he remains Scotland's champion.

Appendix One

The Declaration of the Clergy, 1309–10

By 1309 King Robert was secure enough in his kingship to order his first parliament to St Andrews. There, following three years of war and attrition, he was able to call upon those present to give public recognition to the legitimacy of his rule. It was a highly significant moment. On 17 March, the clergy banded together and issued a significant declaration which set out to rationalise events since the death of Alexander III, King of Scots, and outline King Robert's sole right to the throne. The terms were clear and unequivocal. The document, sealed by twelve members of the clergy, remains intact, but the individual seals have long been lost. Surviving documents like this one give real insight into the minds and arguments of those caught up in Robert's story. Their voices leap from the page.

> We, the bishops, abbots, priors, and other clergy in the realm of Scotland, give greeting, in the name of the Author of salvation, to all the faithful in Christ to whose notice the present document shall come. Be it known to all of you, that when there arose a subject of dispute between John Balliol, lately installed as King of Scotland *de facto* by the King of England, and the late Robert Bruce, of honourable memory, grandfather of Robert who is now the king, concerning which of them had the better title, by right of birth, to inherit the rule over the people of Scotland, the faithful people always believed without hesitation, as they had understood from their ancestors and elders, and held to be the truth, that Robert, the grandfather, was the true heir, and was to be preferred to all others as ruler of the realm, after the death

of King Alexander, and of his granddaughter, the daughter of the King of Norway. But because the enemy of the human race has sown tares, and because of the divers stratagems and tricks of Robert's rivals, which it would be tedious to describe one by one, the matter has turned out otherwise and, by his deprivation and loss of the royal dignity, grievous harm has since come to the realm of Scotland and to its inhabitants, as experience of events, our mistress in politics, now often repeated, has manifestly shown.

Therefore the whole people of the realm of Scotland, wearied with the stings of many tribulations (for this John was taken by the King of England, for various reasons, and imprisoned, and deprived of his realm and people, and the realm of Scotland was lost to him, and reduced to servitude, laid waste by great slaughter, and imbued with the bitterness of heavy sorrow, made desolate by the lack of true governance, exposed to every danger, and given up to the despoiler, the inhabitants deprived of their property, tortured with strife, made captive, bound and imprisoned, oppressed with untold killings of blameless people, and with continual burnings, subject and in bonds, and nigh to perpetual ruin unless by divine counsel speedy provision were made for the restoration of a realm so afflicted and desolate, and of its government, by the providence of the King most high, under whose authority kings rule, and princes govern), this people, being unable any longer to endure injuries so many and so great, and more bitter than death, which were being continually inflicted on their property and their persons for lack of a captain and a faithful leader, agreed, by divine prompting, on Lord Robert who now is king, in whom reside and remain uncorrupted, in the general opinion, the rights of his father and his grandfather to the kingdom; and with their knowledge and approval he was received as king, that he might reform the defects of the realm, correct what had to be corrected, and direct what was without guidance. By their authority he was set over the realm, and formally established as King of Scots, and with him the faithful people of the realm wish to live and die, as with one who, by right of birth and endowment with other [*sic*] cardinal virtues, is fit to rule, and worthy of the name of king and of the honour of a realm since, through the grace of the Saviour, he has saved from injury and restored with his sword the kingdom thus damaged and decayed, as many princes and Kings of the Scots had formerly by the sword restored, gained, and held in ancient times the said kingdom, which of old was often in jeopardy, as is contained more fully in the ancient and splendid histories of the Scots, and as the warlike efforts of the Picts against the Britons, and of the Scots against the Picts, who were expelled from the realm, and many others who were put to fight, conquered, and expelled with the sword in olden days, clearly testify.

If anyone, however, defends his claim to the realm by producing sealed letters from the past, which record the consent of the whole people, be it known that this entire business was in fact carried through by force and violence which nobody could then resist, and by intimidation and many tortures of the body, and by various threats which were able to pervert the senses and the minds of even the best men, and to afflict the steadfast. We, therefore, the bishops, abbots, priors and other clergy aforesaid, knowing that these statements are founded upon the truth, and heartily approving of them, have sworn fealty due to Lord Robert, our illustrious King of Scotland, and we agree, and bear witness by the text of this document, that the same should be done to him and his heirs, by our successors in future. And we have caused our seals to be added to this document, as a sign of our testimony, and in approval of all the aforesaid, being not constrained by force, or seduced by craft or lapsing into error, but acting with pure, perpetual, and spontaneous freewill. At a Scottish general council, celebrated in the church of the Friars Minor of Dundee, 24 February A.D. 1309, in the fourth year of the reign of the same [king].[1]

Appendix Two

The Declaration of Arbroath, 1320

By the dawn of 1320, King Robert's legitimate right to the crown and the independence of the kingdom of Scotland remained a matter of continued dispute and conjecture. Pope John XXII had already issued a papal decree of excommunication and had laid Scotland under the severe penalty of interdict. In March, King Robert ordered a Great Council to assemble at Newbattle Abbey near Edinburgh for Easter. Three letters were commissioned there: one from Robert himself, one from the clergy and one from the king's lay magnates. The latter is the only one to survive, and since the nineteenth century it has been remembered to history as the Declaration of Arbroath, the place where the barons' seals were attached to it.

The letter was an expertly crafted document, designed to appeal to the pope and written in the rhythmic Latin used among the Curia, to be read aloud in front of a full papal court. Its form, written by an eloquent Latinist – perhaps Bernard, Abbot of Arbroath or Alexander Kinninmonth, later Bishop of Aberdeen – goes to the heart of King Robert's, and indeed Scotland's, determination to assert and defend its independence from England. Today, the declaration remains one of Scotland's most prized constitutional documents.

To the most Holy Father and Lord in Christ, the Lord John, by divine providence Supreme Pontiff of the Holy Roman and Universal Church, his humble and devout sons Duncan, Earl of Fife, Thomas Randolph, Earl of Moray, Lord of Man and of Annandale, Patrick Dunbar, Earl of March, Malise, Earl of

Strathearn, Malcolm, Earl of Lennox, William, Earl of Ross, Magnus, Earl of Caithness and Orkney, and William, Earl of Sutherland; Walter, Steward of Scotland, William Soules, Butler of Scotland, James, Lord of Douglas, Roger Mowbray, David, Lord of Brechin, David Graham, Ingram de Umfraville, John Menteith, guardian of the earldom of Menteith, Alexander Fraser, Gilbert Hay, Constable of Scotland, Robert Keith, Marischal of Scotland, Henry St Clair, John Graham, David Lindsay, William Oliphant, Patrick Graham, John Fenton, William Abernethy, David Wemyss, William Muschet, Fergus of Ardrossan, Eustace Maxwell, William Ramsay, William Mowat, Alan Murray, Donald Campbell, John Cameron, Reginald Cheyne, and the other barons and freeholders and the whole community of the realm of Scotland send all manner of filial reverence, with devout kisses of his blessed feet.

Most Holy Father and Lord, we know and from the chronicles and books of the ancients we find that among other famous nations of our own, the Scots, has [have] been graced with widespread renown. They journeyed from Greater Scythia by way of the Tyrrhenian Sea and the Pillars of Hercules, and dwelt for a long course of time in Spain among the most savage tribes, but nowhere could they be subdued by any race, however barbarous. Thence they came, twelve hundred years after the people of Israel crossed the Red Sea, to their home in the west where they still live today. The Britons they first drove out, the Picts they utterly destroyed, and, even though very often assailed by the Norwegians, the Danes and the English, they took possession of that home with many victories and untold efforts; and, as the historians of old time bear witness, they have held it free of all bondage ever since. In their kingdom there have reigned one hundred and thirteen kings of their own royal stock, the line unbroken by a single foreigner.

The high qualities and deserts of these people, were they not otherwise manifest, gain glory enough from this: that the King of kings and Lord of lords, our Lord Jesus Christ, after His Passion and Resurrection, called them, even though settled in the uttermost parts of the earth, almost the first to His most holy faith. Nor would He have them confirmed in that faith by merely anyone but by the first of His Apostles – by calling, though second or third in rank – the most gentle Saint Andrew, the Blessed Peter's brother, and desired him to keep them under his protection as their patron for ever.

The Most Holy Fathers your predecessors gave careful heed to these things and bestowed many favours and numerous privileges on this same kingdom and people, as being the special charge of the Blessed Peter's brother. Thus our nation under their protection did indeed live in freedom and peace up to the time when that mighty prince the King of the English, Edward, the father of the one who reigns today, when our kingdom had no head and our people harboured no malice or treachery and were then unused to wars or invasions, came in the guise of a friend and allay to harass them as an enemy. The deeds of cruelty, massacre, violence, pillage, arson, imprisoning prelates, burning down monasteries, robbing and killing monks and nuns, and yet other outrages without number which he committed against our people, sparing neither age nor sex, religion nor rank, no one could describe nor fully imagine unless he had seen them with his own eyes.

But from these countless evils we have been set free, by the help of Him Who though He afflicts yet heals and restores, by our most tireless Prince, King and Lord, the Lord Robert. He, that his people and his heritage might be delivered out of the hands of our enemies, met toil and fatigue, hunger and peril, like another Maccabaeus or Joshua and bore them cheerfully. Him, too, divine providence, his right of succession according to our laws and customs which we shall maintain to the death, and the due consent and assent of us all have made our Prince and King. To him, as to the man by whom salvation has been wrought unto our people, we are bound both by law and by his merits that our freedom may be still maintained, and by him, come what way, we mean to stand.

Yet if he should give up what he has begun, and agree to make us or our kingdom subject to the King of England or the English, we should exert ourselves at once to drive him out as our enemy and a subverter of his own rights and ours, and make some other man who was well able to defend us our King; for, as long as but a hundred of us remain alive, never will we on any condition be brought under English rule. It is in truth not for glory, nor riches, nor honours that we are fighting, but for freedom – for that alone, which no honest man gives up but with life itself.

Therefore, it is, Reverend Father and Lord, that we beseech your Holiness with our most earnest prayers and suppliant hearts, inasmuch as you will in your sincerity and goodness consider all this, that, since with Him Whose vice-gerent on earth you are there is neither weighing nor distinction of Jew and Greek, Scotsman or Englishman, you will look with the eyes of a father on the troubles and privations brought by the English upon us and upon the Church of God. May it please you to admonish and exhort the King of the English, who ought to be satisfied with what belongs to him since England used once to be enough for seven kings or more, to leave us Scots in peace, who live in this poor little Scotland, beyond which there is no dwelling-place at all, and covet nothing but our own. We are sincerely willing to do anything for him, having regard to our condition, that we can, to win peace for ourselves.

This truly concerns you, Holy Father, since you see the savagery of the heathen raging against the Christians, as the sins of Christians have indeed deserved, and the frontiers of Christendom being pressed inwards every day; and how much it will tarnish your Holiness's memory if (which God forbid) the Church suffers eclipse or scandal in any branch of it during your time, you must perceive. Then rouse the Christian princes who for false reasons pretend that they cannot go to the help of the Holy Land because of wars they have on hand with their neighbours. The real reason that prevents them is that in making war on their smaller neighbours they find quicker profits and weaker resistance. But how cheerfully our Lord the King and we too would go there if the King of the English would leave us in peace, He from Whom nothing is hidden well knows; and we profess and declare it to you as the Vicar of Christ and to all Christendom.

But if your Holiness puts too much faith in the tales of the English tell and will not give sincere belief to all this, nor refrain from favouring them to our prejudice, then the slaughter of bodies, the perdition of souls, and all the other misfortunes that will follow, inflicted by them on us and by us on them, will, we believe, be surely laid by the Most High to your charge.

To conclude, we are and shall ever be, as far as duty calls us, ready to do your will in all things, as obedient sons to you as His Vicar; and to Him as the Supreme King and Judge we commit the maintenance of our cause, casting our cares upon Him and firmly trusting that He will inspire us with courage and bring our enemies to nought.

May the Most High preserve you to His Holy Church in holiness and health and grant you length of days.

Given at the monastery of Arbroath in Scotland on the sixth day of the month in April in the year of grace thirteen hundred and twenty and the fifteenth year of the reign of our King aforesaid.[1]

Appendix Three

Terms of negotiation between Robert I, King of Scots and Andrew Harclay, Earl of Carlisle, 1323

By 1323, permanent peace between the kingdoms of Scotland and England looked as elusive as ever, despite King Robert's ardent attempts to broker it. His recent failed mission to capture Edward II at Rievaulx Abbey in Yorkshire nevertheless humiliated the English king, coming hot on the heels of a failed attempt to invade Robert's kingdom. While Edward licked his wounds, Andrew Harclay, recently elevated to the earldom of Carlisle, sensing the futility of further stalemate, took it upon himself to open negotiations with the King of Scots without a legal mandate. Harclay believed that if he reached an agreement for a permanent peace, he could convince Edward II of its merits afterwards. It was a dangerous game, and one for which Andrew Harclay paid with his life, being executed in March 1323. However, the terms that were drawn up between Robert and the rebellious earl were sensible, and later formed the basis of a final peace between the two kingdoms detailed in the Treaty of Edinburgh sealed in 1328. Those early terms have survived, copied and attached to a writ issued under Edward II's privy seal.

Edward II's response to Andrew Harclay's Anglo-Scottish 'Treaty', 1323

We, Edward, by the grace of God, King of England, lord of Ireland, and duke of Aquitaine, give greeting to our beloved and faithful subjects, the treasurer and his lieutenant, the barons of our exchequer, and the others of our council who are at York. We are sending you enclosed here a copy of an indenture between

Andrew Harclay, earl of Carlisle, and Robert Bruce, a thing which seems to us, and to our council, to bode great evil. We have therefore ordered our beloved and faithful William Latimer to stay in the city, with some men-at-arms, to look after its safety. We command you, accordingly, to be in good heart in the meantime and to reassure our good people of the city, offering help and advice in every way that you know, or can contrive (as we trust you to do) to William, in matters which affect the safety of our city, and of our courts and our treasury, which are there, and of the surrounding districts. Stow Park, attested by our privy seal, 19 January, in the sixteenth year of our reign [1323].

~

These are the details of the agreement made between Robert Bruce, on the one hand, and the earl of Carlisle, on the other, on behalf of all those in England who wish to be spared and saved from war with Robert Bruce and all his followers:

First, because both kingdoms prospered so long as each kingdom had a king from its own nation, and was maintained separately, with its own laws and customs, let it again be done in the same manner. For this reason, all those who are parties to this agreement shall give all possible counsel and aid to Robert, and his heirs, so that they may be able to hold the realm of Scotland freely, entirely, and in liberty, and they shall pursue all those who are unwilling to agree to this, as enemies of the common good of the one realm and of the other. The king and the earl wish to assure and to satisfy those who are willing to commit themselves to this, that they will advise, maintain, and assist them in everything that can be to the common profit of the realm of England, according to the decision of twelve persons sworn for this purpose, six of whom shall be chosen from the people of the king, and six chosen by the earl. By these twelve or the majority of them, if need be, everything that has to be done for the common profit of both realms shall be negotiated, ordained, and settled. And the magnates shall be bound to execute their decisions and their ordinances in every detail. All those who wish to take part in this agreement shall have, from the King of Scotland and the earl, such security as the aforesaid twelve persons shall say that there should be. As for those who do not wish to consent to this agreement, all the others who partake in it shall pursue them, and the king and the earl [shall act] likewise. If the King of England is willing to consent, within one year after the making of this agreement, that the King of Scotland shall have his realm, free and quit for himself and his heirs, as is said above, the King of Scotland shall do for him the things which follow, that is to say: he will found an abbey in Scotland with a rent of 500 marks sterling for the souls of those who were slain in the war, and within ten years he will grant him also 40,000 marks sterling, that is 4,000 marks each year; and the King of England shall have the marriage of the heir male of the King of Scotland, to be married, in some suitable place, to one of his kindred, if it is the opinion of the twelve persons aforesaid that this should be done, for the common advantage of both [realms]. If the King of England does not wish to accept these offers within a year, the King of Scotland shall be bound no further, but the twelve persons shall act according to their judgement for the common profit of one realm and the other. And note that if agreement is reached between the kings, as God grant, neither of them on this account shall be bound to receive in his realm a man who has been opposed to him, nor to render him the lands that he or his ancestors had in his realm, if he does not wish to do it of his special grace.

The earl of Moray had sworn on the soul of the King of Scotland that he will maintain all those who wish to take part in this agreement against all men, and that the King of Scotland will never make peace with the King of England, unless all those who are concerned in this agreement are included in his peace. Likewise the earl of Carlisle has sworn to maintain all those who are concerned in the agreement.[1]

Notes

Abbreviations

Ann Lond: *Annales Londonienses, 1195-1330*
Ann Paul: *Annales Paulini, 1307-1340*
Barbour: *The Bruce, John Barbour* (ed & trans A.A.M. Duncan)
Barrow: G.W.S. Barrow. *Robert the Bruce & The Community of the the Realm of Scotland*
Barrow, Kingdom: G.W.S. Barrow. *The Kingdom of the Scots*
Bingham: Caroline Bingham. *Robert the Bruce*
Carpenter: David Carpenter. *The Struggle for Mastery: Britain 1066-1284*
CCR: *Calendar of Close Rolls*
CChR: *Calendar of Charter Rolls*
CDS: *Calendar of Documents Relating to Scotland. Volumes i-v*
CFR: *Calendar of Fine Rolls*
CPL: *Calendar of Papal Letters*
CPR: *Calendar of Patent Rolls*
Davies: R.R. Davies. *The First English Empire: Power and Identities in the British Isles 1093–1343*
Duncan, Scotland: A.A.M Duncan. *Scotland: The Making of a Kingdom*
Flores: *Flores Historiarum, vol. ii-iii* (ed. H.R. Luard)
Foedera: *Rhymer's Foedera, Conventiones, Litterae, vol i-ii*
Fordun: *Johannis de Fordun. Chronica Gentis Scotorum, vol ii* (ed W.F. Skene)
Froissart: *Jean Froissart, Chronicles of England, France and Spain* (trans T. Johnes)
Guisborough: *The Chronicle of Walter of Guisborough* (ed. Harry Rothwell)
Lanercost: *The Chronicle of Lanercost, 1272–1346*, (trans. Sir Herbert Maxwell)
Langtoft: *The Chronicle of Pierre de Langtoft* (ed. T. Wright, 2 vols)
Le Bel: *The True Chronicles of Jean le Bel* (trans Nigel Bryant)
McNamee: Colm, McNamee. *The Wars of the Bruces: Scotland, England and Ireland, 1306–1328*
Morris: Marc Morris. *A Great and Terrible King: Edward I and the Forging of Britain*

m:

Palgrave: *Documents and Records illustrating the History of Scotland* (ed. F. Palgrave)

Parl Writs: *Parliamentary Writs and Writs of Military Summons, Edward I and Edward II* (ed F. Palgrave)

Penman: Michael Penman. *Robert the Bruce: King of the Scots*

Phillips: Seymour Phillips. *Edward II*

Powicke: F.M. Powicke. *The Thirteenth Century, 1216–1307*

Prestwich: Michael Prestwich. *Edward I*

PROME: The Parliamentary Rolls of Medieval England

Rishanger: *Willelmi Rishanger, Chronica et Annales* (ed. H.T. Riley)

RPS: *The Records of the Parliaments of Scotland to 1707* (ed. K.M. Brown et al.)

RRS: *Regesta Regum Scottorum, v: The Acts of Robert I, 1306–29* (ed. A.A.M. Duncan)

Scalacronica: *Scalacronica - The Reigns of Edward I, Edward II and Edward III by Sir Thomas Gray* (trans Sir Herbert Maxwell)

Scotichronicon: *Scotichronicon*, Walter Bower (ed. D.E.R. Watt)

Spinks: Stephen Spinks, *Edward II the Man: A Doomed Inheritance*

Stevenson: J. Stevenson, ed. *Documents Illustrative of the History of Scotland, 1286–1306*

Stones: E.L.G. Stones, *Anglo Scottish Relations, 1174–1328: Some Selected Documents*

The Great Cause: E.L.G. Stones & G.G. Simpson, *Edward I and the Throne of Scotland 1290–1306. An Edition of the Record Sources for the Great Cause*

Vita: *Vita Edwardi Secundi* (ed. N. Denholm-Young)

1. Scotland

1. *Geoffrey of Monmouth, Historia Regum Britanniae.* trans, Lewis Thorpe. (London, 1966), 90.
2. Lord Cooper, 'The Numbers and Distribution of the Population of Medieval Scotland', *SHR 26*, (1947) 2–9.
3. Bingham, 7–8.
4. Ibid, 8.
5. McNamee, 11.
6. Bingham, 8. Legge, M.D. 'La Piere D'Escoce'. *SHR 38*, (1959), 109–13. Davies, Empire, 47. Morris, 245.
7. Bingham, 8–9. Morris, 241.
8. McNamee, 5,9. Barrow, 4.
9. Morris, 242. Bartlett, *The Making of Europe: Conquest, Colonization and Cultural Change 950–1350* (London,1993), 274–7.
10. Barrow, 6. Barrow, *The Anglo-Norman Era in Scottish History* (Oxford, 1980), 201–3.
11. Morris, 243. Barrow, 23, 26.
12. Barrow, 6.
13. Carpenter, 180–2.
14. Barrow, 6.
15. Ibid, 7.
16. Prestwich, Plantagenet England, 233. Barrow, 9–10. James W. Dilley, 'German Merchants in Scotland, 1297–1327', *SHR 27*, 153–4.

17. Duncan, Scotland, 336.
18. Davies, Empire, 47. Powicke, 593–4. Morris, 245. Bingham, 8. M.D Legge. 'La Piere D'Escoce', *SHR 38.* (1959), 109–13. McNamee, 11.
19. Prestwich, Plantagenet England, 228. Barrow, 11.
20. Barrow, 3.
21. Ibid, 3.
22. Barrow, Kingdom, 83–90.
23. Carpenter, 180. Barrow, 8.
24. Barrow, 8.
25. Prestwich, Plantagenet England, 228.
26. Keen, M. *Chivalry* (London, 1984), 203–12.
27. Carpenter, 182. Barrow, 16. McNamee, 4–5.
28. McNamee, 6.
29. Barrow, 3. McNamee, 9.
30. Carpenter, 142–3.
31. Ibid, 142–3, 178–82. Morris, 242.
32. Carpenter, 166.
33. Ibid, 195, 220.
34. Prestwich, Plantagenet England, 229. Powicke, 586–7. Davies, Empire, 11–14, 64–5. Morris, 244.
35. Bingham, 9.
36. Ibid, 9. Duncan, Scotland, 578.
37. Bingham, 10.
38. Ibid, 10.
39. Barrow, 11. Duncan, Scotland, 581. Prestwich, Plantagenet England, 230. Bingham, 10.
40. CCR, 1251–3, 12. Bingham 5.
41. Bingham, 5. Morris, 244. Duncan, Scotland, 560 citing *St Altars Chronicle.*
42. Barrow, 13 citing Matthew Paris, *Chronica Majora*, v, 505.
43. Lanercost, 9.
44. Duncan, Scotland, 589–90. Morris, 247.
45. Foedera, I, ii, 563. Bingham, 13. Barrow, Kingdom, 218–20.
46. Bingham, 13 citing *Cartulary of Dunfermline.*
47. Stones, 40–1. Bingham, 13–14. Barrow, 12. Morris, 248.
48. CDS, ii, no 253. Prestwich, Plantagenet England, 230.
49. Stones, 42–3. Bingham, 15.
50. Bingham, 16. Barrow, 13.
51. Lanercost, 41–2.
52. Ibid, 43–4. Barrow, 15. Bingham, 20.
53. Barrow, 15.

2. The Bruces of Annandale

1. Barrow, 20. Bingham 23. Barrow, Kingdom, 322.
2. Bingham, 24.
3. Barrow, 20. Barrow, Kingdom, 281, 322–6.
4. Barrow, 20.
5. Bingham, 26.
6. Ibid, 31.

7. Ibid, 24.
8. Barrow, 21.
9. CDS, i, nos 1429, 1431, 1503. Barrow, 21. Penman, 14.
10. Lanercost, 114.
11. Ibid, 111–12.
12. Bingham, 26–7.
13. Palgrave, 29.
14. Bingham, 27. Barrow, 23.
15. CDS, i, nos 1994, 2472, 2034.
16. Barrow, 23.
17. Penman, 14.
18. Flores, ii, 488.
19. Bingham, 27.
20. CDS, i, no 2575.
21. Macquarrie, A. *Scotland and the Crusades, 1095–1560* (Edinburgh, 1985), 56–65.
22. Lanercost, 112–3.
23. Ibid, 114. Bingham 28.
24. Barrow, 25.
25. Scotichronicon, vol v, 383–5. Bingham 28–9.
26. Fordun, 299–300.
27. Penman, 14. Bingham, 28. Barrow, 25.
28. Penman, 15.
29. CChR, 183. CDS, ii, nos 236, 237.
30. Corser, P. 'The Bruce Lordship of Annandale, 1124–1296' in R.D. Oram and G. Stell, eds *Lordship and Architecture in Medieval and Renaissance Scotland*. (Edinburgh, 2005).
31. Lanercost, 69, 72.
32. Barrow, 26. Bingham, 30.
33. Bingham, 31.
34. *Chronicon Galfridi le Baker de Swynebroke*, ed. E.M. Thompson (Oxford, 1889), 38.
35. Guisborough, 296. Penman, 13. Barrow, 26. Bingham, see footnotes, 339.
36. Barbour, 122, 132. Penman 16. Bingham, 33.
37. Penman, 18. Bingham, 33.
38. Penman, 19.
39. Ibid, 19.
40. Ibid, 19.
41. CDS, ii, no 1516.
42. Penman, 17.
43. Barrow, 26. Penman, 19. Bingham, 34.

3. The Great Cause

1. Fordun, ii, 306. Scotichronicon, vol 6, 7, 9.
2. Palgrave, 42. Scotichronicon, vol 6, 9.
3. Bingham, 36.
4. Stevenson, i, 4–5. Penman, 23–4. Bingham, 36.

5. Bingham, 37.

6. *The Exchequer Rolls of Scotland*, ed. J. Stuart et al (Edinburgh, 1878–1908), vol i, 36–41. Bingham, 37. Penman, 24.

7. Bingham, 37. Powicke, 597–8. Duncan, A.A.M. 'The Community of the Realm of Scotland and Robert Bruce', *SHR 45* (1966), 188.

8. Ibid, 25.

9. Penman, 25–6.

10. Ibid, 25–6.

11. Scotichronicon, vol 6, 3. Bingham, 37–8. Penman, 25.

12. CDS, ii, no. 386.

13. Penman, 28.

14. Foedera, I, ii, 719–20. Scottish Historical Documents, 38–9.

15. Stevenson, i, 134. Bingham, 39. Penman, 28.

16. English Historical Documents, vol 3, 1189–1327, ed Harry Rothwell (London, 1975), 467. Stevenson, i, 162–73. RPS,1290/7/1. Prestwich, 361. Penman, 29.

17. Stevenson, W. 'The Treaty of Northampton (1290): A Scottish Charter of Liberties', *SHR* 86, (2007), 1–15.

18. Prestwich, 362. Bingham, 40.

19. CPR, 1281–92, 386. Stevenson, i, 156–7, 161–2.

20. Bingham, 40. Barrow, 29.

21. Annales Monasterii de Waverleia, A.D, 1–1291; *Annales Monasteri*, ed. H.R. Luard (Rolls Series, 1864–9), ii. Prestwich, 356.

22. Binghàm 41.

23. Foedera, I, ii, 741. Letter of Bishop of Bergen, dated 1 February 1320, *Proceedings of the Society of Antiquaries (1874)*, X, 417, 418. Bingham, 41.

24. Foedera, I, ii, 741. The Great Cause, 5–6. CDS, ii, no 459. Bingham, 42–3. Penman, 29–30.

25. Stones, 44–50. Penman, 30.

26. Cockerill, Sara. *Eleanor of Castile: The Shadow Queen.* (Stroud, 2014), 343.

27. Bingham, 44.

28. *Song of Lewes*, ed and trans, C.A. Kingsford (1890), 18. Bingham, 42.

29. Duncan, A.A.M, 'The Process of Norham, 1291', in P.R. Coss and S.D. Lloyd, eds, *TCE*, V (Woodbridge, 1995), 207–30. Duncan, Archie, 'Revisiting Norham, May–June 1291', in Chris Given-Wilson, Ann Kettle and Len Scales, eds, *War, Governance and Aristocracy in the British Isles, 1150–1500* (Woodbridge, 2008), 69–83.

30. Bingham, 44–5.

31. Stones, 54–5.

32. Barrow, 33. Bingham, 45.

33. Bingham, 46.

34. Lanercost, 81. Penman, 33.

35. Bingham, 47. Penman, 33.

36. Prestwich, 366.

37. Bingham, 48.

38. Ibid, 47.

39. Simpson, G.G. 'The Claim of Florence, Count of Holland to the Scottish Throne, 1291–2', *SHR* 36, (1957), 111–23. Prestwich, 367.

40. Penman, 32.

41. Ibid, 34.
42. Ibid, 34.
43. Ibid, 34.
44. Scotichronicon, vol 6, 21–5.
45. Ibid, vol 6, 31.
46. Bingham, 50.
47. Simpson, G.G. 'The Claim of Florence, Count of Holland to the Scottish Throne, 1291–2', *SHR* 36, (1957), 111–23. Bingham, 50–1.
48. Scalacronica, 12.
49. Prestwich, 368–9. Penman, 36.
50. Guisborough, 239. The Great Cause, 252–3.

4. A Nation in Peril

1. Lanercost, 145. Rishanger, 371.
2. Penman, 38.
3. RPS, 1293/8/8. Penman, 39.
4. Bingham, 56–7.
5. Ibid, 57.
6. Scotichronicon, vol 6, 41.
7. Lanercost, 102.
8. CPR, 1292–1301, 69. CCR, 1288–96, 295, 367. Penman, 41.
9. Bingham, 58. Prestwich, 375.
10. CDS, ii, no 695. Foedera, ii, 804.
11. Prestwich, 372–3.
12. Langtoft, 216. Prestwich, 220–24. Morris, 275–80.
13. Lanercost, 114–5. Langtoft, 223. Bingham, 58–9.
14. Guisborough, 270.
15. Bingham, 59–60. Nicholson, Ranald, 'The France–Scottish and France–Norwegian Treaties of 1295', *SHR*, *vol 38* (1959), 118.
16. Lanercost, 111–12. Guisborough, 259.
17. Lanercost, 103.
18. CDS,ii, no 675.
19. CDS, ii, nos 236–7, 716. CPR, 1292–1301, 147.
20. CDS, ii, nos 718, 736. Lanercost, 128–9. Fordun, ii, 318.
21. Guisborough, 270–1. Lanercost, 115–16. Penman, 44.
22. Lanercost, 129.
23. Bingham, 63–4.
24. Prestwich, 470.
25. Guisborough, 283–4. Stones, 68–9. Bingham, 72–3.
26. Guisborough, 272–4. Lanercost, 135–7. Bingham, 65. Prestwich, 471.
27. Lanercost, 134. Scalacronica, 15.
28. Scotichronicon, vol 6, 59. Lanercost, 135.
29. Bingham, 66.
30. Lanercost, 135–8, 168. Guisborough, 274–5. Fordun, ii, 318.
31. Stones, 73–4.
32. Guisborough, 277–8. Bingham, 68.

33. CDS, ii, nos 742.
34. Ibid, nos 736.
35. Stones, 73–4. Bingham, 68.
36. CDS, ii, nos 821. Blount, M.N. 'The surrender of King John of Scotland to Edward I in 1296: some new evidence', *BIHR, xlviii* (1975), 94–106.
37. Scalacronica, 17.
38. Penman, 46. Prestwich, 473.
39. CDS, ii, no 839.
40. Scalacronica, 17.
41. Rishanger, 191.
42. Penman, 46.
43. Stones, 73–6.
44. Scalacronica, 17. Penman, 47. Bingham, 72. Prestwich, 474.
45. RPS, A1296/8/1.
46. CDS, ii, no 823. Scalacronica, 18. Prestwich, 94. Bingham, 72.
47. Scotichronicon, vol 6, 75. Morris, 290.
48. CDS, ii, no 853. Penman, 47.
49. CDS, ii, nos 852.

5. Precarious Ambition

1. Lanercost, 163.
2. Scotichronicon, vol 6, 83.
3. Prestwich, 477. Bingham, 79.
4. Bingham, 82.
5. Prestwich, 477. Penman, 54.
6. Penman, 48. Bingham, 82.
7. Guisborough, 296.
8. CDS, ii, no 910. Penman, 54. Bingham, 84.
9. CDS, ii, no 933, 961. CFR, 1272–1307, 392.
10. Bingham, 85.
11. CDS, ii, no 917. Bingham, 86.
12. Prestwich, 478.
13. Guisborough, 300.
14. Bingham, 88.
15. Scalacronica, 19. Lanercost, 164. Prestwich, 478.
16. Barrow, 90. Bingham, 89.
17. Guisborough, 303–8. C. McNamee, 'William Wallace's Invasion of Northern England, 1297', *NH, xxvi* (1990), 40–58. Prestwich, 478.
18. Rishanger, 384. Penman, 57.
19. Guisborough, 324–5. Parl Writs, i, 309–12. Prestwich, 479.
20. CDS, ii, no 997. CPR, 1292–1301, 344.
21. Bingham, 91.
22. Fordun, ii, 323. Scalacronica, 21. Guisborough, 323–8.
23. Bingham, 92.
24. Guisborough, 325–8. Bingham, 92. Prestwich, 481.
25. Barrow, 136–8. Penman, 59. Bingham, 92.

26. Scalacronica, 22.
27. CDS, ii, 1978.
28. Bingham, 93–4. Barrow, 140–2.
29. CCR, 1296–1302, 379. Prestwich, 484.
30. Lanercost, 170. Scalacronica, 23.
31. *Rolls of Arms of the Princes, Barons and Knights who attended Edward I at the Siege of Caerlaverock*, ed. T. Wright (London, 1864). Spinks, 36.
32. Prestwich, 487. Bingham, 95.
33. Guisborough, 334–38. Lanercost, 171. Prestwich, 490–1.
34. Bingham, 96.
35. Foedera, i, 924. CDS, ii, no 1163–4. Guisborough, 334.
36. Foedera, i, 932–3. Guisborough, 338–44. Scotichronicon, vol 6, 113–7.
37. Scotichronicon, vol 6, 183. Prestwich, 495.
38. Spinks, 37–41.
39. Prestwich, 493.
40. E.L.G. Stones, 'The Submission of Robert the Bruce to Edward I', *SHR xxxiv*, 132–4. Stones, 118–9.
41. Penman, 70. Bingham, 98.
42. Bingham, 101.
43. CDS, ii, 1657. Penman, 71. Bingham, 102.
44. CDS, ii, no 1516. Langtoft, ii, 336–7. Bingham, 102–3.
45. Penman, 72.
46. Foedera, i, 942.
47. Bingham, 104. Prestwich, 497. Barrow, 162–5.
48. Spinks, 47. Penman, 126. Barrow, 126. Bingham, 104.
49. CDS, ii, no 1334.
50. Parl Writs, i, 366.
51. CDS, ii, no 1385, 1420, 1437. Bingham, 104–5.
52. CDS, ii, no 1375.
53. Prestwich, 499. Penman, 75.
54. Barrow, 128. Palgrave, 333.
55. Scalacronica, 23.
56. Foedera, i, 949. Bingham, 106.
57. Palgrave, 276. Bingham, 106.
58. Bingham, 106. Prestwich, 500.
59. CDS, ii, no 1465.
60. CDS, ii, no 1433, 1493, 1495, 1540.
61. CDS, ii, no 1510.
62. Scalacronica, 25.
63. Flores, 320. Prestwich, 501. Bingham, 109.
64. Spinks, 46–7.

6. A Champion Arises

1. CDS, ii, no 1817. Palgrave 323–5.
2. CDS, ii, no 1651, 1652, 1653. PROME, Edward I, Roll 12, no 14.
3. Barrow, 134. Penman, 83.

4. Palgrave, 293. Barrow, 189. Penman, 84.
5. Palgrave 293. CDS, ii, no 1691.
6. Stones, 121–2. Bingham, 113.
7. CDS, ii, 1691. Palgrave, 293. Stones, 122. Barrow, 134–5, 189. Prestwich, 504.
8. Prestwich, 504.
9. Langtoft, 362. Barrow, 136. Bingham, 110. Prestwich, 502–3.
10. Ann Lond, 139–42. Flores, 321. Prestwich, 503. Penman, 84. Lanercost, 176 claims William Wallace's left foot was displayed at Aberdeen.
11. Guisborough, 366–67. Scalacronica, 29.
12. Scalacronica, 29. Barbour, 70–80. Flores, 322–23. Fordun, 333.
13. Scotichronicon, vol 6, 303–7. Barbour, 70–72.
14. Barbour, 74–76. Langtoft, 364–7, 380–1.
15. Fordun, 332–3.
16. Stones, 133. Bingham, 123.
17. CDS, ii, no 1828. Palgrave, 340–50. Penman, 94.
18. Barrow, 150. Bingham, 123–4. Penman, 93.
19. Bingham, 122. Barrow, 148.
20. Barrow, 148. Penman, 93.
21. Bingham, 123. Penman, 95.
22. Barbour, 86. Bingham, 124.
23. Penman, 100. Barrow, 154–60.
24. Penman, 100.
25. Ann Lond, 144. Fordun, 333–4 although Fordun dates the inauguration incorrectly to 27 March which is in fact the date of the Bishop of St Andrew's Inauguration Mass.
26. Ibid, 97.
27. Guisborough, 367. Scalacronica, 30–31.
28. Bingham, 125.
29. Ibid, 98.
30. Stones, 135–9.
31. CDS, ii, nos 1746, 1747. Palgrave, 335.
32. Prestwich, 505.
33. Parl Writs, i, 374. Guisborough, 367.
34. CDS, ii, nos 1782, 1787, 1908.
35. Barbour, 32. Barrow. 153. Bingham, 131.
36. Spinks, 52. CPR, 1301–7, 424.
37. Ann Lond, 146.
38. Scalacronica, 33. Spinks, 51–53. Bingham, 129. Prestwich, 121.
39. CDS, v, no 492. Prestwich, 506.
40. Penman, 99. Bingham, 131.
41. CDS, ii, 1786, 1813, 1815, 1824, 1827, 1828.
42. Bingham, 131–2.
43. Ann Lond, 148.
44. Barbour, 92–102.
45. Scalacronica, 32. Bingham, 133.
46. Spinks, 53–4. Prestwich, 506, 508.
47. CDS, ii, no 1811.

48. Barrow, 161. Penman, 103.
49. Scalacronica, 33.
50. Ann Lond, 148–9. Lanercost, 178–80.
51. Bingham, 137.
52. Ann Lond, 147.
53. Barbour, 112–20. Barrow, 160–61. Bingham, 137.
54. Barrow, 106–7. Bingham, 140.
55. Penman, 102.
56. CDS, ii, no 1829. Penman, 103.
57. Scotichronicon, vol 6, 323.
58. Lanercost, 179. Guisborough, 369. Flores, 135. Ann Lond, 149, Scalacronica, 33. Prestwich, 508
59. Guisborough, 368. Scalacronica, 32.
60. C.J. Neville, 'Widows of War: Edward I and the Women of Scotland during the War of Independence', in S.S. Walker, ed. *Wife and Widow in Medieval England* (London, 1993), 109–39.
61. Scalacronica, 32.
62. CDS, ii, no 1963. Guisborough, 368–9. Prestwich, 508–9. Bingham, 142.
63. CDS, ii, no 1910.
64. Scalacronica, 31. Prestwich, 508.
65. Scalacronica, 31.
66. Guisborough, 368–9. Rishanger, 229. Flores, 324.
67. Guisborough, 369. CDS, ii, no 1910.
68. Bingham, 142–3.
69. Ibid, 147. Penman, 102.
70. Penman, 102.
71. Barrow, 163–4. Bingham, 147.

7. The Turn of the Tide

1. Barrow, 163, 169. McNamee, 36.
2. S. Duffy, 'The Bruce Brothers and the Irish Sea World, 1306–1329' in *Cambridge Medieval Celtic Studies* (1991), 64–5. Penman, 104. Barrow, 314. Bingham, 150.
3. Barrow, 170. Bingham, 151. Penman, 104.
4. Penman, 104. Jo Lydon, 'The Scottish Soldier Abroad: The Bruce Invasion and the Galloglass' in G.G. Simpson, ed *The Scottish Soldier Abroad, 1247–1967* (Edinburgh, 1992), 1–15.
5. Guisborough, 369–70.
6. CDS, ii, nos 1888, 1889, 1893.
7. Lanercost, 179. Guisborough, 370. Scalacronica, 34. CDS, ii, 1905. Barrow, 361.
8. Bingham, 153–4.
9. Barbour, 196. Barrow, 171. Bingham, 155.
10. Scotichronicon, vol 6, 320. Barrow, 171.
11. CDS, ii, nos 1895, 1896.
12. Bingham, 157.

13. Ibid, 164.
14. Scalacronica, 34 states that Valence rode for Ayr. Bingham, 164. Barrow, 172.
15. Guisborough, 378. Scalacronica, 35.
16. Barrow, 172–3. CDS, ii, no 1926.
17. Guisborough, 379. Scalacronica, 36. Prestwich, 556–7.
18. Spinks, 62–4.
19. Penman, 106. Barrow, 173–74.
20. Bingham, 171–2. Barrow, 174.
21. McNamee, 40–1.
22. Barbour, 206–10. Bingham, 180.
23. Bingham, 182.
24. Barrow, 175, 179.
25. Barrow, 179 citing PRO, c.47/22/6, no4. CDS, iii, no 80. Barrow provides the better translation.
26. CDS, iv, nos, 14, 1837. Barrow, 175.
27. Fordun, ii, 336–7. Barbour, 320.
28. Penman, 107.
29. Fordun, ii, 337. Scotichronicon, vol 6, 329.
30. Scotichronicon, vol 6, 341–3. Fordun, ii, 337. Bingham, 175–6.
31. Scotichronicon, vol 6, 343. Bingham, 176. Penman, 107.
32. Barrow, 176.
33. Bingham, 178.
34. W. Standford Reid, 'Truce, Trades and Scottish Independence', *Speculum, xxix (1954)*, 210–21.
35. Barbour, 334. Penman, 109. Barrow, 182.
36. Scotichronicon, vol 6, 345. Bingham, 185.
37. Penman, 107. Barrow, 181.
38. Fordun, ii, 338. Scotichronicon, vol 6, 345. Penman, 107.
39. Fordun, ii, 337. Lanercost, 185. Scotichronicon, vol 6, 343–5.
40. Bingham, 186. Barrow, 182.
41. Penman, 109.
42. Ibid, 108. Barrow, 177. Bingham, 186–7.

8. A Kingdom Reclaimed

1. Lanercost, 189.
2. RPS A1309/1. Penman, 110.
3. Bingham, 188. Barrow, 183.
4. Penman, 113. Bingham, 188–9.
5. Foedera, I, ii, 79.
6. Acts of Parliament of Scotland, ed. C. Innes, vol I, 459. Penman, 111. Barrow, 183.
7. R. Tanner, 'Cowing the Community? Coercion and Fabrication in Robert Bruce's Parliaments, 1309–18', in K.M. Brown and R.J. Tanner, eds, *Parliament and Politics in Scotland, 1235–1560* (Edinburgh, 2004), 59–61.
8. RPS A1309/2. A.A.M. Duncan, 'The Declaration of the Clergy, 1309–10' in G. Barrow, ed, *The Declaration of Arbroath: History, Setting, Significance*

(Edinburgh, 2003), 32–49. Acts of Parliament of Scotland, vol I, 459. Bingham, 189. Penman, 112.

9. Barrow, 185.
10. Penman, 116.
11. Ibid, 116.
12. Bingham, 191. Penman, 116.
13. Penman, 116.
14. Guisborough, 383. Spinks, 64–5. Phillips, 130.
15. J.S Hamilton. *Piers Gaveston: Earl of Cornwall, 1307–1312: Politics and Patronage in the Reign of Edward II* (Detroit and London, 1988), 39, 140. Spinks, 64, 68.
16. Spinks, 75–6.
17. Vita, 3. Ann Paul, 255, 259. Phillips, 134–5.
18. Spinks, 81–6.
19. Lanercost, 190. McNamee, 46.
20. CDS, iii, no 95.
21. McNamee, 49. Bingham, 195–6.
22. McNamee, 48–9. D. Simpkin, 'The English Army and the Scottish Campaign of 1310–11', in A. King and M. Penman, eds, *New Perspectives: England and Scotland in the Fourteenth Century* (Woodbridge, 2007), 14–39.
23. McNamee, 49.
24. Vita, 13. Bingham, 196. McNamee, 49, Penman, 121.
25. Lanercost, 191.
26. Vita, 12.
27. Ibid, 13.
28. CDS, iii, no 197.
29. Lanercost, 191. McNamee, 51. Bingham, 198.
30. CDS, iii, no 203. Penman, 123.
31. Spinks, 92–3. J.R. Maddicott, *Thomas of Lancaster, 1307–1322: A Study in the Reign of Edward II* (Oxford, 1970), 23.
32. CDS, iii, no 202.
33. McNamee, 52. Bingham, 199.
34. Lanercost, 194.
35. Ibid, 194–5. Penman, 123.
36. Lanercost, 194–5.
37. Vita, 31, 48. Lanercost, 195.
38. CDS, iii, no337. Lanercost, 195. Barrow, 188.
39. Spinks,100. Penman, 122–3, 125–6. Bingham, 202–3.
40. Vita, 48.
41. CDS, iii, no 279. Vita, 48. Penman, 127.
42. Lanercost, 197.
43. Ibid, 199–200.
44. Bingham, 204.
45. Lanercost, 200.
46. CDS, iii, no 279.
47. Barrow, 55, 59.
48. CDS, iii, no 279.

49. Penman, 127–8.
50. Barrow, 201.
51. Ibid, 200.
52. Bingham, 207.
53. Lanercost, 201. Vita, 48.
54. Scotichronicon, vol 6, 347. Barrow, 194.
55. Penman, 130.
56. Bingham, 208–9.
57. Ibid, 209.
58. CDS, iii, nos 279, 304. Scotichronicon, vol 6, 349. Bingham, 209.
59. Scotichronicon, vol 6, 349. Penman, 130–1.
60. Arthur.W. Moore, 'The Connexion between Scotland and Man', *SHR vol iii,* 405.
61. Barrow, 193. Bingham, 210.
62. Barbour, 367–70. McNamee, 59.
63. Vita, 48. Barbour, 378–86. Scotichronicon, vol 6, 351. Lanercost, 204.
64. Vita, 48.
65. Barbour, 386–96. Scotichronicon, vol 6, 351. Bingham, 214. Barrow, 195–6.
66. *The Political Songs of England from the Reign of King John to that of Edward II, ed.* T. Wright (London, 1839), 216.

9. Divine Providence

1. Barrow, 203. Bingham, 217.
2. CCR, 1313–18, 86. Spinks, 116.
3. Barbour, 496–7.
4. Scotichronicon, vol 6, 368. Barbour, 408.
5. Bingham, 217–18. Spinks, 117.
6. Vita, 50. Prestwich, Armies & Warfare, 117. Phillips, 226.
7. Barrow, 204. Bingham, 219.
8. Bingham, 219.
9. Vita, 50–1. Bingham, 220.
10. Vita, 50.
11. Scalacronica, 52–3. Spinks, 115. Penman, 138.
12. Spinks, 117. McNamee, 60–1. Barrow, 209. Penman, 116.
13. Vita, 50.
14. Barbour, 414. Barrow, 209.
15. Nusbacher, The Battle of Bannockburn, 130.
16. Bingham, 222. Barrow, 208.
17. Barbour, 420. Barrow, 210.
18. Barrow, 210. Bingham, 223.
19. Scotichronicon, vol 6, 345.
20. Barbour, 416. Barrow, 209. Spinks, 117.
21. Barbour, 428.
22. Barbour, 422. Barrow, 210.
23. Spinks, 117.
24. Penman, 141.

25. Spinks, 117.
26. Bingham, 224. Barrow, 210.
27. Scotichronicon, vol 6, 363.
28. Ibid, 118. Barrow, 217.
29. Flores, 158. Vita, 51, Barbour, 412.
30. Barbour, 448–52. Vita, 51. Barrow, 218.
31. Spinks, 118–9.
32. Barrow, 218–20. Bingham, 228.
33. Vita, 51. Scalacronica, 53–4.
34. Spinks, 119.
35. Scalacronica, 55.
36. Barbour, 456. Barrow, 222. Nusbacher, The Battle of Bannockburn, 122–23. Spinks, 120.
37. Penman, 142.
38. Barrow, 223. Phillips, 231. Nusbacher, The Battle of Bannockburn, 126. Spinks, 120.
39. Vita, 52.
40. Scotichronicon, vol 6, 365.
41. Penman, 139. Barrow, 225.
42. Barbour, 468. Bingham, 232.
43. Scotichronicon, vol 6, 363–4. Barrow, 225 in whose translation I have chosen to use here.
44. Barrow, 225.
45. Barbour, 470. Nusbacher, The Battle of Bannockburn, 130–1.
46. Scalacronica, 55. Nusbacher, The Battle of Bannockburn, 125. Spinks, 120–1.
47. Barbour, 472. Barrow, 225–6. Phillips, 232. Spinks, 121.
48. Spinks, 121.
49. Vita, 52–3. Barbour, 480–1. Prestwich, Armies and Warfare, 223.
50. Lanercost, 208. Vita, 52–4. Scotichronicon, vol 6, 375.
51. Spinks, 121.
52. Lanercost, 208.
53. Barrow, 228. Bingham, 234.
54. Scalacronica, 56.
55. Lanercost, 208. Vita, 54.
56. Barbour, 496.
57. *Johannis de Trokelowe et Henrici de Blaneford Chronica et Annales*, ed H.T. Riley, Rolls Series (London, 1866), 86. Scalacronica, 56. Spinks, 122.
58. Lanercost, 209. Scalacronica, 56. Barbour, 494–7.
59. Spinks, 122.
60. Barbour, 499–500, 508.
61. Ibid, 508–10. Scalacronica, 57. Lanercost, 209.
62. Barbour, 508.
63. Barrow, 231.
64. Scotichronicon, vol 6, 365. Barbour, 504.
65. Penman, 140. Barrow, 231–2. Bingham, 237.
66. Spinks, 122–3.
67. Ibid, 123.

10. Brothers, Kings, Countrymen

1. CDS, v, no 593. McNamee, 77–8.
2. Lanercost, 210–11.
3. RRS, vol v, no 40.
4. Phillips, 239. Penman, 151.
5. CDS, iii, nos 371–2, 393. Foedera, II, i, 256.
6. McNamee, 78 Penman, 151.
7. RPS, 1314/1. RRS, vol v, no 41. Penman, 151–2.
8. Penman, 153–4.
9. Ibid, 154–5.
10. Ibid, 152–3.
11. CDS, iii, no 476.
12. Bingham, 247–8. McNamee, 79.
13. Penman, 157.
14. Bingham, 239. Barrow, 162. Penman, 158.
15. Barrow, 278. Bingham, 239–40.
16. Penman, 158.
17. RPS, 1315/1. RRS, vol v, no 58.
18. Scotichronicon, vol 6, 377–81.
19. RRS, vol v, no 391. Penman, 161.
20. Penman, 161–2.
21. Barrow, 323.
22. Penman, 164.
23. J.R.S. Phillips, 'The Irish Remonstrance of 1317: An International Perspective' in *Irish Historical Studies, xxvii* (1990), 112–29.
24. Barbour, 521. Bingham, 251.
25. Scotichronicon, vol 6, 381. Spinks, 129.
26. Spinks, 129.
27. Vita, 61.
28. Foedera, II, i, 318–19. RRS, vol v, no 571. McNamee, 192.
29. McNamee, 194. Bingham, 252.
30. CDS, iii, no 549.
31. McNamee, 191.
32. RRS, vol v, no 101.
33. CDS, iii, no 455.
34. Vita, 69–70. Ann Paul, 278. Scotichronicon, vol 6, 411.
35. Penman, 166.
36. Barbour, 564. Bingham, 253.
37. Bingham, 253. Penman, 166.
38. Guisborough, 396. Lanercost, 213. Bingham, 248.
39. Lanercost, 213. Bingham, 253–4.
40. Lanercost, 215.
41. Penman, 167.
42. Ibid, 168.
43. Bingham 254.
44. Barbour, 566–70. CDS, iii, no 470, 477.

45. Barbour, 578.
46. McNamee, 81. Penman, 169.
47. Lanercost, 216.
48. Ibid, 216. Bingham, 255. McNamee, 82–4.
49. Lanercost, 217. Vita, 76.
50. Penman, 171. McNamee, 180. Bingham, 256–7.
51. Spinks, 135.
52. Ibid, 136.
53. Bingham, 257. Penman, 173.
54. McNamee, 182.
55. Ibid, 182. Bingham, 257.
56. Barrow, 316. Bingham, 258. Penman, 173–4.
57. Fordun, ii, 340.
58. *Annals of Connacht (AD 1224–1554)*, ed A.M. Freeman (Dublin, 1944), 233.
59. Lanercost, 218.
60. Barbour, 596–604. Scalacronica, 58.
61. Scotichronicon, vol 6, 383.
62. Ibid, 383.
63. Foedera, II, i, 321–2, 327–8. CPL, ii, 127.
64. Penman, 175, 177.
65. RRS, vol v, no 113.
66. Ibid, no 115–16. Penman, 178.
67. Penman, 178.
68. Ibid, 180.
69. Scotichronicon, vol 6, 385–405. Penman, 181–2.
70. RRS, vol v, 127–8, 131, 499. Penman, 183.
71. Lanercost, 220.
72. CDS, iii, no 599.
73. Lanercost, 221. Bingham, 262.
74. Penman, 183.
75. Bingham, 261–2. Barrow, 281.
76. Foedera, II, i, 115–2. Ann Paul, 283. Lanercost, 224–5. Vita, 89.
77. Penman, 186.
78. Lanercost, 225. Scalacronica, 57. Ann Paul, 284. Vita, 90. Bingham, 262–3.
79. CCR, 1318–23, 141. Vita, 88. Spinks, 149–50.

11. United We Stand

1. RPS, 1318/30. RRS, vol v, no 301. Scotichronicon, vol 7, 39–43.
2. Penman, 190.
3. RRS, vol v, no 301. RPS, 1318/30.
4. Penman, 202.
5. Lanercost, 227–8.
6. Penman, 206.
7. RRS, vol v, no 152, 404. Penman, 206–7.
8. *Anonimalle Chronicle 1307 to 1334 from Brotherton Collection MS 29*, ed W.R. Childs and J. Taylor (Yorkshire Archaeological Society Records Series 147, 1991), 95–7. Vita, 94–5.

9. Lanercost, 227–8. Spinks, 153.
10. Ann Paul, 286.
11. McNamee, 218.
12. Anonimalle, 97.
13. Spinks, 153.
14. Scalacronica, 66. Anonimalle, 97.
15. Ann Paul, 287–8.
16. Vita, 95.
17. Ann Paul, 288. Vita, 95. Flores, 189.
18. Lanercost, 227. Spinks, 154.
19. McNamee, 94–5. Bingham, 265–6.
20. Penman, 208.
21. Vita, 98.
22. Ibid, 102.
23. Foedera, II, i, 404. McNamee, 95.
24. Lanercost, 227–8.
25. RRS, vol v, no 148, 203–6, 157–8.
26. CDS, iii, no 738.
27. RRS, vol v, no 162.
28. Lanercost, 228. Penman, 212.
29. Foedera, II, i, 407–8. 412–13. Lanercost, 229. Penman, 212–3.
30. RPS, 1320/3/1. Barrow, 304. Bingham, 271.
31. G. Barrow, ed. *The Declaration of Arbroath: History, Setting, Significance* (Edinburgh, 2003). Bingham, 271.
32. Bingham, 271. Penman, 216. *The Declaration of Arbroath, 1320.* ed & trans, Sir James Fergusson (Edinburgh, 1970), 9.
33. Ibid, 9.
34. Ibid.
35. Bingham, 272.
36. Ibid.
37. RRS, vol v, no 440. Penman, 215.
38. Barrow, 308–9. Bingham, 273.
39. Penman, 218.
40. Ibid, 214–5.
41. RRS, vol v, no 569. Barrow, 314.
42. Penman, 220.
43. Scotichronicon, vol 7, 3. Penman, 199, Bingham, 274.
44. Barbour, 700.
45. Fordun, ii, 341.
46. Penman, 222. Bingham, 274.
47. Scotichronicon, vol 7, 3. Fordun, ii, 341.
48. Fergusson, 4.
49. Barbour, 702.
50. Ibid. Scotichronicon, vol 7, 3.
51. Fordun, ii, 341. Penman, 223–4.
52. CDS, iii, nos 43, 121, 219, 235, 373–4.
53. Penman, 204.
54. Barbour, 702–6.

55. Penman, 227.
56. G. Donaldson, 'The Pope's Reply to the Scottish Barons in 1320', *SHR* *XXIX*, 119–20.

12. Towards Peace

1. RRS, vol v, no 170. Penman, 229.
2. Penman, 230.
3. Foedera, II, i, 441.
4. Penman, 234.
5. Ibid, 233.
6. RRS, vol v, nos 29, 195–6.
7. Ibid, no 196.
8. McNamee, 96–7.
9. CDS, iii, no 745.
10. Vita, 120–1. Bingham, 279.
11. Bingham, 279. Barrow, 242.
12. Lanercost, 230–1.
13. Spinks, 174.
14. Vita, 123–4.
15. Spinks, 174–77.
16. Foedera, II, i, 479.
17. CCR, 1318–23, 532.
18. Spinks, 181.
19. Lanercost, 238. Penman, 237.
20. Lanercost, 238.
21. Penman, 236–7.
22. CDS, iii, no 752.
23. Spinks, 181–2.
24. Barbour, 680. Scotichronicon, vol 7, 11. Fordun, ii, 342.
25. Scotichronicon, vol 7, 11, 13. Scalacronica, 69. Barbour, 681–2.
26. Scalacronica, 69.
27. McNamee, 99.
28. Bingham, 284.
29. McNamee, 100. Bingham, 284.
30. Scalacronica, 69. Bingham, 284.
31. Barbour, 685. Barrow, 243.
32. Lanercost, 240.
33. Ibid, 240.
34. Scalacronica, 69.
35. Barbour, 690. Bingham, 285–6.
36. Lanercost, 240. Spinks, 182.
37. Spinks, 183.
38. Bingham, 287. Barrow, 284.
39. Lanercost, 240–1.
40. Penman, 239.
41. Lanercost, 241.
42. CDS, iii, no 745.

43. Lanercost, 241. Bingham, 288.
44. Stones, 154–7. Bingham, 289. Penman, 239.
45. CDS, iii, nos 800, 801, 802.
46. Bingham, 290.
47. Lanercost, 245, fn.
48. Penman, 242–3. Bingham, 291.
49. Bingham, 292. Penman, 241, 243.
50. Foedera, II, i, 541. RRS, vol v, no 450. Penman, 246.
51. RRS, vol v, no 240.
52. Penman, 247.
53. Ibid, 248. RRS, vol v, no 44.
54. Penman, 248.
55. RRS, vol v, no 253. Penman, 248.
56. Scotichronicon, vol 7, 15, 176–7. Fordun, ii, 343.
57. Fordun, ii, 343.
58. Foedera, II, i, 541. Barrow, 250. Bingham, 294–5.
59. Bingham, 295.
60. Vita, 132.
61. Foedera, II, i, 595. Vita, 133.
62. Penman, 256. Barrow, 250. Bingham, 295.

13. Bruce Victorious

1. Penman, 257.
2. RRS, vol v, no 263.
3. Spinks, 190–4.
4. Bingham, 296. Penman, 261.
5. Penman, 260–1. Bingham, 296.
6. RRS, vol v, nos 127, 281. Penman, 263.
7. Vita, 143. Spinks, 197–99.
8. CDS, v, nos 702–3.
9. Penman, 263–4.
10. Ibid, 264.
11. RRS, vol v, no 299. McNamee, 239. Bingham, 300–1.
12. CDS, iii, nos 882–3.
13. Fordun, ii, 343. Penman 269. Bingham, 298.
14. RRS, vol v, no 302.
15. CDS, iii, nos 887–9. CPR, 1323–27, 85. Foedera II, ii, 164.
16. Foedera, II, i, 639. RRS, vol v, no 453.
17. *The Brut*, ed F.W.D. Brie, Early English Text Society, cxxxi, part I (London, 1906), 240. Spinks, 211.
18. Lanercost, 253.
19. Spinks, 213–4.
20. Lanercost, 256. McNamee, 240. Bingham, 304.
21. Bingham, 305.
22. Scotichronicon, vol 7, 35. Barbour, 708–10. Penman, 279.
23. Le Bel, 34–5.
24. CDS, iii, nos 907–8, 913–4.

25. Penman, 280. McNamee, 243. Bingham, 305.
26. Penman, 281. Bingham, 306.
27. Bingham, 306. Barrow, 252.
28. Barbour, 712.
29. Lanercost, 257. Le Bel, 47.
30. Scalacronica, 80.
31. Barbour, 722–4. Lanercost, 257, Barrow, 253. Bingham, 308.
32. Scalacronica, 81. Lanercost, 258, Le Bel, 47–8.
33. Lanercost, 258. Le Bel, 49, Scalacronica, 81.
34. Penman, 281.
35. Barbour, 742. Penman, 282. Bingham, 309–10.
36. Bingham, 310. Penman, 280. Spinks, 222–3.
37. Spinks, 223.
38. Edward II in fact survived his alleged murder in 1327 even though he no longer played a part in English politics. See Spinks, 221–36. Mortimer, Ian. *The Greatest Traitor: The Life of Sir Roger Mortimer, Ruler of England 1327–1330* (London, 2003). Mortimer, Ian. *Medieval Intrigues: Decoding Roya Conspiracies* (London, 2010). Warner, Kathryn. *Long Live the King: The Mysterious Fate of Edward II* (Stroud, 2017).
39. Stones, 158–160. Barbour, 742–4. RRS, vol v, no 326. Penman, 283. Bingham, 313. Barrow, 254–5.
40. Foedera, II, i, 728.
41. Barrow, 255.
42. Hailes, *Annals of Scotland, II* (1779), 93–4. Stones, 161–3.
43. Penman, 279, 285. Bingham, 316–7.
44. Bingham, 317–8. McNamee, 243.
45. PROME, Edward III, 24 April – 14 May.
46. RRS, vol v, no 343. Penman, 286. Barrow, 260.
47. Bingham, 318, 382 fn 14. Penman, 285.
48. Penman, 291.
49. Bingham, 318–9.
50. McNamee, 253. Bingham, 319–20. Penman, 294.
51. Penman, 296.
52. Ibid, 296.
53. RRS, vol v, no 156. Penman, 297.
54. Le Bel, 52–3. Barbour, 752. Penman, 300.
55. Barbour, 754. Fordun, ii, 345. Penman, 302.

14. Aftermath

1. Barbour, 758. Bingham, 325–6.
2. Penman, 307.
3. Scotichronicon, vol 7, 45 –51.
4. CPL, ii, 289, 290.
5. Penman, 306.
6. Bingham, 383, fn 8.
7. Penman, 305.
8. Lanercost, 257. Froissart, 26.

Notes

9. Penman, 302–3.
10. Bingham, 334.
11. Barbour, 744–46.
12. Penman, 304.
13. CDS, iii, nos 990, 991. Bingham, 327.
14. Froissart, 28.
15. Ibid, 28.
16. Barbour, 770.
17. Penman, 326.

Appendix One

1. *Anglo-Scottish Relations 1174–1328: Some Selected Documents*, ed by E.L.G Stones (London, 1965), 140–3.

Appendix Two

1. *The Declaration of Arbroath, 1320.* ed & trans, Sir James Fergusson (Edinburgh, 1970), 5–11.

Appendix Three

1. *Anglo-Scottish Relations 1174–1328: Some Selected Documents*, ed by E.L.G Stones (London, 1965), 154–7.

List of Illustrations

Bibliography

Primary Sources

Anglo-Scottish Relations 1174–1328, Some Selected Documents, ed. E.L.G. Stones (London, 1965).

Annales Londoniensis 1195–1330, in W.Stubbs, ed. *Chronicles of the Reigns of Edward I and Edward II, Vol I, Rolls Series, lxxvi* (London, 1882).

Annales Monasterii de Waverleia, A.D, 1–1291; *Annales Monasteri,* ed. H.R. Luard (Rolls Series, vol ii, 1864–9).

Annales Paulini 1307–1340 in W. Stubbs, ed. *Chronicles of the Reigns of Edward I and Edward II, Vol I, Rolls Series, lxxvi* (London, 1882).

Annals of Connacht (AD 1224–1554), ed A.M. Freeman (Dublin, 1944).

Anonimalle Chronicle 1307 to 1334 from Brotherton Collection MS 29, ed W.R. Childs and J. Taylor (Yorkshire Archaeological Society Records Series 147, 1991).

Calendar of Charter Rolls (London, HMSO, 1903–).

Calendar of Close Rolls (London, HMSO, 1892–).

Calendar of Documents Relating to Scotland (5 vols, 1881–88), ed. Joseph Bain (Edinburgh, 1887).

Calendar of Fine Rolls (London, HMSO, 1911–).

Calendar of Patent Rolls (London, HMSO, 1891–).

Calendar of Entries in the Papal Registers Relating to Great Britain and Ireland: Papal Letters, 1305–1341, ed. W.H. Bliss (London, HMSO, 1895).

Chronicle of Walter of Guisborough, ed. H. Rothwell, Camden 3rd Series, lxxix (London, 1989).

Chronicon Galfridi le Baker de Swynebroke, ed. E.M. Thompson (Oxford, 1889).

Documents Illustrative of the History of Scotland, ed. J.Stevenson, 2 vols (1870).

Documents and Records illustrating the History of Scotland, i, ed. F. Palgrave (1837).

Edward I and the Throne of Scotland, 1290–1306. An Edition of the Record Sources for the Great Cause, 2 vols, ed. E.L.G. Stones and G.G. Simpson (Oxford, 1978).

English Historical Documents, vol 3, 1189–1327, ed Harry Rothwell (London, 1975).

Flores Historiarum, vol ii–iii, ed. H.R. Luard. Rolls Series (London, HMSO, 1890).

Bibliography

Foedera, Conventiones, Litterae et Cujuscunque Generis Acta Publica, ed T,Rymer vol I, ii (London, 1816–20).

Geoffrey of Monmouth, Historia Regum Britanniae. ed & trans. Lewis Thorpe (London, 1966).

Hailes, *Annals of Scotland* (1779).

Jean Froissart, Chronicles of England, France and Spain, trans T. Johnes (London, 1839).

Johannis de Fordun, Chronica Gentis Scotorum, ed. W.F. Skene (2 vols, Edinburgh, 1871–72).

Johannis de Trokelowe et Henrici de Blaneford Chronica et Annales, ed H.T. Riley, Rolls Series (London, 1866).

Parliamentary Rolls of Medieval England, 1275–1504, vol iii, iv, ed. J.R.S. Phillips (Woodbridge, 2005).

Parliamentary Writs and Writs of Military Summons, Edward I and Edward II, ed F. Palgrave, 2 vols, Record Commission (London, 1827–34).

Regesta Regum Scottorum, v: The Acts of Robert I, 1306–29, ed. A.A.M. Duncan (Edinburgh, 1986).

Rolls of Arms of the Princes, Barons and Knights who attended Edward I at the Siege of Caerlaverock, ed. T. Wright (London, 1864).

Scalacronica: The Reigns of Edward I, Edward II and Edward III by Sir Thomas Gray (trans Sir Herbert Maxwell (Glasgow, 1907).

Scotichronicon, Walter Bower, ed. D.E.R Watt, v, vi, vii (Aberdeen, 1988–91).

Scottish Historical Documents, ed. Gordon Donaldson (1970).

Song of Lewes, ed and trans, C.A. Kingsford (1890).

The Bruce: John Barbour, ed. A.A.M. Duncan (Edinburgh, 1999).

The Brut, ed F.W.D. Brie, Early English Text Society, cxxxi, part I (London, 1906).

The Chronicle of Lanercost, 1272–1346, ed. Herbert Maxwell (Glasgow, 1913).

The Chronicle of Pierre de Langtoft, ed T. Wright, 2 vols (Rolls Series, 1886).

The Declaration of Arbroath, 1320, ed & trans, Sir James Fergusson (Edinburgh, 1970).

The Exchequer Rolls of Scotland, ed. J. Stuart et al (vol I, Edinburgh, 1878–1908).

The Political Songs of England from the Reign of King John to that of Edward II, ed. T. Wright (London, 1839).

The Records of the Parliaments of Scotland to 1707, ed. K.M. Brown et al (St Andrews, 2008–).

The True Chronicles of Jean le Bel 1290–1360, trans, Nigel Bryant (Woodbridge, 2011).

Vita Edwardi Secundi, ed. N. Denholm-Young (London, 1957).

Willelmi Rishanger, Chronica et Annales, ed. H.T. Riley (Rolls Series, 1865).

Secondary Sources

Barrow, G. ed. *The Declaration of Arbroath: History, Setting, Significance* (Edinburgh, 2003).

Barrow, Geoffrey W.S. *Robert the Bruce & The Community of the Realm of Scotland* (Edinburgh, 1988).

Barrow, Geoffrey W.S. *The Anglo Norman Era in Scottish History* (Oxford, 1980).

Barrow, Geoffrey W.S. *The Kingdom of the Scots* (London, 1973).

Bartlett, *The Making of Europe: Conquest, Colonization and Cultural Change 950–1350* (London,1993).

Bingham, Caroline. *Robert the Bruce* (London, 1998).

Blount, M.N. 'The surrender of King John of Scotland to Edward I in 1296: some new evidence', *BIHR, xlviii* (1975).

Carpenter, David. *The Struggle for Mastery: Britain 1066–1284* (London, 2003).

Cockerill, Sara. *Eleanor of Castile: The Shadow Queen.* (Stroud, 2014).

Corser, P. 'The Bruce Lordship of Annandale, 1124–1296' in R.D. Oram and G. Stell, eds *Lordship and Architecture in Medieval and Renaissance Scotland.* (Edinburgh, 2005).

Davies, R.R. *The First English Empire: Power and Identities in the British Isles 1093–1343* (Oxford, 2000).

Dilley, James W. 'German Merchants in Scotland, 1297–1327', SHR, 27.

Donaldson, G. 'The Pope's Reply to the Scottish Barons in 1320', *SHR XXIX*.

Duffy, S. 'The Bruce Brothers and the Irish Sea World, 1306–1329' in *Cambridge Medieval Celtic Studies*, 1991.

Duncan, A.A.M. *Scotland: The Making of a Kingdom* (Edinburgh, 1975).

Duncan, A.A.M. 'The Community of the Realm of Scotland and Robert Bruce', *SHR 45* (1966).

Duncan, A.A.M. 'The Declaration of the Clergy, 1309–10' in G. Barrow, ed, *The Declaration of Arbroath: History, Setting, Significance* (Edinburgh, 2003).

Duncan, A.A.M. *The Nation of Scots and the Declaration of Arbroath* (Historical Association, 1970).

Duncan, A.A.M, 'The Process of Norham, 1291', in P.R. Coss and S.D. Lloyd, eds, *TCE*, V (Woodbridge, 1995).

Duncan, Archie, 'Revisiting Norham, May–June 1291', in Chris Given-Wilson, Ann Kettle and Len Scales, eds, *War, Governance and Aristocracy in the British Isles, 1150–1500* (Woodbridge, 2008).

Hamilton, J.S. *Piers Gaveston: Earl of Cornwall, 1307–1312: Politics and Patronage in the Reign of Edward II* (Detroit and London, 1988).

Keen, M. *Chivalry* (London, 1984).

Legge, M.D. '*La Piere D'Escoce*'. SHR 38, (1959).

Lord Cooper, 'The Numbers and Distribution of the Population of Medieval Scotland', *SHR 26*.

Lydon, Jo. 'The Scottish Soldier Abroad: The Bruce Invasion and the Galloglass' in G.G. Simpson, ed *The Scottish Soldier Abroad, 1247–1967* (Edinburgh, 1992).

Macquarrie, A. *Scotland and the Crusades, 1095–1560* (Edinburgh, 1985).

Maddicott, J.R. *Thomas of Lancaster, 1307–1322: A Study in the Reign of Edward II* (Oxford, 1970).

McNamee, Colm. *The Wars of the Bruces: Scotland, England and Ireland, 1306–1328* (East Linton, 1997).

McNamee,C. 'William Wallace's Invasion of Northern England, 1297', *NH, xxvi* (1990).

Moore, Arthur.W. 'The Connexion between Scotland and Man', *SHR vol iii*.

Morris, Marc. *A Great and Terrible King: Edward I and the Forging of Britain* (London, 2008).

Neville, C.J. 'Widows of War: Edward I and the Women of Scotland during the War of Independence', in S.S. Walker, ed. *Wife and Widow in Medieval England* (London, 1993).

Nicholson, Ranald, 'The France–Scottish and France–Norwegian Treaties of 1295', *SHR, vol 38* (1959).

Nusbacher, A. *The Battle of Bannockburn 1314* (Stroud, 2005).

Penman, Michael. *Robert the Bruce: King of the Scots* (London, 2014).

Phillips, J.R.S. 'The Irish Remonstrance of 1317: An International Perspective' in *Irish Historical Studies, xxvii* (1990).

Phillips, S. *Edward II* (New Haven & London, 2010).

Powicke, F.M. *The Thirteenth Century, 1216–1307.* 2nd ed, (Oxford, 1962).

Prestwich, M. *Armies and Warfare in the Middle Ages: The English Experience* (New Haven & London, 1996).

Prestwich, M. *Edward I* (2nd ed, Yale, 1997).

Prestwich, M. *Plantagenet England 1225–1360* (Oxford, 2005).

Simpkin, D. 'The English Army and the Scottish Campaign of 1310–11', in A. King and M. Penman, eds, *New Perspectives: England and Scotland in the Fourteenth Century* (Woodbridge, 2007).

Simpson, G.G. 'The Claim of Florence, Count of Holland to the Scottish Throne, 1291–2', *SHR* 36 (1957).

Spinks, Stephen. *Edward II the Man: A Doomed Inheritance* (Stroud, 2017).

Standford Reid, W. 'Truce, Trades and Scottish Independence', *Speculum, xxix* (1954).

Stevenson, W. 'The Treaty of Northampton (1290): A Scottish Charter of Liberties', *SHR* 86 (2007).

Stones, E.L.G. 'The Submission of Robert the Bruce to Edward I', *SHR xxxiv.*

Tanner, R. 'Cowing the Community? Coercion and Fabrication in Robert Bruce's Parliaments, 1309–18', in K.M. Brown and R.J. Tanner, eds, *Parliament and Politics in Scotland, 1235–1560* (Edinburgh, 2004).

Index